THE CLUB-FIGHTERS OF THE AMAZON
Warfare among the Kayapo Indians of Central Brazil

Gustaaf Verswijver

THE CLUB-FIGHTERS OF THE AMAZON
Warfare among the Kayapo Indians of Central Brazil

With a preface by Carlos Fausto

Turuti Books
Almeria

Cover photo: Bô-te leaving on a hunt carrying his *kô* round club. PI Mekranoti, 1978. © Gustaaf Verswijver.

First printing in 1992. Re-edition in 2018, with a new preface and editorial changes.

Verswijver, Gustaaf
The Club-Fighters of the Amazon; Warfare among the Kayapo Indians of Central Brazil / Gustaaf Verswijver. - Almeria: Turuti Books, 2018.
376 p. — (Amazon Indians Monographs, vol. I)
Includes bibliographical references.
Includes annexes.

ISBN 978-84-697-9204-9

To Prof. Simone Dreyfus,
who initiated me into the world of the Kayapo,
and to René Fuerst,
who encouraged my work among the Kayapo

Table of Contents

Foreword to the new edition

The original version of this book was written in 1985 under the title *Considerations on Mekrãgnoti Warfare*, and was submitted as my doctoral dissertation at the University of Ghent (Belgium). For its publication in 1992, a few changes were made: the title was altered to *The Club-Fighters of the Amazon*; the text was slightly adapted for edition purposes, and an additional chapter and a series of photos were added. Unfortunately, the distribution of the book was very poor, which is one of the reasons why it didn't get the necessary feedback. Indeed, recent scholars rarely seem to get access to it, and therefore often resort to secondary sources. Quite ironically, without consulting the original source, some of the secondary sources came to predominate, pushing the original work even more into oblivion — a phenomenon which, unfortunately, is the fate of many ethnographic works.

This does not mean that the original book remained entirely unnoticed. Paul Henley (1996), for instance, included it in a list of five selected works to illustrate the new lines of research in the anthropology of Amazonia, and Terence Turner based several articles almost entirely on the data presented in The Club-Fighters of the Amazon and in the preceding dissertation version. Most importantly, however, the book and the dissertation version were fundamental tools in the process leading to the official recognition and demarcation of three indigenous lands: Terra Indígena Menkragnoti (4.914.000 ha), Terra Indígena Bau (1.541.000 ha) and Terra Indígena Capoto/Jarina (635.000 ha) — and this is, in itself, of course the highest reward any ethnographic study can get!

Yet, in spite of the positive references, Carlos Fausto of the Federal University of Rio de Janeiro was right to state that "The Club-Fighters of the Amazon is one of the best historical ethnographies of an Amazonian people. One day this fact will still be recognized" (pers. comm.).

This all being said, the problem of the poor accessibility of the book is a real issue, and that is why I decided to publish it once again: thirty-three years after its first version, it is now available as a Print-on-Demand publication.

Upon republishing a book, one is inevitably confronted with the dilemma to either leave the text untouched, or rework the content to include new data and new insights. I decided to opt for the first solution, only changing the orthography of the names of some tribes and replacing a few photos with more recent ones. There are several reasons why I chose to leave the text as it was. One of these is that updating the book seemed like an insurmountable task in the view of the significant amount of new data I gathered during the last three decades. Another reason was that, upon rereading the book, I realized how up-to-date many arguments still are. This is particularly so regarding several processes I tackled in the final chapter (e.g. the change in leadership; the growing emphasis on ceremonies organized along the lines of kinship; the ongoing process of village schisms...) and which are still very contemporary. It therefore seemed correct to leave the text of the book untouched.

Yet, in the meantime the need emerged to present the manifold new data I collected on the history of the Mekranoti and of the Kayapo in general. I therefore decided not only to republish The Club-Fighters of the Amazon, but also to make it the first volume of a series of ethnographic monographs on the Kayapo and neighbouring tribes. The series is named Amazon Indians Monographs. In this ambiguous project, it is the aim to publish several monographs, in which I will present, among others, translations of Kayapo myths, statements, life-stories and songs ; various aspects of Kayapo material culture; the diaries covering the three years I worked as a coordinator for the Raoni Institute (2003-2005); an in-depth analysis of Kayapo (ethno) history in the period 1930-1960, and so on. All this because I firmly believe in the importance of publishing basic ethnographic material. In a time when ever fewer anthropologists invest in lengthy fieldwork, the importance of (and the need for) basic ethnographic material simultaneously increases. Also, the rapid changes noted in the societies where I did (and still do) fieldwork seems to make the divulgation of basic ethnographic material all the more pertinent,

I hope you enjoy reading this first volume.

Gustaaf Verswijver
8 February 2018

Preface

IN PRAISE OF THE CLUB-FIGHTERS

It is hardly possible for me to talk about *The Club-Fighters of the Amazon* without a feeling of nostalgia. I read Verswijver's Doctoral thesis (on which the book is based) in the late 1980's, when I was just beginning my fieldwork among the Tupi-Guarani speaking Parakanã. The book was published a couple of years later, and I re-read it when I was still struggling with my data on the Parakanã's equally belligerent history. At the time, so-called 'primitive warfare' was one of the hottest subjects of Amazonian ethnology, and many different intellectual traditions competed for explicative preeminence in the field. Even so, there were few monographs dealing with warfare from a consistent historical perspective, particularly one based on indigenous oral history. This is an irretrievable loss. In the 1980's, there were still many living individuals, from different Amazonian peoples, who had actually participated in warfare events. Most of them are dead by now.

Verswijver's book is the best example of a solid, empirically based work, which took the pains of reconstructing events and patterns of indigenous warfare (in this case, Kayapo and more specifically Mekranoti) from oral history. When I say 'took the pains' I really mean it. He not only conducted fieldwork in difficult situations and during difficult times, spending almost three years in the field between 1974 and 1981, but also painstakingly collected different sorts of data, and managed to crosscheck them, producing a rich and convincing depiction of Kayapo history since the early 19th century. Having myself tried to follow Verswijver's steps in the reconstruction of Parakanã history, I thoroughly appreciate his feat. I am well aware of the methodological pitfalls involved here, and the time-consuming character of such research.

When The Club-Fighters was written, it was generally thought that

Amazonian peoples had a very shallow history, a fact which would be made evident by their purported genealogical amnesia (i.e., the fact that people seldom remember their relatives beyond the second ascending generation). Verswijver proved this to be a hasty generalization. He collected data from many sources (major political events, raids, the name of men's societies, the performance of major ceremonies, life-histories, genealogical information etc.), and established a relative chronology, which he could partially map onto our own chronology. Unfortunately few ethnographers emulated Verswijver's example. Until the 1988 Brazilian Federal Constitution, the main legal argument for the demarcation of indigenous lands was the traditional occupation of a territory, which had to be asserted by historical documents. Deemed inaccurate and subjective, oral history was hardly ever accepted as proper evidence. Works such as The Club-Fighters offered a vivid corroboration that oral history could serve as a legitimate proof for the recognition of indigenous lands.

Verswijver did research before post-modernist epistemological anxiety took flight. He feels no need to apologize for doing his job, and almost never presents his own self to the reader. After so many years of (too much) reflexivity, I found his style refreshing. He talks about the Kayapo in a very straightforward way, which I imagine would also please this very straightforward people. Since the 1950's, the many existing Kayapo subgroups have received excellent anthropologists, who made a joint contribution to the understanding of this extremely sophisticated and self-affirming people. Besides Verswijver, Simone Dreyfus, Terence Turner, Lux Vidal, Vanessa Lea, Darell Posey, William Fisher, Cesar Gordon and others offered us rich portraits of these people, who had been originally classified as a 'marginal tribe' in the fourfold typology of the Handbook of South American Indians (Steward 1948). Since then, we have discovered that they are rather a paradigm of complexity!

Verswijver makes clear that such complexity is simultaneously the product of a structural pattern and an evenemential history. The Kayapo are divided into matrilineal segments that own ritual prerogatives and privileges, transmitted across generations. This system of ceremonial privileges — which includes ornaments, songs, ritual lore, forms of decoration, graphic motifs etc. — can be augmented by innovation and/or incorporation of new items from non-Kayapo peoples. The author gives a number of extraordinary examples of this practice, which also marks the introduction of new tangible and intangible items from national society. As time goes by, however, some of these ritual privileges dissolve into common usage, and are no longer restricted to specific segments or individuals anymore. This 'communalization', as Gordon (2006) phrases it, is counteracted by a centrifugal force, which prompts the Kayapo to constantly acquire new items in the exterior. Traditionally, this could be attained through different strategies, such as 'silent exchange', pacific interaction, and warfare.

The richness and diversity of Kayapo material culture, as well their spectacular ritual life, is a consequence of this process. As Verswijver indicates, a suitable justification for raiding a non-Kayapo people could be to bring back captive women and learn their songs. Actually, about 40% of the all-important Kayapo naming ceremonies are said to have an external origin. Another distinctive features of this outward movement was the Kayapo capacity for collectively absorbing and internally transmitting the newly acquired valuables. This was also true in the case of war captives. The outward movement was met with a powerful machine of incorporation, one that had no equivalent in the Parakanã case. The Kayapo considered it viable to 'kayapo-nize' any person, including non-indigenous individuals. In the 20th century, the Mekranoti resorted to the abduction of white children in the hope they would serve as intermediaries in the contact with non-indigenous settlers — although to no avail.

This structural pattern of appropriating and taming persons, songs, and artefacts (which can be read as an example of what I called 'familiarizing predation') is not, however, outside history, but is instead necessarily open to history. It is modulated according to the people with whom the Kayapo interact, and to the historical situations in which they become entangled. This is clearly shown by Verswijver's wonderful analysis of the different modalities of warfare, which vary according to the enemy and which fluctuate in tune with different historical contexts. Moreover, warfare was but one of the strategies for promoting innovation within Kayapo society, one which became prevalent in the 20th century, as the contact with national society grew into a necessity (not only because settlers were closing in, but also because firearms had increasingly entered indigenous conflicts). The portrait Verswijver gives us in the book is not a frozen image of Kayapo bellicosity. Rather, it is an image sensible to time, context, and also individual histories of great chiefs, unfortunate warriors, abducted boys and girls, who traversed a huge territory from the savannahs east of the Tocantins to the dense forested zone of the Xingu basin in search of a place to keep producing beautiful people: *mereremex* ("those who show off beautifully", as Verswijver glosses the term).

Today, all surviving Kayapo subgroup have succeeded in guaranteeing their territories, and protecting them against the advancement of the colonizing frontier. Verswijver's story ends in late 1980's, which proved to be a central decade in the reconfiguration of Kayapo political strategy.

After the devastating effects of epidemics just after sustained contact, they had already recuperated their pride and developed a new politics of self-representation towards Brazilian society (Turner 1991). They played a central role in the struggle for securing indigenous rights in the 1988 Federal Constitution, and in blocking the construction of a hydroelectric plant in the Xingu River (which sadly, however, was built 25 years later). After the proclamation of the new Constitution, they became the most successful people in terms of the demarcation of indigenous lands. Instead of abducting non-indigenous boys and girls to act as translators between them and the whites, they sucked in new people (not only anthropologists, but also pop stars like Sting), and also captured the Global imagination. In doing so, they paved the way for other indigenous people in Brazil, who had their lands subsequently recognized by the State.

We should all praise the club-fighters of the Amazon.

Carlos Fausto

Professor of Ethnology at the Graduate Program in Social Anthropology at the National Museum, Federal University of Rio de Janeiro.

Acknowledgements

The research upon which this essay is based was made possible through grants from the NFWO (National Science Foundation-Brussels), the Leopold III Foundation for the Conservation and the Exploration of Nature (Brussels) and the FAPESP (Fundação de Ámparo à Pesquisa de São Paulo). Sponsorship in Brazil was provided by the Museu Paulista and authorization to carry out field research was granted by the Presidents of FUNAI (Fundação Nacional do Índio, the Brazilian Indian Foundation, Brasília) and by CNPq (Conselho Nacional de Pesquisas, the National Science Council, Brasilia). I am indebted to these institutions for their cooperation and assistance.

This book, the product of consecutive field-work terms, depended on the generous participation of many people. Although I cannot adequately thank all those who gave me their practical and intellectual support during the many years involved in the elaboration of this project, I would like to acknowledge those who have been particularly helpful in seeing me through the various stages of my research.

I am most grateful to Jacques and Maureen Bisilliat who were not only wonderfully hospitable by accommodating me during my often lengthy stays in São Paulo, but likewise were an invariable stimulus for my research. Without the inestimable help of these friends, several field-work terms simply would have been impossible.

I am particularly indebted to Prof. Simone Dreyfus who initiated me into the world of anthropology and whose inspired advice, as well as thorough supervision and guidance, have encouraged me in the pursuit of my studies. I likewise extend my thanks to Prof. Thekla Hartmann, my Brazilian sponsor, for her kind hospitality and the interest she has constantly shown in my work.

I thank Prof. Hendrik Pinxten for his warm receptivity and unfailing intellectual encouragement. He deserves special credit for guiding me through my doctoral degree. To Prof. Renate Viertler, Prof. Manuela Carneira da Cunha and Prof. Lux Vidal, my thanks for their support throughout the lengthy process of my field-work research.

My hearty thanks to Prof. Darrell Posey who helped me with specific parts of this essay, and to Ruth Thomson of the Summer Institute of Linguistics (SIL) who was not only extremely helpful in the field, but also was willing to gather some ethnographic data for me after I concluded my field research.

My thanks to Prof. Anthony Seeger and to my good friend and colleague Dominique Gallois for the many pleasant and instructive moments we had discussing indigenous cultures in Brazil. To the FUNAI staff in Brasilia (in particular Prof. Olímpio Serra, Conceição Militão Rocha and Delvair Melatti), to Mickey Stout and Kathleen Jefferson of the SIL, and to all those whom I encountered in the field, my gratitude.

Last but not least, special mention and my deepest thanks to René Fuerst, who stimulated my research among the Kayapo, and to Orlando and Claudio Villas Boas who, through their very existence, made my project possible.

Finally, I thank the Mekranoti for their generous and amiable treatment towards me during my numerous stays in their villages. Whilst all members of the various villages contributed in various ways, special thanks are required for Bepgogoti (the old village chief) and his family, who often shared their food with me; to Karadja, Bemoti-re, Pakyx, Mey-re, Kremôr and Kruma-re (all senior tribesmen and among my main informants) who patiently faced the arduous task of opening up the mind of the persistent white man; to dear old Pănhngri and her husband Bàjkà-re, who not only adopted me as their real grandson but who also did everything possible to integrate me into Mekranoti society, even conferring upon me specific privileges related to their household; and to Pykati-re, for his happiness in times of total confusion.

Orthography

In 1974, an official Brazilian orthography was devised through the combined efforts of the Brazilian Indian Foundation (FUNAI) and the Summer Institute of Linguistics (SIL). That orthography is used throughout this book for Kayapo words.

Consonants

		bilabial	alveolar	palatal	Velar
Stops	voiced	b	d		g
	unvoiced	p	t		k
Affricates	voiced				dj
	unvoiced			x	
Nasals		n	n	ñ	nh
Semivowels		w	r	j(h)	

Vowels (oral)

	front (unrounded)	central (unrounded)	back (unrounded) (rounded)	
High	i		y	u
Medium	ê		ỳ	ô
Low	e	a	à	o

Vowels (nasal)

	front	central	back	
High	ĩ		ỹ	ũ
Low	ẽ	ã		õ

Notes on the accentuation of Kayapo words:

- the emphasis is invariably put on the last syllable: e.g., *meõtoti* should be read as *meõtotí*;

- hyphen [-] marks the beginning of a suffix which is not emphasized: e.g., *mekra-re* should be read as *mekrá-re*;

- in end syllables ending with a vowel followed by a "r", the vowel should be read again: e.g., *gor* should be read as *góro* (this, while the same syllable in a word is spelled out: *gorotire*).
- glottal stops are indicated with a single inverted comma: e.g., in *me'ôkre*, a glottal stop precedes the "ô".

New to the 2018 edition:

For names of non-Kayapo Indian tribes, I have followed the orthography of the Instituto Socioambiental in São Paulo[1] without, however, using the accent marks. As such, Kayapó becomes Kayapo. I draw attention to the fact that the orthography used by the Instituto Socioambtental is not always consistent, using alternatively the "y" and the "i" for the same consonant (cf. Kayapo and Wayana, versus Kamaiura). To avoid this confusion, I used the orthography Kaiapo in the earlier version of this work. Since, however, the term is written Kayapo in nearly all scientific literature regarding this indigenous nation, I will follow this custom and will also write "Kayapo".

To facilitate lecture, the names of the different Kayapo subgroups are invariably written according to an easier orthography, most commonly used by FUNAI members. As such, Mekrãgnoti becomes Mekranoti, Kubẽkrãkênh becomes Kubenkranken, Kôkrajmôr becomes Kokraimoro and Goroti-re becomes Gorotire. Likewise, Irã'ãmranh-re becomes Ira'amranh.

In the course of the last decades, several indigenous peoples have opposed to the fact that their group is designated by a term given by oyther peoples, and prefer that their selfdesignation is used. Therefore, in this new version of the book, I have changed the designation Kreen Akrore (or Krãjôkàr) to Panara. In the same way, Suya became Kisedje, Juruna became Yudja, and Karaja became Iny Karaja. If I continue to use the term Kayapó instead of their self-designation Mebêngôkre, I do so largely because the Indians concerned also still often use this designation: they realize that the term Kayapo is associated with their warlike past and, hence, commands respect...

Introduction

1. ON FIELD-WORK TERMS

The present essay is an updated version of my doctoral dissertation. It deals with warfare among the Kayapo (Mebêngôkre), a Ge-speaking tribe of Central Brazil. The Kayapo live divided among fifteen villages, belonging to several subgroups. Field-work was carried out most of all among the Central Mekranoti, but I also spent short periods of time in other Kayapo communities such as the Northern and Southern Mekranoti, the Kubenkranken and the Gorotire.

Originally, I planned to work on Kayapo material culture. While visiting European museums and consulting the existent bibliography, I realized that the few works on Kayapo material culture dealt either with a Kayapo group which by 1940 had become extinct, or with the Kayapo-Xikrin, the smallest of the two contemporary Kayapo groups. On the numerous Kayapo of the Xingu villages not a single specific study on material culture existed.

My plan was formulated in early 1973, and I arrived in São Paulo on March 28, 1974. With the help of Orlando Villas Boas (Director of the Xingu National Park), Prof. Lux Vidal (USP — University of São Paulo) and Prof. Olímpio Serra (FUNAI), the authorization to carry out this research among the Txukarramãe was granted by FUNAI. Txukarramãe is the name by which the Southern Mekranoti are often referred to in literature. It is the southernmost group of the Kayapo of the Xingu. I arrived in their village at Pôsto Indígena Kretire (Xingu National Park) in early May, and found out soon that field-work would be difficult. I was lodged at the FUNAI post, some six hundred meters from the village. Not being allowed to go to the village without the Indian chief's permission, in the space of three weeks I was only able to spend some twenty hours in the village. Since no improvement came after three weeks, and unexperienced as I was in coping with this uncomfortable and apparently dead-end situation, I felt field-work to be impossible at that time[1]. I decided to return to Brasilia where I asked for authorization to work in another Kayapo village.

FUNAI granted me authorization to work among the Central Mekranoti, close relatives of the Txukarramãe, living in the most isolated circumstances of all the Kayapo of the Xingu villages. Due to lack of finances, I was unable to hire a plane to reach the Central Mekranoti village. I made two unsuccessful attempts at arriving there. In early December 1974, after receiving further financial support, I was able to hire a single-engined plane. On arriving in Mekranoti, the Indians were cheerful and friendly, but I was told that most of the men were out of the village collecting Brazil nuts some hundred and fifty kilometers to the north. The village was only inhabited by women, children and a handful of elderly men. Contrary to the information given to me in Brasilia, no FUNAI agent or SIL missionary was present. To make things worse, Pykati-re, the only Central Mekranoti who spoke Portuguese, was also out of the village. Since I only spoke a few words of Kayapo, initial conversation was based on mimicry.

The fact that I was planning to stay in the village soon became obvious since the pilot, impatient to depart, threw my luggage out of his plane and took off. As I was told later on, the Indians were confused about why I came. Since I had not arrived on the official FUNAI airplane, they initially took me to be a missionary and indicated that I could stay in the SIL house. But when I did not operate the SIL radio, it became obvious that I was not a missionary. Treating successfully a child for worms, they then took me for a doctor. Immediately about thirty to forty Indians came to my house daily for medical treatment. Luckily, no serious health problem arose. Yet, providing medical assistance enabled me to learn the people's names and to acquire a basic Kayapo vocabulary.

The quiet and monotonous daily life suddenly gained a new dimension when, at the end of January, the men returned from their Brazil nut collecting. Within two weeks, not only the men returned, but the FUNAI agents and SIL missionaries also appeared. Since the SIL missionaries returned to their house, the Indians sheltered me in an old, abandoned

---

1   It was only later that I found out that these Indians had killed five Brazilians near a road during my stay in the village. The Indians were afraid that I would spread this news, endangering their relationship with the Brazilians. Furthermore, they feared a violent counter-attack and thought that the FUNAI post was a safer place for me to stay.

house where the village chief stored his rice. The house was infested by rats and insects, there was no table to work or eat on, and no bench to sit on. But I soon learned to live with these practical problems, and continued living in this fashion for over three months. Things slightly improved when, in early February, an elderly Indian man proposed to work for me as a cook, simultaneously performing some practical jobs such as clearing the surroundings of the house (to keep the various snakes, insects and spiders away) and building a primitive outhouse.

My project was to adapt to the circumstances. During my first stay, two naming ceremonies were held. Since none of these ceremonies had been described before in ethnographic literature, I decided to work on naming practices. Through the ceremonies, however, I managed to learn a lot about material culture, only to find out that the use of ornaments was much more complicated than expected (Verswijver 1983a). I also started working on Mekranoti ethno-history (Verswijver 1978b, 1978c), since the existing literature made it clear that much confusing data existed concerning the division and origin of this particular Kayapo group.

Although I made many friends and had been adopted as the village chief's son, a greater affinity was to grow when the Indians discovered that I was one of the few *kubẽ* ("non-Kayapo") to return again and again to their village. They thus included me within the category of "our non-Kayapo" (*meba nhõ kubẽ*), which is the category of specific friends of the community and which includes only a handful of "Whites". The Indians then proposed to improve my accommodation by reinforcing the walls of my house, building a table and benches, and fixing the leaking roof.

I was to go to the Mekranoti ten times, staying there for over thirty months in all, sojourns that were interrupted by trips to Brazilian towns or to Belgium, and by short visits to other Kayapo villages. Field-work terms fluctuated between one and seven months and I carefully planned my stays so that an almost equal time was spent in the dry season and the rainy season.

Besides working with informants, I occasionally joined the men on hunting trips, went with the women to the gardens, participated in long forest treks, was often invited to participate in ritual life, and provided medical assistance when the FUNAI and SIL members were out of the village (which frequently occurred in the period from 1974 to 1977).

By Amazon Indian standards, the Central Mekranoti village is relatively large: in 1974 it numbered two hundred and thirty-nine Indians, and in 1981 the population had increased to three hundred and sixty. In such a village, the distribution of commodities always poses a problem, not only in practical terms, but also in terms of maintaining a balanced relationship with the entire community. All village adolescents and adults want to acquire at least one important item (such as an axe, pan, cloth, etc.), and each individual tries to get as many commodities as possible for himself. The result is that, as long as commodities are available, the Indians continuously ask for more. Laboring under acute financial difficulties, anthropologists invariably cope with the problem of not being able to please each and every Indian in the community. A firm economical system, therefore, has to be established. Though not planned as such, my economical system ended up consisting of four ways of distributing commodities: each time I arrived in the field, a bag with numerous small items was delivered to each of the two village chiefs, who distributed the goods to their followers; some commodities were kept aside to "pay" the informants who worked for days on end in my house; the remainder of the commodities were given, little by little, to those whom I knew that would compensate for my gifts by spontaneously bringing food; since I was adopted by Bepgogoti, my numerous "sisters" and "brothers" freely provided me with any type of food I needed. These "kinsmen" often came to my house to see whether I was in need of anything in particular. On leaving the field, I asked them what they most eagerly wanted me to bring them as a present, trying, within my financial limits, to fulfil their demands.

The research developed in several phases. At first I adopted "participatory observation", which enabled me to get to know the people, to get acquainted with their environment and to learn their language. Having what is commonly referred to as "a good ear", I picked up the Kayapo language rather rapidly. After five months, I was able to hold a conversation, and to catch the essence of formal speeches and mythology. In this phase I started to work with informants, though I almost never really chose the informant since the Indians usually indicated the people who were said to be a specialist on the various topics which I wished to discuss.

A normal day in the field would start at about six a.m. When the Indians noticed that I was awake, some men usually came over to my house for a cup of coffee. Bepgogoti was the most regular visitor at this early hour, bringing along a huge cup and taking the coffee to his house for his kinsmen to drink. Aside from these morning visits, the chief was one of the people who least frequented my house.

Before noon, I worked with several informants, usually one after the other. After dinner, I would pay a visit to the Indians in their residential households, go to the men's house to chat and have my daily bath. After supper I used to visit my "kinsmen". Seated in front of the residential house, this proved to be one of the most agreeable moments of the day. Enjoying the pleasant temperature and without the irritation of mosquitos, I usually chatted for an hour or two with my kinswomen. Although we usually joked a lot at such reunions, the women profited from these moments to ask about my family, my personal life, city life and about Western civilization in general. They often drew parallels or would draw attention to dissimilarities between their culture and mine. In this way, I learned a lot about family structure, domestic life, sexual intrigues and kinship. When the women withdrew for their night's rest at about nine p.m., I would return to my house and run over my notes in order to prepare the work of the next day.

This procedure, nevertheless, was not as strictly followed as described. During ceremonies, when illness came or when a visitor arrived, my schedule adapted itself to the circumstances. And during forest treks I would not work with specific informants, rather I would discuss the topics within the sphere of the men's groups.

The essence of my discussions with the informants developed as I was to "grow up". Not only because I gradually became more fluent in the language, or because I had by now learnt "how to ask a question" so as to obtain exact information, but also because the informants adapted the extent of their answers to my acquired knowledge on Kayapo culture. Similar questions asked twice, with an interval of one year or more in between the two occasions, were to reveal that, during the second occasion, much more detail was given. Upon asking the Indians why they had not told me these details before, they replied that "I would not have understood, yet". The Mekranoti's concept of my "development" came hand in hand with my knowledge of their language and their culture, and was simultaneously accompanied with a strengthening of friendship ties which we were able to build. As the Indians told me, when I arrived in the village in 1974, I was considered a child: I did not know how to speak, nor how to behave. By the time I left the field in 1981, I was considered an adolescent, ready to engage in marriage and to start my own nuclear family.

2. ON METHODOLOGY AND THE DELIMITATION OF THE THEORETICAL GOALS

Various publications (Nimuendajú 1952; Moreiro Neto 1957; Sick 1960; Ribeiro 1970; etc.) as well as numerous press-clippings illustrate that, during several periods of this century, the Kayapo have brought about displacements of Brazilian population in large areas of Central Brazil. Consequently, the Brazilians living in the interior of the country consider the Kayapo to be one of the most warlike of Brazilian Indian tribes. In the various anthropological studies which have resulted from field-works among the Kayapo, the importance of warfare in Kayapo society is often referred to, although up to the present date no one focused theoretical research directly on the socio-political implications of warfare on this society. Directed toward the theme of inter-tribal contacts and acculturation processes, this essay stands as an attempt to understand the mechanisms of Kayapo warfare.

In practical terms, I proceeded to subdivide the present essay into three basic sections: a preliminary ethnographic treatise; an analysis on the types and motivations of warfare; and a brief survey of recent acculturative processes.

Chapter 1 provides the ethnographic data which serve as a background for further analysis. Throughout the essay, numerous references are made to ceremonies, trekking patterns, political men's associations and chieftaincy. I therefore considered it not only useful, but also imperative, to prepare the reader by including a chapter in which several socio-political aspects of Mekranoti culture are dealt with. Most of these aspects have been described in former publications (see Dreyfus 1963; T. Turner 1965 and Vidal 1977), but despite the apparent analogy with the already published material, Chapter 1 represents a personal elaboration on Mekranoti ethnography. I must emphasize, however, that my ethnographic data are, at times, in disagreement with data published by Dreyfus (1963) and T. Turner (1965). To be sure, these disagreements can partially be ascribed to dissimilarities in cultural expressions of different Kayapo groups: each anthropologist having worked in different Kayapo groups. Since it is not my aim to accentuate and discuss in this essay the various dissimilarities, I have avoided as far as possible specific cross-references to these.

Many aspects of my analysis of Kayapo warfare are based upon ethno-historic research. The reconstruction of the complex Kayapo-Mekranoti ethno-history has been divided into two parts: the first one (Chapter 2) represents a general survey of the complicated process of migrations, fissions and fusions of the many Kayapo subgroups since the early nineteenth century; the second one (Appendix A) provides a detailed description of the ethno-history of the Mekranoti throughout the twentieth century. Due to the fact that informants had actually witnessed the post-1900 events, this historical period contains many more details than the pre-1900 period. Nevertheless, a methodological problem arose:

how was I to assimilate the abundance of data, simultaneously allowing for a chronological ordering of events? Terence Turner (1965: 48-78) had presented Kayapo history by focusing on important events such as major splits or fusions. Basing his research on the names given to the men's associations, he analyzed the political configuration functioning at the time of these events.

In an initial stage I adopted a fairly similar procedure. However, unfamiliar as I was with Mekranoti history, I based reconstruction of political configurations on the few important events which I was able to identify through preliminary bibliographic research. Dates could be fixed for each of the following events: 1900 or shortly thereafter (when the Mekranoti separated from the Kayapo-Gorotire); 1936 (when the Gorotire village broke up into several smaller communities); 1953 (when the Mekranoti were peacefully contacted by the Villas Bôas brothers); and 1957-1958 (when the SPI[2] inspector Fransisco Meirelles first visited the Mekranoti area). From 1958 on, several other dates were available, referring to visits of missionaries as well as SPI or FUNAI agents.

Following T. Turner's method, reconstructions were made of the existing men's societies that prevailed during the above mentioned periods. In doing so, I hoped to achieve a representative, general view of Mekranoti history. During a second phase I decided to collect short life-stories. I did this in order to cross-check my data as well as to obtain further data regarding the continuity of membership in political men's associations. Yet, asking several elder men to which men's associations they had belonged during their life-time, I suddenly realized that they mentioned numerous names of men's associations I had never heard off. Furthermore, I began to realize that Mekranoti history was characterized by a great number of schisms and regroupings: Mekranoti history seemed, in fact, to be dominated by many more fissions and fusions than any other Kayapo group, and it became essential to include these data in any historical reconstruction I would attempt.

Considering the many information gaps, I devised another methodology which, this time, would base historical reconstruction upon village names. I proceeded to ask informants about which village the Mekranoti constructed first after their separation from the Gorotire. The result was that all informants agreed that it was a village called *arerek-re*. I then proceeded by asking where they had moved to upon leaving that par-

---

2   SPI is the commonly used abbreviation for "Serviço de Proteção aos Índios", the Brazilian government agency which was founded by General Cândido Rondon in the beginning of this century. The SPI was active until 1967, when it was replaced by the "Fundação Nacional do Índio" (FUNAI).

ticular village. This procedure was repeated over and over again, until I managed to obtain a rough idea of Mekranoti history[3]. The major problem related to this methodology seemed to be obtaining data referring to village occupancy or, in other words, how long the Indians lived in each village. The informants often came up with contradictory answers which really confused me until I realized that, while inhabiting a given main village, the Mekranoti often moved to temporary villages, eventually returning to their main village. In an attempt to answer my queries, I assembled several informants to join discussions on the matter. I was then to observe that the Mekranoti, among themselves, discussed village occupancy by referring to seasons and to major ceremonies performed[4]. Distinction between the numerous ceremonies was possible as informants invariably mentioned the names of the sponsors or of the honored children. These discussions proved to be the key to further elaboration of Mekranoti history.

I then decided to apply yet another methodology: taking an elderly man as an informant, I asked him in which village he had been introduced into the men's house. I then inquired as to what season this event took place, if any ceremony had been held during that specific season and, if so, who had sponsored it or who had been honored during it. Similar questions were asked about each of the following seasons. Little by little, the informants spontaneously started referring to raids undertaken, to internal strife that had occurred, to the numerous splits and fusions and to the major economic activities and migrations. Repeating this procedure with twelve informants, I managed to get a detailed picture of Mekranot history and, much to my surprise, the intervals of seasons between 1918 (the year of a particular Mekranoti raid I was able to trace in bibliography) and 1936 (the year of the Gorotire splits), between 1936 and 1953 (the years of "pacification") and between 1953 and 1974 (the year of my first journey among the Mekranoti) coincided and fitted our "calendar". I thus realized that I had succeeded in elaborating a rather effective method of reconstructing Kayapo history. I applied the same method in reconstructing Kokraimoro history later on, and managed to get a substantial idea of

3   See Verswijver (1978b) where the results of this attempt at a reconstruction of Mekranoti history have been published.

4   The following quotation illustrates such a discussion between several informants: "No, it was already the rainy season when we moved to *krãnhmrôpryjaka*. Then, Kaprãndjêdjà sponsored the *kwỳrỳkangô* ceremony. Your father only returned during the dry season, after the conclusion of the ceremony. He and his followers killed Katàmkrãmêx and only then did we move to *kapôtnĩnõr*." [free translation of a taped discussion].

their history in just a few weeks' time.

The ethno-historical reconstruction obtained in this way was to allow me to analyze several aspects relevant to this essay, such as (1) the frequency of raids; (2) whether or not warfare was related to territorial conquest; and (3) the eventual evolution of war patterns in the course of this century. Future analyses might also bring out any relationship between war expeditions and the performance of major ceremonies. Through this reconstruction I was also able to establish the age of most Mekranoti Indians with a certain amount of accuracy, and to understand the mechanisms inherent in several of the recent changes in Mekranoti society.

Chapter 3 deals with Kayapo warfare. In an interesting survey, Otterbein (1973) distinguishes among sixteen approaches regarding the study of "primitive warfare". Basically these approaches can be grouped into two major categories: those who emphasize the causes of war and those who emphasize the effects of war. Naturalists, for instance, emphasize the zoological property of the human species and view warfare as a consequence of an innate aggression; marxists see warfare as a result of the scarcity of available material goods; and defenders of political-exchange theories feature the social relationships by focusing upon the relation between warfare and exchange.

Among the most recent schools of thought, I should mention the analyses provided by ecologically minded anthropologists such as Harris (1977, 1979 and 1980), who emphasize the ecologically adaptive functions of warfare. These anthropologists take primitive warfare as a phenomenon caused by population pressure on the natural environment: band and village societies are said to use warfare as well as post-conception controls such as abortion, female infanticide and the systematic neglect of unwanted (female) children readily to keep their population below carrying capacity. This is done in order to guarantee the quantity of animal protein sources and to improve the quality of their diet. Although endowed with a refreshingly nondeterministic ecological materialism, such an approach is strongly contested and has been the subject of numerous basic criticisms (see especially Sahlins 1979). Indeed, although ecological constraints do evidently exist, the inhabitants always have the possibility of adapting to the particularities of their natural environment. As such, protein deficiencies are often to be taken as a mere artifact of theoretical perspectives.

Sociologically minded anthropologists, on the other hand, have suggested several approaches. A recurrent theme which runs through their analyses is the focus upon the symbolism of aggression. In their point of view, this aggression makes of the enemy the figure which is necessary for the construction of a collective identity. Warfare would therefore be closely related to the notions of identity and ethnicity, having profound sociopolitical and ritual foundations (e.g., Siverts 1979, Chaumeil 1985, Taylor 1985, Carneiro da Cunha and Viveiros de Castro 1985, Overing 1986, Erikson 1986).

Otterbein (1973) and Ember and Ember (1971) distinguish between "internal warfare" (i.e., warfare between political communities within the same cultural unit) and "external warfare" (i.e., warfare between culturally different political communities). In the present essay, I show that such a distinction is also applicable on Kayapo warfare.

Based on the date on Mekranoti history and additional data provided by informants, I first examine several practical aspects of warfare to show that the acquisition of booty and the capture of women (girls) are essential for explaining the inducement to military participation in "external warfare"; by contrast, "internal warfare" is shown to be a means of assuring social cohesion.

I then proceed by analyzing the fortunes and the misfortunes related to participation in warfare. Featuring the socio-political impacts of warfare on Kayapo society, particular attention is repeatedly drawn to the special status given to successful warriors. This can be explained by the fact that it "is the most effective means of socializing a new generation into military activity" (Goldschmidt 1988: 57).

The ritualistic character of Kayapo warfare is dealt with in Chapter 4, where a detailed analysis is provided of the ritual performed on the occasion of the return of the warriors. This part of the essay emphasizes several aspects related to the notion of the construction of the individual.

Directly or indirectly, regular peaceful contact with Brazilian society has brought about the suppression of warfare, a severe reduction in population and the introduction of new socio-political values. Radical modifications to the "pre-contact form" have resulted. Concerning recent economic and political changes, I endeavor in Chapter 5 to explain the adaptive processes taking place in, for example, sedentary village life, riverine village settlement and alterations in leadership. Chapter 5 can, therefore, be taken as a contribution to the study of acculturative processes in Indian societies.

Yet, an additional note is in order here. I would like to add that data on Mekranoti warfare were gathered with a certain difficulty. Initially, the older men willingly and patiently provided me with data on warfare patterns. They did this until the younger tribal members reacted. In an endeavor to live on peaceful terms with the Brazilians, the younger men did not greatly appreciate the idea of me "asking questions on ancient raids".

Young men considered warfare an element of the past and regarded it as the immediate cause of the numerous pre-contact village disputes, of the numerous killings in that period, and of the splitting of the once huge Kayapo villages into several smaller communities. Furthermore, they did not want me to have the impression that the Kayapo, in pre-contact times, "only made war". And this rightly so, since in the Mekranoti village I knew between 1974 and 1981, little real evidence of a warring past was to be perceived. A discussion then began in the men's house and, as a result, for months on end the elder men avoided any further commentaries on this topic. I thus started working on ceremonial life and on name transmission until things started to change at the end of 1978 when an internal village dispute was about to break out. Suddenly, at this point, informants turned automatically to talking about warfare once again and the younger men, although ashamed of this tricky situation, no longer reacted in a disapproving manner.

Although the Central Mekranoti had not undertaken one raid since 1973, things were different for several other Kayapo groups such as the Southern Mekranoti and the Gorotire. These groups live under the constant threat of invasion of their reserves. This pressure led to violent clashes with pioneering members of the national society in the early 1980s.

CHAPTER I

THE KAYAPO AND THEIR HABITAT

1. GEOGRAPHY AND ENVIRONMENT

Situated some six hundred meters from the right bank of the Galça creek (also called Rasgado), the village is erected some forty kilometers due west of the Xixê River, the nearest main water-course. It is located on the Central Brazilian plateau, near the southern border of the State of Pará and at 8°39'54"S and 54°12'36"W. Elevation of the site is approximatively four hundred meters (IBGE maps).

The village at Pôsto Indígena (PI) Mekranoti consists[1] of a ring of twenty-two residential households built around a circular, central and cleared plaza and has a diameter of about two hundred meters. For years, the Indians called it "the place of the Brazil nut tree" (*pi'ydjãm*), a reference to a high and dried Brazil nut tree which stood alone west of the village. In 1978, the FUNAI agents asked the Indians to cut down this tree so as to use it for firewood; the name of the site was then changed to *mryretitetyk'ô*, after the leaves of a type of shrub that grows luxuriantly in the area.

It is a mountainous country: a chain of hills with a maximum elevation of some five hundred and fifty to six hundred meters above water-level lies on a north-south axis and constitutes the natural division between the watersheds of the Curua and Xixê Rivers. These are the two main rivers which, from a hydrographic point of view, dominate the area and are fed by an innumerable series of creeks and minor rivers which sprout in the hilly zone and cross it on an east-west axis. These creeks are often

---

1   Unless stated otherwise, the period from 1974 to 1982 is taken as the ethnographic present throughout this essay.

so small that several of them have, as yet, barely been discovered by the Brazilians and therefore remain unnamed.

Kayapo villages have traditionally been built on open grasslands or savannah (cerrado in Portuguese) near the edge of the tropical forest. This allows for exploitation of both ecosystems and maximizes resources (Posey 1979b: 21). Although the contemporary village near PI Mekranoti was rebuilt on several occasions, since 1956 it has been located on more or less the same site, in the dense Amazon forest, with the nearest savannah at a distance of about hundred and fifty kilometers.

A year is marked by two seasons: the dry season or "winter", from May to October, and the rainy season or "summer", from November to April. The dry season is characterized by hot, windy days, cool nights and the almost total absence of mosquitos. This is by far the more pleasant period and is therefore called "when it is good" (amex kam) by the Indians. The rainy season, on the other hand, is characterized by heavy rainfall, the flooding of most creeks and rivers and by the unpleasant presence of several types of mosquitos and other biting and sucking insects. The Indians refer to this period simply by "when it rains" (na kam). Annual rainfall is high: approximatively two thousand five hundred millimeters, which is about twenty-five percent more than in PI Gorotire, a Kayapo village located more to the east. The average temperature is about 25-29° C.

In September, at the end of the dry season, the creeks surrounding the village dry up and become stagnant pools, leading each year to serious problems of stomach infections, diarrhea and amoebic dysentery. When the rains come, however, large areas of forest become flooded: from November to April, one has the impression that the village is located on an island surrounded by large areas of flooded forest.

From a geographical point of view, the Mekranoti village can be considered the most isolated of all contemporary Kayapo villages. São Felix do Xingu and São José do Xingu are the two nearest "civilized" agglomerations. Yet their distance from the village is no less than two hundred and fifty kilometers as the crow flies. Only Cachimbo — a military basis of the Brazilian Air Force (FAB) — lies at a range of hundred and ten kilometers, but it is never visited.

Fluvial access to the village is very difficult. Such a venture by canoe or by a typical Amazon river boat is almost never undertaken since it is considered too time-absorbing and, above all, too dangerous. Even so, this would only be possible during the rainy season, as in the dry season it is virtually impossible to cross the many river rapids on the upper Iriri and Xixê Rivers.

Due to these circumstances, access to the village is practically limited to air transport. The airstrip near the village is thousand two hundred and fifty meters long and twenty meters wide, and was built by the Indians. Yet, given the excessively high prices of gasoline in the interior of Brazil, flights are reduced to the very minimum.

This all results in the fact that the Mekranoti, until 1982, had very little contact with the local Brazilian population. But farmers and other groups of local Brazilians have, little by little, started to penetrate the Mekranoti territory. In 1978 a farmer settled at a short distance north of the confluence of the Iriri and Xixê Rivers. The farm was, nevertheless, abandoned two years later. SIL missionaries and FUNAI delegates are, therefore, the sole agents of Western civilization with whom the Mekranoti maintain regular contact: they erected posts near the village in 1970 and 1973, respectively. However, to meet certain needs of the community, the Mekranoti sometimes venture to sites as distant as hundred and fifty kilometers (or more) from the village. I here refer to seasonal migrations which are undertaken to gather palm material (straw, leaves and oil) or feathers (usually of specific parrot species which are scarce in the near vicinity of the village); palm material is fetched near the village of PI Bau (another Mekranoti village), while feathers are gathered along the Iriri River.

Sale of handicrafts and Brazil nuts through FUNAI representatives constitute the sole money earnings for the village that are worth mentioning. Important concentrations of Brazil nut trees exist near distant rivers, such as the lower Bau and mid-Iriri, which are about one week's walk from the village. Once every year or so, the Mekranoti go to such sites to collect Brazil nuts in large quantities. On such occasions, groups of men are sent out to spend a month or two near these locations to do the collecting, which invariably occurs in the rainy season. It is at these locations that the Indians come into direct contact with the local Brazilian population, mining companies, teams of gold seekers and farmers. Although during these contacts some trade takes place (during which the Indians usually get cheated), the consequence of these contacts are generally of minor impact on communal, village life. At least, that was the situation up to 1982...

2. MORPHOLOGY OF KAYAPO SOCIETY

As many publications make clear, early visitors to Central Brazil were repeatedly struck by the formal and impressive morphology of Gê villages. Even today, decades after these earlier testimonies, aerial photographs provide views of almost perfect circular, sometimes spooked-wheel villages with large, cleared plazas that still greatly impress spectators.

In the tradition of Radin (1923), Malinowski (1927) and others, Nimuendajú (1946) called attention to the formal layout of Gê villages. Ever since, analysis of Gê social organization has often focused on correlations with the physical layout of their villages, and with good reason, as the ideal and actual configurations of space are quite consistent and clear in these societies.

Common to all Gê societies is the distinction between the village center and the periphery, also referred to as the public and private domain respectively. This distinction is no mere artefact of theoretical perspective but is an analytical restatement of the village physical layout. All traditional Gê villages are composed of circular or semi-circular rings of regularly spaced households around a large, cleared plaza.

The center is the symbolic locus of the renowned organizational complexity of Gê societies and their moiety systems. The periphery, on the other hand, is constituted by a circular or semi-circular arrangement of uxorilocally based households that are conceptually female areas concerned with essentially "female matters" such as cooking, consumption, and the rearing of children. As Heelas (1979: 63) pointed out, the importance of these pervasive and fundamental distinctions between center and periphery is such that an understanding of spatial order is necessary before discussing virtually any aspect of the society.

2.1 — The village

Each Kayapo village community is a politically independent and economically self-sufficient unit and is the largest internally integrated unit of Kayapo society: it is the center of its own universe. Partly due to the great distances which separate Kayapo village sites — usually hundred and fifty kilometers or more — and partly due to the hostility that prevails after a village schism, village endogamy is the normal pattern, but it is not a definite rule. Some intervillage marriages occur after (lengthy) visits of tribesmen or families to another community. In addition, Kayapo communities are strongly affected by their relations with other Kayapo groups and that is why individuals, nuclear families, or even entire dissident groups who separate from a Kayapo village, are usually granted shelter in another Kayapo community. The recently introduced facilities for speaking with members of other communities by wireless radio, and the facilities of air travel by planes of FUNAI — and recently of the Kayapo themselves since the Gorotire bought a plane in 1986 — have led

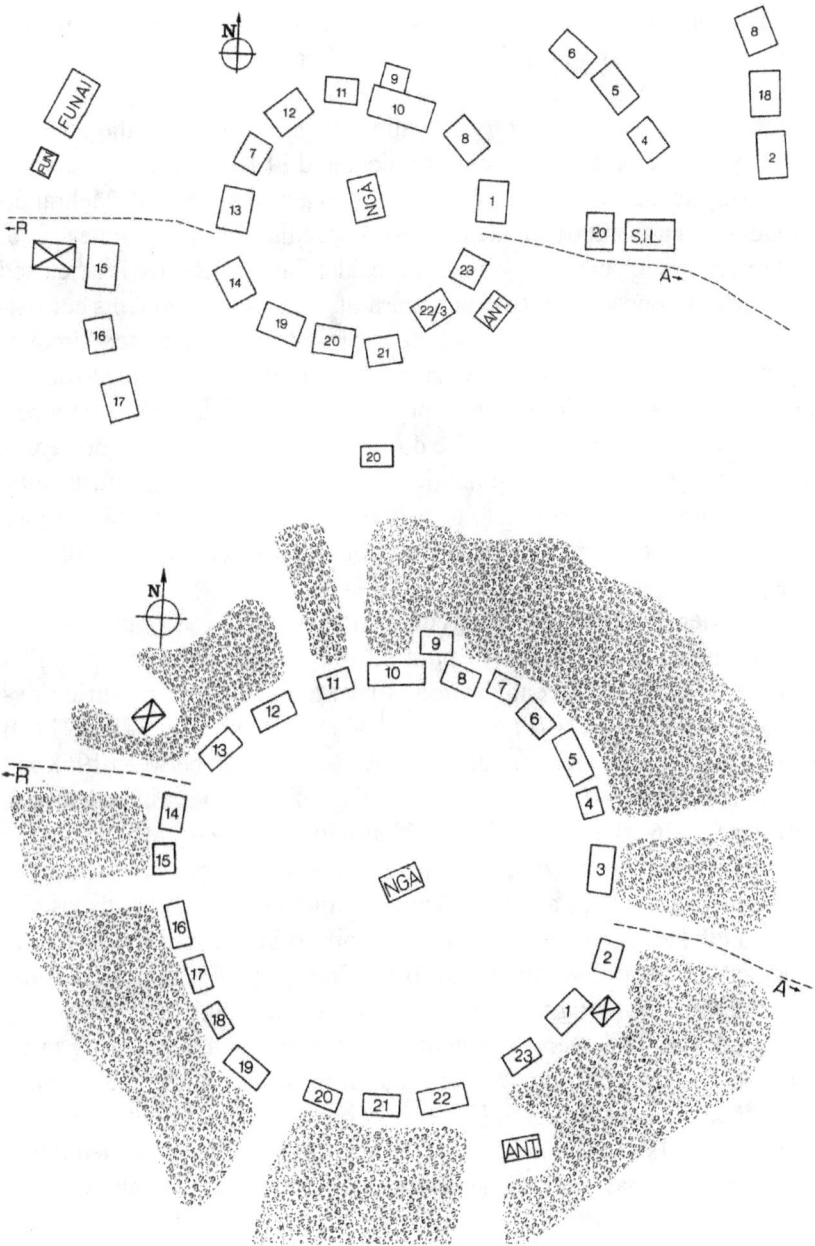

Figure 1 — Lay-out of the Central Mekranoti village.
(a) in 1974; (b) in 1980. A: main path to the airstrip; R: main path to the river

to an increased ethnic solidarity in which intervillage conflicts and hostile attitudes decline and in which both intervillage visits and marriage have become more frequent. I will return to this important aspect in Chapter 5. Although some contemporary Kayapo villages — such as the ones located near PI Gorotire, PI Kubenkranken and PI Kokraimoro — consist of two or more rows of residential houses in a grid pattern, all Mekranoti villages still are laid out in the traditional circular form. Da Matta (1976: 67) refers to such circular settings of residential households as a "closed pattern", as opposed to the open pattern of Brazilian settlements consisting of streets. Apparently, the Kayapo commitment to a closed circle of residential houses makes their village pattern highly susceptible to demographic fluctuations. For instance, problems related to the conservation of circular villages are likely to arise due to sudden demographic decreases after a village split or an epidemic. In such cases, several houses may become unoccupied leading to gaps in the ring of houses. Some families are consequently deprived of having contiguous neighbors, leading to relative social isolation.

Another disadvantage of circular villages is that, as population increases, new houses have to be built behind the already established ring of houses. The most recent Kayapo village to have two concentric rings of residential houses was the one located near PI Mekranoti in 1977. It consisted of a closed inner circle of twelve houses built between 1968 and 1972, and an almost complete second ring of residences built between 1973 and 1976 when population suddenly increased — partly due to the arrival of several immigrant families from other Mekranoti villages. Informants regarded this as an unfavorable situation, since those tribesmen living in the outer ring were deprived of observing activities which took place on the central village plaza. By 1976, many Indians spoke of the necessity of rebuilding the village with only one, single ring of houses. Yet, as the Indians were repeatedly preoccupied with executing tasks requested by FUNAI agents, the rebuilding of the village was always postponed. Things changed, however, when a fire broke out in the village in July, 1978. The entire northern half of the village burned down and this unfortunate incident led eventually to the effective rebuilding of the village (see figures 1 and 2 representing the village at PI Mekranoti in 1977 and 1980).

But the question remains whether the problems related to the maintenance of a closed circular village pattern have not become more significant since pacification. Mekranoti oral history indicates that in the period from 1920 to 1953 — corresponding to the pre-contact era on which substantial data are available — this group showed a highly developed form of mobility.

In former times, Mekranoti were more nomadic and new villages were frequently built. The problem of maintaining a complete village circle was, therefore, not as acute since the majority of their villages was only inhabited for one year or so: villages could, as such, easily be adapted to demographic fluctuations. Contemporary villages, on the other hand, are not easily rebuild. This is due to the fairly recent adoption of the neo-Brazilian house construction consisting of rectangular, pitched roof thatch huts. The building of such houses requires much more labor than the traditional Kayapo houses which consisted of long and shallow, lean-to-like constructions with curved roofs.

Villages where people remained for longer periods (e.g., *pykatôti, krãnhmrôpryjaka, rojkô-re*) are considered to be "beautiful villages" (*krĩ mex*) or, more specifically, "old beautiful villages" (*krĩ mex tũm*). This is opposed to the more temporary villages or settlements (*krĩ*) and forest camps (*adjôre*). The term *krĩ* (village) refers to a social space, constituted of at least two specific areas which are omnipresent in drawings made by informants when discussing historic and contemporary village layouts. In the literature, these two areas are referred to as private and public domains being, respectively, the ring of residential households and the village plaza with the men's house(s) (see figures 3, 4 and 5).

The private domain consists of a ring (or rings) of uxorilocal residential households and is related to domestic activities, a person's biological development, and incorporation through kinship. When not away from the village for gardening, gathering wood or wild food, women spend most of their time in or around the house spinning cotton, taking care of their children, preparing food, or simply conversing with members of their own family. Most men's activities are away from the house: hunting, fishing, trekking, manufacturing handicrafts or tools in the men's house, or simply spending their idle evening hours chatting in the men's house.

The Kayapo distinguish between two terms for their houses. First, *kikre*, means "hole/ place of the earth oven" and refers to the house as a building and to the *ki*, the traditional Kayapo earth-oven in which packages of manioc or corn flour (usually mixed with slices of meat or fish) are put between pre-heated stones to roast. This earth-oven is related to typical domestic, and therefore female activity. *Nhyrykwã* or *ũrũkwã*, the second term, means approximatively "sitting site" or "one's site" and refers to the house as a residence and social space.

The Kayapo village periphery, or private domain, is considered to be less socialized than the more socialized village center or *ngà ipôk-ri*. This latter is the public domain and is related to specific male activities (meetings, speeches, ceremonies and public rituals), to the men's house and the men's societies, and to incorporation through fictive kinship or friendship ties.

The public domain or center of Kayapo social space consists of two areas: the village plaza on which public activities and transactions take place, and the men's house(s). As will be apparent in the following sections, this village configuration neatly reflects the Kayapo conception on different stages of socialization.

The village represented in figure 3 is a reconstruction by one of the informants of the ancient village at *krãnhmrôpryjaka* — a term meaning approximatively "mountain base with white savannah". The village in question was inhabited by the Mekranoti in the period 1936-1938 and it was viewed as the most traditional of all Mekranoti villages since the split from the Gorotire in about 1905; it is therefore often referred to by informants when discussing traditional customs. All essential areas are reproduced in this drawing: in the center stands the huge men's house (A) in which four corporate men's groups are indicated; a ring of residential households (B) surrounding the circular village plaza; five dots (C-G) situated in the transitional zone between the village and the surrounding nature indicate the places where groups of women executed their body painting sessions; and the mountain (H) after which the site was named. Another drawing (figure 4) represents the Mekranoti village at *arerekre*, which was inhabited about 1925. On this figure, two men's houses (A and B) were specified; in between was the circular dancing area (C); several lines (D-F) connect the men's houses with specific houses in the village circle, those belonging to the most important chiefs at that time; the circle represents the ring of households (G); the path (H) connecting the village with the riverside is also reproduced.

2.2 — The village center

The village center is often designated by the Kayapo as *ngà ipôk-ri* ("center"). Depending on the context, this term may refer to the circular area which is confined by the ring of residential households, or just to the very center of the circle. A more commonly used term is "village clearing" (*krĩkarêr*).

In the rainy season, herbs, grass and weeds grow luxuriantly and the women of the respective households regularly have to remove the excessive vegetation from the area just in front of their houses. Besides this cleared ring, the paths leading from each house to the village center as well as the village center itself are occasionally cleared from obstructive

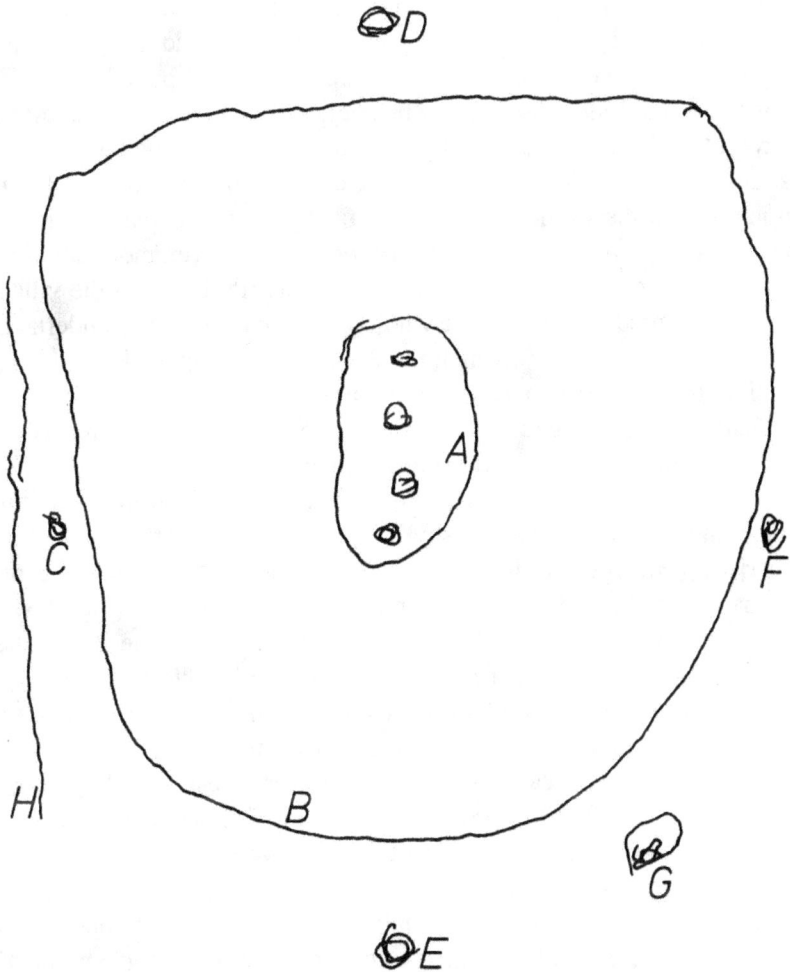

Figure 2 — Informant's drawing of the village of *krãnhmrôpryjaka* as occupied in 1937-1938.
(A) the big men's house with four sitting places; (B) the ring of residential houses; (C) site of the body painting sessions of the pubescent girls; (D) site of the body painting sessions of the *mekruwakopkê* (the wives of the men of the *menokà-re* men's society); (E) site of the body painting sessions of the *mebêmryti* (the wives of the men of the *menhakrekroti* men's society); (F) site of the body painting sessions of the adolescent girls; (G) site of the body painting sessions of the young married women.

vegetation. This is done especially during the period of the most intensive ceremonial activities which coincides with the rainy season.

While the Timbira settlements, due to their neat and sharp delimitation of paths and center area, are often spoken of as "spoked-wheel villages", such a designation cannot be applied to the Kayapo villages; the Kayapo prefer village plazas that are entirely cleared. Although this ideal is rarely obtained, the beginning of the dry season is marked by a common effort of the women to weed practically the whole plaza, allowing only some fruit trees to remain. Some women, however, more laborious than others, see to it that the area between their houses and the village center is cleared throughout the whole year. This is not only undertaken to provide "a nice view", which the Kayapo highly appreciate, but also to diminish the risk of snakes and insect pests that thrive in it.

The Kayapo recognize only two directions which, to be sure, are not cardinal points as conceived of in our society but are rather arcs determined by the daily course of the sun: the east is referred to as the "tip, beginning or lower part of the sky" (*kàjkwakrax*) or as "there where the sun rises" (*mytapôxdjà*); the west is referred to as the "root, ending or upper part of the sky" (*kàjkwanhôt*) or as "there where the sun goes down" (*mytngjêdjà*). North and south are both alluded to by the same term: either "the edge of the sky" (*kàjkwa nhire*) or "the sides" (*tikiai*).

In former times, when Kayapo villages numbered up to a thousand or more Indians, such villages often had two men's houses erected on the village plaza: an eastern and a western one, respectively *ngàkrax* and *ngànhôt* (see figure 5 where both these men's houses are given emphasis). All contemporary Kayapo villages have only one men's house and, although this may under some circumstances be erected in the very center of the village plaza, it is usually located somewhat to one side of the center: this in symbolic recognition of the (absent) opposite men's house. The *ngà ipôkri* area is, therefore, conceptually divided into an eastern and a western half.

Yet, this diametric division of the village plaza does not affect the ring of residential households since men's houses and their corresponding men's associations are exclusively related to the village center. The Kayapo merely draw a distinction between the different areas of the settlement or, more specifically, between the village plaza and periphery.

The men's associations of the village center do not regulate marriage nor any kin-based activity. The introduction of a novice to the life of the men's house occurs on the basis of a nonkinsman and incorporation into the political, mature men's associations (the men's societies) is a nonkinship-based matter. The village periphery and its

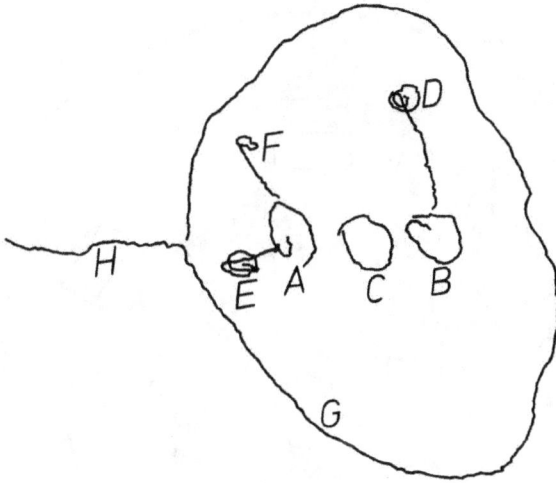

Figure 3 — Informant's drawing of the village of *arerek-re* as occupied in 1925.
(A) western men's house; (B) eastern men's house; (C) central dancing area; (D) house of chief Mote-re; (E) house of chief Pănhkĭ; (F) house of chief Ôket; (G) boundary of the village; (H) path to the river. Note that the informant explicitly drew the limit of the village behind the ring of residential houses, including, therefore, the *atyk-mã* as an essential part of the village.

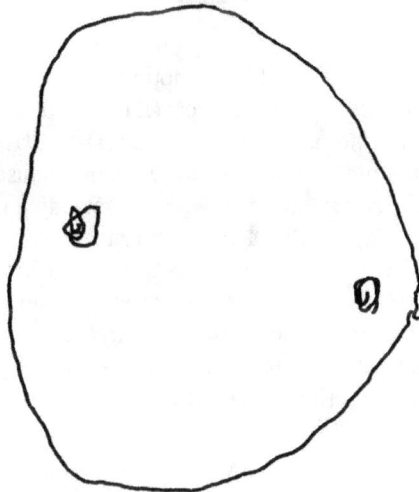

Figure 4 — Informant's drawing of a traditional Kayapo village with two men's houses.

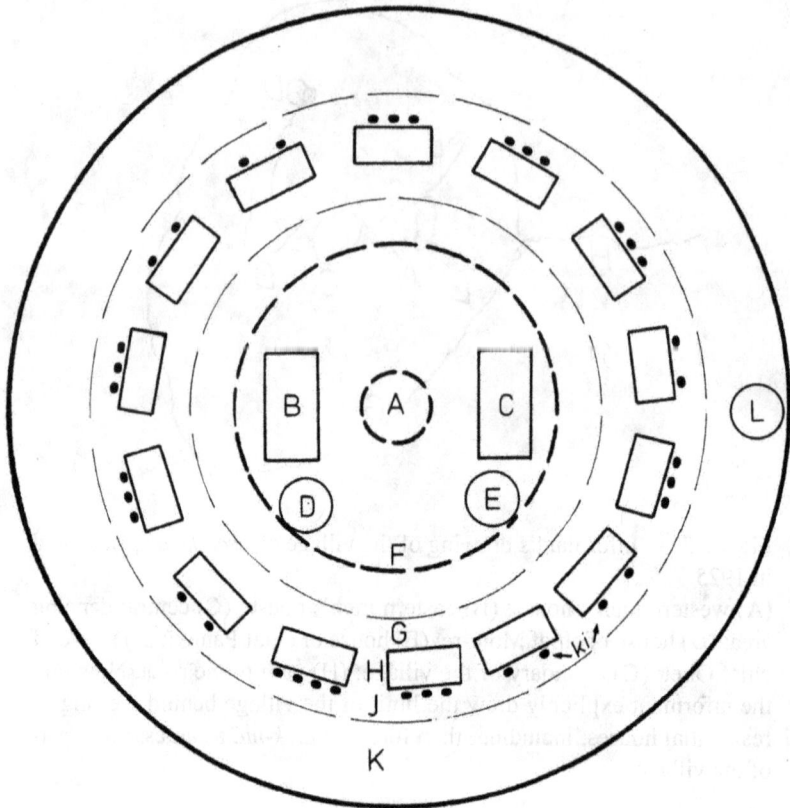

Figure 5 — Model of an ideal Mekranoti village.
(A) *metorodjà*, the central dancing area; (B) *ngànhôt*, the western men's
house; (C) *ngàkrax*, the eastern men's house; (D) *ngakrax me jã ku'êdjà*,
the "standing place of the men of the eastern men's house" where several
rituals begin; (E) *ngànhôt me jã ku'êdjà*, the "standing place of the men
of the western men's house" where several rituals begin; (F) *metorodjà*,
the main dancing circle; (G) *kikrekabe-'ã*, the area in front of the residential houses; (H) *kikre*, the (ring of) residential houses; (J) *kikrebu-
rũm*, the area just behind the houses; (K) *atyk-mã*, the transition area
between the village and the surrounding nature; (L) *me'ôk-re ngreredjà*,
the early morning gathering site of the boys of the *me'ôk-re* age grade.

related activities, on the other hand, are characterized by organization
based on kin groups.

The men's house (*ngà-be*) is rarely totally empty; it is one of the most animated of all sites in a Kayapo village. In the early morning or late afternoon, it is the meeting place where important oratories may be given by the village elders or by the chiefs, and where communal activities as well as politics are discussed. During the daytime, it may serve as the place where handicrafts are manufactured; at night unmarried men, as well as some married men with pregnant wives or new-born children, may sleep in it in observance of pre- and post-natal restrictions. During periods of ritual performances, the men's house bursts with life.

The area where most dances and communal, public ritual activities take place is located between the two men's houses or, in a single men's house village, in front of its main entrance. The latter invariably faces the village center and is, as such, positioned opposite to the nearest set of residential households.

Posey (1980: 33) mentions a path connecting both men's houses (if both are existent) and referred to it as the "chief's path", being the trail the chiefs of both men's houses cross to discuss matters of common, communal interest. No Mekranoti informant ever referred to such a path and it is possible that such a path only existed in huge villages like *pykatôti* which no Mekranoti informant ever actually saw, but which are still remembered by several older Gorotire and Kubenkranken informants.

Being above all associated with the men's associations, the village center is pre-eminently a male domain. Except on rare (ritual) occasions, women and girls are chased away from the men's house. Consequently, when a woman has to cross the village to go to the river or the gardens, or to go on a visit to another household, she usually avoids coming anywhere near the men's house by making a detour around it. She will generally follow the cleared area in front of the ring of residential households, referred to as "next to the houses" (*kikre kabe-'ã*). It is the area where the women also group in the evening to talk. After a hard day's work and when weather permits, they sit on household mats and avail themselves of the tranquility and the open air to talk about matters of common interest. Some older women may chant or relate a myth, while the younger women listen and children play, always within a certain secure and visible range of their mothers or other kinswomen.

The women's associations also have meeting places; these are located on the *kikre kabe-'ã*, just in front of the ring of houses. This location reflects the Kayapo conception of the women's relatively unsocialized nature, as opposed to the more socialized nature of men who are associated with the very center of the village or social universe.

2.3 — The village periphery

The Kayapo village periphery consists of a set of residential households which accommodate the extended families. The basis of the household structure is the uxorilocal post-marital residence pattern where women remain living in their mother's household. Men move in with their wife at the consummation of marriage. Therefore, each of the uxorilocal extended families consists ideally of one or more older sisters, their daughters, granddaughters and respective husbands and offspring.

It sometimes happens that after a certain time, a given extended family has become too numerous to remain in a single household. In such cases, big houses may split up: those who are leaving will usually build a new house beside or behind the original house. It is therefore common to find a set of houses in which the women are all related matrilineally to each other. Following Melatti's terminology (Melatti 1979: 51), such house sets are called a "residential segment". Up to 1980, that is before the village of PI Mekranoti started splitting up, each of its fifteen[2] residential segments numbered between one and five houses (see figure 7). The Kayapo term for residential segment (or briefly, segment) is *rwỹkdjà* (which literally means "birth-place"), referring to the place in the village circle in which a person was born or, in other terms, to a person's natal household.

Each of these residential segments is associated with a number of personal names, ritual privileges (such as the right to perform specific dances or specific ritual functions), rights to wear specific items of personal adornment or to keep such ornaments stocked in the house after use, rights to receive specific parts of certain animals in ritual food distribution and rights to raise certain domestic animals (Verswijver 1983a, 1983b).

Residential segments are not named as such, but may be referred to by the enumeration of some of the most important items of personal adornment or ritual privileges[3]. Such references to residential segments are particularly common when visiting other Kayapo villages: visitors will list a number of personal adornments or ritual privileges associated with their "birthplace" (i.e., their natal household) so as to discover which

---

2   *Krãnhmrôpryjaka*, the Mekranoti village occupied in the period of 1936-1937, numbered twenty such residential segments. The villages of PI Bau, PI Kretire and PI Jarina respectively numbered six, twelve and five residential segments in 1980 (Verswijver 1983a: 318-320). After consulting habitants of other non-Mekranoti Kayapo villages, it appears that *pykatôti* had many more of these segments.

3   Due to the existing taboos against reciting one's personal names, they are never used in this context.

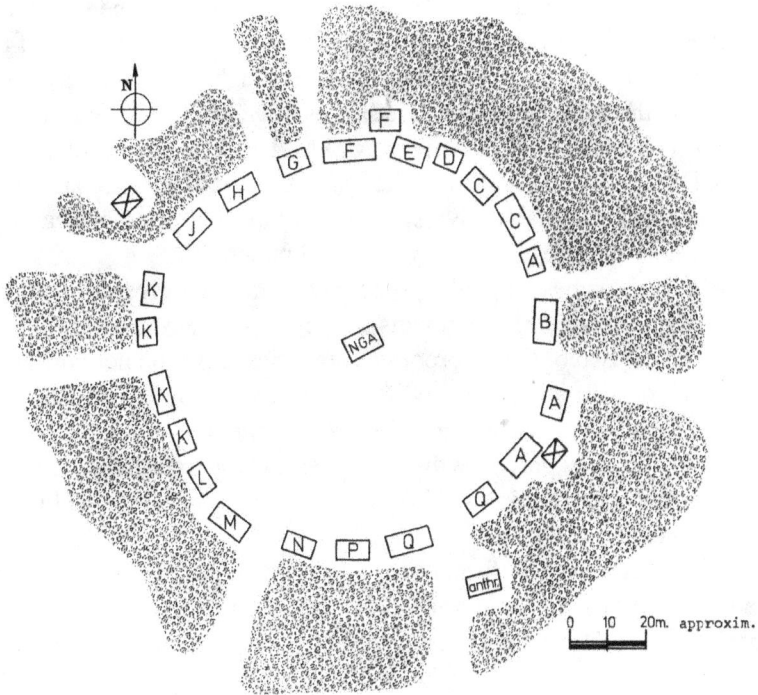

Figure 6 — Distribution of the residential segments throughout the Central Mekranoti village (1980). Each letter represents another segment.

house(s) in that village is of his/her residential segment. It will be in this house that the visitor will be housed and fed for the duration of the visit (see App. B: 7 for an account of a man visiting another Kayapo village).

But this is only one of the ways of referring to a given residential segment. The Kayapo will often also respond to a question concerning their *rwỳkdjà* by pointing to the appropriate house(s) within the village or by indicating its position in relation to the course of the sun.

There are, therefore, two ways to refer to residential segments: the first way reflects the association of segments with items of personal adornment and other ritual privileges, while the second reflects their spatial organization.

The arrangement of residential segments is fixed and is maintained when a new village is constructed and also during most treks.

It should be emphasized, however, that being born in a given segment does not in and of itself confer all rights and personal names associated with that specific residential segment: rather, these must be transmitted in order for a person to have the right to use them. Transmission of personal names and other ritual paraphernalia through individuals is effected bilaterally through kinship and dyadic ties of *ingêt* (FF, MF, MB) to male *tàbdjwỳ* (SS, DS, ZS), or *kwatyi* (MM, FM, FZ) to female *tàbdjwỳ* (DD, SD, BD). Cross-sex siblings of the parents as well as grandparents are therefore potential name-givers and these kinsmen often play a major ritual role in the lives of the Kayapo, until puberty.

Although names as well as other rights may be given to members born in other residential segments, the cycle of transmission involves no more than two of these corporate categories: a person not born in the "owning" residential segment will, after receiving such a name or right, have to retransmit these to a member of the original "owning" segment. Transmission rules prescribe that such elements be transmitted to a child who has the relationship of *tàbdjwỳ* to the person who received it from that segment.

The ceremonial confirmation of "beautiful names", as well as the transmission of social status and ritual paraphernalia, always occurs before puberty and before a person formally joins the men's or women's associations.

On a secular basis, a man's share in the food provision (meat and fish) is often shared with co-habitants of his wife's segment, as well as with members of other residential segments to which the man or his spouse may owe meat or fish. Thus, under propitious economic circumstances, the network of exchange results in the fact that a man may not necessarily have to go out hunting or fishing every day.

Residential segments, therefore, constitute a higher level of economic organization than the nuclear family, since they involve a more complex set of social relations than the nuclear family.

The nuclear family is the smallest recognizable group in Kayapo society, serving as the basic unit of secular economic production and procreation.

Informants' views on conception are not unanimous, since two different versions were collected in the field. A first one relates how the man's semen mixes with the woman's milk and how this mixture then drips from the latter's breasts, inside her body, into her womb. Both parents, therefore, provide liquid substances which, once mingled, gradually "make" the child's body. In another account, the man's semen blackens inside the woman's womb and gradually constitutes the body of the child. Thus the father provides the bones, flesh and skin, while the mother provides the blood. Although both versions differ relative to the ascription of the individual contribution of each of the partners in the conception of a child, both agree that the monogamous couple provides the essential fluid substances (blood, milk and semen) and that numerous sexual acts are required to construct a new human being. As the Kayapo say, the little quantities of semen gradually "make" the child's body. In Kayapo opinion, then, neither short-lived adulterous liaisons nor a single amorous adventure can engender a child. The establishment of permanent sexual relations between a man and a woman, therefore, constitute the first and decisive stage in the formation of a new nuclear family. The birth of a child confirms and consolidates the union or "marriage".

Siblings are said "to have appeared together" (*atxikôt kator*) which refers to the fact that these persons have "turned up" out of the same womb. Siblings are linked by a biological bond and, therefore, observe periods of restrictions on behalf of each other, just like parents do for their children in order to assure the growth and survival of the child.

The nuclear family is not only defined on account of its potential for procreation or its biological link, however, but also by its relative economic independence. While the husband provides the meat, fish, necessary tools, and handicrafts to sustain his family, the wife goes almost daily to her garden(s) accompanied by her daughters to harvest the crops. She may also leave on short gathering trips to collect wild fruits, nuts or medicinals. The nuclear family, therefore, is considered as a potentially independent economical unit and may go into the forest for a few days or weeks, surviving exclusively on its own daily production. I emphasize the word "potentially" since reference here is made exclusively to the most basic, secular level of economic activities. On a higher level, each nuclear family is intricately related to others through the permanent network of food exchange: i.e., the constant process of receiving and giving. On a community level this network expands to ritual obligations, the "payment" of consulted specialists and retribution for services rendered.

In general, the man's economic contribution is less than that of the woman. Men may go out hunting or fishing every other day or so, but the woman's agricultural tasks are daily, since women's economic tasks include food production and processing, and the supply of water and firewood. Other female activities are delousing and painting their kinsmen, and the socialization of young children. This is not only expressed in breast-feeding — a kind of external pregnancy which is seen as the natural continuation of procreation itself — but also by the education and permanent caretaking of their children. The women's activities are therefore mainly restricted to the sphere of the village periphery.

In summary, it can be said that the fundamental transactions performed in the village periphery are essentially organized on the basis of kin ties. The ring of residential households establishing the village periphery, thus, constitutes the sphere of domestic and kin-based activities.

2.4 — A model of concentric spatial order

A model of Kayapo cosmological conceptions can best be illustrated by a series of concentric circles. Of all forms, the circle is the primary symbolic figure. Circles are omnipresent in Kayapo society: the sun and the moon — both spheres viewed as mythological beings — are circular, as are the courses of these two heavenly bodies. A great number of ritual artifacts — such as feather headdresses, bracelets and necklaces — are circular, as are some objects of daily use such as baskets, spindles and music instruments. Most dances and ritual expressions are performed in a circular configuration, whether through a circular movement or by a grouping in circles by protagonists. Earth-ovens are circular as are gardens, villages and most forest camps.

The village is the center of Kayapo cosmology and is considered to be made up of three main areas: the village center, the circle of residential households and the transitional zone between the village proper and the surrounding nature. The village itself has been dealt with more deeply in the foregoing section and I will now, in the following pages, exclusively deal with concentric zones beyond the ring of residential houses. All the numbers mentioned refer to the ones displayed in the figure 8.

I. the transitional zone atyk-mã

Beyond the houses lies the *atyk-mã*, the "black" or asocial part of the village. It is the transitional zone between the village, the most highly socialized of all spaces, and the fully natural area of the forest and savannah.

The *kikrebu-rũm* or "behind the house" is a narrow stretch behind the ring of houses and has to be taken as a zone that is marginally *atyk-mã*. In this *kikrebu-rũm*, each matrilineal dwelling has a *ki* (the traditional earth oven), and it is the arena of such collective activities as female body paintings. The former daily, early morning meeting of the boys of the *mebôkti-re* and *me'ôk-re* age grades also took place in this area — this meeting place used to be located to the east of the village and was named *atyk-be*, literally "to be (located) in the black or dead ground".

Since rubbish is thrown in the *kikrebu-rũm*, this area is often a bit messy. Women therefore prefer to hold their body painting sessions in front of the houses, while *ki* earth-ovens are either placed in front of the houses or (and this during the rainy season) inside of these houses.

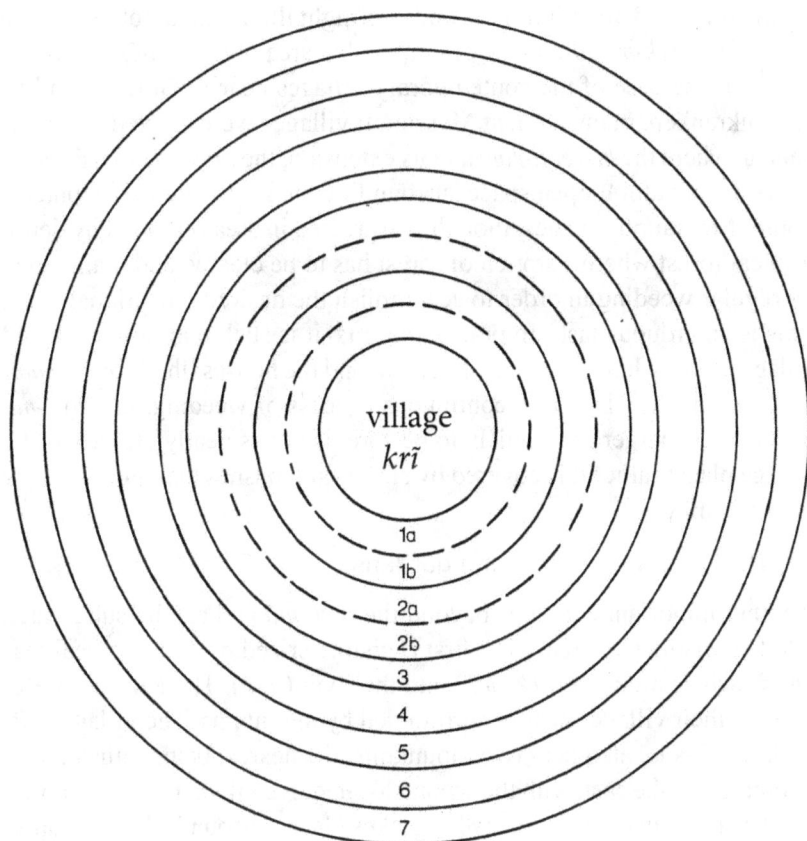

Figure 7 — Concentric categories of space.
(1a) *kikrebu-rũm*; (1b) *atyk-mã*; (2a) *ngô* (river) and *krãnh* (mountains); (2b) *pur* (gardens); (3) *kutakẽnhtxdjà*; (4) *meba nhõ pyka*; (5) *me-bêngôkre nhõ pyka*; (6) *bà kakrit*; (7) *krĩ rax* (cities) and *ngô rax* (ocean).

The *atyk-mã* is the extension of the *kikrebu-rũm* and consists of a fairly broad area behind the houses. Depending on the age of the settlement as well as the energy of the inhabitants of the village, the width of this area may range from fifty to five hundred meters or more. In the *atyk-mã* the dead are buried, returning hunters or warriors sing their songs to inform villagers of the results of their ventures, some dances originate, the jaguar is prepared by young men, animal skins are hung out to dry and most children are born[4]. It is here too that small camps are erected

4   For obvious reasons of safety against jaguars, snakes and other dangerous

during the boys' initiation ritual and overnight illicit sexual relations take place. The *atyk-mã* is also the principal play area of the *mebôkti-re* boys.

As is the case of the contemporary villages near PI Gorotire and PI Kubenkranken, many ancient Mekranoti villages were erected in the savannah where the *kikrebu-rũm* and its extension, the *atyk-mã*, consisted of a broad and natural open space surrounding the ring of houses. Contemporary Mekranoti villages, though, are erected in areas covered by dense tropical forest where a stretch of forest has to be cleared and maintained by regular weeding in order to accomplish the desired transitional zone. This is an arduous task. In practical terms, it is such that newly erected villages merely have a narrow stretch behind the houses (the *kikrebu-rũm*) properly cleared. Due to a continuous process of weeding, the *atyk-mã* expands to a larger area which, to be sure, is not as neatly cleared as the village plaza: rather it is covered by shrubs and bushes that quickly grow after weeding.

II. rivers, mountains and gardens

Another important zone lies beyond the *atyk-mã* and can be subdivided into two distinctive areas. The first is characterized by geographical features such as mountains (*krãnh*) and the river (*ngô*). The Kayapo prefer to build their villages near or surrounded by mountains. The village at PI Mekranoti is located near two mountains, the nearest being situated two kilometers to the east, with the second located five kilometers to the north.

The river, in which daily bathing takes place, surrounds the Mekranoti village on three sides. The most important of several bathing places is to the west of the settlement. It is also one of the most desired playgrounds for children, the place where drinking water is acquired and where most village inhabitants take their daily baths. The river has an important social function for the Kayapo. Women are deprived of an institutional meeting place such as the men's house, but they usually meet at the bathing place. At certain times up to twenty or more women can be found at this site eating sweet potatoes, gossiping, commenting on village activities as well as domestic affairs, and sometimes even discussing village politics.

The numerous paths which connect the village with the many river crossings, and the presence of a dense gallery forest offer favorite hidden meeting places for illicit sexual intercourse during the daytime.

Behind the river and the mountains and connected with the village by a network of broad, cleared trails lies the second area. This second area

---

animals which often wander around in the *atyk-mã* at night, nocturnal birth usually occurs inside the houses.

is dominated by gardens. Fields are usually laid out at distances between two and six kilometers from the village, although some are more distant. For the village at PI Mekranoti the farthest gardens are situated near the Xixê River, at approximatively forty kilometers to the east of the village, where several annual treks pass for fishing and hunting.

Like the houses, gardens belong to the women. Almost daily the women wander to these fields to gather manioc, sweet potatoes, bananas, corn or other garden products. Gardens are places to withdraw to for those seeking isolation from village activity. They are also favorite sites for sexual intercourse.

For fear of spirits (*karõ*), women rarely go alone to their fields. Small groups of women leave together for their daily journey of hard work and these women are frequently related: sisters usually have contiguous gardens laid out around that of their mother.

The more distant gardens are only visited by (groups of) nuclear families or a group of women, all members of the same women's society. Indians generally spend several days or sometimes even a few weeks in distant fields, and have small houses built near or on these gardens. Fields are laid out in a circular form and the cultivars are planted in concentric patterns.

III. the well-known forest

Beyond the ring of mountains, rivers and gardens, where women daily venture without male company, is a huge area of tropical forest (*bà*), sometimes alternating with open spaces of grassland (*kapôt*). The Kayapo distinguish between four categories of forest and as many categories of open grassland (Posey 1981ms: 20). Innumerable narrow trails, most of which are hardly perceivable by people not accustomed to jungle life, crisscross this domain. The men are very familiar with this area since they penetrate it almost daily in search of game or, to a lesser extent, for fish.

Seasonal or ceremonial treks[5] always take place within this zone. The course of such treks is usually circular. During the treks, it is rare nowadays that a group of Kayapo will travel further than sixty kilometers from the village, the distance men can cover in a day's walk. By referring to this zone as *kutakẽnhtxdjà* ("return sites"), the Kayapo make clear

---

5   As will be explained in Chapter 5, seasonal treks *(meyh* or "the people's trekking") are performed to collect wild fruits or some specific material such as palm oil or palm leaves. Similar treks may also be undertaken in the dry season to areas where fish and meat are more abundant. Ceremonial treks *(õntomõr,* "to go on a journey for a number of nights") are performed to obtain the necessary quantity of meat or fish for the conclusion of a major ceremony.

that the outer limit of this domain is where the village can no longer be reached in one day's walk.

During seasonal treks, small circular camps are usually built, frequently with a men's house in the center. If not rendered impossible by obstructive existing vegetation, the arrangement of uxorilocal houses, as found in the village, is maintained in such temporary forest camps.

In the *kutakẽnhtxdjà* zone most places are named: rivers, creeks, areas of specific vegetation, areas where certain fruits are abundant, mountains, hillsides, areas of open grassland, or old campsites all have names. The sources of the great variety of such place names can mainly be reduced to first, those of a descriptive nature, such as *kukryt nhõ ngô* ("the water of the tapir") or *krãnhmrôpryjaka* ("mountain base with white open grassland"), and secondly those with an anecdotal nature, referring to a specific event which took place at a given spot. Within this last category of place names, the possibilities are numerous as illustrated by the following examples: *bekwỳnhtetxô kam* ("at Bekwỳnhtetxô") referring to the place where a girl named Bekwỳnhtetxô was born during one of the many forest treks; *ropdjãmdjà* ("standing place of the jaguar") referring to the place where years ago a hunter sighted a jaguar; *kikretxêt kam* ("there where houses burnt") referring to the place where once a village burned down. Such place names are kept alive in tribal memory, and it is obvious that over time, the whole area becomes a cultural map in which many names refer to historical events. In Kayapo oral tradition, many such references to place names are made. While referring to those periods when the Kayapo still lived along the Xingu, Fresco and Araguaia Rivers — far to the east of the current area — older Mekranoti informants often provide names of places which they never actually saw. Seeger (1977: 353-355) noted that through the naming of places, a large geographical area is in a sense socialized and familiarized.

New place names are constantly given, some older ones forgotten, but there is no doubt as to the importance of such names in the recalling of events and to their contribution to tribal history. This is because, when travelling in this zone of daily penetrated forest, older tribal members usually recall such names and tell them to their younger companions. Reference is then often made to the meaning of the name whereby old memories are revived. Wandering in the forest with a senior tribesman is therefore not only a lesson in the ecological knowledge of these people — since all sorts of comments are made on plants and their uses — but also a lesson in Kayapo history; it also means a journey through time, where present and past become reality and form one consistent entity.

IV. Mekranoti land

The next important zone is the area called *meba nhõ pyka* ("our land"), which refers to the whole stretch of land the Mekranoti have occupied since their separation from the main Kayapo of the Xingu group in about 1905. This huge area of about sixty thousand square kilometers, reaching from PI Kretire in the south to a little ways downstream from PI Bau along the Curua River in the north, and from the Liberdade River in the east to the Jamanxim River in the west, represents in fact the whole area in which both ancestral and contemporary Mekranoti villages and gardens were and are located.

Partly because communities generally lived on hostile terms after village schisms, and partly because each Kayapo village is an autonomous social, political and ceremonial unit, the Mekranoti did not really consider this whole area as one closed entity in pre-contact era. Today, however, common problems have arisen which reinforce the ethnic solidarity between Kayapo groups. With the ever increasing number of invaders and neo-Brazilian settlements, the ownership of land has become a problem bringing about the necessity of defining native territory.

A main obstacle in the process of Mekranoti land demarcation by the Brazilian government concerned the definition of an area referred to as *meba nhõ kapôt djwỹnh* ("our real savannah"). This is an almost circular area of open grassland some thirty kilometers in diameter, and situated between the upper Iriri Novo and Jarina Rivers (see map 2). Although a considerable number of ancient or historical villages were built at distances of up to two hundred kilometers from this savannah area, the relatively small area in question is considered the core of traditional Mekranoti land by all contemporary Mekranoti Indians. In it, most ancestral villages were built, most ancient gardens were laid out, most attacks were suffered, most Mekranoti were buried and most currently living adults and elders were born. It is also said that the village of the dead — the "spirit place" (*mekarõ nhyrykwã*) — is situated in one of the many hills that are located in that area. The *meba nhõ kapôt djwỹnh*, therefore, is by far the most important of all ancient sites to the Mekranoti.

In the 1960s and 1970s no Mekranoti village was erected in the *meba nhõ kapôt djwỹnh*. In spite of Mekranoti insistence that it should be included within Reserve boundaries, the Indian Reserves the Government had proposed excluded this area of savannah. After years of demands and after pressure from the Southern Mekranoti, in May 1984 the Brazilian Government finally annexed this area to the Xingu National Park.

V. Kayapo land

The *meba nhõ pyka* nor the following zone called *mebêngôkre nhõ pyka* ("the land of the Kayapo") are geographically circular zones (see maps 5 and 7) but these are conceptually seen as such by the Mekranoti. The "land of the Kayapo" is a huge geographic area composed of the tribal territories of all contemporary Kayapo villages. It is, in other terms, the sum of the *meba nhõ pyka* of each and every one of the Kayapo groups. The zone in question is only penetrated for visiting other communities or, in former times, for raiding. Vanishing narrow trails, old camp sites overgrown by forest, hardly recognizable old gardens and so on, recall the historic occupation by the Kayapo. In the early twentieth century, this almost contiguous area ranged over about hundred and forty thousand square kilometers. Today, the *mebêngôkre nhõ pyka* has been reduced to some seventy thousand square kilometers, being the sum of the designated Kayapo Reserves and of additional areas which the Kayapo claim but which have still not been demarcated. This area is being severely threatened by encroaching farms, neo-Brazilian settlements and, more particularly, huge industrialization projects.

Although the Indians are familiar with the dangers of these two zones, the forest has always been considered as an anti-social domain in which people may be transformed into animals or spirits, may become mad, and kill kin members, or where unknown animal-like humans may live. The farther one withdraws from the center of the Kayapo universe — that is, the village center — the less socialized and the more dangerous the environment becomes. This is clearly represented in narrative 3 of Appendix B where a Kayapo group distances itself from the tribal territory, gradually penetrating more and more into unknown areas. The group first encounters species of sweet potatoes, jaguars and snakes (elements known by the village habitants), then unknown strangers and finally the "area of the perpetual night" which is feared and which the contemporary, surviving Kayapo are said not to have traversed.

VI. the distant forest

The distant forest (*bà kakrit*), the next important zone, is a domain which is inhabited by strangers (*kubẽ*) and by enemies (*mekurêdjwjỳnh*). It is greatly feared and only penetrated by raiding parties. It extends from Kayapo known land to White inhabited areas.

VII. cities and big waters

Brazilian and other cities (*krĩ rax*, "big villages") — including any country the Mekranoti have heard of — and the ocean and big rivers (*ngô rax*, "big water") are considered by the Mekranoti as the last zone. Monsters of various types, animal-like humans and unknown animals lived in this area until, as the Indians say, the Whites killed most of them.

3. THE AGE GRADES

Division into sex and age grades are the two major criteria by which all individuals in Kayapo society are classified. From birth to death, all males and females are classified through a series of conceptual categories of social age called age grades. Each age grade is named, is ritually distinct, has a peculiar set of behavioral rules, and is visibly distinguishable by specific ornaments, body painting styles and hair-cuts.

Progression from one age grade to the other is marked by an individual socially determined or timed biological event such as attaining basic motor skills, the girl's first menstruation, the birth of a first child in wedlock, and so on, and therefore is not automatic.

Since many detailed descriptions of Kayapo age grades and their relation to family and community have already been published[6], I will, in this section, limit the following presentation to a brief survey of the basic characteristics of each age grade. Also, as the central theme of this essay is pre-eminently a male matter, the female life cycle will not be discussed in this essay. Table 1 offers a general view of the male age grades. In addition, more detail on the several rites of passage marking the transition from early puberty to manhood will be given in Chapter 4, where these passages are discussed in the perspective of warfare.

3.1 — The *meprĩ-re*

From birth until the time a child is fully "able to walk" (*aryp mrãnh kam*) children of both sexes are referred to as "little ones" (*meprĩ-re*). During the first year of life, which corresponds to the period when the father temporarily takes up residence in the men's house to observe post-natal restrictions, the child is often called "suckling person" (*mekarà*).

Biologically undifferentiated from its parents — and more specifically, from its mother — the child's existence is limited to the sphere of its parental nuclear family. Carried in a sling, the child is breast-fed while the mother transports the child wherever she goes. And when she is oc-

6   For more detailed analyses on Kayapo age grades, see especially Dreyfus (1963: 71-77), T.Turner (1965: 103-403) and Vidal (1977: 87-174).

Table 1 — The male age grades with corresponding residence pattern and sitting place in the men's house.

MALE AGE GRADE	STATE OF LIFE CYCLE	AGE RANGE approx.	RITE DE PASSAGE	RESIDENCE	SITTING PLACE IN MEN'S HOUSE
meprĩ-re	infancy	0-3	no rite (cut hair, remove ear-plugs	maternal house	
mebôktí-re	childhood	3-8	me'ôk (painting by "substitute father")		
me'ôk-re	early puberty	8-12			sitting place of "substitute father"
menõrõny-re	adolescence, sociological adulthood	12-20	mydjê (receiving of penis sheath) followed by 'ôk oinore-re (last painting by "substitute father")	men's house	sitting place of young men of his age grade
mekra-re	married men with children in wedlock	20-45	no rite (birth of first child in wedlock)		sitting place of men's society of his choice (junior group)
mebêngêt	old man	45 +	no rite (old age and becoming grandfather)	wife's house	sitting place of men's society of his choice (senior group)

cupied with a task in or just in front of her household, the child may crawl around to discover its new environment, but this is invariably within a secure range of a few meters from its mother who promptly presents the breast whenever the little one starts crying.

The earlobes of girls, as well as the earlobes and lower lip of boys, are pierced a few days after birth. Cotton strings are put into the holes to prevent them from healing-over, and those in the earlobes are then replaced by little, cigar-shaped earplugs of reddened wood which are gradually replaced by larger ones that increase the size of the hole in the earlobe.

Children of the meprĩ-re age grade are generally elaborately painted and are characterized by the profusion of bodily ornaments, such as earplugs, slings and belts made of numerous strings of glass beads, and cotton arm and leg bands. The first earplugs, the first cotton arm bands and the umbilical cord are kept in a small bag made of palm fibers and called prôdjà. Afterwards, this bag is placed near a stone or suspended in a hardwood tree in the atyk-mã area, an act which is believed to transmit the "strength" or "hardness" (tỹx) of these natural elements to the child.

The hair of the new-born is usually not cut during its first year, and even later is left long at the back and sides.

3.2 — The *mebôkti-re* or *mebêngàdjy-re*

From early childhood to early puberty, the boy is referred to as *mebôktire* or as *mebêngàdjy-re* ("the one who is about to enter the men's house"). The transition from *meprĩ-re* to this age grade is marked by the removal of the earplugs and the cutting of the hair.

The *mebôkti-re* boys gradually become more and more independent of their parents and often engage in playing soccer or *rõnkrã* ("babassu palm head"), a traditional hockey-like Kayapo game. These boys usually walk about with a small group of their peers, often forming small cliques of close friends.

In an initial phase, their range of action is confined to the village plaza. By growing older, however, they little by little shift this boundary to the *atyk-mã* around the village. After a first, hesitating exploration of this area — by which they are usually chased away by the elder age grade mates — they gradually spend more of their time along the riverside playing and fishing, and finally end up by appropriating the *atyk-mã* as well as the area around it as their play-ground. There, they hunt small birds, build small camps, imitate the mature men's dances, etc. Several references in Kayapo tales refer to the fact that these boys, as constant occupants of the immediate vicinity of the village, often detect the arrival of visitors or enemies (see App. B: 6-8).

Due to their relative freedom, these boys are in a marginal position, between the natal household — with which they gradually loosen ties — and the men's house — of which they are not yet members, but which they will join soon.

During this phase of the life cycle, "beautiful names", which have been transferred after birth, will be ceremonially confirmed during one of the elaborate naming ceremonies. The relationship between a boy and his several *ingêt* (MF, FF, MB) is expressed and emphasized in many rituals during this particular phase of his life and is seen as a gradual deflection of the major social responsibilities of the boy from the parents to this specific kin category.

3.3 — The *me'ôk-re* or *megôrômãnõr*

Early puberty (at the approximate age of eight to twelve) is marked by a brief rite of passage. A nonkinsman[7] will go to the boy's natal household.

---

7   This nonkin is a man who stands in no genealogical relationship with the boy and who preferably is one of the men who has carried forest turtles during the naming ceremony in which the boy was honoured while a *mebôkti-re*.

He addresses the boy's father saying, "I will keep painting your son" and leads the boy to the men's house. While both the father and the mother ritually wail over the separation of their son from the natal household, the nonkinsman paints the boy's body black. After this brief and solemn rite of passage, called "the people's painting" (*me'ôk*), the boy is a full member of the *me'ôk-re* ("painted people") age grade.

Through this ritual act, the nonkinsman in question assumes the role of "substitute father" (*bãm ka'àk*) for the boy. The Mekranoti say it is preferable for a *menõrõny'ãtũm* or "old (senior) adolescent" to assume this role of tutor, i.e., of "substitute father". Mature men with children who are members of one of the existing men's societies may also be tutors, but this occurs much less often.

Once *me'ôk-re*, the boy will use the men's house for sleeping until he fathers his first child in wedlock. Since these boys sleep collectively in the men's house, they are often referred to as "those who sleep together" (*megôrômãnõr*). Although they regularly continue to frequent their natal household, they cease to be considered full members of that domestic group. As a member of the *me'ôk-re* age grade, a boy sits in the men's house slightly behind his tutor. The "substitute father" instructs the boy in the creation of handicrafts, in the knowledge of some medicinal plants and in ceremonial lore. The boy is also regularly painted by his "substitute father", who is therefore often referred to as "the father who paints me" (*ibãm kute ijôk*). Yet, the tutor has no particular obligations towards the boy other than occasional painting — an act which must be seen as the semi-permanent confirmation of this symbolic and ritual adoption — and introducing the boy to some practical knowledge. The boy's true mother and sisters continue to supply the boy with food and firewood.

On the other hand, the boy is in a way subordinate to his "substitute father" in the sense that the latter will make use of him as a messenger, an errand-boy or, more comprehensively, as a general practical aid. Many references to these tasks of the *me'ôk-re* boys exist in Kayapo mythology (see, for example, Wilbert 1978: 104-105, 177-179, 355-356), but it is a position which not always pleases the subordinate. A boy may refuse to carry out what he is asked but frequently other men of his tutor's men's group reinforce the demand so that finally the boy will go and fetch or do what he is asked for. On two occasions I witnessed a newly incorporated *me'ôk-re* who was reluctant to carry out these duties and systematically refused to come near the men's house. These boys returned to join the younger *mebôkti-re* in their daily ventures outside the village, thus avoiding coming anywhere near the men's house. The concerned "substitute fathers" reacted almost indifferently and said that the boys were still too young or too lazy[8] and they temporarily renounced their ritual responsibilities. In both cases, it took about one year before the established ritual tie became effective; then the boys started to frequent the men's house as did their age grade mates.

3.4 — The *menõrõny-re*

At puberty another brief but important ritual takes place during which all those boys who are considered of age are given a penis sheath (*mydjê*) to wear. The penis sheath consists of a strip of palm leaf, folded into a conical form and through which the prepuce is pulled. Traditionally, from that occasion on, a man is never seen without this little piece of clothing which only covers the glans penis. Nowadays, with the introduction of western clothing, most Mekranoti men constantly wear shorts but may, on ritual occasions, still put on their *mydjê*.

The bestowal of the penis sheath reflects the formal recognition of the boy's sexual potential — that is, his biological maturity — and corresponds to his initiation into regular sexual relations. It therefore seems appropriate to refer to these young men with the term bachelors.

Those bachelors who recently received their penis sheath are often referred to as "those with the new penis sheath" (*memydjêny-re*) a term which does not correspond to an age grade but rather to the sub-category of the *menõrõny-re* age grade embracing all these newly incorporated youngsters. As bearers of the penis sheath, the *menõrõny-re* are socially defined as marriageable but the Kayapo consider it desirable for them to wait as long as possible before marrying.

The *menõrõny-re* continue to sleep in the men's house, but due to their series of sexual liaisons, they often sneak out of the men's house at night to visit the girls in their houses. They are out of these houses and back into the men's house before the girl's parents awake in the morning. The term *menõrõny-re* (literally "those who sleep in a new way") is clearly an allusion to this particular form of semi-permanent residence in the men's house.

A newly introduced member of the *menõrõny-re* age grade establishes sexual liaisons with several girls. These liaisons are not binding and after some years, the man will establish a more or less monogamous relationship with one girl. As this union becomes more firmly established, he is gradually allowed to spend some time with his girlfriend in her house during the daytime: at first when his future parents-in-law are out work-

8   I often had the impression that "readiness" to become a *me'ôk-re* was related to the boy's maturity of refraining from playing with his age mates.

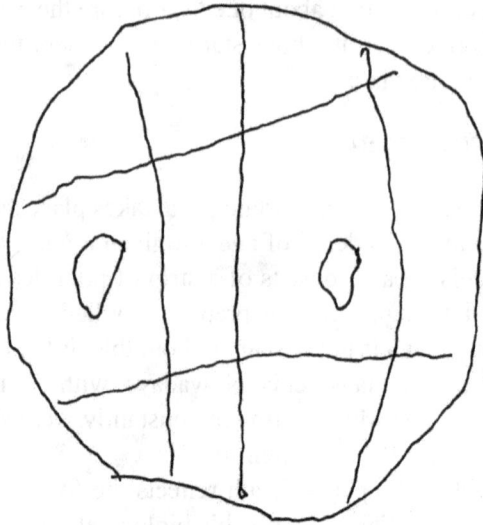

Figure 8 — Informant's drawing while discussing marriage patterns.

ing, and later even in their presence.

After some years a bachelor may father a child with a girl he is not willing to marry. Such men with children out of wedlock usually wait a long time before effectively marrying and consequently become known as "old (senior) *menõrõny-re*" (*menõrõny 'ãtũm*), a term which corresponds to yet another subcategory of the *menõrõny-re* age grade.

No marriage or sexual relations are allowed with kindred or, in other words, with a person's "real kin" (*õbikwadjwỳnh*)[9]. In general terms, *õbikwa* refers to all those individuals whom ego recognizes and calls by a relationship term (Bamberger 1979: 135). Marriage is said to be consummated with a member of "the other side of the village" (*kĩkjê- 'ã*), not alluding to any diametric spatial division of the village periphery but rather to the prescribed rule of marriage to a non-kin. Figure 9 shows the connection of the houses of marriage partners as seen by an informant and

9   As T. Turner (1974ms: 78) has put it, *õbikwa* is a term which can be used on three levels: meaning "kinsmen", as opposed to "nonkinsmen" *(meba 'itêm,* "people beside my people"); meaning "true kinsmen" *(õbikwadjwỳnh* or *õbikwakumrenhtx)* as opposed to "false" or "adoptive kinsmen" *(õbikwaka'àk* or *õbikwakajgo);* and meaning "consanguinal kin" as opposed to "kinsmen by marriage" *(abenwỳr mõr kam õbikwa).*

revealing the conceptual, genealogical distance between the components of a couple.

The *menõrõny-re* have their hair cut semi-short. Within the men's house they occupy a separate "sitting place" (*krĩdjà*). Generally located in the center of the men's house and surrounded by the sitting places of the mature men's societies, this separate setting symbolizes the relative independence of these young men. No longer under the ritual tutelage of their "substitute father", the *menõrõny-re* are characterized by their collectivity. Most of the activities these bachelors undertake are performed by the collective group of men of their age grade: they usually paint each other, dance and sing together, often go bathing jointly, or take off on long hunting or gathering expeditions. This constant state of togetherness and mutual solidarity often leads to the building up of strong individual bonds between pairs of young men, a mutual friendship which often lasts an entire lifetime. This particular relationship is given emphasis and expression in the Kayapo word *inhikjê*, a term indicating symmetry, reciprocity, "my other half" or, more generally, "my good friend".

Not yet burdened by the duties and responsibilities which are inherent to those men who already have set up their own nuclear family, the *menõrõny-re* are the most mobile men's group in Kayapo society; Mekranoti history shows that these bachelors may jointly leave the village to stay away for periods of up to a year or more, covering hundreds of kilometers. They are also expected to be the most enthusiastic and energetic participants in communal activities such as ceremonies, hunting, trekking and raiding — activities through which they gain esteem of the married women, who often have *menõrõny-re* as lovers.

The bachelors are cast in a marginal status referent to village politics: they are subordinate to the mature men and this status is accompanied by a certain rivalry and antagonism between these two men's groups (T. Turner 1965: 279).

3.5 — The *mekra-re*

Once a woman has a "big swollen belly" (*tyjarô rax*), marking her sixth or seventh month of pregnancy, both she and her husband are designated as "those with a swollen belly" (*metyjarô*). After the birth of the child and during its first year — while it is referred to as "suckling person" (*mekarà*) — both parents are referred to as "those with suckling children" (*mekrakarà*).

While they are *metyjarô* or *mekrakarà*, the man refrains from maintaining sexual relations with his wife, and the woman is prohibited from having any sexual intercourse until the child is considered strong enough. The length of this period of sexual abstinence varies from case to case. The decision as to when this period ends is taken by the woman who will, at that time, apply a specific body painting as a sign that she will now fully participate in communal life again. In general, however, a period of about one year seems to be the average. During this time, the husband takes up residence in the men's house and maintains occasional sexual intercourse with a "substitute" or "unreal spouse" (*prõ ka 'àk* or *prõ ka-jgo*) who usually belongs to the group of *kupry*: unmarried women who have had children out of wedlock and who are associated with a given men's society which they may join on treks.

The pre- and post-natal restriction period in question is equally observed during the following births and is generally only dropped after the fourth child. One Mekranoti man who had procreated seven children up to 1981, still periodically observed these restriction periods and was considered by the village population as the sole man to really "act according to Kayapo custom" (*mekukràdjà kôt*) in this respect.

The Kayapo term for marriage is *aben wỳr mõ* (literally "coming together") and clearly reflects the nature of this betrothal. Marriage is considered to be consummated only when the wife has born a child: until then the union is easily broken off. The solemnization of marriage through the birth of a child permits the man to progress to the age grade of the "fathers" or of "those with new children" (*mekrany-re*) and "those with many children" (*mekrakramtĩ*), the latter referring to those men who have fathered four or more children in wedlock.

Progression to the *mekra-re* age grade marks the transition to mature manhood. On becoming a "father", the young man goes to the men's house and formally joins one of the existing mature men's societies, membership in which is restricted to and emblematic of the men of the "fathers" age grade. The man then moves his belongings to his wife's household — if he has not yet done so already when he was a *menõrõny 'ãtũm* — and thus occupies the status of newly incorporated son-in-law in his wife's household.

Fathers with new-born children are the junior members of the men's societies and still conduct a rather passive role in village politics. It is only upon attaining the status of "father with many children" that men will fulfil a more assertive role in village politics. Then they may actively participate in daily oratory, which is the principal constituent of the male council, and become part of the more dynamic group of political leadership in the community.

The accomplishment of this status parallels the man's position in his affinal household: a *mekrany-re* is characterized by his subordinate role, both economic and positional, to his parents-in-law, but when attaining the age grade of *mekrakramtĩ* the man's position both in his affinal household and his men's group are fortified. Likewise, the *mekrany-re* do not have any prestige within the *mekra-re* age grade and, as such, do not have any prestige on the political level. They do not, thus, differ much from the *menõrõnyre* in this aspect.

3.6 — The *mebêngêt*

Upon becoming a grandfather, a man is referred to as *mebêngêt* ("those who are old"). No rite of passage marks the transition from the *mekra-re* — or, more specifically, from the *mekrakramtĩ* sub-category — to this age grade. One becomes a *mebêngêt* by attaining the status of village elder and by communal accordance of great prestige. These men may continue to be active in oratory, but their political role is often more passive than that of the *mekrakramtĩ*. The *mebêngêt* mainly act as appeasers for disputes and as articulators of tribal tradition and of the community's moral values. This passive role is symbolized by separate sitting places in the men's house, apart from the more active men of their men's society.

4. POLITICAL ORGANIZATION

4.1 — Men's houses and men's associations

In former times, some Kayapo villages with a population of five hundred or (many) more Indians had two men's houses erected on the village plaza: an eastern (*ngàkrax*) and a western (*ngànhôt*) one. Due to the many consecutive splits in these huge villages, as well as to the relative low population in the new communities, all contemporary Kayapo villages have one, single men's house. Built on the village plaza, it still may stand to one side, in symbolic opposition of the (absent) other men's house. This location of the single men's house indicates the descent from the ancestral two men's house village from which the given community separated. So, for example, the ancient Mekranoti village of 1937 had two men's houses. The contemporary village of PI Bau is a descendent of the western men's house, since at the time of the split from that ancient, main village, all men of the dissident group were members of that western men's house. All other Mekranoti villages are descendants of the eastern men's house. The single men's house in PI Mekranoti is, therefore, built on the eastern

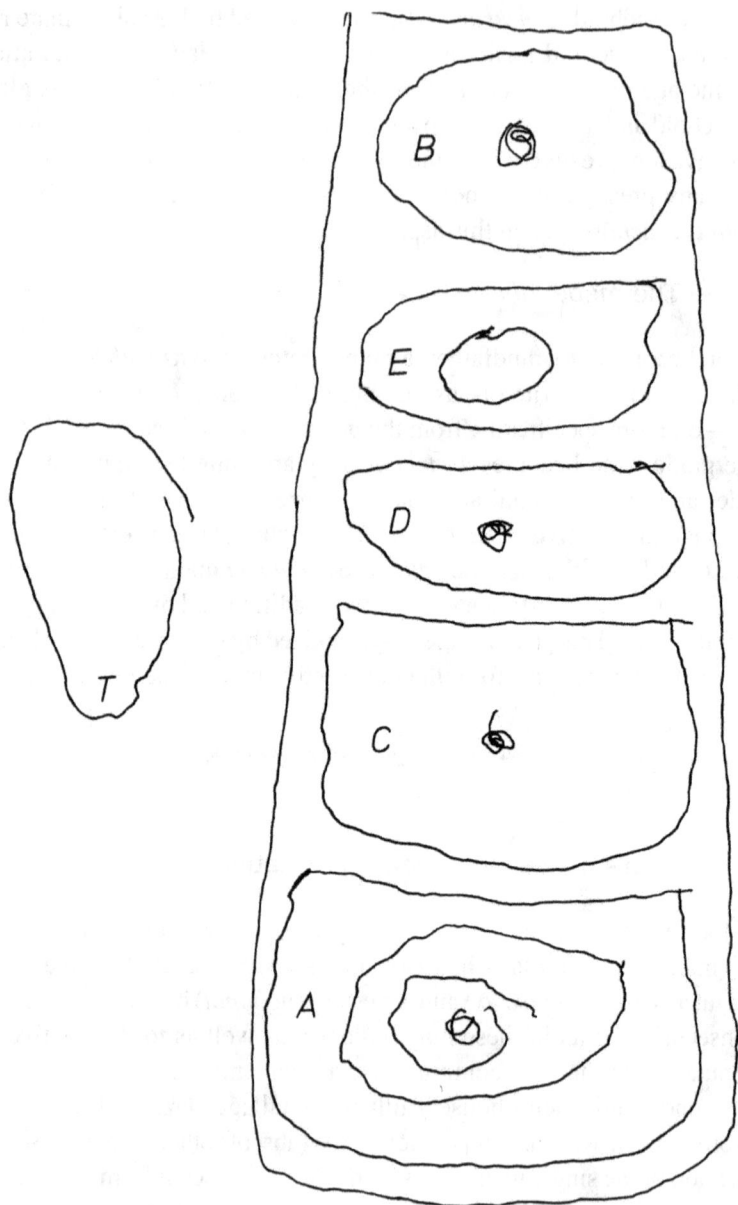

Figure 9 — Informant's drawing of the men's house of the village at *krãnhmrôpryjaka* (1937-1938). (A) the *menokà-re* ("eyebrow people") men's society; (B) the *menhakrekroti* ("stinking nose people") men's society; (C) the *memydjêny-re* (i.e., the junior m*enõrõny-re*); (D) the *memydjê'ãtũm* (i.e., the *menõrõny-re*); (E) the *menõrõny'ãtũm* (i.e., the senior *menõrõny-re*); (T) *metorodjà*, the central dancing area.

side of the village plaza, with its main entrance facing the central located dancing area which is situated to the west of it — see figures 1 and 2. This definition of descent from a given men's house has no influence whatsoever on intervillage relations. Rather, it is only defined as such to reproduce visually this descent by erecting the single men's house on its appropriate space on the village plaza.

Internally, the men's house is spatially divided into several "sitting places" (*krĩdjà*): the one of the *menõrõny-re* age grade, usually either centrally located or facing the main entrance, is surrounded by the various men's societies. T. Turner (1965: 40) defined a men's society as "a corporate group which is named, has a distinct sitting place within the men's house, acknowledges a common leader or leaders whose position is institutionalized, engages in collective activities such as dry season treks, and manifests solidarity and mutual support vis-à-vis other men's societies in disputes".

Men's societies are the basic political units of Kayapo society, membership in which is restricted and imperative to all the men with children in wedlock (i.e., *mekra-re* and *mebêngêt*). Upon establishing a nuclear family of his own, the young man chooses which of the existing men's societies he will join. This choice often seems influenced by the individual relations built up during a man's initial stages in the men's house, that is, while a member of the *me'ôk-re* and *menõrõny-re* age grades.

Frequently it is mentioned that a man opted for a specific men's society in order to remain with his *ikjê* ("good friend"), in order to join his colleagues or for all those who "collectively and jointly received their penis sheath" (*ro-'ã mydjê*, which is put on a par with *ro-'ã abatàj* or "jointly grown up"), to remain together. Besides these factors based on friendship or the sharing of a common event, preference for a given chief is equally mentioned in some villages. I noticed this in the Kubenkranken village, but never heard such a statement in the contemporary Mekranoti village. This can probably be explained in the light of the rivalry between the three Kubenkranken chiefs in 1976, while such rivalry did not exist in Mekranoti. Therefore, in Kubenkranken, the men often referred to a men's society as "the followers/workers[10] of X" (X *nhõ àpêx*, where X stands for the name of a chief), references which the Mekranoti informants equally made for certain periods in their history.

The number of men's societies varies from one to three for each men's house. Each of these mature men's associations has a separate sitting

---

10   In this case, the term *àpêx* ("to work, to make") seems to refer to communal labours such as the work on the men's society's garden(s) or house building.

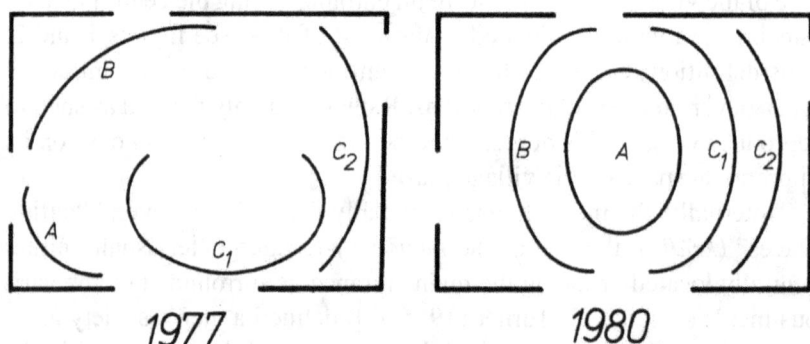

1977 **1980**

Figure 10 — Lay-out of the "sitting places" in the men's house of the village at PI Mekranoti. Situation in 1977 and in 1980.
(A) the adolescents (*menõrõny-re*); (B) the members of the *mepa'ãkadjàt* men's society; (C) the members of the *meõtoti* men's society; (C1) the *me'õtõtikry-re* (the junior members of the *meõtoti* men's society); (C2) the *meõtoti* (the senior members of the *meõtoti* men's society).

place and is named. In fact, it is more accurate to say that each sitting place is named. Such names are usually given in a mocking way and the word *mekrãgnoti* ("people with a big red facial paint") refers to one such historic men's society.

All men who constitute one single sitting place are referred to as "those who sit together" (*me kute ro-'ã krî*). Big men's societies of around thirty or more men tend to split up and divide between two sitting places, a fact which seems common both in pre- and post-contact eras and which equally effected the *menõrõny-re* sitting place. In figure 10, the inform-ant displayed the spatial division of all sitting places in the men's house of 1937-1938. The two outer groups are the two men's societies (named *menokà-re* and *menhakrekroti*) while the three center groups reflect the division of the *menõrõny-re* age grade along its sub-categories: the *me-mydjêny-re*, the *memydjê'ãtũm* and the *menõrõny'ãtũm*. Census data on that period reveal that there were eighty-one *menõrõny-re* and seventy *mekra-re* and *mebêngêt* in that village.

In 1980, the Mekranoti village had two men's societies, named *mepa'ãkadjàt* ("people with cotton string around their arms") and *meõ-toti* ("people with big tongues"), numbering twenty-four and thirty-four men, respectively. The *meõtoti* men's society was divided between two sitting places: one exclusively made up of nine elder men of the *mebêngêt* age grade, the other by the *mekra-re*. The latter sitting place was named *meõtotikry*-re ("small people with big tongues"). A similar phenomenon was observed by Dreyfus (1963: 76) in the Kubenkranken village of 1955, where the major *mekrãngrãngrã* ("people with green/ yellow head") men's society had a second sitting place for the men of the *mebêngêt* age grade. This latter group was called *mebêmôpdjôti* ("the big yam people"). In 1976, in that same village, I observed three men's societies, each divided over two sitting places with one exclusively for the *mebêngêt* men.

The *mebêngêt* act as peace-makers and appeasers of disputes and play a pacifying role within their men's society and the community as a whole. They are said to stand above any involvement in factional disputes. It is, therefore, considered normal for these elders to occupy a place distinct from the other members of their men's society, but this seems only to be put in practice when the men's society is big enough to allow such a sub-division.

Distinct sitting places within a single men's society are not seen as a recognition of a socially distinct group and, if such separate groupings receive different names, they are only to differentiate between the two settings. In some cases such informal groupings of a few men within a men's society may lead to the formation of more comprehensive social assemblage: gaining some social status, they may eventually lead to the breaking up of the men's society. In such cases, the initial cluster of men who identify themselves differently are *mekra-re*. Such an instance occurred in Kubenkranken sometime between 1969 and 1973. A clique of a few *mekra-re* of one of the two men's societies called themselves by a different name. At first, these men did not consider themselves to be beginning a men's society, but later on they separated from the big men's society. After some time, this group of men began to act independently and a chief was indicated: a new, third men's society had emerged. Informal processes of differentiation may, therefore, lead to the formation of a new men's society.

Yet, such a process is only possible when the demographic situation allows such a separation of a men's society. The demographic position of a community greatly influences the political set-up of the corporate men's groups. As stated, in 1937 the Mekranoti had three separate sitting places for their numerous *menõrõny-re*. The Mekranoti village in 1974 only numbered a few *menõrõny-re* who were seated in one of the men's house corners (see figure 11a). Informants said that they were too few to sit in the center. In 1978, a discussion arose on the fact that the *mekrany-re* should join the few *menõrõny-re* and form one separate, corporate group as opposed to the *mekrakramtî* and *mebêngêt* (see Chapter 5, where this event is explained in more detail). This reformulation did not occur, but after a village split in 1980, the *menõrõny-re* — in the meanwhile more numerous — had moved to the very center of the men's house (see figure 11b). After the split, the numerical equilibrium between the two men's societies was almost effected.

But it is not only the composition and the setting of the men's groups which is influenced by particular demographic situations. The formation process of new men's societies or the fission of existing ones is also biased by populational fluctuations, as shown in the Kubenkranken case mentioned earlier. Since about 1930, the Mekranoti history is one succession of splits and regroupings. This instability and its consequent demographic changes have led to the constant reformulation of the mature men's associations: in the period 1930-1955, not one political arrangement remained for longer than five years and in this period of twenty-five years, no less than eight rearrangements of the political groupings occurred. This inconsistency may give the impression that the men's societies are pre-eminently temporary cliques rather than (strong) political factions. Yet comparisons with other Kayapo groups as well as with the current Mekranoti situation show that this incongruity was the result of a series of historical accidents and that it should not be taken as the normal course of affairs. While discussing with informants, I had the impression that, ideally, membership in a political named faction is considered a life-time matter; each generation a new subgroup of such faction would emerge, with its proper name.

The *menõrõny-re* form a separate corporate group with roughly the same autonomy, except during certain ceremonies when the opposition of two numerically balanced men's groups occurs. During communal labor, these young men also join the smallest of the two men's societies — this was the case in the Mekranoti village in 1974-1982 — or may be divided along the existing men's societies — as in the village of Kubenkranken[11].

Furthermore, the *menõrõny-re* are subordinate to the mature men

11   As mentioned earlier, the village at PI Mekranoti numbered relatively few *menõrõny re* in the period from 1974 to 1980 and all *menõrõny-re* joined the smallest of the two men's societies in order to obtain the numerical dualistic balance. This is an unusual process, undoubtedly the result of this temporary and uncommon demographic situation. In the Kubenkranken village of 1976, three men's societies existed: one major one and two smaller ones. The numerous *menõrõny-re* were divided along the three men's associations, and the major one stood in ritual opposition to the combined units of the two smaller men's societies. On this occasion, each *menõrõny-re* joined the men's society of his preference. This same procedure was observed among the Mekranoti in 1989, when a numerical balance existed between the two existing men's societies and when the number of *menõrõny-re* had increased considerably.

and lack any prestige at the political level. Yet, in Kayapo history and at two events (in about 1850 and again in 1956) the *menõrõny-re* became a strong political faction which separated from the main village. Such splits, usually due to the reaction of these young men to their subordinate role, were only possible since some *mekrakramtĩ* and *mebêngêt* men formed an alliance with these younger men.

Each men's society acts autonomously as a military unit, may go on separate hunting, fishing or gathering trips, and plants its own communal garden(s). Society members also cooperate in other communal labors such as house-building or may form separate teams during games of soccer or *rõnkrã* (the native hockey-like game). Each men's society also functions as a council, meeting frequently and at length in the early morning and, more specifically, in the late afternoon. But during periods of ceremonial activities, the men's house bursts with action: ornaments are made; elderly men tell stories which are related to the specific festival and may even occasionally discuss the performance of the ceremony; oratories are nearly constantly given by *mekrakramtĩ* and *mebêngêt* men.

When men are reunited in the men's house, the members of each of the men's societies tend to respect formally the other societies. This form of inhibition is expressed in the Kayapo term of *piaàm* ("shame, respect, restraint of open hostility"). But, as is frequently shown in Kayapo history, men's societies often developed a corporate spirit of rivalry against other such societies. This process occasionally breaks out into manifest opposition, followed by collective club-fights (*aben tak* or "hitting together"). *Aben tak* is a formal, stylized combat between two men or between the members of two men's societies. Armed with heavy spatulate clubs (see Chapter 3 and fig. 14a-c), the men stand in pairs and take turns striking each other at a point between the shoulder and the elbow, until one of the combatants is unable to continue (after having broken his arm, for instance) or until some kinsmen or others intervene to stop the fight[12].

Adulterous relations are often cited as the immediate cause of such violent expressions of antagonism. Field-data indicate that individual clubfight(s) between men caught in the very act of adultery by the cuckolded husband were often no more than an overt vindication for preceding

---

12   On some occasions it happens that — due to emotional involvement — the rules are not strictly followed and someone gets hit on the head. In this way, a man can be killed during combat, as happened in the Southern Mekranoti village at PI Jarina in 1980. I never witnessed such a club-fight since none had occurred in the Central Mekranoti village in the period from 1973 to 1983.

acts of aggression. But such individual and abrupt physical confrontation — often very agitated and explosive — can then be an inducement to a sudden and instantaneous collective club-fight.

Tension between two men's societies can, moreover, arise on account of motives other than those related to domination over women. I refer to various causes such as, for example, friction between chiefs due to political ambition; opposition of men's societies in sports such as the abovementioned *rõnkrã* game; and any political discussion in the men's house affecting the community as a whole.

After an "individual" club-fight between two men in which both members belong to one and the same men's society, one of them will leave "in shame" (*piaàm*) and change membership by joining another men's society. The society which loses a "collective" club-fight is said to have too much *piaàm* to remain in the village with the opposing faction(s): a village split follows. Such village splits therefore tend to occur along the lines of the men's societies. Yet, not all men of the departing society leave the village at the moment of the separation. Some men, if they have numerous kinsmen on the winning side, may opt to remain, much in the same way as some men who belong to the winning group may opt to join the departing group.

The separating group builds a new village, often at a safe distance of hundred and fifty or more kilometers from the original village. From then on, open hostility between the two villages remains.

Such drastic occurrences as a village split are, nevertheless, often (temporarily) prevented by several forces such as the relationship of *piaàm* towards the other men's societies, the pacifying role of the village elders, the fact that the ties of kinship and marriage cross-cut the men's political associations (since recruitment occurs on the basis of friendship rather than kinship), and the fact that chiefs tend to establish a network of inter-relations between the several men's societies by using men of other such societies than their own to perform some practical jobs for them. At such crucial occasions as an approaching village split, all these elements may function as stabilizing forces to maintain the community unity by re-establishing the peaceful equilibrium between the corporate men's groups.

4.2 — On important men and prestige

Each Kayapo community has a group of people collectively known as *merax* (literally "great people"). The term does not relate to physical size, or to the *mebêngêt* who, due to their old age, have status at both a domestic and political level. Rather, *merax* refers to those people who are renowned for their leading roles, ritual functions, or a specific knowledge, statuses through which a man acquires or increases his prestige within the community. Except for the function of chief of a men's society, which is the highest status possible, one can distinguish five categories: shamans/ sorcerers, orators, ritual specialists, scouts and leaders. Most of these functions are held by men of any age grade (i.e., *menõrõny-re* or older); only oratory and shamanism/sorcery seem to be held exclusively by the senior men. Most of these functions are not hereditary, but rather are held because of personal traits such as bravery, eloquence, as well as the display of ambition and exemplary behavior.

I. *metema-ri* ("healers") and *wajanga* ("shamans")

This category includes two distinct levels. The first level relates to the specific knowledge of medicinal plants, leaves, roots or fruits of medicinal plants which are eaten, rubbed on some parts of the body, or drunk in mixtures. This process may be executed to lead to a successful hunt or raid, or to cure a certain disease. Illness is usually diagnosed as proceeding from eating or touching a given animal, or from the animal's spirit which is believed to have entered the sick person's body. Diseases are referred to as *kanê* and usually have animal names, such as *pàt kanê* ("the illness or indisposition caused by the anteater").

A connoisseur of such skills is referred to as "he who knows X" (*kute X ma-ri*, where X stands for the specific animal which is believed to have caused the particular disease); the group of connoisseurs and practitioners of such skills is referred to as *me(ku)tema-ri* ("those who know"). Although nearly all men have been taught at least one of these skills, most of them have been instructed in a wide series of these specialties and one Mekranoti elder, for example, is reputed to be acquainted with no less than twelve such specific skills.

Knowledge is passed between the kin categories of *ingêt* (FF, MF, MB) to male *tàbdjwỳ* (CS, ZS) and this invariably occurs while the apprentice is unmarried. However, out of respect for the senior tribesmen and being subordinate to these elders on both a political and a domestic level, the younger men do not yet display or put into practice the knowledge they have acquired. They rather wait until becoming a *mekrakramtĩ* or a *mebêngêt*, that is when their *ingêt* — who taught them the skills — are no longer present or no longer actively practice this knowledge. Since *metema-ri* specialists are often asked to treat nonkinsmen, they gradually acquire a prestige which transcends the limits of their own kindred: this steadily increases their status within the community.

The second and higher level of prestige is the shaman (*wajanga*). Besides knowing the use of medicinal plants, these men (and women) are said to be able to contact, see and consult human and/or animal spirits. In talking to these spirits, they may learn new remedies, inquire about their names which they eventually transmit to their *tàbdjwỳ*, ask about the location of enemies (see App. B: 16), and so on. Men usually become *wajanga* when they are a *mekrakramtĩ* or *mebêngêt*, and usually after a personal experience such as a serious illness, when their spirit is believed to have left their body and returned. Their knowledge in performing sorcery and breaking sorcery spells as well as activating the return of a spirit which has left a sick person, distinguish them from other members of society.

Yet, the term *wajanga* is only used for a person who uses these powers for the social benefit since; if it is used to cause injuries or death, the person is often referred to as an *udjy*. The latter are seen as a danger to the community and are often expelled. Such an instance is illustrated in narratives 10 and 11 of Appendix B, where a *me bê udjy ma-ri* ("he who knows the *udjy*") was said to be banished and continued living alone with his family at a great distance from the community.

When consulted, both the *metema-ri* and *wajanga* usually require payment for the application of their skills. Such rewards may vary from gifts of food to gifts of trade goods, the latter being more common nowadays.

II. *mekabẽndjwỳnh* ("orators")

As stated when discussing the male age grades, only the senior men — that is the *mekrakramtĩ* and *mebêngêt* — give formal speeches. Not all of these men do so: in the Central Mekranoti village of 1980, only seven out of the seventeen *mebêngêt* and three out of the eighteen *mekrakramtĩ* effectively and at regular intervals gave orations. They are said to be "real speakers" (*mekabẽndjwỳnh*). Being a haranguer is often on a par with being a "great person" (*merax*). When I asked some elders why they never gave formal speeches in the village, they often replied "I'm not a great one" (*djam irax got*) and added that they would feel ashamed to do so.

This function is not hereditary, but a direct consequence of verbal eloquence and ambitions to display prestige and influence. Being an orator therefore seems a privilege, as well as a moral obligation for the most prestigious men in the community. As a junior *mekrakramtĩ*, a man may make an attempt to give an oration while on a trek where such discourses are less formal. If he fails, not succeeding to interest his fellow tribesmen, he will not repeat such attempts back in the village.

In Xikrin society, the function of *mekabĕndjwỳnh* is passed on from *ingêt* to male *tàbdjwỳ* and seems more restricted since it involves only the right to perform the ritual *bĕn* (Vidal 1977: 146-147), speeches which in Mekranoti are delivered by the chiefs of the men's societies.

III. *mengrenhõdjwỳnh* ("ceremonial specialists")

The function of ceremonial specialist or ritual leader is in fact the most prestigious of all ritual rights which are passed on between the *ingêt* and *tàbdjwỳ* kin categories: it is one of the many values which is "owned" by residential segments.

The Kayapo term I refer to as ceremonial specialist is *ngrenhõdjwỳnh* ("the real singer") or *ngôngredjwỳnh* ("the real singer of the water"). It is probably a reference to the specialist's performance during the timbo fishing ritual of which the origin is told in a myth (see Wilbert & Simoneau 1984: 211).

Ritual leaders are specialists of those songs which are invariable, meaning those songs which represent a fixed pattern and that do not change at each performance of the ceremony (Verswijver 1988: 20-24). The men in question are often consulted on this matter: they are the repositories of knowledge about most dances and songs, and their presence is an essential part in some major ceremonies. At the conclusion of the *pãnh-te* naming ceremony, as well as during several phases of the *tàkàk*, *bep* and *kôkô* naming ceremonies or the important timbo fishing ritual, for instance, these specialists perform a series of small rituals or may lead the dancing men. Such performances are paid for with gifts of food or trade goods by the sponsoring parents of the ceremony. The specialist may refuse to perform the ritual performance for the child(ren) if gifts are not provided or if the mother of the honored child(ren) refuses to have sexual intercourse with him during the course of the ceremony[13].

This function likewise involves the performance of "blessing songs" at the occasion of the first harvest of a newly ripened crop in the gardens. Each nuclear family brings a few of these crops to the ritual specialist who then, with a rattle in his hand, "blesses" this sample by singing a

13   In the course of every naming ceremony, the female sponsors are willingly supposed to allow the men to have sexual intercourse with her. This intercourse never takes place in the village, but rather when the woman is alone near the riverside, out in the forest to cut firewood, and so on. The husband is aware of this procedure but, as the Mekranoti say, he is always busy hunting and "he pretends not to see/ realize it" *(ate krã)*. The Mekranoti explain that the men who go to these women are those nonkinsmen who will help the sponsors by carrying the heavy loads of forest turtles during the long forest trek. If a woman refuses, the men may equally refuse to help.

short song: for each type of crop, a specific song exists. In compensation for his act, the ritual specialist usually acquires this food sample for personal consumption.

IV. *meoprãr-re* ("scouts")

Those men who are sent ahead to go and spy on the enemy before an attack, or who are sent ahead of the group of men when penetrating unknown territories, are referred to as *meoprãr-re* ("those who flatten", which probably is a reference to their office of preparing the venture by opening the way for other members of the group), or as *meàpkàràdjwỳnh* (a term I am unable to translate).

This function is not hereditary but rather held by those men who display bravery by proposing to go ahead of the other men. It is held by senior as well as junior men (*menõrõny'ãtũm* or older) and some junior men use this opportunity to gain prestige at a fairly young stage of their life.

V. *meobadjwỳnh* ("leaders")

The *me'ôk-re* age grade, each sitting place of the *menõrõny-re* age grade as well as occasionally the *mekrany-re* group within a men's society, may have one or more leaders, which the Mekranoti refer to as *meobadjwỳnh* ("those who really go about with the others"). A distinction should be drawn between leaders and chiefs: while the latter conduct the mature men's societies, are formally installed in office and remain in office throughout their lifetime, leaders conduct the junior men. They often do so only while belonging to these specific junior age grades. Although not taken as a formal rule, leadership may denote a preliminary step towards becoming a chief at a later stage in the man's life. Very few exceptions seem to exist in the sense that most chiefs were leaders while a member of the junior age grades. Yet, not all *meobadjwỳnh* become a chief of a men's society.

Not charged with several ceremonial duties and not necessarily required to have broad knowledge on traditional culture (as is the case for chiefs), leaders usually hold this function due to a general, often spontaneous agreement within their group of young men. Leaders usually reflect exemplary behavior, have the capacity of coordinating the corporate activities of their group, are among the most active men and are respected for their decisions. A man thus becomes leader through the support of his fellow age mates. Since chieftaincy is the sole institutionalized office of political command, leadership can be seen as a less formal form of that office. Leaders lead their group during treks and other corporate activities.

When asking informants about who usually becomes a leader, the answer often seems to relate to the fact that the young man in question was brave, and therefore a *meoprãr-re* or scout. In analyzing the many leaders in Mekranoti society in this century, it appears that these men often were the protégés of the chiefs of the men's societies in the sense that they were related to these chiefs through kinship, or had been presented by the senior men as a potential successor.

Leaders often consult the chiefs of the men's societies, and this relative hierarchical position reflects the subordinate role of the young men towards senior tribesmen. Leaders also often tend to specialize in a specific activity such as "leading the forest treks" (*meyh kadjy meoba*), "leading the labor" (*meàpêx kadjy meoba*), "leading the raids" (*mekurêdjwynh kadjy meoba*), etc.

4.3 — On chiefs

Each men's society has at least one active chief, but may occasionally have two, each of these leading his own group of followers within that society. Before turning to the succession process of chieftaincy, I will discuss the chief's ritual and politico-juridical functions. It is interesting to broach this analysis through presenting the Kayapo view on the matter. When asking a Mekranoti what qualities and skills a chief should have, he is very likely to mention six points, each of these representing a different and specific aspect of the office in question:

I. a chief should "know the *bẽn*" (*bẽn ma-ri*)

Bẽn refers to a specific from of oratory, consisting of a stylized speech which is performed at a wide variety of specific occasions, such as the return of the men from a trek, the end of a major ritual or dance, the appearance of a rare natural phenomenon, etc. Each of these types has a specific name which refers to the occasion, such as "the *bẽn* of the meteor" (*akrã-re 'ã bẽn*) or "the *bẽn* for the meat" (*mry-'ã bẽn*). Performed while standing, with the right leg somewhat backward, the man slightly moves up and down and in a see-sawing motion. Holding a club or a firearm in his hand, he then utters the short speech, which may last less than thirty seconds. This brief ritual is accomplished facing the participants of the specific event. Whenever performed preceding a collective activity, these *bẽn* speeches are called *nojarêt* (literally "to pull out the eye").

Another type of *bẽn* consists of a series of recitative-like addresses which are seen as an integral part of several major ceremonies. This type of *bẽn* may last a few seconds, or ten or more minutes.

In regard to content, both types of *bẽn* may include one or more of

Table 2 — The correlation between the chief's esteemed knowledge and qualities, and the specific functions of several categories of "great" or "important" men.

Chief's knowledge	Corresponding function of "great men,,
bẽn ma-ri	ceremonial specialist *(ngrenhõdjwỳnh)*
pidjỳ ma-ri	conoisseur of medicinal plants *(kute ma-ri)* — pioneer *(oprãr-re)*
àkre *kukràdjà ma-ri* *kabẽn mex*	{ orator *(kabẽndjwỳnh)*
õdjàj	leader of junior age grades *(obadjwỳnh)*

the following elements: moral admonitions; encouragements towards the people to prepare for the actual dancing, to dance properly, to put on the appropriate ornaments, and so on; and ritual formulae to reverse a calamity forecasted by a natural phenomenon.

The performance of the *bẽn* is one of the basic ritual functions discharged by a chief, as is denoted in the Kayapo term for the office: *bẽnjadjwỳr* ("he who really delivers the *bẽn*") or *ir-re* (the abbreviation of *bẽndjir-re*, "he who places the *bẽn*").

II. a chief is supposed to "know all about Kayapo culture" (*me kukràdjà ma-ri*)

It is obvious that this statement should not be interpreted *ad litteram*, since no person fulfils such requirement. Rather, it has to be taken as a reflection of the fact that the person should have a profound knowledge of the culture, that he should display an interest in it, that he should be endowed with a certain intelligence and that he should know the specific knowledge related to chieftaincy. His knowledge is vast, and comprises the acquaintance of myths and tales, of ceremonial lore, of the *bẽn* speeches and songs, and of a specific type of blessing songs which only chiefs perform. Younger chiefs may often consult the *mebêngêt* of their men's society on such matters, but during their oratories a well as at decision-taking, they have to be able to display admonitions of moral value which are often illustrated by reciting myths and tales.

III. a chief has to "talk good" (*kabẽn mex*)

This is a reference to his eloquence as well as to the content of his speeches or to the moral value of his decisions. Since chiefs have no formal means to force followers to obey them or to act according to their decisions, they use oratory as the primary instrument of persuasion. During oratory, they articulate their decisions which in turn reflect the consensus within their men's society. Such consensus is often attained in conjunction with the senior men of the men's society. Through orations the articulation of moral values and the interests of their men's society, chiefs exercise their influence and their prestige in order to get their suggestions or ideas accepted and in order to prevent individual strives from developing into collective disputes which may endanger the unity of the community. Not all chiefs are endowed with exceptional talents of verbal eloquence, but such deficiencies may be compensated by a capacity for decision-taking or other remarkable qualities.

IV. a chief has to "know the remedies" (*pidjỳ ma-ri*)

This refers to those remedies or medicinal plants used during raids, such as "to kill people" (*meparidjà*), "to weaken people" (*meuabôdjà*) or "to scare people" (*meumadjà*). This point reveals the condition that chiefs have to be *metema-ri* — connoisseurs of a specific knowledge related to the use of medicinal plants — of the war-related techniques, since they are the military leaders of their men's society.

V. a chief has to be "bellicose" ('*àkrê*)

Since "only tough people are chiefs" (*metỳx bit ne me bẽnjadjwỳr*), this is a reference to the function of military leader of the men's society.

VI. a chief has to be "generous" (*õdjàj*)

To keep his followers united, a chief has to distribute the trade goods he acquires.

As shown in this list, as well as in table 2, a Kayapo chief is supposed to represent and personify all the possible functions which lead to the recognition of a man as a "great person" (*merax*). A chief, therefore, has to reflect all the ideal Kayapo male values such as knowledge, eloquence, bellicosity, solidarity and generosity. Men who tend to accumulate several of these functions may increase their influence within the community. And chiefs, who personify all of these functions, invariably figure among the most prestigious men in the community.

Conspicuous to the office of chieftainship is the apparent paradox that chiefs should be bellicose and tough on the one hand, and "talk good" and be an appeaser on the other. While the first refers to the male virtues of physical strength, insensibility to pain, the capacity of being a good warrior, and the ability aggressively to assert the interests of both his men's society (against threats from another men's society) and the community at large (against threats from the enemy), the latter clearly alludes to his duty to strive for the maintenance of a balance between both the preservation and the promotion of unity, a phenomenon which is equally reflected in the requirement of being generous. Chieftainship is therefore marked by a certain form of ambiguity: the office requires a pacific behavior on the one hand, and a pugnacious, (aggressively) affirmative conduct on the other hand, representing, respectively, a fusional and a fissional influence on the community. One must be aggressive to outsiders but affirmative within the village.

As already stated, chiefs tend to prevent the development of individual conflicts into collective disputes which threaten the unity of the community. It is therefore considered highly hazardous to this unity for chiefs to get involved in such conflicts, whether personally through an individual clash, or in the function of chief of his men's society, coming up for the interests of his men's society. Chiefs are therefore expected to avoid such entanglements, and Mekranoti history shows that the more bellicose chiefs often led to temporary or even permanent splits within the community. It is considered a primarily requirement that the chiefs of the several men's societies should have a good mutual understanding as this diminishes the risks of conflicts between these men, consequently reducing the possibilities of overt antagonism between the men's societies. Yet, chiefs tend to specialize in one of these two roles: only very strong chiefs, such as Bepgogoti of the contemporary village at PI Mekranoti, are able to represent both the more bellicose and the pacific roles related to that office. As will be shown now, striving for a good understanding between the chiefs of the different men's societies is an important aspect in the succession process of chiefs.

No formal rule exists for the establishment of the succession of Kayapo chiefs. In the pre-contact period, young men were initiated in the knowledge of chieftainship by their father (whether real or fictive), by their *ingêt* (FF, MF, MB) or by one of their ritual friends (*kràbdjwỳ*)[14]. The normal procedure for someone becoming a chief is, de facto, a long process, beginning at early puberty (*me'ôk-re* age grade) and which is affected by a wide variety of influences.

⋈ the *me'ôk-re* stage

Nearly every evening, two or three *me'ôk-re* boys may visit the senior chief in his house. The latter patiently teaches these youngsters the vast

14   Nowadays it is thought appropriate for a chief's son (whether real or fictive) to become a chief. I will discuss this change of emphasis in more detail in Chapter 5.

repertory of specific knowledge which a chief is supposed to possess, such as the numerous types of *bẽn*, the remedies, and many aspects of Kayapo culture. These boys may be real or fictive sons — such as the "adoptive son" of the *me'ôk* rite of passage — or nephews of the old chief. The parents of the boys have to remunerate for these teachings with gifts of food. Such training usually takes years and I was told that it invariably occurs in the village, never in the forest or while on a trek.

¤ the *menõrõny-re* stage

The instruction continues while the boy is a *menõrõny-re*. But during this stage, some of the trained young men usually become a leader (*meobadjwjỳnh*) of their age grade. This greatly depends on the boy's personal ambition as well as on the support he may win from his comrades. It is therefore not imperative for all these trained boys to become leaders, nor is it such that only these boys can occupy that function. Yet, it is considered normal that some of these boys hold the function in preparation for becoming a chief later.

¤ the *mekra-re* stage

When becoming a *mekrany-re*, the young man joins one of the men's societies and the training is stopped. Informants stated that the instructed men usually join the men's society of the old chief who has trained them. All of these trained young men may occasionally perform the *bẽn* speeches for the men's society, but as yet no definition is taken as to which of the men will succeed the old chief.

Although still often referred to as *meobadjwjỳnh*, that trained young man who wins the support of his age mates within the men's society may occasionally be referred to as "new" or "young chief" (*bẽnjadjwỳrỳny*). Several of these "young chiefs" may be named within one men's society.

Once a *mekrakramtĩ*, the man who has developed himself as the most qualified and most broadly supported of the "new chiefs" goes to the old chief who had trained him to ask to become a real chief. The old chief then consults the chief of the other men's society and, if the latter agrees on the choice, it is he who will formally install the chosen man as chief. He does so by officially proclaiming his support. He is from then on referred to as a *bẽnjadjwỳr kumrẽnhtx* ("genuine chief") of his men's society at large.

¤ the *mebẽngêt* stage

At reaching the *mebẽngêt* age grade, he will be referred to as *bẽnjadjwỳrỳ'ãtũm* ("old chief ' or "chief for a long time") and starts teaching some boys in the lore of the office. Due to his advanced age, the *meobadjwỳnh* or the younger chiefs (*bẽnjadjwỳrỳny*) will effectively lead

Table 3 — Model of the evolution of a chiefs political career.

AGE GRADE	FUNCTIONS AND EVOLUTION OF LEADERSHIP	TYPE OF LEADERSHIP
me'ôk-re	training by an old chief (benjadjwỳrỳ'ãtum)	may be a leader (meobadjwỳnh) of his age grade companions
menõrõny-re	training stopped ; builds up support of his age grade companions by examplary conduct	may be a leader (meobadjwỳnh) of his age grade companions
mekra-re mekrany-re	keeps building up support ; may occasionally perform the bẽn speeches or songs	becomes known as "little" or "new" chief (benjadjwỳrỳ-ngri or benjadjwỳrỳnỳ) of his men's society
mekrakramtĩ	formally installed in office by a chief of another men's society ; proceeds to oratory to increase influence and status ; very active political role and literally leader of the corporative activities of his men's society	referred to as "real" or "great" chief (benjadjwỳr kumrẽnhtx or benjadjwỳr rax) of his men's society
mebêngêt	becomes less active, taking the position of counselor ; trains new young men and indicates chief(s) of other men's societies ; has reached the height of his political power and, together with the mebêngêt, figures among the appeasors of major communal strives	referred to as "old" chief (benjadjwỳrỳ'ãtim) of his men's society and, to a lesser extent, of the village at large

the men of his men's society during dangerous ventures such as raids, or during laborious tasks such as some economical activities. The "old chief" mainly acts as counsellor of the men's society and of the community at large and especially of these younger leaders and chiefs.

Although several boys may be trained for the office, a person's ambition greatly influences his nomination. Werner (1980: 181) also referred to ambition as one of the characteristics of Kayapo chieftaincy. In PI Mekranoti there are four men who have the necessary training but as yet show no ambition of becoming a chief. This is not uncommon as some men display such ambitions only at a later stage in life — for instance at the occasion of changes in the community's political configuration due to village splits or fusions — and eventually becoming a chief after all. A good example of such a late installation as a chief is Bepgogoti, currently the "old chief" in the village at PI Mekranoti. Trained by his uncle in his childhood, he later became a renowned leader as a member of the *menõrõny-re* and *mekrany-re* age categories. But he never really acted as "new chief" nor did he, as I was told, really show any ambition to become one. Bepgogoti himself always responded to this by stating that two main chiefs already existed in that period: Kreti-re (an age-mate of Bepgogoti) and Kremõr (about ten years younger). When the village started splitting up in 1956, Bepgogoti moved with his followers to a new site, a few months later followed by Kreti-re and his group. In this new village, and at the age of approximatively fifty years, Bepgogoti was officially installed as chief (*bẽnjadjwjỳr kumrẽnhtx*).

In addition to ambition and the necessary training, support from comrades of the men's society is another essential prerequisite for becoming a chief. This support is not only gradually acquired through exemplary behavior, but also through the display of generosity. Generosity is seen by the Kayapo as one of the main characteristics of solidarity, and therefore is one of the more influential requirements for becoming a chief. Only those men who are considered to personify the ideal male values such as generosity, the exemplary behavior, bellicosity, etc., can attain this support. Showing his capacity of good understanding with his companions, executing his activities with responsibility and enthusiasm, proving his qualities of aggression during raids and displaying his intelligence at suggesting corporate activities: all these factors are important for a man to increase his potential to be backed up. The winning of the support of his companions, however, is only formally reinforced when the man is installed into office when being proclaimed by another chief — generally the chief of another men's society — who supports his nomination.

Support from the chief of another men's society is imperative, as proved by a case I witnessed in the Mekranoti village. Around 1962-1970, Bepgogoti, the old chief of the major men's society, had trained three young boys: two of his youngest sons (Bepkũm and Bõti-re) and his nephew Beptykti-re. In the period of 1974-1980, the latter showed no ambition to become a chief; Bepkũm had won some support from his companions, and had acted as a *meobadjwỳnh* of the younger men of that men's society, but showed little ambition to proceed in his function; his younger brother, Bõti-re was greedy and often displayed a conduct which was not always appreciated, such as neglecting his wife to constantly maintain adulterous sexual relations, often displaying a volition to go to the cities and remain there as long as possible and, above all, exhibiting little enthusiasm to accompany the men during their corporate activities. One day, Kôkôrêti, the chief of the other men's society, formally reproved Bõtire's lack of interest and disapproved of his individual conduct. This act of reprimand by one chief to another is called "shout at" (*kũm aki-ja*) and is very rarely performed. Bõti-re, ashamed, avoided the men's house for a long time and about a year later he moved to the Southern Mekranoti villages, where he still lives. In 1983, three years after this event, Bepkũm was formally installed in office as chief of the major men's society.

As I already mentioned, the necessity of being proclaimed by a chief of another men's society seems to be performed to avoid late, overt antagonism between the chiefs, and therefore between the men's societies.

Yet, it is only when a man has reached the *mekrakramtĩ* age grade that he may be officially installed as chief: up to then, he may be a leader (*meobadjwỳnh*) or a leader who occasionally delivers the *bēn* speeches (*bēnjadjwỳrỳny*). The *mekrakramtĩ* are indeed the most active in politics and it is therefore a normal procedure that being a chief of that age category relates to chieftaincy of the whole men's society, since the younger age grades are subordinate to the *mekrakramtĩ*. Interesting, though, a man is therefore officially installed as a chief before he really has developed his ability at oratory: once he is a "real chief", he will increase his prestige even more by giving speeches, displaying his knowledge, his abilities and his influence and becoming, in this way, a "great chief" (*bēnjadjwỳr rax*) — see table 3.

5. THE RITUAL CATEGORIES OF "BEAUTIFUL" AND "COMMON" PEOPLE

From the moment a child has developed basic motor and linguistic skills, or it is *kàtỳx kam* ("having a strong skin"), until the youngster formally joins the societies associated with the village center, both boys and girls may be "honored" in one of the many major ceremonies. The Kayapo term I refer to as "honoring" is *mereremex* (literally "those who show off beautifully"), a reference to the often elaborate way these youngsters are ornamented during the final phase of the ceremony. The *mereremex* act as focal points in nearly all major Kayapo rituals.

There are several ways for a person to become honored, but by far the two most important ones are through a naming ceremony and through initiation.

5.1 — Naming ceremonies

The Kayapo distinguish between two categories of personal names: "common names" (*idjikakrit*, where *kakrit* denotes more or less "of no special value" or "less important") and "beautiful" or "great names" (respectively *idjimex* and *idjirũnh, idjirax* or *idjikati*).

Common names may refer to something in the environment such as Ngôtire ("big water") or to some body part such as Inhyngri ("little upper lip"). Other common names may make reference to some life experience such as Kubẽpa-ri ("killer of strangers"), simply be a word such as Akamàn ("night"), or represent a metaphysical conception such as Pykàr ("the crying annatto"). Brazilian names for people (e.g., Orlando), animals (*mutum*, the curassow bird) or things (*machado*, the axe) are often incorporated nowadays, generally after undergoing the necessary phonetic adaptation to Kayapo language. The number of common names is vast.

Beautiful names consist of two parts: (a) a ceremonial prefix and (b) a *kakrit* (common) suffix as, for example, in Beptyk (*bep*: the ceremonial prefix; *tyk*: suffix meaning "black") or Irekro (*ire*: the ceremonial prefix; *kro*: suffix meaning "smell, odor"). There are eight ceremonial prefixes: *bep* (also *bemp* or *beb*), *tàkàk* (both exclusively male), and *kôkô, ire, nhàk, bekwỳnh, pãnh* and *ngrenh* (for males and females). With the exception of *nhàk* — being related to *tàkàk* (Verswijver 1981) — each of these ceremonial prefixes is associated with a specific naming ceremony in which only names based on that prefix are conferred and transmitted. Besides these seven ceremonies, which I will refer to as "specific naming ceremonies", there are four others in which names based on any and all of the ceremonial prefixes may be confirmed and transmitted and which I will refer to as "comprehensive naming ceremonies". The latter are named *kwỳrỳkangô* ("manioc liquid"), *bô kam me tor* ("dance with the straw"), *memybijôk* ("the painted men") and *menibijôk* ("the painted women").

As a rule, both beautiful and common names are passed down between the kin categories of *ingêt* (FF, MF, MB) to male *tàbdjwỳ* (CS, ZS), and between a *kwatyi* (MM, FM, FZ) and her female *tàbdjwỳ* (CD, BD). The only exception to this is that of the transmission of names to one or more nonkinsmen, in which case a tie of fictive kinship is established.

Parents, as well as their parallel-sex siblings, who are classificatory parents to the child, never pass their own names, either common or beautiful, to their children. To do so is thought to kill the child. Theirs are, however, the households that provide the sizeable economic support necessary for the performance of the ceremony. The comprehensive naming ceremonies are characterized by the fact that the parents of the honored children are always siblings (real or classificatory) of the same sex.

A few days after the birth of a child, several *ingêt* and/or *kwatyi* will pass on a number of both common and beautiful names to the child. Beautiful names based on several ceremonial prefixes will normally be given at this time. Although either a common or a beautiful name may be used to refer to the child, a beautiful name, if not later confirmed ceremonially, will be considered an *idjimex kajgo* ("falsely given beautiful name"). Each child should therefore ideally be honored with several namings. The number of honored children in such ceremonies varies from one to eleven, with usually two to five.

5.2 — The *mei'ĩtyk-re* rite

The *mei'ĩtyk-re* ("people with black bracelets") ritual for the boys simultaneously involves an initiation, a ritual marriage, and may denote the rite of passage from the *mebôkti-re* to the *me'ôk-re* age grades. This ritual is never celebrated separately but is always incorporated in the *bep* or *tàkàk* naming ceremonies, or in the *ngô-re* fishing ceremony. *Mei'ĩtyk-re* is considered to be the most prestigious way of becoming a *mereremex*, but it is only performed about every five to ten years. Only five to eight boys are so honored at each ceremony and thus not all boys become *mei'ĩtyk-re*: only twenty-seven percent of the adult Mekranoti men have been so honored.

All those people who in one or another (or even several) of these occasions have been a *mereremex* are collectively referred to as *memex* ("beautiful people"), as opposed to the *mekakrit* ("common people") who have never been honored in such a ritual.

The social category of *memex* is characterized by the phenomenon that they have "slept with ornaments" (*nêkrêx kam ikwã*). This expression is a paraphrase of various principles of becoming a *memex*: the wide variety of ornaments (*nêkrêx*) that are worn when being honored (Verswijver 1983b) and the long duration of the ceremonies (often several weeks or months), an aspect which is reflected in the term *ikwã* ("to sleep" or "to remain"). The term *nêkrêx kam ikwã* also denotes a distinction between being honored in a *mereremex* ritual or in a rite of passage related to age grades: in the latter rites, few or no ornaments are worn and the duration rarely exceeds an hour or so.

Beautiful names (*idjimex*) and ornaments (*nêkrêx*) are considered to be intrinsically "natural": i.e., "wild" and dangerous ('*àkrê*). Naming ceremonies should therefore be considered collective acts of socialization of these "wild" names and ornaments (T. Turner 1987ms: 27).

Not all people become *memex*: in the Mekranoti village in 1980, only twenty-eight percent of the adults (i.e., people with children) had been honored by one of the above-mentioned ceremonies, and eight percent of these persons had been honored on more than one occasion. These numbers are almost equally divided over the two sexes, since fifty-one percent of the *memex* are male and forty-nine percent are female. However, there is currently a relative tendency for more people to become *memex*. And this not only because such ceremonies are more regularly held than in various pre-contact eras, but also because the number of children honored in each of these ceremonies is higher. During the period of 1924-1968, the Mekranoti celebrated an average of 1.2 naming ceremonies a year; more recently (1968-1980) an average of 1.7 such ceremonies have been performed. The average number of children being honored yearly was 3.8 in the period of 1924-1968, and 7.0 in more recent times — this, in spite of the fact that the contemporary Mekranoti villages number fewer inhabitants than in most of the pre-contact era.

The parents of the "honored" child(ren) act as sponsors of the ceremonies; they are referred to as *mekrareremex* ("those who show off their children beautifully"). Certain ceremonies may last up to three or even four months and the parents of these children have to provide enormous quantities of food to all the dancers during the course of the ceremony. It is common for parallel-sex siblings — whether female, residing in one and the same residential segment, or male, living dispersed in several segments — to cooperate in providing the necessary economic support for sponsoring such a major ritual to honor their children.

All *memex* are said to observe strict food taboos, eating only what is referred to as "fine" or "beautiful animals" (*mry mex*), such as turtles and most large game animals. No such dietary restrictions are laid on common people, who may eat *mry mex* as well as "common animals" (*mry kakrit*, a term which refers to small food animals such as birds, monkeys, etc.). Yet, this is no more than a general rule since specific, supplementary food taboos are imposed according to the ceremonial prefix of the conferred names.

Beautiful people are, therefore, referred to as *mejangri tỳx* ("those who observe strong dietary restrictions"). Not observing the food taboos is believed to result in skin diseases of the "beautiful" person but, in practice, these food taboos are in no way strictly observed. They are, rather, either put into practice or accentuated during the course of the ceremony by those people who became honored in a previous performance of that same ceremony. Besides these food taboos, *memex* are also on some occasions expected to observe other restrictions more strictly.

Being a *memex* carries with it ritual prestige and denotes a symbolic assertion of the Kayapo ideal of the ritual relations which are established, activated or confirmed. The distinction between *memex* and *mekakrit* has no impact on every-day social relations but, rather, is the expression of the economic support which both the parents — the sponsors of the ceremonies — and their parallel-sex siblings have displayed during the expression between a person and his grandparents or his parents' cross sex siblings.

The collective celebration of kin relationship in naming ceremonies (through the very act of naming) and in the *mei'ĩtyk-re* rite (through its ritual marriage) amounts to the reintegration of the segmentary and communal level of social organization: the center of the village — where association is based on friendship and non-kin — becomes the locus of kin-based organization.

If numerous references to the *mei'ĩtyk-re* rite are made in ancient tales (App. B: 6-7), they are no less than an expression of the Kayapo ideal of people becoming *memex*.

CHAPTER II

KAYAPO HISTORY SINCE THE EARLY NINETEENTH CENTURY

Many confusing situations arise when examining the existing literature on Central Brazilian Indian tribes: different authors used different names to designate what later often appeared to be one and the same tribe. Consequently it is not easy to work on an ethno-historical reconstruction of such tribes, and in the case of the Kayapo we are not spared these difficulties.

Gorotire, Mekranoti, Kubenkranken, Kayapo of the Xingu, Txukarramãe and Kayapo of the Pau d'Arco are but a few of the many names that appear in the literature to designate the many Kayapo groups and subgroups which have emerged in the course of the last two centuries as the Kayapo split up into many subgroups which, in turn, often split up into several villages. The situation, therefore, is confusing to the degree that even many scholars are puzzled by it. In these pages I will try to clear up this confusion by giving a quick review of the complex entity of the still existing Kayapo groups and subgroups frequently mentioned throughout this book.

Existing ethno-historical essays on contemporary Kayapo groups are usually limited to the presentation of events which took place during the twentieth century, and often focus upon one particular Kayapo subgroup. In the first pages of this Chapter, I will deal with early Kayapo movements, emphasizing some of the historically more important passages that occurred in the nineteenth century. The aim of this section is twofold: to outline the origin of the three major Kayapo groups known in the literature as Gorotire, Xikrin and Ira'amranh; and to give a general picture of the major migrations undertaken by the Kayapo during that period. Furthermore, I consider this section necessary for the reader to clearly understand the extremely complex composition of the Kayapo tribe.

A major part of this Chapter, though, deals with the history of the

Kayapo in the twentieth century. The numerous schisms, the often calamitous consequences of so-called "pacification" of the various Kayapo
groups and other major events are described here. A much more detailed
version of the history of the Mekranoti and Kokraimoro in this century
can be found in Appendix A.

1. ON THE NORTHERN AND SOUTHERN KAYAPO

The most ancient bibliographic reference to the term *kayapo* probably
dates back to 1607 (Carvalho Franco 1953: 101, 340): it was used to
designate an important ethnic group already known as *bilreiros* ("club
wielders" in Portuguese). These Indians occupied an extensive territory
near the lower course of the Paranahiba River and its tributaries (Southeastern Brazil). There they lived dispersed throughout many villages with
a population of six hundred or more inhabitants to each community. Neme
(1969) estimated their total population at some ten thousand to fifteen
thousand, whereas Hemming (1978: 493-494) evaluated it to be some
forty-seven thousand.

In the early nineteenth century, another Ge tribe, living almost thousand five hundred kilometers north of the Bilreiros, was called by the
same name, Kayapo. Reports mentioned "Kayapo" (also spelled Kaiapo,
Caiapo or Cayapo) or "Gradáu" (also spelled Gradaho or Kradáu) Indians
living between the lower Araguaia and mid Tocantins Rivers. Both the
Bilreiros and the "Kayapo/Gradáu" were said to be "the same people,
speaking the same language" (Castelnau 1850 part I [2]: 115). To distinguish between both of these "Kayapo" groups, the first (Bilreiros) is
known in ethnographic literature as the Southern Kayapo and the second
as Northern Kayapo.

The Southern Kayapo became extinct at the beginning of this century
(Lowie 1946: 519) and whenever the term Kayapo is used in this book, it
refers to the Northern Kayapo unless explicitly stated otherwise.

2. EARLY NORTHERN KAYAPO MIGRATIONS

In 1824, Cunha Mattos (1874: 392-393) mentioned the Gradáu between
the lower Araguaia and mid Tocantins Rivers, north of a small settlement named Santa Maria do Araguaia (see map 3). Mattos wrote that
these Indians were "Kayapo of origin" (using the term *kayapo* in reference to the Southern Kayapo), a statement which was later confirmed

by Castelnau (1850 part I [2]: 115). In his study on the Kayapo, Krause (1911: 368) not only agreed with Mattos' remark but went on to suggest that the Kayapo had undertaken a westward migration: coming from the east of the Araguaia River they had moved to the west of this same river, where he found them in 1909.

Kayapo oral tradition seems to confirm Krause's observation. Field data repeatedly mention that the Kayapo refer to the crossing of a big river in historical times. This river, called *kôkati* ("huge stick") is difficult to identify: some Indians claim it is their designation for the Tocantins River, others speak of the Araguaia. These statements are not necessarily in contradiction since it is possible that both these rivers were conceived by these Indians as one single river: the same is true for the Xikrin who refer to both rivers in question as *byti* (Vidal 1977: 21), a term other Kayapo groups use to designate the Xingu River.

Kayapo oral history consequently confirms Krause's observation. But, in order to find any further bibliographic reference to a Kayapo presence east of the Araguaia, it is necessary to give a short ethno-historical survey of the area where I state the Kayapo were supposed to have lived in that period.

At the turn of the eighteenth to nineteenth century, seven tribes were said to have lived between the lower Araguaia and mid Tocantins Rivers (Nimuendajú 1946: 36). In addition to the Xambioa (a Iny Karaja subgroup), the following Ge tribes occupied the area in question: Krahô or Makamekra, Kanakateye, Pórekamekra (all Eastern Timbira groups); Apinaye (a Western Timbira group); Gradáu (the Iny Karaja-Xambioa designation for the Kayapo) and Nhyrykwãye (a tribe supposedly belonging to the Eastern Timbira).

Of all these tribes, the Apinaye, Krahô and Gradáu (Kayapo) still exist, while the Kanakateye, Pórekamekra and Xambioa have become extinct. Little data are available on the fate of the Nhyrykwãye.

In 1810, Jose Pinto de Magalhães founded São Pedro de Alcántara, a settlement today called Carolina. Officially, São Pedro was a military outpost, established in order to provide protection against Indian attacks to the farmers who were settling in the area. However, Magalhães was also a merchant, trying to make as much profit as possible from this double occupation. Shortly after his arrival in that area, Magalhães began friendly relations with his nearest neighbors, the Krahô. He used these Indians as allies to obtain captives from the surrounding tribes. These captives were either used on the large plantations he himself wished to lay out in order to expand his economic monopoly of the territory, or sent to Belem or Piaui to be sold as slaves.

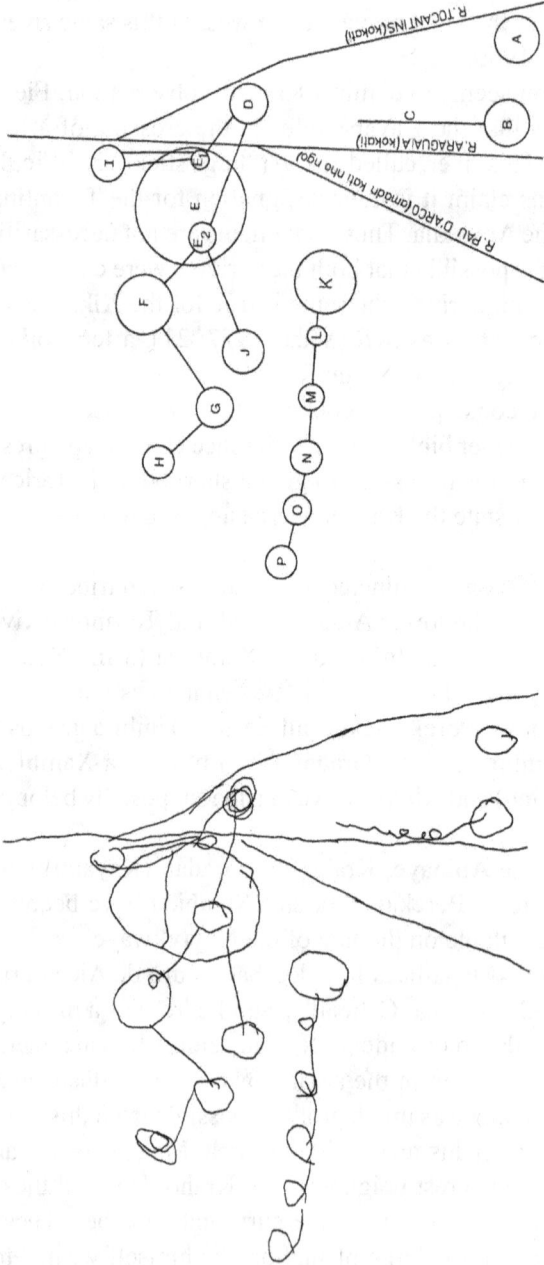

Figure 11 — Map showing the informant's interpretation of the successive schisms in the Kayapo groups. (left) original map; (right) complementary explications given by the informant. (A) village of the Kubêpa-ri Kam No (a mythological tribe); (B) village of the Goroti Kumrênhtx; (C) path of the northward migration; (D) village of the Kayapo (period when referred to in literature by the terms Nhyrykwãye and Gradau); (E1) village of chief Kongrãti; (E2) village of chief 'O-jore; (E) huge village after the fusion of both groups (E1 and E2); (F) separation of the Porekrô (Porekry); (G) village of the Xikrin of the Catete River; (H) village of the Xikrin of the Bacaja River; (I) temporary village of the Ira'amranh; (J) separation of the Gorotire from the Goroti Kumrênhtx; (K-P) successive villages of the Gorotire during their westward migration

Magalhães undertook several major expeditions, raiding the Krõrekamekra, Pórekamekra and other surrounding villages. Three of these expeditions were specifically against the Kanakateye and the Nhyrykwãye. On these occasions,

> ... 52 Indians of the mentioned nations were captured and were immediately divided among the neighboring farmers to be educated in the essential knowledge of our language, the Christian dogma and our customs. (Almeida 1851: 51 — translation mine)

Based on Ribeiro (1841: 83) and Almeida (1851: 55), Nimuendajú wrote the following passage on one of Magalhães' raids on the Nhyrykwãye:

> Pinto de Magalhães places [the Nhyrykwãye] among the tribes between the Tocantins and Araguaia, from São Pedro de Alcántara to the confluence of these rivers. He reports how more suo he had tried to make friends with them by aiding the Krahô in a raid against the [Nhyrykwãye] and sending back to their own people two of the three women that were made captives. This seems to have occurred in 1810 or a little later. (Nimuendajú 1946: 36)

The sole significant later reference to this Nhyrykwãye tribe that Nimuendajú was able to trace back dates from 1824, when these Indians are said to have attacked the Xerente. The number of warriors involved was estimated at two hundred: I therefore assume that the Nhyrykwãye village numbered at least eight hundred inhabitants[1].

But after 1824 the Nhyrykwãye are no longer mentioned. Even Nimuendajú — unquestionably the main ethno-historian of that particular part of Brazil — seemed puzzled about the later situation of this tribe. I consider Nhyrykwãye to be another ancient designation which was given to the Kayapo. This hypothesis may easily be contestable since very little evidence seems to exist but, as I will endeavor to show, this premise appears to be fully acceptable. To prove it, I have to, once more, take a close look at the Kayapo oral tradition.

The Kayapo narrate how, in the period when they still lived near the kôkati river, their tribe was first visited and later raided by "Whites" who

---

1   Analyzing the census of twelve Central Brazilian Indian tribes, I calculated that a factor of four can be used as an average to obtain the total village population based on the number of warriors in a given community. To obtain this factor, I compared the total village population with the number of men between fifteen and forty-five years of age. Although these age limits for potential warriors can be questioned, it is not necessarily so that all these men leave together on a raid and the factor, therefore, may well be an underestimation. The censuses were drawn from Ribeiro (1970: 292-300) and Dreyfus (1963: 196) and were taken from villages without an expressive demographic expansion. In the Mekranoti village of 1981, where the village population was steadily on the increase, a factor of more than seven could be applied!

were accompanied by non-Kayapo Indians. According to the Kayapo, the latter lived divided over several villages. I take the view that the visiting Indians mentioned were no less than the Krahô and that the so-called "Whites" probably were Magalhães and his companions. This hypothesis is based on several correlations between Kayapo oral history and the existing bibliography:

— The Kayapo say that two of the captured women as well as a girl managed to escape (App. B: 4) while, in his writings, Magalhães spoke of the voluntarily return of two women (Almeida 1851: 55);

— A man called Kĕnngà-re is said by the Kayapo to have visited two of the Indian villages (App. B: 4-5) and it is known that the Krahô lived divided over several villages near Magalhães' settlement (Ribeiro 1874: 66);

— The Kayapo also say that Kĕnngà-re killed several "men with pans on their heads" (*kubẽ krã kam ngôj*, a term the Kayapo still use today to refer to soldiers or members of the police force) and Ribeiro (*ibid.* 70-72) mentions that the majority of Magalhães' companions were soldiers.

Geographical evidence can also be cited, since the territory the Nhy-rykwãye occupied at that time fully corresponds to the area inhabited by the Kayapo according to their oral tradition (see figure 12).

The Kayapo oral tradition furthermore relates how, after their unfortunate contact with the "Whites" and out of fear for these "strangers who possessed firearms" they migrated to the west and crossed the *kôkati* (Araguaia?) River (App. B: 4-5; Wilbert 1978: 355-356). The expeditions of Magalhães took place in the period from 1810 to 1820. Since the Kayapo were undoubtedly already reported on the left bank of the Araguaia River in the 1840s (Gomes de Siqueira), their crossing of the *kôkati* may have occurred between, say, 1820 and 1840.

This crossing apparently did not occur during a single phase (App. B: 6-8). Two major villages were built "one next to the other" (*aben kuri*). Figure 12 shows that the informant, departing from a single village in the area between the lower Araguaia and mid Tocantins Rivers, refers to two separate villages on the left bank of the Araguaia. After the killing of Kôngràti (chief of the easternmost village) the two groups seemed to have reunited into a single, large village. This phase is strikingly accentuated by my informant in figure 12 by drawing a huge circle for the village of the Goroti Kumrẽnhtx, where both groups lived together.

Oral history further relates how a split occurred after internal strife between the members of the two men's houses (App. B: 10-12): the members of the western men's house left and moved westward; the other group first performed a short northward migration and then returned to the traditional setting near the Pau d'Arco and Arraias Rivers. This was the important split between two major Kayapo groups: the Gorotire moved to the west, towards the Xingu River; and the Ira'amranh remained along the Araguaia River. This split probably occurred between 1840 and 1860.

The Ira'amranh started maintaining more or less friendly contacts with the Brazilians in the 1860s, but it was not until the 1890s that these relations were intensified:

> *In 1893, the first abiding contacts between these Indians [the Kayapo] and the Civilized were established. These contacts were the result of an initiative of the people of Barreira, and of Father Gil de Vilanova, who undertook three expeditions in the area (in 1891, 1896 and 1897) ... (Coudreau 1897b: 220, my translation)*

Based on the data provided by the Dominican missionary Gil de Vilanova, Coudreau gave the first classification for the Kayapo groups which, at that time, all lived west of the Araguaia. He distinguished between the following Kayapo subgroups:

> *1. The Cayapós [Kayapo of the Araguaia, or Ira'amranh] (Pau d'Arco and Chicão): 1,500 Indians;*
> *2. The Gorotires [Goroti Kumrẽnhtx] to the west of the Cayapós: 1,500 Indians;*
> *3. The Purucarus [Purukarwỳt] to the northwest of the Cayapós (they would have no contact with the Indians of the two former groups): 1,500 Indians;*
> *4. The Chicris [Xikrin] to the northeast of the Cayapós, in the big forest of Itaipava: 500 Indians. (Coudreau 1897b: 204, my translation)*

I will now proceed by discussing these groups separately.

3. THE PURUKARWỲT AND/OR KAYAPO-XIKRIN

Several designations were used in the literature to refer to the Kayapo-Xikrin. Coudreau (1897b: 204) mentioned two groups living north of the Ira'amranh and called them Chicrís (Xikrin) and Purucarus (Purukarwỳt or Putkarôt). Later, two more names were used: Djo-re and Porekry (Porekrô). In the 1940s and 1950s, the two subgroups as mentioned by Coudreau were commonly referred to as Xikrin and Djo-re.

In the literature, four designations thus appeared whereas only two subgroups seemed to exist. It took years before this confusing situation was cleared up. Fuerst (1966: 19) first reported that Xikrin and Djo-re were not two different groups, but one and the same subgroup. A few years later, Vidal (1977: 25-42) gave a detailed survey of Xikrin history. In a way she confirmed Fuerst's observation, but added that the ancestral group called Porekry or Porekrô split up into two groups: one called Kôkôrekre and which separated into two villages (Mebũmtire and Xikrin/Djo-re, which both became extinct by the beginning of this century); and another called Purukarwỳt, the ancestral group from which the contemporary Kayapo groups in the area of the Itacaiunas and Bacaja Rivers are descendants. In addition, my reconstruction of Kayapo history (field notes) revealed that other Kayapo groups used the terms Djo-re and Porekry (Porekrô) to refer to the Xikrin and Purukarwỳt, respectively. The original version as proposed by Coudreau seems to be, therefore, very accurate, despite the early date of his observations.

Thus, in fact only the Purukarwỳt still survive. Yet, since the name Xikrin is still in common usage in ethnographic literature and current reports, I will also follow this custom.

The Mekranoti informants seemed puzzled and confused regarding the exact period of the Xikrin split from the main Kayapo group called Goroti Kumrẽnhtx (see figure 13). Some informants claimed that this split occurred before their westward migration (App. B: 3); others said that it took place after this migration — i.e., after they became established on the left bank of the Araguaia River around 1820-1850 — and still others related this event to a mythological period ref erred to as "the cutting of the corn" (*bày ta kam*)[2].

In her monograph on the Kayapo-Xikrin, Vidal (1977: 27) wrote that the great-grandfather of Bepkaroti — a Xikrin chief who died in 1971 at the age of approximatively eighty-five — was alive then and living near the Catete-Itacaiunas Rivers where these Indians still abide. This means that the Xikrin probably already occupied this area around 1810-1820 and that they had probably separated from the other Kayapo prior to that date. The manifold differences between the Xikrin and the other Kayapo in such important aspects as political organization, body painting, material culture and ceremonial life, may indeed support the hypothesis of a remote separation. This would confirm the version in which the referred to split occurred before the crossing of the Araguaia River by the other main Kayapo group(s).

---

2   This myth relates how corn was introduced into Kayapo society and how, after this phenomenon, the population split up into many different tribes, Kayapo as well as non-Kayapo. If the split between the Xikrin and the other Kayapo groups is referred to in this mythological episode, I can but paraphrase this train of thought as a way of saying that the event happened a long time ago and that the Indians had nothing more to add,

In any case, the separation of the Xikrin occurred a very long time ago: any estimation or historical reconstruction remains merely speculative, as Xikrin oral history is apparently mute on the matter (Vidal 1977: 25-26). Today, there are two Xikrin groups: (1) one major one, located along the Catete River, a tributary of the upper Itacaiunas River. This group was contacted in 1953 and numbers little more than three hundred Indians, living divided over two villages; (2) a second group — located near the Bacaja River — was contacted in 1961 and numbers some two hundred Indians.

4. THE IRA'AMRANH OR KAYAPO OF THE ARAGUAIA

After the split between the Gorotire and the Ira'amranh around 1840-1860, the latter again split up into several minor communities which, in the literature, are usually referred to by the names of the respective tributaries near which their villages were located: the Kayapo of the Pau d'Arco, the Kayapo of the Arraias, the Kayapo of the Chicão, and so on. A more general, overall designation is the Kayapo of the Araguaia, as all the mentioned rivers are tributaries of the main Araguaia River. In the recent literature, this particular Kayapo group is also known as Ira'amranh or "those who walk on clear grounds" referring probably to the huge, open grassland which characterizes their territory. This term is the designation other Kayapo groups used in reference to the group in question. Other names such as Nhangagakrĩn, Kubẽ Kẽn Kam Me Mranh ("the strangers who walk on stones"), Mejôtỳr ("the people with growing hair on top of their head") and Mejôkrejabjê ("the people with long tufts of hair on top of their head"), mentioned by Gallais (1942: 240-241) and Vidal (1977: 21), may well be self-designations of different subgroups.

Travelers already mentioned the Kayapo west of the Araguaia in the 1840s. They were said to live a few days' march west of the presidio of Santa Maria (see map 3). The Capuchin friar Francisco had a brief encounter with these Indians in 1859 (T. Turner 1965: 2). The contact was limited to the friendly reception of some Kayapo men in Santa Maria do Araguaia. Such occasional contacts — during which the Indians traded wild pigs in exchange for metal tools and glass beads — continued during the following decade.

In the early 1870s, several Ira'amranh and Gorotire children were taken to a school called Santa Isabel de Leopoldina, founded by Couto de Magalhães and located upstream of Santa Maria. Soon, some of the children died of malaria, but a few remained and learned to speak Portuguese. Later-on, some of them fled back to their ethnic groups.

Skirmishes between the Ira'amranh groups and the Gorotire continued in that period. In 1876, chief Wanaô led a hundred of his men and thirty women on a reprisal raid against the Gorotire. Twenty days later, Wanaô returned with only eight followers: he had been defeated by the Gorotire and the rest of his group had stayed there, either dead or as captives (Gallais 1942: 83-85).

The Ira'amranh greatly suffered from the national colonists who were settling in the area and who were armed with rifles. In 1879, the President of the State of Goyás met the chiefs from five Ira'amranh villages and proposed that they move closer to the presidio of Santa Maria. One Ira'amranh group settled a few miles west of the presidio, but the experiment was short-lived. In 1881, when the Ira'amranh made a surprise attack on a Iny Karaja group, the commander of Santa Maria went to chide them, but the Indians had already escaped to the west. When the German ethnologist Paul Ehrenreich sailed down the Araguaia in 1888, there was no direct contact anymore between the Brazilians and the Ira'amranh (Ehrenreich 1891).

The earlier, frail contacts between the Brazilians and the Ira'amranh were consolidated at the very end of the nineteenth century. In 1896, some five years after a first, failed attempt, the Dominican missionary Gil de Vilanova visited Barreira de Santana near Santa Maria do Araguaia, where a few of the local settlers had been very recently in peaceful contact with a neighboring Ira'amranh group led by Pakaranti (Audrin 1946: 78). Both Pakaranti and Kôngri (a chief of another Ira'amranh group), who were to become Vilanova's right-hand men, had been educated in the school of Santa Isabel de Leopoldina some twenty-five years before (Gallais 1902: 40).

Through these contacts, Vilanova managed to visit several Ira'amranh villages. He founded Conceição do Araguaia, a new missionary post located some fifty kilometers to the north of Santa Maria and, as such, much closer to the Indian villages. From there, Vilanova regularly maintained contact with these Kayapo groups and built a missionary school in the post. Indian children were abruptly withdrawn from their villages, were dressed and put in school to "civilize" them. This, at least, was Vilanova's goal and aspiration (Gallais 1902: 5-8).

Coudreau visited the area in 1897 and, based on Vilanova's experience, the French geographer published a survey dealing with the division of several Ira'amranh villages. Four villages seemed to have existed at that time with a total population of some thousand five hundred Indians (Coudreau 1897b: 204). Later-on, Vilanova re-evaluated his initial opinion on the Ira'amranh population and estimated their total number at some two thousand to two thousand five hundred divided over five villages (Gallais 1902: 240-241; Moreiro Neto 1959: 51; Ianni 1979: 20): some even speak of an original number of three thousand Ira'amranh (Audrin 1946: 130).

The overall assistance provided by the Dominicans to the Indian population proved insufficient, if not totally and inexcusably limited: Vilanova was indeed simply and solely concerned with the "salvation" of the Indian soul and tried to baptize and convert as many Indians as possible into the "truth". No attention at all seemed to have been paid to the physical survival of the natives through medical care[3] and the devastating consequence was that the mortality rate was enormous. In but a few years more than half of the population succumbed to European diseases against which the American aborigines had/have no resistance.

In the first year of its existence, Conceição do Araguaia was a missionary post almost exclusively occupied with the Kayapo Indians. But this situation didn't last for long. The news soon spread that the "savage Kayapo" had been peacefully contacted by the missionaries and that they no longer had to be feared. In no time, the post became a center of attraction for the nearby colonists: two years after its foundation, nearly thousand Brazilians had settled in or near Conceição. This situation worsened when rich concentrations of rubber were discovered in the forests to the west of the Pau d'Arco River. Rubber gatherers promptly arrived from distant areas and Conceição do Araguaia turned into one of the most significant rubber centers in the State of Pará. By 1911, over fifteen thousand Brazilians had settled in and near Conceição do Araguaia (Audrin 1946: 85, 102). These Brazilian settlers soon invaded and appropriated the Indian lands. A road, built in 1908 to connect Conceição do Araguaia with newly established settlements along the Fresco River, simply passed through the Ira'amranh villages. On their way through, the Brazilians made a habit of stopping in the villages for a rest and a meal. These increased and uncontrolled contacts led to an even swifter depopulation of the Ira'amranh due to constant disease.

Kissenberth visited the area in 1908. He encountered only three Kayapo villages, the smallest being made up of merely three huts. A year later, Kissenberth revisited the area to find only two villages (Hartmann 1982: 162). There was talk of a fusion between these surviving groups

3   Although medicines were only introduced on a large scale in a later era, the reports of Vilanova and his confreres clearly indicate that this essential part of assistance was but a minor aspect of their worries.

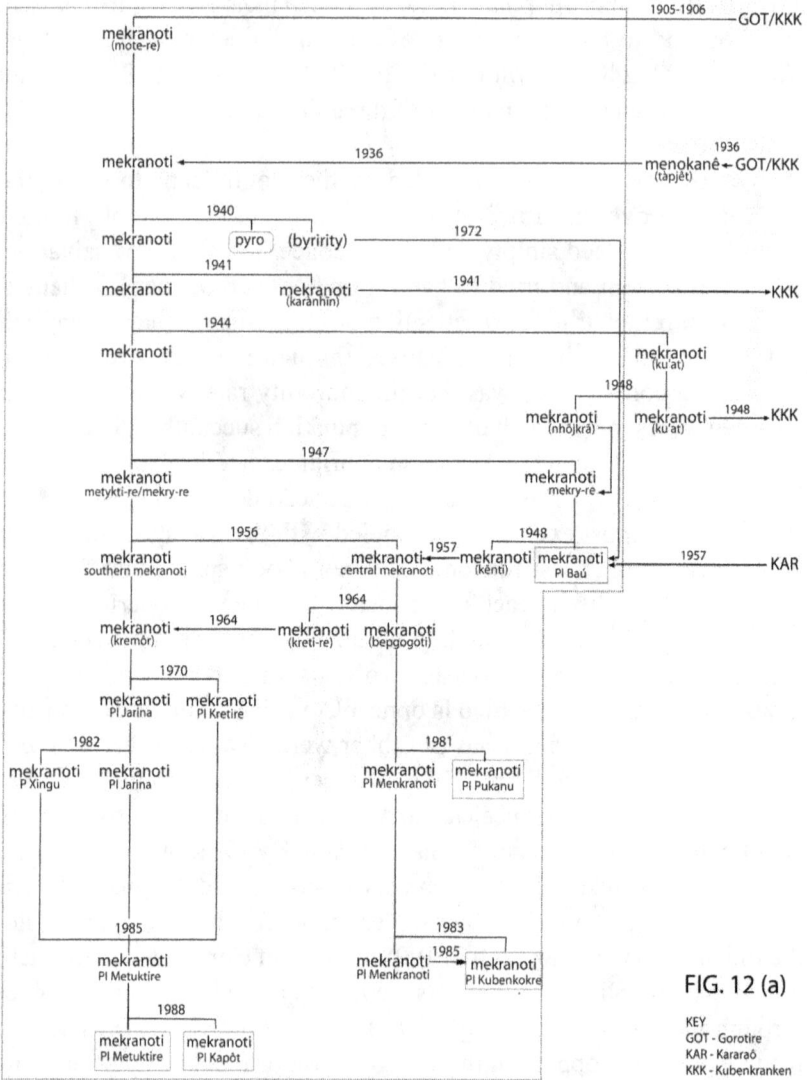

FIG. 12 (a)

KEY
GOT - Gorotire
KAR - Kararaô
KKK - Kubenkranken

Figure 12 — Schematic representation of the main schisms and fusions of the Kayapo groups in the course of the last two centuries (situation updated until 1988). (a) The Mekranoti groups; (b) the Gorotire groups.

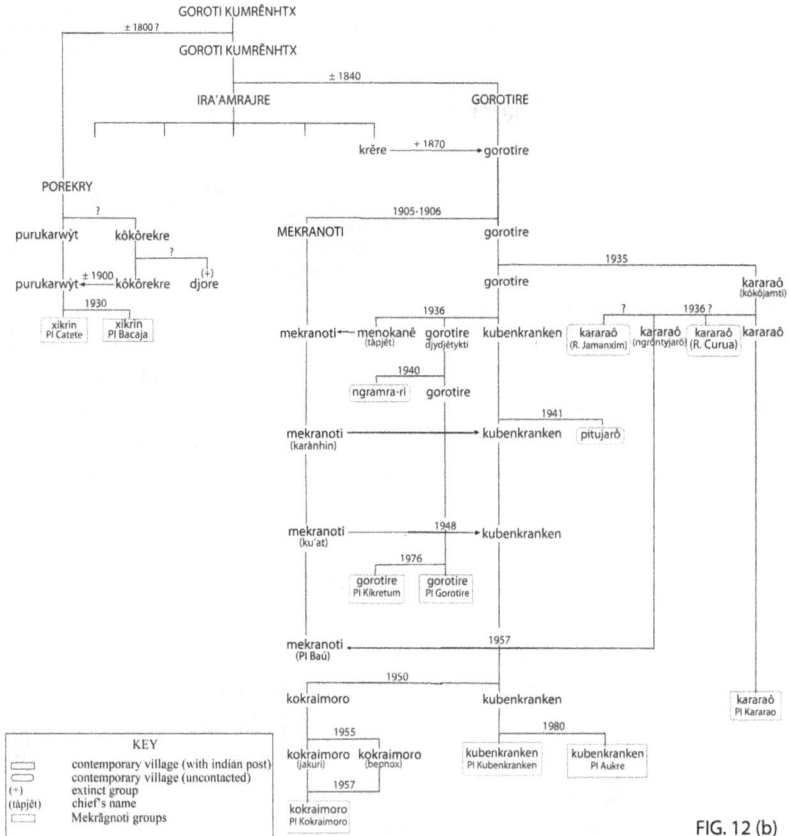

GOROTI KUMRÊNHTX
± 1800 ?
GOROTI KUMRÊNHTX
± 1840
IRA'AMRAJRE   GOROTIRE

krêre ——— + 1870 ——→ gorotire

POREKRY
?   1905-1906
purukarwỹt   kôkôrekre   MEKRANOTI   gorotire
                    ?   1935
purukarwỹt ←± 1900 kôkôrekre (+)djore   gorotire   kararaó
        1930   (kôkôjamti)

xikrin   xikrin   1936
PI Catete   PI Bacaja   mekranoti ←— menokanê gorotire kubenkranken kararaó kararaó kararaó kararaó
                              (tâpjêt) djydjêtykti   (R. Jamanxim) (ngróntyjaró) (R. Curua)
                                    1940
                              (ngramra-ri) gorotire
                                                      1941
                              mekranoti ————————→ kubenkranken (pitujaró)
                              (karànhin)
                                          1948
                              mekranoti ————————→ kubenkranken
                              (ku'at)
                                    1976
                              gorotire   gorotire
                              PI Kikretum PI Gorotire
                                                      1957
                              mekranoti ←——————
                              (PI Baú)
                                    1950
                              kokraimoro   kubenkranken   kararaó
                                                                          PI Kararao
                                          1955   1980
KEY   kokraimoro kokraimoro   kubenkranken kubenkranken
contemporary village (with indian post) (jakurá) (bepnox) PI Kubenkranken PI Aukre
contemporary village (uncontacted)   1957
(+) extinct group   kokraimoro
(tâpjêt) chief's name   PI Kokraimoro
Mekrãgnoti groups

FIG. 12 (b)

into a single village, a union which took place in 1921.

In the early 1930s, the people at São Jacintho (the name of the last Ira'amranh village) formulated a request to the government of the State of Para to have the area around the village officially recognized as a reserve (Mensageiro do Santo Rosario 1933: 99). The request was not complied with.

In 1940, Nimuendajú found only six (!) surviving Ira'amranh Indians, who were living together with the local Brazilian population (Nimuendajú 1940ms: 3). The last survivor of this Kayapo group, an old woman, died in the village of Gorotire in 1961.

This once numerous and important Kayapo group thus became extinct because of a basic lack of interest on the part of the missionaries. Once this group had arrived at a "good" relationship with the members of Western society, some two thousand (or more?) Indians died due to insufficient assistance in a space of less than fifty years.

5. THE GOROTIRE OR KAYAPO OF THE XINGU

We now come to the numerically most important of the still surviving Kayapo groups, the one which, not surprisingly, has received greater scientific attention.

As far as I can tell, the Kayapo were first mentioned near the Xingu River around 1750. Based on data provided by the German Jesuit Roque Hunderpfund, Father José de Morães reported the following:

> *The Indians of the Caraja-uçu nation live in the savannah near the Tocantins River, where they have been sighted occasionally. They have been warring with the Jurunas. (Morães 1860: 505, my translation)*

Three observations have to be considered regarding this citation:

1. Once again, another designation is used in reference to the Kayapo: Karaja-uçu ("big Karaja" in Tupi language). At the end of the nineteenth century, the Kayapo were often mistaken for a Iny Karaja group. I believe this is mainly due to the similarity of weapons used during raids, especially round war clubs (see Chapter 3) which, according to Kayapo customs, are left near the body of the slain victim. Such Kayapo clubs are almost identical to Iny Karaja ones;

2. The above mentioned quotation clearly states that the Kayapo lived near the Tocantins River, thus once again endorsing the observation made earlier that the Kayapo lived east of the Araguaia prior to 1859;

3. It may seem inconceivable that the Kayapo attacked the Yudja (Juruna) tribe which lived along the Xingu River, at no less than five hundred kilometers from the Kayapo habitat in those days. In Appendix A it is shown, however, that even in the course of this century, several Kayapo groups undertook raids as far as six hundred kilometers as the crow flies from their village.

The split between the Gorotire and Ira'amranh occurred around 1840-1860: the former attacked the Ira'amranh, who fled temporarily to the north. While the Gorotire moved further west towards the Xingu River, the Ira'amranh returned to their former habitat, splitting up into several minor villages (map 3) and came into peaceful contact with the Brazilians shortly afterward.

In 1843, when Prince Adalbert of Prussia went up the Xingu River to 4° southern latitude, the Yudja provided him with an impressively long list of tribes inhabiting that river. One of the tribes listed was *ticuapam-oin*, the Yudja designation for the Kayapo which is commonly spelled in contemporary ethnographic literature as Txukarramãe, Tshukahamai or Xukahahamei. According to the Yudja, this was the most important of all Xingu tribes and was located near the mid-course of the Xingu River (Adalbert of Prussia 1847). It must therefore be understood that, in 1843, the Gorotire already lived near that river or had, at least, already frequently crossed it.

According to Kayapo oral tradition, for years the Ira'amranh did not risk a counter-attack on the Gorotire out of fear for Kubẽdjàgogo, the main Gorotire chief; instead, one of the Ira'amranh groups led by Krẽ-re joined the Gorotire.

The death of Kubẽdjàgogo, however, initiated a period of overt hostilities between the Gorotire and Ira'amranh. During this time the Gorotire started to attack some of the Brazilian settlements along the Xingu River, acquiring in this manner their first firearms.

6. THE MEKRANOTI SEPARATE FROM THE GOROTIRE (1900-1935)

At the end of the nineteenth century the Gorotire occupied a single, huge village called *pykatôti*. It was located on the open grasslands near the headwaters of the Riozinho, a tributary of the Rio Fresco. The village had two men's houses, each housing several men's societies, and probably had a population of about two thousand Indians. It was not constantly inhabited by the entire village population, though, as it was not uncommon for the men of a men's society and their dependents to temporarily leave the main village. Such bands often wandered around in the large area between the Fresco and Xingu Rivers, eventually returning to the main village.

One of the men's societies of the western men's house lived aside in this way for a few years. The group was led by Mote-re and was called *mekrãgnoti* (Mekranoti), after the name of the men's society. They lived in a temporary village named *krã'ãbõm*. It was erected some fifty kilometers north of *pykatôti* and near the site of the contemporary village at PI Kubenkranken. This location allowed the Mekranoti to visit the nearby Yudja tribe more often.

Ever since the eighteenth century, the Yudja were traditional enemies of the Kayapo. At the end of the nineteenth century, the two hundred and five Yudja lived dispersed over five small villages along the mid Xingu River. By moving to *krã'ãbõm*, the Mekranoti wanted to engage in more frequent exchanges with the Yudja who, by that time, already had peri-odic contacts with the Brazilians and who, as such, already possessed firearms and other commodities. The Kayapo were especially interested in the glass beads, then and today a highly prized trade good. Both the Gorotire of the main village and the Mekranoti visited the Yudja but the Mekranoti did so much more often and some of them eventually ended up learning the Yudja language (see App. B: 14).

Early explorers of the Xingu River either referred to the exchanges that took place between the Kayapo and the Yudja (Coudreau 1897a: 22, 34- 36, 52-54, 59, 87-88) or to the fact that some Kayapo captives were found among the Yudja (Von den Steinen 1886). These "captives" prob-ably were Ire'ôti and Mrykarà, two young Mekranoti women who lived for years among the Yudja (see App. B: 14).

Around 1905, the earlier tensions between the Kayapo and the Yudja emerged again due to a clash between the Gorotire and the Yudja. A Goro-tire man was killed and decapitated, allowing the Yudja to perform their war rite in which the skull of a slain enemy takes a prominent part (Nim-uendajú 1948: 235-236; Kräutler 1979: 41-42). After this incident, the Mekranoti returned to live in the main village, but not for long, however. Within a year, Mote-re got into a fight with a man of the eastern men's house over an adulterous relationship. This led to a collective club-fight between the men of Mote-re's men's society and those of the opposite men's house. In the aftermath of this fight, Mote-re left again with his men's society. The dissident group built a new village in a small area of savannah to the west of the Xingu River. About a year later, 'Ôket, Pãnhmoti and Karànhĩn, all important chiefs of the western men's house, joined the Mekranoti with a group of their followers. By then, the Me-kranoti had a population of about hundred and ninety Indians.

After a few years, the Mekranoti moved south to a bigger area of savan-nah located between the Jarina and Iriri Nova Rivers. This was to become the core of the Mekranoti area: although many villages were erected in the nearby and distant forests, the Mekranoti somehow always returned to that area which they up to the present refer to as "our real area of savannah" (meba nhõ kapôt djwỳnh). The period between 1906 and 1934 was one of relative internal peace within the Mekranoti community. To be sure, some attacks or raids took place, some captives were taken, and some club-duels occurred within the community, but no permanent schism resulted, nor, apparently, was there any case of homicide. The population increased at a fast and steady rate and, by 1934, the group was about five hundred and twenty strong.

The attack against the Panara (Kreen Akrore) undertaken in 1921 proved to be a significant landmark in Mekranoti history: the assaulted tribe took revenge and the Mekranoti were attacked in their own village by a non-Kayapo group. This had never happened before in their history. The Mekranoti, therefore, considered the Panara to be among the most feared and respected enemies. The 1921 attack marked the beginning of an enduring animosity between the two Gê tribes. This particular enmity had a significant impact on the pre-contact history of the Mekranoti: especially in the period between 1921 and 1930, Mekranoti movements seem to be marked by episodes of fear for Panara (counter) attacks and several of the migrations in that period were almost entirely due to the hostilities between the two tribes.

7. THE GOROTIRE COME INTO CONFLICT WITH ENCROACHING COLONISTS (1905-1935)

In the first years of this century, numerous rubber gatherers settled in the area near Conceição do Araguaia. Soon, a number of them marched further inland towards the nearby Fresco River, an area particularly rich in latex (Audrin 1946: 95). In no time, three agglomerations emerged: São Felix do Xingu (named after the patron saint of the rubber gatherers and located at the confluence of the Fresco and Xingu), Nova Olinda (near the mouth of the Riozinho) and Novo Horizonte (along the upper Fresco and not far from the agglomerations along the tributaries of the Araguaia River). These agglomerations served as commercial centers for the many rubber gatherers living dispersed throughout the area.

At that time, some minor skirmishes occurred between the Gorotire and the rubber gatherers. During these skirmishes the Gorotire — still living in the area between the Fresco and Xingu Rivers — sacked the settlements of the itinerant rubber gatherers but it was generally accepted that "the Gorotire still were in peace" (Nimuendajú 1952: 428).

This situation didn't last for long, however. The supply of commodities and the export of rubber proved to be a serious problem for the rubber gatherers who were living quite isolated along the Rio Fresco. Due to the many river rapids, river transport along the Xingu was not only time-consuming but also very dangerous. Also, it was only feasible during a few months of the year when the water-level was at its highest. The only viable solution to year-round communication appeared to be the widening of an existent narrow trail connecting Conceição do Araguaia with Novo Horizonte.

These road construction projects were completed in 1908. A small band of Gorotire temporarily lived near the Ribeirão das Antas (a right tributary of the upper Fresco River) and had peaceful contact with the Brazilians at that time (Nimuendajú 1932: 553). The number of rubber gatherers continued to increase at an appalling rate and the trail soon developed into an extremely busy transport route. Numerous muleteers traversed the area with their pack animals transporting food and other merchandise to sell to the rubber gatherers along the Fresco River. Corn was the stock food for the mules. As food was a problem in the area, the mules soon started invading the nearby gardens of the small Gorotire band. The Indians killed some of the mules. The muleteers, upon returning with a heavy load of rubber, found their pack animals slain and immediately attacked the neighboring Gorotire, killing some of them (Cavalcanti 1981: 18).

The Gorotire were taken by surprise and immediately suppressed by the well-armed Brazilians. They feared further conflicts with Brazilians, as they remembered all too well the dreadful experiences of their ancestors along the Araguaia River about a century before. So these Gorotire turned around and went back to the main village site of *pykatôti*. Immediately afterwards, the Gorotire were raided twice in their village by the rubber gatherers who, led by a certain Antônio Firmino, burned down the village and destroyed nearly all the provisions (Nimuendajú 1932: 555). This raid turned out to be a significant event which greatly influenced the further development of relations between the Gorotire and the surrounding Brazilians.

After the punitive expedition of the Brazilians, the number of Gorotire attacks on Brazilian settlements increased markedly. Brazilian settlements along the Xingu and further to the west were being harassed, but those suffering the most were the Brazilians living along the Fresco and the Pau d'Arco Rivers. These perpetual raids inflicted heavy casualties on both sides but despite the insecure situation in the area, Brazilian colonization endured. Soon, several other settlements emerged along the mid Xingu River, in addition to the earlier mentioned agglomerations along the Fresco. The most important of the new settlements was led by a man called Constantino Viana who, for years, was the southernmost Brazilian settler along the Xingu River. He considered himself *amansador dos bichos* ("animal tamer")[4] in reference to the Indians

4   Constantino Viana lived along the mid Xingu since about 1910. Sometime around that date, he got involved in a slaughter of numerous Juruna (Yudja) Indians. By 1915, the few Yudja survivors enlisted the aid of Viana and his laborers for massive raids on the Kisedje (Suya) Indians and on the peaceful Kamaiura and Wauja (Waura) of the upper Xingu River area (Nimuendajú 1952: 432-433; Seeger 1981: 52).

(Nimuendajú 1952: 432-433).

Between 1931 and 1935, Dom Frei Sebastião Thomas, Bishop at Conceição do Araguaia, undertook three journeys to the Fresco to try to "pacify" the Gorotire. Assisted by a few Ira'amranh men, he entered into peaceful contact with groups of Gorotire along the Fresco and Riozinho. During his last brief visit, he managed to convince the Indians to let him take along five children to be educated in the missionary school at Conceição do Araguaia[5]. These children, however, fled at the first opportunity and returned to their village (Sebastião Thomas 1936: 85).

In 1935, less than two months after Dom Thomas' last trip, three British missionaries (often referred to as the "Three Freds") travelled up to the Riozinho River and reached the Cachoeira da Fumaça ("Smoke Falls" in Portuguese), near the old Mekranoti village site of *krã'ãbõm*, where they were killed by the Gorotire (Nimuendajú 1952: 429; Banner 1963, 1975).

8. FURTHER SCHISMS IN THE GOROTIRE VILLAGE AND THE FIRST PEACEFUL CONTACTS WITH THE BRAZILIANS (1935-1947)

For the Gorotire, the period from 1908 to 1935 had been particularly tenuous due to enclosing colonization, contacts with missionaries and the introduction of diseases. In 1935, their main village was still located at *pykatôti*, while other temporary villages existed in the surroundings — one of these being *krã'ãbõm*, the site occupied by the Mekranoti at the end of the nineteenth century. There were probably over thousand five hundred Gorotire.

Pykatôti had two men's houses. Kjêkjêk, one of the senior chiefs of the eastern men's house, had already suffered some skirmishes with Kôkôjamti, a young leader of the *mebêkararaô* men's society in the western men's house. Kôkôjamti was often referred to as *mebĩdjwỹnh* ("real killer") because of his belligerence, not only towards non-Gorotire, but also within the community: Kôkôjamti had undertaken many club-fights to settle disagreements.

One day in 1935, Kôkôjamti took his men out into the forest on a hunting party for a few days. Kjêkjêk died during that interval and his

---

5   In a small booklet, Dom Thomas described the weal and woe of his third brief visit to the Gorotire. It is clear that this aspiration of taking along Gorotire children to the missionary school of Conceição do Araguaia was a major preoccupation of the Bishop. Those Indians who handed over the children were "abundantly rewarded" with gifts (Sebastião Thomas 1936: 57-71).

Table 4 — Presentation of the demographic evolution of all known Kayapo villages since the date of "pacification".

KAYAPO GROUP	SUBGROUP	VILLAGE	POPULATION		
			AT PACIFICATION	IN 1965	IN 1986-1990
GOROTI-RE	Goroti-re	PI Gorotire PI Kikretum	844 (1936)	302	695 316
	Kubēkrākênh	PI Kubenkrankein PI Aukre	300 (1952)	253	203 202
	Kokraimor	PI Krokraimoro	137 (1957) 97 (1957)	170	182
	Kararaô	PI Kararaô (Ngrõntyjarô)	30 (1970) 38 (1957)	(30)	38
MEKRÃGNOTI	Northern Mekrãgnoti	PI Bau (Kenti)	130 (1957) 68 (1957)	} 60	60
	Central Mekrãgnoti	PI Menkranoti/PI Kubenkokre PI Pukanu	360 (1953)	} 220	391 90
	Southern Mekrãgnoti	PI Kapot/PI Mentuktire	210 (1953)	170	364
XIKRÎN	Xikrîn	PI Catete PI Bajaca	300 (1953) 200 (1957)	102 110	304 194
TOTAL			3114	1427	3032

followers accused Kôkôjamti of having killed their chief by sorcery in order to steal his young wife. In revenge, Kjêkjêk's men killed Pidjôpari, Kôkôjamti's brother, and hatched a plan to kill Kôkôjamti upon his return to the village. A group of women and children, all kin members of Kôkôjamti and his followers, then left the village and met the hunters in the forest. This group, called *mebêkararaô*[6] after Kôkôjamti's men's society, then fled to the west and crossed the Xingu River with the intention of joining the Mekranoti. They made peaceful contact with a group of Mekranoti men who were out on a hunting trek, but this union didn't last long: that same night, one of the Mekranoti men killed Kôkôjamti in his sleep and his followers fled to the north, where they split up into several small bands. In contemporary literature, this Kayapo group is known as the Kararaô (see further).

Back in the main village, Tàpjêt was a Gorotire chief who had always sided with Kôkôjamti, but had not joined the Kararaô during their schism. A few months after the separation of the Kararaô, Tàpjêt separated from his wife Krãdjàbyr and joined the *menokanê* ("people with eye disease"), the younger men's group of his western men's house. Immediately afterwards, he left with his men for a raid on the Brazilian settlements along the Jamanxim River. He raided one settlement and captured a girl of about twelve years of age. The girl was named Irekàrênh. On his way back to the village, he met a group of Mekranoti men, spent a few days with them and managed to convince a Mekranoti man (Kopo'yr) to join him and visit the Gorotire.

During his absence, Krãdjàbyr, upset by the divorce, declared herself "wife of the eastern men's house"[7], a highly embarrassing deed for Tàpjêt. This eventually led to open conflict: Tàpjêt and his men called for a collective club-fight with those who had had intercourse with his ex-wife. Greatly outnumbered by the men of the opposite men's house, Tàpjêt and his *menokanê* men were beaten. They left the village and were joined by Bepkamati, a chief of another men's society of the same men's house. Kopo'yr, the Mekranoti man, led the dissident group of some hundred and fifty Indians to his village. The separation of Tàpjêt from the main village occurred at the end of 1936.

6   *Kararaô* is a non-Kayapo word often used by them as a "shout" during warfare.

7   Without openly declaring themselves as such, adolescent *mekrajtyk* girls as well as *kupry* women are "wives" of a men's house or of a men's society. Krãdjàbyr belonged to neither of these two categories. Her unusual act of openly declaring herself available to the men of the opposite men's house was clearly meant as a calculated affront to Tàpjêt.

A few months later, a new, major dispute broke out in the Gorotire village. Yet another schism ensued, during which almost the entire group of men from the eastern men's house left with their kin members. This group, led by Takwỳr, Bemajti and Txikatô, was called *mebêdjydjetykti* ("big black bow people") after the major men's society. Those who remained in the area of *pykatôti* were called *kubẽkrãkênh*[8] ("baldheaded non-Kayapo") by the other Kayapo groups.

The mebêdjydjetykti set up a temporary shelter near the Fresco River. From there, a group of warriors took off to the north, raided some Brazilian settlements along the lower Xingu, and eventually attacked the Asurini, a Tupi tribe living along the Ipixuna River. When the warriors returned, the entire band left the Fresco River and, after attacking two Brazilian settlements along that river, proceeded to the savannah west of the Araguaia River. There, they tried to enter into peaceful contact with the local population but the Brazilians reacted hostilely and the Indians retreated to the Fresco River.

A small band of some forty Gorotire men led by Vicente — a Brazilian who as a boy had been taken captive by the Gorotire along the Triunfo River in about 1925 — appeared in a small settlement near the Pau d'Arco River. The Indians asked for tools in order to lay out new gardens. One of the Brazilians invited Vicente and his people to come and settle near Nova Olinda (Mensageiro do Santo Rosario 1937, n° 8: 207-208).

Within a month (June 1937), Vicente appeared with nearly eight hundred and fifty Indians at Nova Olinda (T. Turner 1987ms: 83). The Indians proposed to the inhabitants of that agglomeration that they live in peace on the other bank of the river. The people of Nova Olinda accepted this treaty, hoping to achieve peace in the area and to a acquire cheap labor force. But the situation in Nova Olinda soon became intolerable. Instead of gaining manpower, the Brazilians were sacked: the Indians finished off all the food supplies and took all the tools they could get their hands on. Especially firearms and ammunition were highly valued by the Indians who planned an attack on the Kubenkranken.

Afraid of evoking new hostilities, the Brazilians remained quite passive and notified the Serviço de Proteção aos Índios (SPI) of their awkward situation (Nimuendajú 1952: 429-430; Banner 1975: 48). The SPI was particularly slow to react. In the meantime, as no efficient medical care was available at Nova Olinda, diseases swept through this newly contacted Kayapo group. In only a few months' time, many Indians died

8   Following FUNAI orthography, and for reasons of readability, the Kubẽkrãkênh are named Kubenkranken in this work.

(Kräutler 1979: 44).

During this encounter, the Brazilians ignored the fact that this Kayapo group was a but a fraction of the main Gorotire group and that it was called *mebêdjydjetykti*. They therefore called these Indians "Gorotire" and this name has been applied specifically to them ever since.

Occasionally, several Gorotire bands left the village site near Nova Olinda to temporarily wander into the forests, sometimes peacefully visiting small settlements of rubber gatherers along the Fresco and Araguaia Rivers, and sometimes attacking them. The situation in Nova Olinda grew particularly tense when one of these bands killed five Brazil nut gatherers along the Branco River in February 1938 (Kräutler 1979: 45). By then, many inhabitants of Nova Olinda had left the area, taking along about a dozen Gorotire Indians who were engaged in working for them. Yet another ten Gorotire lived with Vicente near Trapiche, a small, local alcohol factory located along the Rio Branco (a left tributary of the lower Fresco).

Tension in the main Gorotire group prevailed and, by mid-1938, there were hardly any Gorotire left at Nova Olinda. The majority of the survivors lived scattered over several groups roaming through the area between the Riozinho and Pau d'Arco Rivers. Reports mention overt clashes between such groups which often were hostile to one another (Nimuendajú 1952: 447-448; Kräutler 1979: 154-155). Some of these scattered groups occasionally visited the few surviving Ira'amranh along the Pau d'Arco River. These visits often led to serious conflicts between the Gorotire and the Ira'amranh. On one particular occasion, some seventy Gorotire Indians established themselves near a minor Ira'amranh settlement. The Gorotire left again after a few days, but returned almost immediately afterwards, and killed ten Ira'amranh and seriously injured three others (Mensageiro do Santo Rosario 1942: 66). With this assault, the number of victims from Gorotire raids in the period from 1930 to 1942 increased to over sixty (*ibid.* 1941: 280).

Those Gorotire who in the late 1930s did remain at Nova Olinda were moved by Pedro Silva, a SPI inspector, to a site further upstream, in the hope of reducing the impact of western diseases. A post was erected on this site: it was called Pôsto do Sôbreiro.

In 1938, Horace Banner of the Unevangelized Fields Mission (UFM) erected a small missionary post along the lower Riozinho River, not far from Nova Olinda. Gradually, some of the dispersed Gorotire bands moved into the post; by the end of 1938, some hundred Indians had already settled there, and this number increased rapidly. Other groups often came to pay a brief visit to the mission.

In October 1939, an important group led by Bemajti roamed to the east of the Fresco River. There the Brazilians killed a pregnant Gorotire woman at a garden site and three Brazilians were killed in revenge. The Brazilians then reacted ferociously: fifty armed men set off and executed three consecutive raids on this Gorotire band. In sum, about seventy Indians were killed, including Bemajti. After this incident, Ngramra-ri separated with a small group of about forty Indians. Up to the present, this small Kayapo group continues to live isolated in the forests, without any known contact with members of Western civilization. The rest of Bemajti's group (about two hundred strong) moved to the missionary post and reunited with the more or less two hundred tribesmen who by then had settled there (Nimuendajú 1952: 431, 443). As such, by 1940, the majority of the four hundred and fifty surviving Gorotire lived at the missionary post.

SPI agents as well as missionaries tried to attract as many Gorotire Indians as possible to their post. This rivalry between SPI and the mission, coupled with insufficient resources to cope effectively with the enormous medical and hygienic problems, had devastating consequences. In 1947 all the surviving Gorotire were reunited and moved once again, this time to Novo Horizonte, by then deserted by the Brazilians. The new village numbered only eighty-nine survivors.

9. THE KARARAÔ (1935-1989)

Several anthropologists have met Kararaô Indians, others have spent a few days in one of the Kararaô villages, but none has done any thorough field-work among these Indians. This explains why the Kararaô continue to be the least known of all Kayapo of the Xingu groups.

I have mentioned that the Kararaô separated from the Gorotire in 1936. They must have numbered about hundred and fifty (or more?) Indians and moved to the east, crossing the Xingu River where they met up with a group of Mekranoti warriors. Kôkôjamti, the Kararaô chief, expressed his desire to move into the Mekranoti village, but he was killed by one of the Mekranoti men that same night. The next day, all but two Kararaô fled to the north.

Soon after arriving near the lower Iriri, the Kararaô began separating into several groups and subgroups. In a first phase, the group split up in two: one of which remained in the area along the lower Iriri, and another which crossed that river and settled in the area along the Jaraucu River.

9.1 — The Kararaô of the Jaraucu River

This group again split up into two villages: one which moved to the Igarapé Penetecaua, a tributary of the Jaraucu River, and another one that moved to the Guajara River. The first one was contacted in the late 1930s. They entered into peaceful contact with the local Brazilian population along the Igarapé Penetecaua. When the German missionary Carlos Borromen Ebner visited these Indians in that period, the group numbered eighty-six Indians (Ebner 1942: 364). He referred to these Indians as "Duludy"[9]. Almost immediately after Ebner's visit, the SPI moved the Indians to the vicinity of Porto de Moz, a small town located along the lower Xingu River. Soon, many of the Indians died of contact diseases, while "a reporter of the newspaper A Noite obtained horrible pictures of the hapless survivors lying together with corpses in the house which served as their habitation" (Nimuendajú 1952: 431-432). Only twelve survived. They fled into the forest, to settle near the town of Altamira in early 1940. There, they were frequently visited by passing Brazilians. On the assumption that they had acquired enough confidence from the local Brazilians, the Indians then moved to Victoria, a small town forty-seven kilometers away from Altamira. While sleeping, they were treasonably attacked by the Brazilians:

> ... a massacre occurred, just as the Indians were preparing to spend the night in the old warehouse. Every door, every window bristled with Winchesters and shotguns. Only by miracle did a solitary man get away alive. (Banner 1963: 25)

This one man, called Õkwa, moved to the Kubenkranken a few years later (*ibid.*: 52).

The group that had moved to the upper Guajara River was contacted in September 1965 by SPI agents. The group numbered forty-eight Indians (Arnaud & Alves 1974: 10). Immediately after "pacification" the SPI moved the Indians to a post located along the mid Jaraucu River. A measles epidemic in 1967 reduced the group to merely eight Indians! In 1970, three of the survivors moved to the Xikrin of the Catete River, while the other five settled among the Xikrin of the Bacaja (*ibid.*: 15-16).

9.2 — The Kararaô of the Iriri River

The main Kararaô group, which at the end of the 1930s had remained in

9   Following Ebner's orthography of Kayapo words, I take the view that "duludy" is a transcription of *tyryti,* the Kayapo word for plantains. This leads me to believe that this group called itself *mebetyryti* ("plantain people").

the lower Iriri River area, split up into at least three small groups. A first one was led by Ngrõntyjarô and numbered thirty-eight Indians. These settled along the Igarapé Limão (a tributary of the lower Curua), where they were contacted in early 1957. Immediately after "pacification" these Kararaô were united with some hundred and fifty Northern Mekranoti and were moved by the SPI to Pôsto Curua. The calamitous after-effects of this move are described in the section on the Northern Mekranoti.

Another part of the Kararaô of the Iriri remained unknown until the construction of the Transamazônica. This group of forty Indians was contacted by FUNAI agents near the lower Iriri in 1970. They were moved to a site along the lower Iriri. A post was built near the small settlement and was called PI Kararaô. As in nearly all other cases, contact diseases almost completely exterminated this small group. In 1978, only twenty-two survived including six adult women and one single man. This man was a Southern Mekranoti who had joined with Kremôr to the Kubenkranken in 1959 and who had managed to escape the 1961 slaughter by fleeing to the Gorotire. From there, he moved to PI Kararaô. In 1978-1979, FUNAI moved these Kararaô Indians into the village of the Xikrin of the Bacaja River, in the hope to settle them there. The Kararaô weren't very pleased with the idea and, due to my protest against FUNAI officials in Brasilia, the Kararaô were moved back to their village. In recent years, a few Xikrin and Gorotire men have settled in the village and current population is estimated at about thirty-five Indians.

At least one, and maybe two small Kararaô groups still remain uncontacted: one of these villages is probably located along the Iriri and is said to consist of nine houses; another one may still roam to the west, along the Jamanxim River.

10. The Menokanê join the Mekranoti and separate again (1935-1947)

In 1937, when Tàpjêt arrived from the Gorotire in the Mekranoti village, it had one men's house and was located in the savannah between the Jarina and Iriri Novo Rivers. At this time, the Mekranoti population numbered some five hundred and twenty Indians, which increased to about six hundred and seventy with the arrival of Tàpjêt and his followers. After Tàpjêt's settlement in the village, the number of Mekranoti raids and attacks undertaken against both Brazilian settlers and the Kubenkranken increased noticeably: hardly any season went by without a war expedition taking place.

In 1941, tension grew in the village and Karànhĩn led a group of hundred and two followers in flight from the Mekranoti village. They set up a separate village near the Xinxim (a tributary of the upper Iriri). Shortly afterwards, this group fled to the Kubenkranken out of fear for a Mekranoti attack.

But tension continued in the Mekranoti village and, in 1942, a new village was built, this time with two men's houses: the eastern one was called *metykti-re* ("big black people") and the western one was called *mekry-re* ("small people"). Almost immediately afterward, Tàpjêt left with a group of men to raid the Brazilian settlements along the Jamanxim River. Upon returning, he was killed by a member of his own raiding party.

The Mekranoti often told me that "after Tàpjêt's death, the good relations ended". Ethno-historic research does seem to support this observation as the event in question was followed by a series of internal disputes and by numerous club-fights during which many Mekranoti were killed. In addition, temporary or even permanent schisms occurred between several factions.

Kreti-re, a young leader of the junior men in the western men's house, had been away on a raid when Tàpjêt was killed. Upon his return, he and his followers killed not only Tàpjêt's killer but also Katàmkrãmex, one of the *metykti-re* chiefs.

Tension grew rapidly and the village broke up along the lines of the two men's houses: the *metykti-re* — led by Bepgogoti and Kremôr — left to the east, while the *mekry-re* — led by Angme'ê, Bepkamati and Kreti-re — settled to the north. Besides these two main groups, two ex-associates of Tàpjêt led their kin away: Byriryti left with his wife and children and moved towards the Curua River; and a man called Pyro left with some twenty followers and fled to the mid Iriri River. The latter has never been contacted.

In the *mekry-re* group, tension continued and in 1944 Ku'at, one of Tàpjêt's earlier companions, fled with a group of about seventy people. They moved to the west, roaming around in the area near the Jamanxim River.

A year later (1945), Bepgogoti took off with his men to attack the *mekry-re* in revenge for the death of Katàmkrãmex. A few months later, however, both the *mekry-re* and *metykti-re* groups reunited in a single village with only one men's house.

Once again, a series of club-duels broke out and the village broke up. First, Kremôr left with an important group of junior men from the *metykti-re* group. They were afraid of being killed and moved to the opposite bank of the Xingu. Somewhat later, during one of the collective club-fights in the main village, Bepkamati and his group were defeated. They were supported by Angme'ê and Kẽnti and left the village, moving to the north and building a village with one men's house. The remaining groups, led by Bepgogoti and Kreti-re, respectively, also left the village and roamed freely in the forests to the north. Sometime later, these latter two groups reunited, but a group of senior men separated to join the junior men still living on the other side of the Xingu River.

It is interesting at this point to have a closer look at the composition of the several resulting factions. Excluding the group led by Karànhĩn, which had fled to the Kubenkranken in 1941, the following factions existed by mid-1947 (the numbers refer only to married men with children and elderly men, excluding as such the *menõrõny-re*):

— The small group which, led by Ku'at, still wandered in the forests along the Jamanxim River. It consisted of nine men;

— The group of Bepkamati, Angme'ê and Kẽnti consisted of thirty-two *mekry-re* and one *metykti-re* men. The schism of this group from the remainder of the Mekranoti was definite. This group is called "Northern Mekranoti" throughout this book;

— Kremôr's initial group consisted of twenty-two *metykti-re* and one *mekry-re*, all members of the *menõrõny-re* age grade. Some months later, another group of fifteen men (all *metykti-re* men of the senior age grades) joined this group;

— Bepgogoti's group consisted of seventeen *metykti-re* men and that of Kreti-re consisted of fourteen *mekry-re*. This total of thirty-one men who lived at *rõntinõr* excludes the fifteen men who joined Kremôr's group.

11. THE RECENT HISTORY OF THE NORTHERN MEKRANOTI (1947-1989)

The group of *mekry-re* led by Angme'e, Bepkamati and Kẽnti remained separate from the other Mekranoti and will from this point on be referred to as "Northern Mekranoti". They were little over two hundred and ten strong at the time of their separation from the main Mekranoti village in 1947.

After separating from the other Mekranoti, they first moved to the north and erected a village on a site which they had previously occupied a few years before. Almost immediately after settling there, however, a club-fight broke out and about a dozen Indians left to move back to the main Mekranoti village. A few months later, the Northern Mekranoti left the area and moved towards the Curua River where they met up with and reabsorbed a small band of some twenty Mekranoti. These formed part of the group which, led by Ku'at, had separated from the main Mekranoti group in 1944 — the other part settled in the Kubenkranken village a few years later (see further).

Internal conflicts persisted in the Northern Mekranoti group. About a year after the reunion mentioned above, the group split up in two: a small group of some seventy Indians, led by Kẽnti, left the village and moved to the east, where they wandered in the forest from one temporary village to another. The main group, led by Angme'ê and Bepkamati, was about hundred and forty strong and moved to the north, settling near some deserted gardens of an abandoned Brazilian settlement.

These two Northern Mekranoti groups remained mutually hostile, and are responsible for many of the raids that were recorded against the Brazilian population west of the Iriri River. The group led by Kẽnti will be discussed in a following section as I will here only be concerned with the vicissitudes of the main group led by Angme'ê and Bepkamati.

In the early 1950s, several rubber gatherers of the Xingu River area and a federal deputy requested the federal government to take the necessary steps, since "the regional economy was near a total breakdown due to the incessant Indian attacks" (Arnaud 1971: 3). A special commission was immediately set up in the State of Pará. Important budgets were set aside and allowed the SPI to intensify their "pacification" procedures against the many tribes which at that time still lived isolated throughout the Xingu River basin.

So, in 1957, Francisco Meirelles (an SPI inspector) set out with some Gorotire men to the area of the Iriri and Curua Rivers in order to "pacify" the last main Kayapo groups which, through their ceaseless attacks on Brazilian settlers and pioneers, threatened the colonization of this large area in Central Brazil. In a period of two years, five major Kayapo groups were peacefully contacted one after the other.

By mid-1957, Meirelles and his team of thirty-six men arrived near the confluence of the Curua and the Igarapé do Bom Futuro. Five Gorotire and six Kararaô men were sent ahead to approach the Northern Mekranoti group led by Angme'ê and Bepkamati. Peaceful contact was easily established and Meirelles and his team stayed for four days among the Northern Mekranoti — which they referred to as the "Mekrononti of the Curua". In his report, Meirelles wrote the following passage on his arrival in the village:

> Upon arriving in the warriors' house [the men's house], we were
> received by Angmuie [Angme'ê], the old village chief. I explained

*in detail the reasons for our visit and revealed our readiness to give
them rifles, munition, axes, knives, beads and other commodities.
The old chief then gave a speech, accepting our propositions and
declaring his willingness to collaborate with us in the pacification
of the other [Kayapo] groups. (Meirelles 1962: 8, my translation)*
On this occasion, the Northern Mekranoti received four shotguns, ten
rifles, hundred machetes, sixty axes, thirty large kettles, hundred knives,
thirty pairs of scissors, ten kilos of glass-beads, clothes and twenty hammocks (Meirelles 1958ms: 9). Almost immediately after these peaceful
contacts, several Northern Mekranoti men joined Meirelles for a few
months during an expedition to peacefully contact the Central Mekranoti
along the upper Iriri.

In the meantime, the Northern Mekranoti village was moved to a
site more easily accessible to the SPI agents. Along with a group of thirty-eight Kararaô Indians contacted near the Igarapé do Limão (a small
tributary of the lower Curua) a few months before, they were settled at
the confluence of the Curua and the Igarapé do Bom Futuro. A post was
erected near the village and was called Pôsto Curua. This may sound pre-
posterous because, in doing so, the SPI settled the Indians exactly on the
opposite bank of a small Brazilian agglomeration known as Bomfim. The
reason for the location of the recently contacted Indians near a Brazilian
settlement was that the SPI hoped in this way to introduce the Indians into
the regional economy as soon as possible. In any case, under these tragic
circumstances, it was to be expected that contact diseases were bound to
thrive among the combined group of Kararaô and Northern Mekranoti.
Chief Angme'ê was one of the first to succumb to the newly imported
diseases, and over fifty of his tribesmen followed within the first year
following the so-called "pacification".

Disappointed by this course of events, several men — including
Kôkôrêti, a son of Angme'ê — and their families migrated to the Central
Mekranoti in 1959. By the end of that year, Pôsto Curua had been abandoned, "not so much for prophylactic measures against new diseases," as
a SPI agent bluntly stated, "but rather because the decomposition of the
barely buried corpses simply turned the place uninhabitable" (Moreiro
Neto 1959: 53, translation mine). Local Brazilians told me that the reason for the transfer of the Indians upriver was to open up the area near
Bomfim for colonization. Whatever the reason, the move to the south
only meant the postponement of the evil day.

The survivors, about hundred and twenty in all, were moved further
upstream to the confluence of the Curua and Bau Rivers. A new post was
built and was called Pôsto Juscelino Kubitschek but was renamed Pôsto

Bau some years later. Aware of the fact that the Northern Mekranoti were no longer hostile, the Brazilians not only occupied the area near Bomfim, but also pushed more and more to the south, penetrating an area they had scrupulously avoided in the past out of fear of the Northern Mekranoti. Soon, Brazilians also settled near the recently established Pôsto Kubitschek and this resulted in a new wave of epidemics among the Indians: in 1962 alone, forty-four Indians died. Chief 'Ykakôr, unsatisfied with the lack of adequate medical care from the SPI, moved with his family to the Central Mekranoti. Two years later, in 1964, the leader Ariwê-re died during yet another measles epidemic. Amikôt then became the new, young leader.

In 1968 the name of the post was changed to Pôsto Indigena (PI) Bau. The people of the village peacefully contacted Byriryti, the man who in 1944 had separated from the main Mekranoti group. Byriryti's small family numbered about thirty persons who were all absorbed in the village at PI Bau[10]. A year later, all but one of these newly contacted Indians had died of influenza. The last survivor, a boy, was adopted by a Brazilian family.

In 1969, Amikôt was hospitalized in the city of Belem and died there. When the news reached the village, Màntino (Tàpjêt's oldest son) became the leader of this small Northern Mekranoti community. That same year, a new epidemic killed forty Indians and reduced the population to about twenty survivors! Due to the low population, traditional ceremonies were no longer celebrated.

Four years later, a mining company (Companhia São Benedito) built a small settlement some eight kilometers to the south of the village. During their explorations, these Brazilians constantly penetrated Indian territory, much to the displeasure of the Indians. In 1979, the Central Mekranoti drove the Brazilians away from their territory, sacking their camp (see further).

By 1981 the population had increased to some sixty Indians. This increase was partly due to better medical care from the FUNAI, and partly to the arrival of some Central Mekranoti families and a few men of a recently contacted Kararaô group.

In 1983, more Central Mekranoti families moved in and by 1989, the village numbered some seventy-five Indians.

---

10   Mr. Earl Trapp, of the Unevangelized Fields Mission, kindly provided me with some data on the small *Byriryti* group, which he visited right after its arrival at PI Bau.

12. the separation and "pacification" of the Central and Southern Mekranoti (1947-1956)

In 1947, Kremôr's group — which consisted of thirty-seven *metykti-re* and one *mekry-re* as well as their families — lived in a small area of savannah to the east of the Xingu. From there, two consecutive raids were undertaken against the Tapirape, a Tupi tribe located along a tributary of the upper Araguaia River. After this second attack, the returning warriors came into conflict with an important group of Xavante Indians. Fearing a counterattack, Kremôr and his people crossed the Xingu River to join the other Mekranoti group in 1948. The latter was led by Kreti-re and Bepgogoti and consisted of fourteen *mekry-re* and seventeen *metykti-re* and their families.

After the reunion, a new village was built and the political groupings were reorganized and renamed. Two new men's societies were established: the *metyk-re* ("black people") were led by Kreti-re, Bepgogoti and Kremôr; the *menhakrekroti* ("people with a stinking nose") were led by Tàkàk'i-re and Karikanã, two younger leaders. The junior men in the men's house were led by Pakyx.

Four years of internal peace followed. But the period from 1952 to 1953 most certainly figures among the most turbulent in Mekranoti history: internal strives, collective club-fights, schisms and fusions occurred one after the other.

It all began when peaceful contacts were established with the neighboring Yudja Indians in 1952 (Villas Bôas 1954: 81). These Yudja informed the Mekranoti of two Brazilians who would come and visit them some time later and who would bring along many gifts. Right after this contact with the Yudja, a fire broke out in the village, burning down nearly all the houses. Tension was high and a collective club-fight followed. This resulted in a split: Kreti-re and Bepgogoti remained with thirty-nine men and their families in the traditional site; Kremôr left with thirty-one men and their families and moved to a site near the Cachoeira Von Martius rapids along the Xingu River. In the literature, Bepgogoti's group is commonly referred to as Mekranoti, while the one of Kremôr is often identified as Metuktire (also Metykti-re or Txukarramãe). Throughout this book, these groups will be called the "Central Mekranoti" and the "Southern Mekranoti" respectively.

In August 1953, Claudio and Orlando Villas Bôas (two SPI agents) entered into peaceful contact with a group of Southern Mekranoti hunters roaming near the mouth of the Jarina River. Seven of them — including

chief Kremôr — accompanied the Villas Bôas brothers to Pôsto Vasconcellos, located along the Tuatuari River, a tributary of the upper Xingu
(*ibid.* 1954: 82). A month later, the brothers peacefully visited Kremôr's
group and, a few days later, also the Central Mekranoti. According to
the Villas Bôas brothers (pers. com.), the groups numbered about three
hundred and four hundred Indians, respectively.

Soon, a series of contact diseases appeared. In spite of the Villas Bôas
brothers' remarkable efforts at keeping down the number of victims as
much as possible, many still died.

During the following three years, the Central and Southern Mekranoti
repeatedly separated and reunited, but both groups kept a certain form
of autonomy, with the distinction, however, that the Central Mekranoti
steadily increased in population as they were joined by several Southern Mekranoti families. In 1956, a permanent schism occurred. After an
internal fight, Pakyx left the village with a number of young men and
their kin. They erected a village at a site called *pi'ydjãm*, located in the
dense forests between the Xixe (a tributary of the upper Iriri) and upper
Curua Rivers. A few months later, Kreti-re and his followers also moved
to *pi'ydjãm*.

Immediately afterwards, Kremôr moved with his group towards the
Cachoeira von Martius rapids, while Bepgogoti and his people remained
for a few months in the area near the Jarina River, but not for long. When
his wife died during one of the epidemics, he also decided to leave the
area. Upon leaving, nine of Kremôr's followers joined Bepgogoti during
his move to Pakyx's village. By the end of 1956, the Central Mekranoti
village numbered about four hundred Indians; the Southern Mekranoti
one, led by Kremôr, was about hundred and twenty Indians strong and
remained in the area around the upper Xingu River.

13. THE RECENT HISTORY OF THE CENTRAL MEKRANOTI (1956-1989)

After many elderly people and children had died in the few years immediately following the first peaceful contacts with the Brazilians in 1953, the
period between 1958 and 1968 was marked by the Central Mekranoti's
search for efficient medical assistance. Indeed, the withdrawal of these
Indians from the Xingu area to the one near the Xixe River can partially
be ascribed to their dissatisfaction with the medical assistance which was
offered in the months following their first contacts with the Brazilians.

The village at *pi'ydjãm* had two men's societies: the one called *metyk-
re* was led by Kreti-re and Bepgogoti; the *menhakrekroti* had no real chief.

The younger men were led by Bekwỳnhti. In 1957, one year after settling in *pi'ydjãm*, the Central Mekranoti went on a trek and encountered those Northern Mekranoti families which, led by Kẽnti, had separated from the one led by Angme'ê and Bepkamati in 1948. The small group was incorporated except for Kẽnti himself who fled to the west with his pregnant young wife. After this reunion, the village population rose to nearly four hundred and sixty.

Under the title of "Indians lived isolated for twenty years" Brazilian newspapers announced that two Kayapo women had been found in the area along the Jamanxim River in early 1988. The two women in question are Kẽnti's wife and daughter who, after the death of Kẽnti in the late 1960s, lived isolated until they were taken to the town of Itaituba by gold-seekers. After a few weeks in town, both women were taken to their kin in PI Kubenkokre.

In 1958, Francisco Meirelles sailed up the Iriri River with the specific aim of entering into peaceful contact with the Central Mekranoti — which he called the "Mekrononti of the Iriri" — who continued to raid local Brazilian settlers along the Iriri and Curua Rivers. Meirelles was aided in this venture by numerous Brazilians and by twenty-two Kayapo (a few Gorotire and Kararaô men, as well as a number of recently contacted Northern Mekranoti men). A post was built and called Pôsto Candoca, after the name of a nearby tributary of the upper Iriri. From there, some Brazilians as well as the accompanying Kayapo men were sent to *pi'ydjãm* to announce Meirelles' presence in the area and to inform them of the peaceful character of his mission. While Bepgogoti remained in the village, Kreti-re and his men went to Pôsto Candoca. They received many firearms, ammunition and other commodities, and then returned to their village.

A year later, Kreti-re visited the Northern Mekranoti who, at the time, still lived near Pôsto Curua. He didn't stay long, but six men and their families swiftly joined him at *pi'ydjãm*.

A few months later, the Central Mekranoti had a clash with the Panara (Kreen Akrore) Indians and, fearing a counter-attack, they all moved to Pôsto Candoca. Soon, many children and older people died of contact diseases and all the survivors returned to their village in 1960. Both Kreti-re and Bepgogoti were amply frustrated by the lack of medical assistance at Pôsto Candoca and they thought that such assistance might be better in the Xingu area after all. That's why, upon leaving Pôsto Candoca, these two chiefs left with the great majority of the Central Mekranoti and moved to their traditional area of savannah near the Jarina River. Just a few families remained in *pi'ydjãm*: they were mostly followers of Kẽnti who preferred to stay behind rather than to confront the people of Kremôr.

Some families of *pi'ydjãm* visited Pôsto Kubitschek (the newly established post near the Northern Mekranoti village), but the old enmity soon reappeared. A Northern Mekranoti man challenged one of Kẽnti's ex-followers to a club-duel to revenge the killing of a kinsman about a decade before. A quarrel over an adulterous relationship then led to a collective club-fight. On that same night, Ngrõntyjarô, the Kararaô chief living in the Northern Mekranoti village, was killed and the aggressor, a Central Mekranoti man, was shot to death in revenge. These events led to new tensions in the area and the small group of Central Mekranoti visitors returned to *pi'ydjãm*.

Alarmed by this course of events and fearing that the Central Mekranoti would start raiding Brazilian settlements again, Francisco Meirelles set up a new expedition to the area. After a brief visit to Pôsto Kubitschek, Meirelles' team continued its journey upriver. A post was built along the upper Curua River, some fifty kilometers south of the Northern Mekranoti village, and was called Pôsto Pitiatia, after the local name for the Curua River. Hilmar Kluck — a SPI agent who had already worked with the Xikrin branch of the Kayapo in the mid-1950s — was sent with a few companions to seek contact with the Central Mekranoti. The eighty or so Indians who were still at *pi'ydjãm* promptly followed Kluck and his team to the new outpost. Many gifts were distributed to consolidate the earlier peaceful relations. Meirelles then asked the Indians to go and fetch Kreti-re and Bepgogoti for them to receive gifts too. Two of Bepgogoti's sons immediately set out to go and fetch their father. The two met up with the main Central Mekranoti group near the Xixe River; the group was on its way back to *pi'ydjãm* after suffering several deaths due to diseases in the Jarina River area.

By the time all the Central Mekranoti had arrived at the Curua River, Meirelles had already left but a few of his agents had stayed behind to distribute the gifts. Within a fortnight, several Indians died of diseases and the Indians refused to stay any longer near Pôsto Pitiatia. The post was abandoned and Hilmar Kluck temporarily moved with the Central Mekranoti to their village in order to provide elementary medical assistance. Pôsto Kubitschek, near the Northern Mekranoti village, thus became the sole post in the area which, to a certain point, remained operative. In search of medical treatment and/or commodities, groups of Central Mekranoti returned three times to Pôsto Kubitschek. Yet, each time, some people died and ancient enmities popped up again. The Central Mekranoti therefore invariably retreated to their own village.

In the meantime, the Xingu National Park had been created: an airstrip was built near *porori* (the small Southern Mekranoti village) and gradually more efficient assistance was provided. Ropni, a Southern Mekranoti leader, came for a visit and asked the Central Mekranoti to move to *porori*. Fearing overt conflicts with Kremôr, Bepgogoti did not fall in with the request. The antagonism between Bepgogoti and Kremôr dates back to 1955, when many of Kremôr's followers joined Bepgogoti in his move to *pi'ydjãm*. Kreti-re, 'Ykakor and Bekwỳnhti, on the other hand, accepted and at the end of 1964 they moved with about hundred and twenty Indians to *porori*.

When Antônio Soares Cotrim (an SPI agent) visited the Central Mekranoti in early 1967, the Indians complained about the lack of assistance provided by the Brazilian Indian agency (Cotrim 1968: 4). At that time, the Central Mekranoti village numbered two hundred and six Indians and had two men's societies: the major one, called *meõtõti* ("people with big tongues"), was led by chief Bepgogoti, the smaller one, called *mepa'ãkadjàt* ("people with cotton strings around the wrist") did not have a real chief but Kôkôrêti (son of Angme'ê, the former Northern Mekranoti chief) was an important young leader in the community.

A few months after Cotrim's visit, Dale Snyder of the Unevangelized Fields Mission (UFM) settled in the village. An airstrip was built and, as such, medical assistance finally reached the Central Mekranoti. In that period, the Indians undertook a massive raid against the Panara Indians, killing about thirty people and capturing four children.

About a year later, an epidemic of malaria with severe complications emerged in the village, killing more than forty Indians. Kreti-re arrived for a visit when the epidemic was still going on. He came to ask the Central Mekranoti to join him at *porori*. Bepgogoti hesitated because of his enmity with Kremôr. But as the missionary was about to leave the area definitively, and as Kreti-re's followers were by then much stronger than Kremôr's, Bepgogoti finally agreed to move to the Southern Mekranoti village a year later. But with the sudden death of Kreti-re a few weeks later, Bepgogoti cancelled his plans and decided to stay in his village.

In 1969, the Central Mekranoti population had dwindled to hundred and thirty six[11] but things changed for the better from 1970 on. At that time, Ruth Thomson settled near the village. She is a missionary from the Summer Institute of Linguistics (SIL) who is entirely dedicated to the well-being of the Indians. Due to her constant care, the number of Central Mekranoti began increasing again. Word of this inestimable assistance

11   Excluding the thirty-four Indians which had moved to *porori* with Kreti-re and which returned almost immediately since Kreti-re had died unexpectedly.

soon spread and a few Southern Mekranoti families (including Bekwỳnhti and his family) returned to *pi'ydjãm*. In 1973, FUNAI erected a post near the village. It was called PI Mekranoti and agents settled more or less permanently in the village. These events concluded these Indians' long search for appropriate medical assistance.

From 1970 on, the Central Mekranoti population increased at a fast and steady rate. In the period between 1974 and 1984, the number of Indians augmented from two hundred and forty to four hundred. But this extremely favorable demographic situation led to a less agreeable pressure: in 1980, over fifty-five percent of the village population was less than fifteen years old. These youngsters were economically in-active but still had to be fed. As a consequence, the adults shouldered a heavy economic burden and that's one of the reasons why a small group of some eighty Indians separated in 1981. The departing Indians were nearly all young families with numerous children. Led by Bekwỳnhti and his brother Ajo, the group moved to the upper Iriri River which abounds in fish. A village was built and called *pykany* ("new land") — the FUNAI post was referred to as PI Pukanu.

The people of PI Mekranoti somehow envied their congeners at PI Pukanu who now and then arrived for a visit. At such occasions, the visitors often enthusiastically described the abundance of meat and fish in their new area. After having lived for nearly thirty years in the same area, meat was hard to find near PI Mekranoti, and consistent amounts of fish could only be caught near major streams such as the Xixe, some forty kilometers from the village. In the preceding years, several FUNAI agents had already proposed that the Central Mekranoti move to a major river such as the mid Iriri, where fluvial access would be possible. Each time, the village elders refused. But the Indians didn't really oppose the move: they just didn't want to go and live near a major water-course because, as the elders always said, people are more likely to become sick near such big rivers. This consideration can be understood in the light of the unfavorable experiences in earlier posts which invariably were erected near big rivers. During my discussions with the Indians, I realized that they would like to move to a site near the Iriri Novo River. The Central Mekranoti had lived in that area a few decades before and the river in question was not judged to be a major water-course. The Indians doubted, however, whether FU-NAI would help them during this move and so I promised them I would discuss the matter with the high officials concerned, which I eventually did. FUNAI guaranteed support for the Indians during their move, and so the main group left the area near PI Mekranoti in 1984 to move to the Iriri Novo River. The post near this village was called PI Kubenkokre, after one of Bepgogoti's names (Kubĕkàk-re). This main group of about three hundred and ninety Indians is led by Bepgogoti, Kôkôrêti, Nikàiti and Bepkũm (the two latter are sons of Bepgogoti). The village near PI Pukanu, led by Ajo and Bekwỳnhti, numbers about ninety Indians.

14. THE RECENT HISTORY OF THE SOUTHERN MEKRANOTI (1956-1989)

The Southern Mekranoti were visited by four Kubenkranken men in 1958. About a year later, a dispute broke out between Kruma-re (a young leader) and Bekwỳnhka, a close kinsman of Kremôr. This fight led to a schism: Kremôr, Bekwỳnhka and eight other men left the village with their families (about sixty Indians in all) and moved to join the Kuben-kranken. Within a year after their arrival, the SPI took Kubenkranken chief Ngroj-re on a visit to the town of Belem. Ngroj-re died there and Ngàp-re, his successor, accused the Mekranoti immigrants of sorcery. The Southern Mekranoti tried to flee but were ambushed by Ngàp-re and his men. About a dozen were killed (Banner 1963: 122) and the rest brought back to the village. Eight of these managed to escape to the Gorotire vil-lage on a Brazilian Air Force plane (T. Turner 1965: 74), while Kremôr as well as three other men — two of whom were Mekranoti born and who had joined the Kubenkranken with Karànhĩn about fifteen years before — and their families managed to escape by land and returned to the small Southern Mekranoti band led by Kruma-re and Ropni. After the reunion, the group numbered no more than seventy Indians and continued to live in the small area of savannah between the Xingu and Liberdade Rivers.

In 1961, the Xingu National Park was created and the Villas Bôas brothers asked the Southern Mekranoti to move within Park boundaries. A new village was built at a site called *porori*, near an old Yudja village site. Three years later, Ropni managed to convince an important group of Central Mekranoti to move into the village at *porori* and, as such, the village numbered some hundred and seventy Indians at the end of 1964.

But Ropni kept dreaming of reuniting as many Mekranoti as pos-sible in one single village. In 1967, he went on a visit to the Kokraimoro and brought back five men — all Mekranoti born who had joined the Kokraimoro in 1950 — and their families. In the meantime, Kreti-re was positively impressed with the relatively ample supply of medical assistance and commodities at *porori*. That's why, in 1968, he went on a visit to the Central Mekranoti to try to convince Bepgogoti and his fol-lowers to settle at *porori*. After some hesitation, Bepgogoti agreed, but the move never occurred because it was cancelled a few weeks later due to Kreti-re's death.

By that time, the Ministry of Interior rerouted the construction of what was to become an important road in the Trans-Amazonian highway system. According to the original planning, the BR 080 — as the road was called — was to cross the Xingu River near the Cachoeira Von Martius, at the northern limit of the Park. Yet, in 1971, construction work suddenly reached the Xingu at a place between Diauarum — one of the two main posts in the Park — and *porori*. In this way, the Park was bisected and the area inhabited by the Southern Mekranoti was separated from the rest of the Park. In spite of world-wide protest, the Ministry of Interior nevertheless removed the land north of the road from the Park and offered it for sale to private Brazilian owners.

The Southern Mekranoti were informed and were told that they would have to move out of the area. Tension grew in the group, as different chiefs held different ideas on how to react to this apparently dead-end situation: while Ropni urged acceptance of the Villas Bôas brothers' proposal — which consisted of moving to the south, back within Park boundaries — 'Ykakor preferred to stand and fight the invaders. In this tense period, a club-duel ensued. The man who was defeated left, only to return at night to settle accounts. He was killed in a gunfight and a split became inevitable: Kremôr and Kruma-re left with some ninety followers and erected a small village near the lower Jarina River; Ropni and the main group of some hundred and sixty followers went south and built a village about twenty-five kilometers to the north of the newly constructed BR 080 road.

Sometime later, Kremôr and his group moved into Ropni's village, only to leave once again after a quarrel between the leaders over the distribution of gifts. Ropni, 'Ykakor and many others left the village and settled some twenty kilometers south of the BR 080 road, back within Park boundaries. A post near that village was called PI Kretire. An airstrip was built and a radio installed.

Ropni's followers never really accepted the fact that they had to give up their traditional land. They also never really resigned themselves to their fate of having to live with Brazilians in their neighborhood. The people of PI Kretire became a constant menace to the pioneering settlers along the road. São José do Xingu[12] — a small agglomeration along the

---

12   Partly because the Brazilians at this agglomeration often walked armed as if they were in western movies, and partly because several people were shot to death during internal strives within the settlement, it was often referred to as "Bang-Bang" by local settlers. "Bang-bang" is the Brazilian term for western movies.

BR 080 and located about two kilometers to the east of the Xingu River — was frequently sacked by Ropni's men and the Brazilians were often harassed. Tension grew in the area and in 1974 five residents of that little town were killed.

Two years later, Ropni's men drove the people out of São José do Xingu, burning down the houses. São Jose was rebuilt forty kilometers from the Xingu River, exactly on the eastern boundaries of the Park. The inhabitants were warned by the Indians never to set foot within Park boundaries again. In 1980, however, a group of lumbermen was working just within Park limits and Ropni's men — aided by men of several other Xingu tribes — killed eleven of them (VEJA 1980: 65-69).

Being located within Park boundaries and relatively close to the important Diauarum post, Ropni's village was regularly supplied with medicines and all kinds of commodities by the Park services. This was not the case for the group led by Kremôr and Kruma-re. These people never shared Ropni's enthusiasm for the Park administration, and this indifference was to worsen when it became apparent that fewer commodities were sent to their village by the Park administrators.

In order to obtain such commodities, the people of the Jarina village frequently visited Agropexin — an important farm located near the Cachoeira Von Martius water rapids, at the site where the Southern Mekranoti had been contacted by the Villas Bôas brothers in 1953. But the Indians were often being betrayed and women were at times abused by the local workmen. Visits to Agropexin and other farms to the east of the Xingu were usually peaceful, but the Indians didn't allow any intrusion on the west bank of the Xingu and upriver of the Von Martius rapids.

An epidemic of measles broke out among Kremôr's people in 1974. This epidemic undoubtedly originated from one of the surrounding farms. During a unique rescue operation, FUNAI sent out airplanes to remove all hundred Indians of that village to a hospital on the Bananal Island (upper Araguaia River). No-one died but, four years later and after yet another epidemic of flu, the Indians attacked Agropexin as well as other farms in the area. Two Brazilians were killed and all of the other laborers were expelled. All material, including a metal canoe, an outboard motor and aluminum roof plates were taken to the village. In addition, the houses of the farms were burned down and the cattle were driven away. This event marked the beginning of overt hostility between this Southern Mekranoti group and the surrounding Brazilian settlers.

By 1979, a small post was built near Kremôr's village and was named PI Jarina. In early 1980, Kremôr and most of his men went on a brief visit to the Kokraimoro. It is known that the latter had never really liked

Kruma-re — a position which can probably be explained by the fact that the Kokraimoro consider Kruma-re responsible for the 1970 split between the villages of PI Jarina and PI Kretire. Using Kruma-re's "greed" as an argument, the Kokraimoro told Kremôr and his fellow tribesmen that they did not really appreciate Kruma-re's position as a leader in PI Jarina. Kremôr took advantage of this situation to fortify his own position. Indeed, his position had weakened a lot since he had lost many of his followers first to Bepgogoti in 1956, and then during his disastrous move to the Kubenkranken in 1959-1960. Kruma-re was the man who somehow benefited from Kremôr's loss of prestige: although not a real chief, he had evolved into an important and highly respected Southern Mekranoti leader who aspired to the position of chief. So, upon his return from the Kokraimoro, Kremôr openly blamed Kruma-re for his "greed" and officially indicated Patỳx (Kremôr's oldest son) as second chief of the community. Kruma-re was angered and upset. Unwilling to accept this defeat, he immediately left the village with his kinsmen and a few of his supporters. The small group erected a small temporary camp within the savannah area, but occasionally returned to the village at PI Jarina to gather food in the gardens.

By the end of 1980, however, things changed drastically. Patỳx, the new young chief, was caught while seducing another woman. During the club-fight between Patỳx and the cuckolded man, the latter was killed. Tension grew in the village and while Kremôr remained aloof — neither to blame or defend his son in this tricky situation — it was Kruma-re who intervened and managed to bring peace to the community. The people feared revenge from Mey-re: a classificatory father of the slain man who had been a leader among the Kokraimoro some thirty years before. Afraid, Patỳx fled to the city of Brasilia. Ropni was invited to appease Mey-re and all those who were bent on revenge. On that particular occasion, Ropni launched the idea of reuniting both the villages of PI Jarina and PI Kretire at a site near the ancient village of *porori*, along the Xingu River. He also openly supported Kruma-re, his classificatory brother, by stating that Kruma-re would become a chief once the new, big village was built. Kruma-re then decided to lay out plantations near the confluence of the Xingu and Jarina Rivers and, in 1982, a small village was built, sheltering the extended families of Kruma-re and 'Ykakor, one of the important leaders at PI Kretire. The small community numbered some thirty Indians and was called Pôsto Xingu by FUNAI.

The Southern Mekranoti began pressuring FUNAI and the federal government to officially demarcate the area of the Jarina and Xingu villages which had been removed from the Park in 1971, and to include the area of savannah between the Jarina and Iriri Novo Rivers (the core of traditional Mekranoti area) within Park boundaries. This new and final campaign involved the members of all three of the villages and ·near its end, a few high-ranking FUNAI officials were held hostages at PI Kretire. The media gave a lot of coverage to the Indian protest and the government seemed annoyed with this situation of chronic conflict with the Indians. In 1984, the government gave in and the Southern Mekranoti finally recovered their land.

Within a year, the members of all three Southern Mekranoti villages reunited and built a new village near Kruma-re's small settlement. Two new men's societies were formed: the *metekrekajrerti*, led by Ngàjremy and the *meparikàjabjê* ("people with long shoes") led by Bep'i. The former chiefs and leaders — e.g., Kremôr, Ropni and Kruma-re — all remain recognized as chiefs of the community at large or as leaders with specific duties. In 1987, the village numbered about three hundred and seventy-five Indians, including twenty-four Western Kisedje (Suya) refugees who had arrived the preceding year (T. Turner 1987ms: 92). The post near the village is called PI Metuktire. The location is infested with malaria, though, and that is why in 1989, about half of the population moved further inland, to the nearby savannah and near the ancient village of *krãnhmrôpryjaka*. The post near the new village is called PI Kapot.

15. THE KOKRAIMORO OR THE MEKRANOTI WHO JOINED THE KUBENKRANKEN (1941-1989)

A year after separating from the main Mekranoti village in 1940, Karanhĩn arrived with his hundred and two followers in the Kubenkranken village. Karànhĩn's small group included young leaders such as Kôkôrêti, Màn-ma-ri, Krã'ãkop and Mey-re who were to become the protagonists in the historical development of the Kubenkranken in the 1940s.

At the time of Karànhĩn's arrival, the Kubenkranken village had three men's societies, the *meuatĩ-re* ("the poor people") who were led by chief 'Ôket; the *mekakôpojti* ("the people with flat disks") led by Ngroj-re and the *meinokrori-re* ("the people with spotted eyes") who were led by Màndjwa-re. In addition, four groups of young men existed, led by Akrua'êtyk, Kôkôryti, Bepkô and Ngôti-re. The immigrant Mekranoti men were evenly divided over these men's groups and the Kubenkranken experienced a few years of internal peace.

In 1944, a group of warriors went on a visit to the Gorotire living near the missionary post along the lower Riozinho River. Another group visited a small Brazilian settlement of rubber gatherers along the mid Xingu River. Nine warriors were killed in an ambush by Ignacio Silva and his fellow workmen. A year later, frictions in the village led to a split. A group of some hundred and fifty Indians moved to the south to live separately for a few years. This secessionist group was led by Kôkôrêti and Mànma-ri, two of Karànhĩn's followers, and included the majority of the immigrant Mekranoti.

Two years later, Ku'at and his fifty followers arrived in the Kubenk-ranken village. Ku'at had been one of Tàpjêt's former followers. Backed by chief 'Ôket, Ku'at organized an attack on the small group led Kôkôrêti and Mànma-ri almost immediately after his arrival. The attack was aimed at the band of Mekranoti that lived in the small secessionist group and was, as such, a retaliation for Tàpjêt's killing a few years before. Back in the village, Ku'at had a conflict with Krã'ãkop, another one of Karànhĩn's ex-followers who, at the time, had become a young leader in the Kuben-kranken village. The reason for Ku'at's anger was that Krã'ãkop had refused to participate in the attack on Kôkôrêti's group. Krã'ãkop then left the village and moved to the other small village which by then reu-nited nearly all the Mekranoti immigrants — i.e., Karànhĩn's and Ku'at's followers.

After living separately for four years, this group of some two hundred returned to the main village in 1949. But the reunion was short-lived. Ku'at insisted that all men's groups jointly attack the Mekranoti, but Bepnox and Kôkrajmôr, two new leaders, left with their followers to attack Brazilians settlements along the Iriri River. 'Ôket and Ku'at were grieved by this lack of solidarity and, while the others still were ventur-ing along the Iriri, 'Ôket's men killed six of Karànhĩn's followers. Upon returning, the men of Bepnox and Kôkrajmôr also killed six of 'Ôket's men. The situation became untenable. Bepnox and Kôkrajmôr decided to leave the village. They were joined by the group which, led by Kôkôrêti and Mànma-ri had already left the village before and, as such, nearly all of the Mekranoti left the Kubenkranken village — only Ku'at and two of his followers remained behind. This time the split was a definite one; it occurred in 1950 and the secessionist group numbered little more than three hundred Indians. The group moved to the west of the Xingu and settled along the Xinxim River, near the site where Karànhĩn had lived from 1940 to 1941. The village had two men's societies: the *meuatĩ* ("the poor people") led by Jakuri and the *mebêkôt-te* ("the similar people") with Moj'y-re as chief. Three groups of younger men existed, led by Bepnox, Kàxwakre and Kôkrajmôr (along with Mey-re). The group was generally called Kôkrajmôr (here, Kokraimoro), after one of the main leaders, but the Kubenkranken also occasionally referred to them as "the people of Mànma-ri" after another leader (Dreyfus 1963).

In 1950, the Kokraimoro attacked the Kubenkranken who temporarily fled to the east, some of them seeking refuge in the Gorotire village. The Kokraimoro also began an intensive period of raiding Brazilian settlements among the Curua, Iriri and Xingu Rivers.

The Kokraimoro village lived in three years of relative internal peace until, in 1953, a series of club-fights broke out. Krã'ãkop was killed during one of these fights and this event led to a temporary split, during which a small group led by Bepnox and Kôkrajmôr left the village. A few months later, the men of the main village attacked and killed Kôkrajmôr, after which both groups reunited. But not for long, though, as a new and more definite split took place in 1954: Jakuri and Moj'y-re remained with some hundred and thirty Indians in the area, while Bepnox, Mey-re and old Karànhĩn moved to the south with about hundred and seventy followers.

The following three years were marked by constant attacks and counterattacks between these two groups and many Indians died during these intergroup raids. In April 1957, Meirelles made peaceful contact with Jakuri's group near a site called Lageiro, on the right bank of the upper Iriri River. The group numbered ninety-seven Indians. In November of that same year, one of Meirelles' assistants peacefully made contact with Bepnox's group of hundred and thirty-seven Indians near the upper course of the Igarapé Porto Seguro, a tributary of the mid Xingu.

Both Kokraimoro groups were reunited and moved to a site along the mid Xingu in March 1958. As was the case for the Northern Mekranoti around the same time, SPI agents moved the Kokraimoro to a site near a Brazilian settlement in the hope of absorbing the Indians as soon as possible into the local economy. As such, the recently contacted Indians were settled in an area where no gardens had been laid out. Food soon became a problem and the Kokraimoro had to go and ask for provisions among the nearby Brazilians. No adequate medical assistance was available in the new post and contact diseases swept through the village. About half of the population had died by the end of 1958 and a year later, only some seventy survived.

In about 1960, Jakuri left for the Gorotire village, where he stayed for some six months. In the meantime, the Kokraimoro village was moved to a site a little further away from São Felix do Xingu, an area the Kokraimoro still occupy today.

The Kokraimoro managed to recuperate from the initial and almost fatal depopulation only after the immigration of several Kubenkranken families in the early 1960s: in 1962, the Kokraimoro village numbered about hundred and forty Indians, half of whom had come from the Kubenkranken village (Fuerst, pers. com.). By then, SPI agents and missionaries of the Unevangelized Fields Mission had settled in the post. In spite of the migration of some twenty-five Indians to the Southern Mekranoti in 1967 and of several other families to the Gorotire village of PI Kikretum in the period from 1980 to 1985, the current Kokraimoro population has increased to about hundred and seventy Indians.

16. THE KUBENKRANKEN OR THE FOUNDATION OF PI KUBENKRANKEN AND PI AUKRE (1940-1989)

Ever since the "pacification" of the Gorotire in 1937, both Catholic and Protestant missionaries were anxious to contact the Kubenkranken. This group was estimated to have a population of about six hundred Indians and was thought of as the last important Kayapo group in the Xingu basin. Through some Gorotire men who occasionally left to visit their kin living in the Kubenkranken village, both missionaries and SPI agents knew the actual situation of the Kubenkranken.

At the time, the Kubenkranken village had one men's house with three men's societies, led by 'Ôket, Ngroj-re and Màndjwa-re. It was erected in the savannah along the upper Riozinho River, near the Cachoeira da Fumaça rapids.

In order to acquire commodities, groups of Kubenkranken occasionally paid peaceful visits to Constantino Viana's small settlement along the mid Xingu River in 1939-1940 (Nimuendajú 1952: 439-441). During these visits, a Brazilian woman who had been taken captive before often served as a go-between. In 1944, a group of Kubenkranken men came to visit the Protestant missionary post along the Fresco River (Banner 1963: 52- 54; Kräutler 1979: 158). Such visits became more frequent once the Gorotire were settled near Novo Horizonte (Banner 1963: 60-61).

Two secessionist groups of Mekranoti arrived in the Kubenkranken village in 1941 and 1948. These groups were led by Karànhĩn and Ku'at, respectively. A series of conflicts arose and led to an important split in 1950, when some three hundred Indians departed and formed the group which is known in the literature by the name of Kokraimoro (see above). After the separation of the Kokraimoro, the political associations in the Kubenkranken village were reorganized. Two new men's societies were formed: the meatwỳrỳngrà ("the people of the old dry leaves") were led by 'Ôket and the mekrãngrãngrã ("the green-headed people") were led by chief Ngroj-re[13].

Fleeing from a massive Kokraimoro attack in 1951, an important group of Kubenkranken sought refuge among the Gorotire where they stayed for a few weeks. This event marked the first step in the "pacification" process of the Kubenkranken. Cicero Cavalcanti who, at the time, was the SPI agent working among the Gorotire, treated the Kubenkranken visitors well and several families remained to live with the Gorotire. When the majority of Kubenkranken returned to their village some weeks later, it was agreed that Cavalcanti would come to visit them a year later. And so, the Kubenkranken were peacefully contacted in their village in 1952. The community numbered about three hundred Indians and an SPI post was erected near the village. It was called Pôsto Nilo Peçanha but was only intermittently occupied. In the first years following "pacification" missionaries only sporadically worked among the Kubenkranken. This lack of assistance had calamitous consequences: about one fifth of the population died during a measles epidemic in 1958 before the missionaries arrived with medical aid.

A year later, Bekwỳnhka and Kremôr arrived with a few Southern Mekranoti families. Ngroj-re, one of the Kubenkranken chiefs, was taken to the town of Belem on a visit and died there. Ngàp-re, his successor, accused the Southern Mekranoti of sorcery and made them responsible for Ngroj-re's death. Ngàp-re's followers launched a slaughter among the immigrant Mekranoti and only a few managed to escape.

By that time, SPI agents and missionaries had more or less permanently settled in the area. Due to proper medical care, the population increased rapidly but, due to the migration of several families to the Kokraimoro and Gorotire villages in the early 1960s, the village population didn't grow very fast.

In 1968, the post was renamed PI Kubenkranken and eight years later, the village numbered about three hundred Indians. At the time, two men's societies existed: the *memyjabjêti* ("people with a long penis") led by Txikiri ('Ôket's successor) and the *meõtõjabjê* ("people with a long tongue") led by Ngàp-re. Tensions existed between Txikiri and Ngàp-re, but overt antagonism was temporarily avoided by the foundation of a third men's society, called *metyk-re* ("black people"). It was led by Kupatôp, one of Txikiri's classificatory brothers.

At that time, Txikiri and his group often left the village for long periods of time, settling in a temporary village located in the forest to

---

13   This was the situation when the French anthropologist Simone Dreyfus undertook her fieldwork in PI Kubenkrankein in 1955 (Dreyfus 1963:28).

the north of PI Kubenkranken. In 1979, however, the separation became definite: a group of hundred and twelve Indians split off and settled to the north. A post was erected near the new village and was named PI Aukre (after the term *à 'uk-re* in Kayapo). The secessionist group mainly consisted of Txikiri's kin and followers. Although Kupatôp himself joined Txikiri in the new village, the majority of his followers stayed behind with Ngàp-re in the old village site. Over the years, however, several families left PI Kubenkranken to settle in the new village. The current population at PI Aukre is about two hundred Indians; an equal number of Indians still live in PI Kubenkranken.

17. THE GOROTIRE AND THE FOUNDATION OF PI KIKRETUM (1947-1989)

In 1947, when the Gorotire were moved to the deserted Brazilian agglomeration of Novo Horizonte, they numbered only eighty-nine survivors. SPI agents and missionaries settled nearly permanently in the nearby post and provided appropriate medical assistance. Over the years, Pôsto Gorotire became an "attraction village" where numerous families of other Kayapo groups — both refugees and others — moved to. In the 1950s and 1960s, important groups of Xikrin, Mekranoti and Kubenkranken moved to the Gorotire village. A census of PI Gorotire of November 1965 offers the following distribution regarding the origin of its inhabitants: hundred and fifty-eight Gorotire, ninety-six Kubenkranken, one Kokraimoro, thirty-three Xikrin, twelve Mekranoti and two non-Kayapo Indians (Peret 1965ms). Of the total population of three hundred and two Indians, forty-nine percent were non-Gorotire! This tendency, although still true today, has for some reason diminished during the last few years (see Chapter 5 where this point is discussed more in detail).

Due to these many immigrations and proper medical care, the Gorotire population grew steadily. In 1954, the village numbered hundred and fifty-five Indians, in 1965 it had grown to some three hundred and in 1976 the Gorotire numbered five hundred and twenty-five Indians. By 1978, the population had augmented to nearly six hundred.

There had long been tensions between Kanhonk and Tut, the two chiefs. This situation exploded in 1978 when Tut became involved in a series of club-fights with Kanhonk as well as with Tôtô'i, the third leading man in the village. Tut then decided to leave the village. Along with some hundred followers, he temporarily moved into the Kubenkranken village and, about a year later, settled along the mid Fresco River, near the site where the Gorotire used to have a village before the so-called "pacification". A post was erected near the new village and called PI Kikretum ("old village"). Due to the immigration of some Kubenkranken, Kokraimoro and Central Mekranoti families, this village now numbers about two hundred and eighty Indians.

In spite of the separation of Tut — who now prefers to be called "Colonel Pombo" — and his group, the number of Gorotire continued to increase at a fast and steady rate: it now has a population of about seven hundred Indians.

CHAPTER III

DIFFERENT ENEMIES IMPLY DIFFERENT GOALS AND DIFFERENT STRATEGIES

"Warfare... is not an analytical category but a word which allows us to talk, in a more or less rough and ready fashion, about a large number of phenomena which, on closer inspection, may turn out to differ significantly among themselves. The point is that these differences can only be arrived at by inspecting the phenomena, and not by defining the word." (K. Fukui and D. Turton 1979: 3)

This Chapter is based on a systematic analysis of the many kinds of data regarding raids and attacks provided through Mekranoti ethno-history (see Appendix A and Chapter 2) and by discussions with informants. Several war-related aspects will be discussed here, such as the history and frequency of conflicts, booty obtained, whether or not captives were taken, and tactics employed during raids for each of the specific enemies the Mekranoti and their ancestors have fought or raided in the last two centuries. I am taking the Mekranoti merely as an exemplar of the Kayapo as a whole and I expect that everything I say of them would be equally true, in the essentials, for the other Kayapo groups.

1. WEAPONS AND THEIR USE

For typical male activities such as hunting, fishing and warfare, the Mekranoti make use of a considerable variety of weapons such as clubs, bows and arrows, lances and, nowadays in an ever increasing way, firearms. The following main categories of weapons can be distinguished:

1.1 — Arms for hand-to-hand fighting

Whether during attacks, while hunting certain animals, or during duels, the Kayapo seem to prefer hand-to-hand fights. For this purpose, the clubs are by far the most favoured of all Mekranoti weapons: they are handled with extreme ability. However, a clear distinction should be drawn between both the use and the form of the different Kayapo clubs (see figure 14 and table 5).

In a broad sense, the term *kô* refers to any kind of stick. In a more specific sense, however, it refers to the most commonly used type of club. It consists of a thick, hardwood stick, about 1.00 to 1.20 m. long and gradually increasing in diameter towards the upper part. This round club is most commonly used for hunting and during warfare. Since these clubs are left behind at the place of the raid, neighbouring tribes often refer to the Kayapo as "club-men" or something like that. The term Txukarramãe, for instance, is often used in the literature to refer to the Southern Mekranoti: it is a Yudja word meaning "people without bows". Certainly the Kayapo do have bows and are good archers but while on a visit or while participating in the men's house meetings, the men usually carry their long and heavy *kô* clubs instead of bows and arrows like other Indians. Owing to the remarkable similarity between the Kayapo round clubs and those made by the Iny Karaja Indians of the mid-Araguaia River, chroniclers and ethnographers in the late nineteenth century often referred to the Kayapo as the "Karaja (Iny) of the Xingu"; the Kayapo were recurrently thought of as a group of Iny Karaja who from time to time left the traditional habitat along the Araguaia to roam freely along the Xingu, assailing its inhabitants (Coudreau 1897a).

New *kô* clubs are usually painted red all over with the urucu (*Bixa orellana L*, also known as annatto) colour dye. A distinct term exists for *kô* clubs with different types of decoration or the wood used: the handle of the *kôkam'yr* is adorned with black and light-brown fibres woven into geometric motives; the upper part (or, in rare occasions, the entire length) of the *kôkangã* is adorned with longitudinal grooves; the *kôtyk* is made of dark wood; and the *kôjaka* is an unadorned club wrapped in palm leaves and provided with a carrying-strap made of bark or fibre. The *kôjaka* is a specific war club from which the cover of palm leaves is removed before the attack.

The *kop* is the largest of all Kayapo clubs. It measures between 1.20 and 1.50 m. and consists of a long piece of wood which is roughly circular

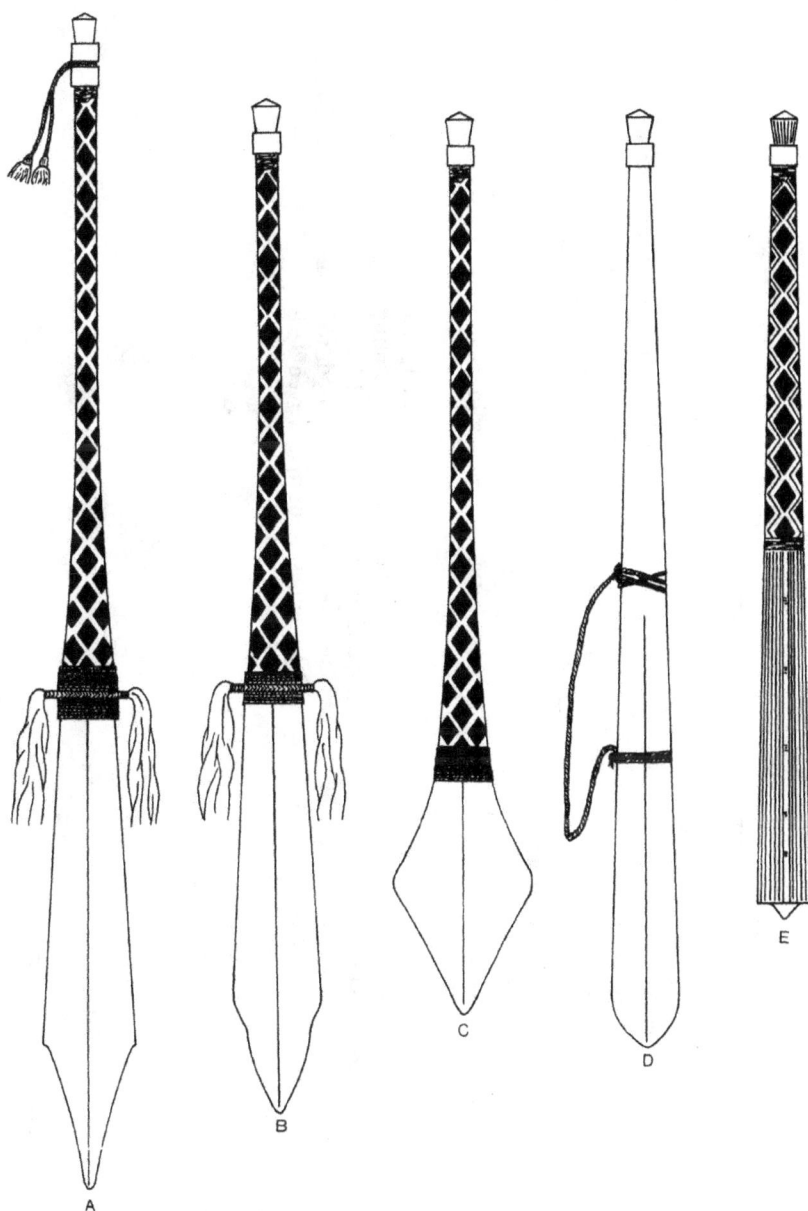

Figure 13 — Five of the most common Kayapo clubs. (A) *kopkam'yr* as used by the Kayapo of the Xingu; (B) *kopkam'yr* as used by the Ira'amranh and by the Kayapo of the Xingu; (C) *kopkrãti* as used by the Ira'amranh; (D) *kop* as used by the Ira'amranh; (E) *kôkangã* as used by all contemporary Kayapo.

Table 5 — Review of the most commonly used categories of Kayapo clubs.

TYPE OF CLUB	DESIGNATION	CHARACTERISTICS
1. *kô* (round clubs)		
kô	"round club"	usually painted red with urucú dye ; smooth surface
kôtyk	"black round club"	made of black wood, and left unpainted
kôjaka	"white round club"	unpainted ; wrapped in leaves
kôkangã	"snake round club"	with bottom part decorated with longitudinal incisions
kôkam'yr	"round club with basketry-work"	handle has decorative woven design
kôkrã	"small round club"	idem *kô*, but smaller in size
kôtykkrã	"small black round club"	idem *kôtyk*, but smaller in size
2. *kop* (sword clubs)		
kop	"sword club"	usually of dark-brown wood, no decorations
koptyk	"black sword club"	made of black wood, red painting on bottom part
kopkamrêk	"red sword club"	made of (red-)brown wood
kopjaka	"white sword club"	made of light-coloured wood, red painting on bottom part
kopkam'yr	"sword club with basketry-work"	handle has decorative woven design
3. *akêïêtyk* (temporary clubs)		
akêïêtyk	"slender black club"	no decorations, not worked on

in diameter at the handle and nearly flat in a spatulate form at the upper part. The upper tip usually consists of a sharp point. This kind of club is used primarily during *aben tak* (club-fights), a formal and stylized combat between two (or more) men or between the members of two men's societies or age-sets. Armed with the heavy spatulate clubs, the men stand in pairs and take turns in striking each other at a point between the shoulder and the elbow. The striking is done with the sharp sides of the *kop* club until one of the combatants is unable to continue (e.g., from having broken his arm) or until some kinsmen or others intervene to stop the fight. Yet, on some occasions it happens that — due to emotional involvement — the rules are not strictly followed and someone gets hit on the head. In this way, a man can be murdered during combat: several such instances are mentioned in pre-contact history of the Mekranoti, and one such case occurred in the Southern Mekranoti village at PI Jarina as recent as 1980. I never witnessed such club-fights since they did not occur in the Central Mekranoti village in the period from 1973 to 1983. *Kop* sword clubs were also occasionally used during warfare, when the adversary was stabbed with the pointed lower tip.

As in the case of the round clubs, there are several types of sword clubs. The Kayapo of the Xingu groups distinguish between the following *kop* clubs: blackwooden clubs (*koptyk-re*), the most common of all; lightwooden clubs (*kopjaka*); brownish clubs (*kopkamrêk*); and those of which the handle is adorned with black and light-brown fibres woven into geometric motives (*kopkam'yr*). In addition to these, the Ira'amranh also manufactured *kop* clubs with a broad and paddle-like upper part and another one which was smaller — about the size of a *kô* round club — but with a flattened, yet curved tip. The Xikrin, on the other hand, only make one particular type of *kop*, which has a concave shape at the upper part.

Consisting of a slender stub or branch of hard and light-brown wood, the *akêtêtyk* (named after a specific type of wood) is a tall club, measuring up to 1.60 m. No decoration whatsoever is applied and the surface often shows many inequalities. The stick is not always straight and the top ends in a rough knob, part of the natural configuration of the stub or branch.

In contradistinction to the "round" or "sword clubs" which are made in the village and in the expectation of a forthcoming raid or hunt, or in the anticipation of a possible club-fight, the *akêtêtyk* is rarely made in the village. Rather, it is made in the forest, often post-haste by those men who do not have a club available when they need one. I personally witnessed such an occasion in 1979 when on trek with a group of Mekranoti men. One day someone spotted a herd of wild pigs. Since very little ammunition was available, it was decided to hunt these animals "in the traditional way", with clubs. Those men who had only brought along their firearms or bows and arrows left the camp to cut long sticks of wood, removing only the bark, branches and other hindrances. The hunt was then performed either with the round clubs (*kô*) or with these freshly made *akêtêtyk* clubs. After the event, nearly all of the latter clubs were left in the forest camp, illustrating my designation as "temporary clubs" for this weapon.

During war expeditions, when the *kô* ("round clubs") and, occasionally, the *kop* ("sword clubs") were left behind on the site of the raid, all warriors made an *akêtêtyk* to return "armed" to the village (see Chapter 5). Some elderly men keep an *akêtêtyk* club and use it as a walking stick. Informants said that in earlier times, young men of the *menõrõny-re* age grade were individually sent into the forest before consummating marriage. Merely armed with an *akêtêtyk* club, they were expected to return to the village only if they brought a major mammal (such as a jaguar, wild pig, tapir or deer) they had managed to kill. It is said that some men, less skilled or unlucky, often remained days or even weeks in the forest before succeeding in their task. This custom is no longer in practice, but was one of the many proofs of strength, speed and agility which the men had to endure in their adolescence.

1.2 — Arms for fights at a distance

Although clubs are by far the most popular of all Kayapo weapons used during warfare, the importance of bows and arrows, lances and firearms cannot be neglected.

Kôtykkrã clubs are identical to the *kôtyk* round clubs, but are considerably smaller: they measure between .40 and .70 m. They are only used during warfare. As evidenced in narrative 9 of the Appendix B, the *kôtykkrã* is a throwing-weapon, launched with great force to the enemy's head.

Two types of lances exist: the *rop'i* and the *nàj*. The *rop'i* ("jaguar bone"), consists of a long, black, wooden shaft, circular in diameter and pointed at both extremities. It is equipped with a sharpened piece of jaguar or deer bone glued on the upper end, next to the decorative part of the black and light-brown fibres which are woven into geometric motives. The *nàj* is made of the same wood but the upper part is flattened into a lanceolate point. Another type of *nàj* is decorated with reddened cotton strings hanging as pendants. This variant is called *àkbĩndjà* ("thing to kill the bird", a reference to a myth in which a big bird was killed by two heroes), and the right to use it is restricted to those men who have inherited a specific ritual right. Lances were occasionally employed in warfare but are no longer in use in the Mekranoti villages: they may, on rare occasions, be carried while dancing.

Kayapo bows (*djydjê*) are simple segment bows where the bow-stave consists of a longitudinal segment cut from a tree trunk. Usually, the wood of the *pau d'arco* tree is used. The cross-section is of the "Peruvian type" (Heath and Chiara 1977: 39): i.e., of an almost rectangular section with rounded edges. The bow nocks have vestigial shoulders on both sides, and the thick bowstring consists of twisted vegetable fibres. Bows are never decorated and the length ranges from 1.80 to about 2.10 m.; they are therefore relatively long in relation to the size of the Kayapo men.

Arrows are somewhat smaller: the average size is about 1.55 to 1.62 m. The shaft consists of an arrow cane, usually of the nodded type: the un-nodded variant being primarily utilized for arrows used for fishing. Basically, there are nine categories of arrows (*kru-wa*) according to the type of arrow-head[1]. The fletching consists of two rounded macaw feathers tangentially bound at the ends. Additional small feathers can be added at the cotton strings holding the fletching. The nock can be a simple notch cut into the end of the shaft or it can be added as a plug in which the notch has been cut. Most arrows are distinctive hunting arrows, which may also be used during warfare. Yet, since the Kayapo prefer to provoke hand-to-hand fights, bows and arrows are only rarely used while attacking.

Story 4 (Appendix B) suggests that, in the early nineteenth century, the Kayapo were already familiar with the existence of firearms (*katõk*). Some informants even related their westward migration at that time to the ancestors' fear of firearms which were constantly used by Brazilians. Although other Kayapo groups may have acquired firearms in earlier stages of their history, the Kayapo of the Xingu groups obtained their first firearms as late as the very end of the nineteenth century. Firearms were used in certain cases of warfare (see further).

---

1   These nine types of arrows-heads are: a simple black hardwooden point (*kruwanotyk*); a white wooden point (*kruwanojaka*); a hardwooden foreshaft with barbs (*kruwakatêrinhôr*); a wooden foreshaft with a bone splinter attached as a side-point (*kruwanhikop*), with the barbed dorsal spine of the stingray (*kruwamjêtxêtper'y*), with a bone at the tip (*kruwa'ã 'i-re*) or with small transverse wooden pins (*kruwakagot*); a bamboo lanceolate point attached to the foreshaft (*kruwapo*); and a wooden foreshaft ending in a lanceolate point (*kruwaby-ri*).

2. HISTORY OF CONFLICTS

In order to acquaint ourselves with the world of Mekranoti warfare, it seems useful to start with a portrayal of the different enemies these Indians have fought or raided in the last two centuries. It is certainly meaningful to examine the history of conflicts before turning to a detailed analysis of the impact of booty, of captives, and so on. The data for the present discussion were nearly all drawn from Mekranoti ethno-history (most dates and events cited can be found either in Appendix A or in Chapter 2) and from subsequent discussions with informants. Through these discussions, it became apparent that the Mekranoti differentiate all human beings living outside the world of their own community into several categories. In the following presentation, I will follow Mekranoti custom by grouping their enemies into four of these categories.

2.1 — The Whites (*kubẽkryt*, literally "light-coloured non-Kayapo")

In the early nineteenth century, the ancestors of the contemporary Kayapo of the Xingu — and, hence, also of the Mekranoti — occupied an extensive area of savannah between the lower Araguaia and mid-Tocantins. After suffering the horrifying consequences of violent encounters with slave-traders, and out of fear for further confrontations with these well-armed Whites, the Indians left their traditional habitat and fled to the west. They eventually settled in a virtually unoccupied area of savannah to the west of the Araguaia. But within a few decades, a new wave of Brazilian settlers appeared. Soon, various small agglomerations emerged and an ever increasing number of navigators started travelling up and down the Araguaia River. Tension in the big Kayapo group led to an important schism: the Ira'amranh remained in the area and the Gorotire left once again, moving further to the west, approaching the dense tropical forests characterizing the Xingu River basin.

In the mid-nineteenth century, the Ira'amranh made peaceful contact with the national society. The Gorotire, however, continued to live relatively isolated for some decades. In the period from 1850 to 1900, groups of Gorotire (the Kayapo of the Xingu) frequently wandered to distant areas, occasionally attacking rubber tappers and in this way obtaining their first firearms, tools, dresses, hammocks, and so on. By the turn of the century, however, an ever greater amount of Brazilians approached the core of Gorotire territory. In reaction to a minor Gorotire aggression against rubber gatherers, the Brazilians mounted a major punitive expedition. This occurred in about 1908, the period when the Mekranoti separated from the main Gorotire group.

The Mekranoti moved further to the west, crossing the Xingu and settling near the upper Iriri River. During the first years following the separation from the main Gorotire group, the Mekranoti made relatively few raids on Brazilian settlements. This is probably due to the fact that numerous rubber tappers and Brazil nut collectors started penetrating the more isolated areas such as the one along the Iriri as late as the 1920s. Moreover, since these invasions ensued from the north, it is very likely that the incessant raids by the more northern Kayapo groups such as Xikrin and Gorotire obstructed the access of many Brazilians to the more southern areas which were dominated by the Mekranoti.

In the 1930s however, Brazilian settlers extended to the mid-course of the Iriri and Curua Rivers, reaching the perambulation area of the Mekranoti. From then on, the Mekranoti undertook numerous raids and several groups of men stayed for months in the forest, wandering from one site to another, executing raids at different sites. This escalation of Mekranoti wars against Brazilians also coincided with the time when Tàpjêt and his followers separated from the Gorotire village and joined the Mekranoti in 1936. Already in the Gorotire village, Tàpjêt had a reputation for being an impassioned leader of attacks on Brazilian settlements. He soon became one of the main Mekranoti war chiefs: in the period from 1936 to 1942, Tàpjêt was not only the instigator but also the military leader of most of the Mekranoti raids. Soon the range of action of this leader and his followers expanded from the regions along the Iriri-Curua to the ones along the Jamanxim and mid-Tapayoz, the latter being located some six hundred kilometres to the west of the core of Mekranoti area.

Tàpjêt's death in 1942 inaugurated a period of drastic change in the Mekranoti community. This event marked the transition from a period of regular raiding on Brazilian settlements to one of internal disputes. Recurrent periods of severe tension within the community followed and led to a series of club-fights which eventually resulted in several splits within a few years' time.

When internal tensions had diminished by the early 1950s, the villages of the Central and Southern Mekranoti were peacefully contacted by the Brazilians. Partly due to the impact of contracted epidemics during the first few years after the so-called "pacification", and partly due to the Indians' search for adequate medical assistance, few raids were undertaken on Brazilian settlers in the period from 1953 to 1970.

In 1971 the BR 080 road was built bisecting the Southern Mekranoti territory. Numerous farmers settled in the area and for over fourteen years these Indians — occasionally helped by other tribes of the upper Xingu area — fought the invaders. A rough estimation leads me to believe that at least thirty-five Brazilians were killed in this tenuous period.

2.2 — The *kubẽkakrit* ("weaker" or "less important non-Kayapo")

By the term *kubẽkakrit*, the Mekranoti refer to a series of Central Brazilian Indian tribes with which they and their ancestors have had some contact during the last two centuries. Although the Mekranoti often enumerated a long list of such *kubẽkakrit* groups, only the following tribes could be identified: Arara, Asurini, Yudja, Iny Karaja (Xambioa), Kuruaya, Munduruku, Parakanã, Tacunhape and Tapirape.

The Arara are known to the Kayapo as *kubẽnhônh* ("vulture people", a term which refers to the cannibalistic practices of this group) or as *kubẽnhakrekamkruwapu* ("people with a piece of bamboo cane in their nose", a reference to an ornament often worn by these Indians). They lived along a tributary of the right bank of the mid Xingu River from where they were dislodged by the Kayapo in about 1850 (Nimuendajú 1946: 223). This period corresponds to my estimation of the Gorotire invasion of that area after their separation from the Ira'amranh (see Chapter 2). The Arara fled to the north and settled along the lower Iriri River, where some groups have been contacted as late as 1980.

The Asurini, Arawete (*kubẽkamrêk*, "red people") and Parakanã (*kubẽakàkakô-re*, "lip plug people") are three Tupi groups that occupy the lower Xingu River and Tocantins River areas and who have suffered several Xikrin attacks (Vidal 1977: 50,155-156). In 1936, the Gorotire attacked an Asurini village.

Kayapo raids on Yudja (*ngôjrẽ*, "rowers") settlements are mentioned as early as 1750. Yet, at the end of the nineteenth century, a small group of Gorotire (Mekranoti) men maintained for years tenuous yet peaceful relations with the Yudja, who at that time lived along the mid Xingu River. After the breakdown of peaceful relations around 1900-1905, the Yudja, distrustful of the numerous Kayapo passages in or near their tribal territory, moved to the south where they were on several occasions attacked by the Gorotire, and three times by the Mekranoti (1910-1920). Some ten years later, the Yudja moved even further to the south and settled near the Manissaua Missu River, in the upper Xingu area.

The Iny Karaja (*kubẽnokàkỳx*) once lived scattered over numerous villages along the mid and lower Araguaia River. Three main Iny Karaja groups can be distinguished: Iny Karaja, living along the mid Araguaia

River; Javahe, living on the Island of Bananal; and Xambioa, living along the lower Araguaia. Given the geographic proximity, the Kayapo maintained more intense contact with the Xambioa than with the other two subgroups. In the nineteenth century, the different Kayapo groups seemed to maintain distinct types of contacts with the Xambioa: the Xikrin maintained friendly relations often visiting and trading with them (Vidal 1977: 49-50); the relationship which the Kayapo of the Xingu and Kayapo of the Araguaia groups had with the Xambioa seemed to have developed from peaceful relations into overt hostility. The Mekranoti relate how their ancestors — at the time still living along the Tocantins River — maintained peaceful relations with the Xambioa. When the Kayapo started moving westward, crossing the lower Araguaia River (i.e., traditional Xambioa tribal territory) around 1810, hostilities between the two groups commenced. These hostilities continued until 1900 or so, when the Xambioa nearly became extinct.

The Xipaya (*ngôjrẽ*, "rowers") are close relatives of the Yudja, and the Kuruaya (*kubẽtekamrêkti*, "people with red legs") are a Tupi group. Both these groups were frequently raided by the Gorotire and Mekranoti: due to frequent Kayapo raids, the Xipaya were forced to leave their habitat along the Iriri River and to move to the northwest in 1885. The Kuruaya suffered the same fate in the period from 1918 to 1934 (Nimuendajú 1946: 219 222). However, Mekranoti informants rarely mentioned these two groups and usually seemed to put them on a par with the Brazilians. This can probably be explained by the fact that, by 1940 or so, the great majority of the members of these two tribes already lived integrated with the local Brazilian population[2].

In the mid nineteenth century, the Munduruku (*kubẽhàngôjrẽ*) population numbered over ten thousand Indians. This made it the most important of all Central Brazilian Indian tribes in terms of population. The Mekranoti relate how "a long time ago", when their ancestors still lived along the *kôkati* (Tocantins?) River, a huge Indian group passed their tribal territory. Informants tend to identify this group as "related to the Munduruku" (*kubẽhàngôjrẽ-re nhõbikwa*) and say that their ancestors fought these invaders and drove them away. A bibliographic reference to this historical passage says that "their [=Munduruku] next expedition, involving an army of some two thousand warriors, is said to have crossed the Xingu and Tocantins Rivers ... the expedition is said to have been defeated and turned back by the Apinaye" (Horton 1948: 273). Nimuendajú

2   A small Kuruaya group continued to live isolated in the area along the lower Curua River. It was contacted at the end of 1988 and numbered about thirty Indians.

cast doubt upon this statement, since Apinaye oral tradition seemed to lack any reference to this major attack; it thus seems reasonable to assume that the Munduruku were defeated by the Kayapo rather than by the Apinaye. In 1941, one of the numerous small Munduruku settlements was raided by the Mekranoti.

The Tacunhape were a Tupi tribe that lived in the area of the lower Xingu River and became extinct by 1920 before any scientist ever visited the group. The literature mentions that these Tacunhape were attacked by the Kayapo shortly before 1842 (Nimuendajú 1946: 223), but I was unable to get any Indian account of this event since I was unable to identify the group in question.

Baldus (1970: 25) mentioned that in the (early?) nineteenth century or before, the Tapirape (*kubẽdjuabô*, "fearful people") lived to the north of their current habitat or, more specifically, near the Pau d'Arco River. At that time, they traded with the Kayapo and regularly maintained peaceful relations. Wagley (1977: 29) mentioned that "the Tapirape spoke of male Kayapo visitors who lived in peace in a Tapirape village for many months" and that "the Tapirape have songs and masked dances which they identify as having been learned from the Kayapo and the Iny Karaja". However, these friendly relations eventually broke down. The Tapirape then moved to the south. It is plausible that this migration is related to the Kayapo migration to the west in around 1820 when these Indians invaded and appropriated the Pau d'Arco River area. In more recent times, the Gorotire occasionally raided the Tapirape, as did the Mekranoti in 1947.

2.3 — The Panara (Kreen Akrore or *Krãjôkàr*, i.e. "[people with] shaven heads")

The Mekranoti do not consider the Panara — a Northern Gê tribe "pacified" as late as 1973 — to be a genuine *kubẽkakrit* tribe. I therefore follow Mekranoti custom by treating the Panara separately.

It was in about 1920 that the Mekranoti noticed the presence of the Panara to the west of their territory. Scouts were sent to spy on their villages in 1921 and an attack was organized. The Panara undertook a counter-attack a year later. Fully taken by surprise, the Mekranoti fled to the northwest but while building a temporary shelter near the Curua River; they were once again attacked. Fearing further Panara aggressions, the Mekranoti then moved to the east and settled along the mid-Iriri River.

In the dry season of 1925, the Mekranoti undertook a massive attack against the Panara. Dreading violent reactions, they moved immediately after the attack to an ancient village, located some hundred kilometres northeast of their traditional territory. For about five years, they constantly moved about, returning periodically to their main village, but leaving each time signs of recent passage by Panara men were sighted.

No further collisions occurred until 1945 when one of the Mekranoti villages (led by Kremôr and Bepgogoti) was attacked by the Panara. Bepgogoti and his followers then left the village with the aim of joining up with another Mekranoti group (led by Kreti-re and Angme'ê) living along the mid-Iriri River. During the trek Bepgogoti's group suffered another Panara attack.

Following a period of relative calm, the Panara killed three Central Mekranoti Indians at a garden in 1959. Revenge was immediately taken and one of the Panara warriors was killed. Fearing new skirmishes, the Central Mekranoti moved immediately after this attack to Pôsto Candôca, where some SPI agents resided. Due to the death of many children in that post, however, they returned to live in their traditional village where, in 1966, some members were killed once again by the Panara near a garden site.

The last and probably most ravaging confrontation between the two groups occurred in 1968 when the Central Mekranoti attacked a Northern Panara village, killing, according to Heelas (1979: 11), twenty-seven men, two women and one child, while capturing eight others. When the Southern Mekranoti heard of this attack, they also set out to attack the Panara, but found only deserted villages and returned with nothing achieved (Cowell 1973: 246-249).

In the period from 1921 to 1968, the Mekranoti suffered six Panara attacks and this led them to identify the latter as their worst enemies. The Panara raids prior to 1946 had the characteristic more of massive onslaughts, during which the assailants bluntly entered the Mekranoti village and promptly provoked man-to-man fights. The more recent raids (1959 and 1966) were limited to the killing of individuals around the villages. This more aloof strategy can probably be explained by the fact that the Mekranoti possessed numerous firearms, whereas the Panara had none. I will return to this important aspect in a later section of this Chapter.

The Mekranoti have attacked only on three occasions, but each time the actions were extremely violent, often with ravaging consequences for the Panara. Thus, the period of tranquillity between 1925 and 1945 can well be explained as a period of necessary recuperation for the Panara after the important attack they suffered in 1925.

2.4 — Other Kayapo groups

Before turning to the intervillage conflicts, it is important to first deal with the mechanism of village schisms. Both features are indeed related because, as stated earlier, Kayapo groups become hostile to each other after such a separation.

Persistent disputes within a Kayapo community often result in collective club-fights where two men's associations or age-sets confront one another in physical combat. Many instances of such club-fights are related to cases of adultery. This can be explained by the disruptive faculty of adulterous relations: one of the major threats to the internal harmony and peaceful relations between the men's associations of a given community is posed by the individual relations of their members to women and to particular nuclear families. Disputes over adultery may therefore threaten the balance between the domestic and communal institutional levels of Kayapo society.

In some cases, tension in the village became so high that the group which was vanquished during a collective club-fight left the village and established a new independent village. Informants often relate the breaking up of villages to disputes over adultery. Yet, adultery is quite a common feature in Kayapo communities, as are club-duels between two (or a few) men. The question can therefore be raised as to why such disputes occasionally led to collective club-fights involving the men's associations or age-sets and leading to village schisms. Upon closer examination, ethno-historical data seem to indicate that several of the major schisms concurred with a far greater danger, one that was induced by forces alien to the community. Indeed, many major schisms[3] coincided with periods where either contacts with members of the national society were approaching or where such contacts had been recently established. While such instances of (approaching) contact with national society cannot be taken in consideration in each of the cases, it is beyond doubt that such contacts generated serious tensions within the community. Once in a while, informants did mention the dissension that arose between opponents and proponents to such contacts. Opponents justified their attitude by referring to the great danger of diseases, while proponents referred to the relative ease with which commodities could be obtained. In any

3   I refer here to the following important schisms: between the Ira'amranh and Gorotire in about 1840; between the Gorotire and Mekranoti in about 1905; between the Kararaô and the Gorotire in 1935; between the Menokanê and the Gorotire in 1937; between the Gorotire and Kubenkranken in 1936; between the Kubenkranken and Kokraimoro in 1950; and between the Central and Southern Mekranoti in 1953.

case, there is no doubt about it that tension must have been high at such moments when extremely important decisions had to be taken. The risk that cases over adultery developed into political issues therefore greatly increased at such particularly tense moments.

Once a village has suffered such a schism, the two resulting groups continue to be reciprocally hostile; surprise attacks are then usually undertaken by the secessionist group that has been forced to leave, initiating in this way a process of occasional mutual attack. Instances where the separated group returns to live with the main group are observed but these are rather rare and usually result in a new separation some time later.

Ethno-historical data also show that small secessionist groups often preferred not to live separately, but rather to join another Kayapo group which lived on hostile terms with the one from which they recently separated. This was particularly so when the split occurred along the lines of families rather than along the men's associations or age-sets as was usually the case[4].

All the cases of fusions of two groups which up to then had lived on hostile terms obviously led to a very tense situation. That is why it was common for members of the arriving group to participate actively in ceremonial life by co-sponsoring the next naming ceremony[5]. In other cases, the arriving group often insisted on a joint attack against the group from which they had just been separated: i.e., the group which had become their common enemy. Both performances were undertaken in order to secure their integration into the embracing community.

But such fusions between two groups didn't always work out: some instances are known where the fusions simply failed, others where the arriving group was not accepted. Of the three Mekranoti groups that returned to the Kubenkranken from 1941 to 1959, the ones led by Karànhĩn and Ku'at were at first integrated but left the Kubenkranken village again a few years later, giving rise to the Kokraimoro; the one led by Kremôr was almost entirely massacred. Likewise, the Mekranoti did not always accept approaching groups: the Kararaô wanted to join them but were

4   The following were instances where Mekranoti secessionist groups were mainly composed of people from one or two families: the group led by Karànhĩn (mainly composed of Karànhĩn's affin and by the kin of Bàka'ê, a trainee by Karànhĩn into chieftaincy); the group led by Nhôjkrã (mainly composed of Nhôjkrã's kin); and the group led by Kremôr (mainly composed of Kremôr's kin).

5   In addition to its political aspect related to integration, this act of co-sponsoring a naming ceremony with members of the embracing group also brought about the integration of the arriving nuclear families in the extended families of the embracing group.

chased away; the groups led by Tàpjêt and Kenti were accepted, but Kenti himself was banished.

In the period from 1905 to 1945 relatively few attacks were recorded between the Mekranoti and the Gorotire/Kubenkranken: both groups undertook on four occasions an attack against this specific adversary. From 1945 to 1956, coinciding with the period of several schisms within the Mekranoti group, seven inter-Mekranoti group attacks were recorded, all against recently split off Mekranoti groups.

3. THE OBTAINED BOOTY: FROM INDIFFERENCE TO TOTAL DEPENDENCE

Excluding garden products and the sporadic appropriation of Brazilian commodities that were found in the attacked village, informants never mentioned that booty was taken during raids against other Kayapo villages. Booty definitely did not figure among the main purposes of intervillage warfare and this is certainly founded on the basis of cultural homogeneity.

Things were slightly different for the Panara (Kreen Akrore), another Gê tribe. Although none of the informants ever actually mentioned it, booty was invariably taken from raided Panara villages. In 1974-1975, items such as weaponry and ornaments obtained during the 1968 attack could still be observed in the Central Mekranoti village. But of all these items, only two seemed to draw their interest: the Panara techniques of featherwork on the arrow ends and the Panara version of the *ikre kam ngàp* ("musselshell in earlobe") ornament which is slightly different from the Mekranoti one. Both elements were incorporated into Kayapo material culture as variants of already existing features.

As in the case of raids on other Kayapo villages, booty seemed of trivial importance regarding the Panara. If little emphasis was put on this aspect by informants, it can be explained by the fact that, in addition to other cultural aspects such as house setting with two men's houses and body paintings, both ethnic groups shared many elements of material culture. Panara artifacts were too similar to their own and provoked little interest.

Things were entirely different for the attacks on non-Gê tribes. The contacts maintained by the Mekranoti and their ancestors with "neighbouring" Indians groups oscillated between a relationship of peace and overt hostility. Peaceful relations were expressed on two levels of contact which I refer to as "indirect" and "direct" contact. The first one will be discussed here, while the latter will be discussed in the next section of this Chapter.

During "indirect contact", the Kayapo left bamboo tubes filled with feathers and closed up with beeswax in designated campsites. The members of the other tribe would reciprocate by leaving other feathers or trade goods. Since such exchanges have not been practised for many decades, it is difficult to imagine how the required items, the agreed to campsites and the timing of the exchanges were arranged between the two groups. Still, it is known that, prior to 1853, the Kayapo left parrot feathers and eagle down to obtain yellow *japu* (*Psarocolius decumanus*) bird feathers from the Arara. Similarly, in the second half of the nineteenth century, macaw feathers were left to obtain glass beads from the Yudja. During these exchanges, the members of the two exchanging groups rarely actually met, which explains the use of the term "indirect contact".

Basically, this type of contact consisted of an indirect or "silent" exchange of materials: it primarily entailed the exchange of primary material such as feathers, seeds and so on. In some cases, Brazilian commodities were also obtained from groups who already made peaceful contact with the local Brazilian population: the Xikrin obtained machetes, axes, scissors and the alike from the Xambioa (nineteenth century), while the Mekranoti obtained glass beads from the Yudja prior to 1885.

Available data show that peaceful contact with non-Gê groups was never maintained for long periods and eventually turned into overt hostility. Kayapo raids on *kubēkakrit* villages seem to be a consequence of a broken peaceful relationship originally established to obtain (among others) some items of material culture.

During the raids on non-Gê Indian groups, the Kayapo always took whatever ornaments and other artifacts they could find in the raided village. The introduction of such artifacts had important consequences for the existent material culture. The fact that, within the group of Northern Gê societies, the Kayapo are known for their elaborate featherwork can be explained by their frequent contacts (whether hostile or not) with non-Gê tribes, and in particular with the Tupi tribes. Featherwork is indeed much less developed in other Northern Gê groups than in the case of the Kayapo. But the incorporation of new elements in material culture was not limited to featherwork: during the last two centuries, many other Tupi, Yudja and Xambioa artifacts such as bamboo flutes, pipes, baskets as well as decorative techniques, have been incorporated into Kayapo material culture. The differences in material culture which are noted nowadays between the several Kayapo subgroups are, among other reasons, due to the contacts each of these communities have maintained with different non-Kayapo cultures.

Booty was also frequently taken during attacks on Brazilian settlements. Firearms, metal tools, pots, hammocks, garments, and so on were highly prized commodities. Of all of these, the firearms were by far the most important: the impact of the introduction of firearms was of incalculable consequences and has to be taken indeed as one of the main innovations in recent Mekranoti warfare.

The importance of firearms is not only related in a myth (Wilbert & Simoneau 1984: 257-259) but its relation to Kayapo warfare can be comprehended in the light of narratives 5 and 6 of Appendix B which relate how these Indians, out of fear for men with firearms, left their traditional habitat along the Tocantins River and fled to the west. Through the acquisition of firearms, the Kayapo were able to overcome their initial military disadvantage in relation to the local Brazilians: they were able to match them on equal terms. More importantly, the appropriation of such weapons led to a more adequate way of defending their villages against Indian enemies who also owned firearms.

Of all the Kayapo groups, the Ira'amranh were probably the first to acquire firearms. Since they used these against the Gorotire and the Xikrin, the latter groups were driven to seize firearms on their own. This process led to an ever increasing need for more firearms and ammunition, which in turn led to more raiding of Brazilian settlements. It was a vicious circle, where more firearms entailed the need for more ammunition, and where the increased possession of such weapons by one group induced the other Kayapo groups to obtain more in turn. The importance of the introduction of firearms can be illustrated by the fact that the Mekranoti still remember that Bepaka and Tàkàknhôti were the first Kayapo of the Xingu men ever to have acquired a firearm. This probably occurred around 1860-1870.

In the beginning of this century, very few firearms existed in the Mekranoti villages and they were not instantly acquired in great quantities. Up to 1936, the Mekranoti made few raids on Brazilians and had obtained relatively few firearms. Informants say that the group led by Tàpjêt possessed as many or even more firearms than the Mekranoti: and this while the entire Mekranoti village was at least four times as large as Tàpjêt's group in terms of population. This is due to the fact that Tàpjêt had been a very active war leader already in the main Gorotire village which was located much closer to approaching national colonists. In the period immediately after Tàpjêt's arrival, the Mekranoti started attacking the Brazilians along the Iriri and Curua Rivers more frequently; the acceleration of the number of raids on Brazilian settlements in the period from 1936 to 1942 led to a considerable increase in firearms in Mekranoti community.

In addition to an ever increasing demand for more firearms, the possession of such weapons in the pre-contact era resulted in a heavy dependence upon contact with the Brazilians. If we consider the numerous schisms and fusions of Mekranoti and Kokraimoro groups in the period from 1905 to 1956 (see Appendix A), then we have data on eighty-two group-years. In that period of years, ninety-two raids were conducted: sixty (sixty-five percent) were against Brazilians; twenty-two (twenty-five percent) were against other Kayapo groups; four (four percent) were against the Panara; and six (six percent) were against non-Gê indigenous groups. The remarkably high percentage of raids against Brazilians (sixty-five percent) indicates that the military hyper-activity of the Kayapo must be understood as a product of Brazilian contact (Turner 1987ms: 76, based on Verswijver 1985). Indeed, the acquisition of firearms for self-defence against aggression by other Kayapo groups quickly became a self-perpetuating and self-intensifying need. Traditional tools and ornaments were produced within the community with the available natural resources, but the acquisition of firearms required more or less regular contact, whether peaceful or hostile, with Brazilians to furnish the necessary supply of ammunition. Since the increased number of attacks on Brazilian settlements led to an increase in casualties, the Mekranoti sought a more convenient way of satisfying their needs for firearms, ammunition and other commodities. That is why, in 1942, Tàpjêt and his men tried to "pacify" the Brazilians: the Indians hoped to enter into friendly relations with the habitants of a small settlement along the Jamanxim River in order to obtain more firearms and ammunition while taking fewer risks. But the attempt failed, and the Indians didn't see any other way out than to continue raiding Brazilian settlements in order to slake their needs.

The need for firearms and ammunition was also one of the main reasons why the Gorotire spontaneously entered into peaceful relations with the Brazilians in 1936. The Gorotire had just separated from the Kubenkranken and tried to obtain as many firearms and ammunition as possible from the people at Nova Olinda. This was done in order to organize a massive attack on the Kubenkranken.

Several main Kayapo groups were peacefully contacted in the 1950s. In addition to a number of Kayapo guides and interpreters, the "pacification" teams mounted by the SPI involved at times about thirty well-armed Brazilians (Meirelles 1958ms: 7). SPI supervisors justified the necessity of such small "armies" as a means of deterring the Kayapo from attacking. Yet, if the Kayapo had really wanted, they could have massacred these approaching teams. This is particularly well illustrated in the case of the "pacification" of the Northern Mekranoti in 1957, when these Indians dictated that the Brazilians leave their arms at a site in the forest before entering their village (Meirelles 1962: 8). This made the SPI team extremely vulnerable to a Kayapo assault, but even so the "pacification" occurred peacefully, just as it did in the case of all the other Kayapo groups. The explanation for this peaceful accommodation was that the interpreters explained that they had brought along many firearms and lots of ammunition as gifts to the community, and that they were to receive even more in the future. In exchange for this "generosity", the Kayapo had to abstain from attacking the Brazilians any further. This was easy to agree upon by the different Kayapo groups because, by accepting the peaceful propositions of the SPI team, they could obtain firearms, ammunition and other commodities, and this in seemingly big amounts. And, most importantly, it apparently involved much less physical risk than raids which at times inflicted heavy casualties on the Indian side. Much to the Brazilians' surprise, the "pacification" of the warlike Kayapo groups therefore went extremely placidly and when the SPI, almost immediately after "pacification", insisted that the Indians collect rubber and Brazil nuts in exchange for more commodities, the Indians willingly did so: at least during the first few years after establishing peaceful contacts with the national society.

Other commodities such as pans, machetes, hammocks and so on were often taken as booty during pre-contact raids on Brazilian settlements: the Mekranoti villages possessed lots of such tools even before the so-called "pacification". All of these commodities were either kept by the man who brought these tools from a raid, or distributed among his kin and affine.

In general, it can be said that the Mekranoti displayed no or little interest in the acquisition of booty during attacks on other Kayapo groups or on the Panara. This is understandable since the Mekranoti share a common cultural background and the resulting material culture. The aggressors, therefore, paid little attention to obtaining objects they themselves made within their own community. Things were, however, completely different during raids on settlements of groups of more distant cultures, such as the *kubĕkakrit* (non Gê groups) or the *kubĕkryt* (Brazilians). On such occasions, booty was not only taken, but this procedure also frequently figured among the main motives for these particular raids.

The importance of the introduction of firearms has already been mentioned, but an additional note should be added on the way other categories of acquired booty were incorporated in Mekranoti society. Two different levels of incorporation should be distinguished, according to the incorporation of either the entire object or applied technique, or of primary materials.

3.1 — Incorporation of the objects or techniques

It is abundantly clear that many objects such as axes, machetes, firearms and so on, taken from Brazilians, were simply adopted as practical and desirable tools. Likewise, some Brazilian "ornaments" were incorporated without introducing any change in the object. The Brazilian female red dresses (*kubẽkàkamrêk*, "non-Kayapo red covering") were brought back to the village for the first time in the mid-nineteenth century. The man who managed to get hold of the first such dress had put it on during several dances and considered it as his *nêkrêx* (ritual wealth). He consequently transmitted the right to wear such a dress to his *tàbdjwỳ* (CC, ZS). In doing so, this ritual privilege became, and still is, associated with a specific residential segment in the village, being that man's segment of birth. In pre-contact times, only the women of that residential segment were allowed to use this specific type of dress on a secular basis. Today, with the sudden and growing import of cloth, many women of various segments wear such red dresses. Yet, in the event of the death of a woman from the original segment which "owns" this privilege, her male relatives — that is, those men who have inherited the right to use the dress during dances — go around the village circle, visiting house to house, collecting all the red dresses which are then buried with the body. Similar limitations exist on the use of red cloth with dots[6] and red cloth hats (*krãdjêkamrêk*, "red head-band").

Brazilian "red dresses" were worn in exactly the same form as they were found. But this apparently stationary process of adopting non-Kayapo items in an unchanged form can not only be attributed to Kayapo unfamiliarity with given techniques. Those techniques used by closer cultural groups, such as the kubẽkakrit (non-Gê tribes), are often very similar to the Kayapo ones and yet, some baskets, clubs, pipes and flutes were copied identically from the ones observed in the original group, using the same technique as the group from which the artefact was taken.

Regarding ornaments obtained from non-Gê tribes, there seems to be a tendency to alter some aspect in order to give the adornment a more (or

---

6   The limitations on red cloth and red cloth with dots explain why many women nowadays prefer to wear blue or orange cloth: blue and red are the most esteemed colours and orange — a variation of red called by the same term (*kamrêk*) — is therefore highly appreciated.

even typical) Kayapo style. Several such instances can be observed: on the small feather headdress (*meàkkà*) which the Kayapo copied from the Yudja, for instance, the general original aspects such as the composition and techniques used were maintained, but were at the same time combined with the typical Kayapo feature of either turning the centre macaw tail feathers with their backside to the front, or attaching additional small feathers to the bottom. On both occasions, this headdress gets a typical "Kayapo style".

3.2 — Incorporation of primary material

Primary material such as cloth, seeds and so on, which are obtained from other cultures, were more easily incorporated into Kayapo material culture than entire objects. Even before initiating the important westward migration in the early nineteenth century, it was apparently already a traditional pattern in Kayapo communities for new ornaments to emerge: the Xikrin narrate, for example, how a variation of an already existing animal teeth necklace emerged when they raided a *kubĕkakrit* tribe (Wilbert & Simoneau 1984: 256-257). Yet, the early nineteenth century westward migration and the following intensified contacts with other societies unquestionably accelerated the introduction process of formerly unknown primary material and led to a consequent increase in the variety of ornaments.

When a person invented a variation of an already existing ornament by changing its form, adding a type of pendant, combining it with other primary materials and so on[7], the newly invented ornament became his particular ritual privilege: it was therefore "owned" by his residential segment at birth. The Kayapo refer to this "owning" of residential segments by *kam ne X krax* or *kam ne X djwỳnh* (literally "there where X originated" or "there where the real X is", where X stands for the type of ornament in question and where reference is made to a residential segment).

Incorporating alien primary materials with existing objects led to these elements being rapidly integrated into Kayapo material culture.

7   It should be emphasized that the development of new ornaments — which become a ritual privilege, owned by a specific residential segment — is not restricted to the incorporation of commodities: many of the Mekranoti adornments currently in use are variations of a few basic ornaments on which some transformation merely in the form, or some alteration in the material used is induced (Verswijver 1984: 39-42). For other commodities obtained during raiding on Brazilian settlements, it is the right to wear them during certain dances which constitutes a ritual privilege.

Yet, once incorporated, a need for that particular primary material was cultivated. Given the differences in ecological zones, some of these materials are not available in the areas inhabited by the Kayapo communities. Things were even more critical regarding materials taken from the Brazilians. In order to get the primary materials they had incorporated, the Kayapo were driven to seek contact with those groups that owned these materials. The white crystal stones necessary to make the esteemed *kruturã* lip-plugs, for example, are only found in the open grasslands along the Araguaia River. In order for the Kayapo of the Xingu groups to obtain this material, they had to contact, peacefully or inimically, those groups that collected this material and that lived along the Araguaia River: that is the Ira'amranh (the Kayapo of the Araguaia), the Xambioa and the Tapirape. Vidal reports how the Xikrin obtained the black seeds they used for the musselshell necklace:

> ...*the Xikrin also made war with the Asurini. The expeditions against these Indians aimed, among other things, at stealing necklaces of black seeds which the Asurini perforated and used as beads. These seeds don't exist in Xikrin land, and were indispensable to accompany the [ngàp] necklace. (Vidal 1977: 50)*

A good example of "primary materials" taken from the Brazilians regards mirrors (*itxe*). These were introduced a long time ago but around 1940, a Mekranoti man made an ear plug of the *ikre kam ngàp* ("musselshell in the earlobe") type for his granddaughter. Rather than gluing a round piece of musselshell at the extremity of a piece of bamboo cane, he used a little round mirror. The new ornament was called *ikre kam itxe* ("mirror in the earlobe"). While the original *ikre kam ngàp* is used only by those persons, both male and female, who have their beautiful names confirmed during any naming ceremony other than *bep*, the *ikre kam itxe* variation became a ritual privilege owned by the man's segment of birth.

Similarly, a variation of a feather headdress came about. The headdress is put on a fine wooden stick of about thirty centimetres and inserted in a hat of beeswax. A man bound a rectangular mirror to such a stick and tied some macaw tail feathers to the two lateral and top sides. The use of this *nhỳnh kam itxe* ("headdress on stick with mirror") is restricted to those men who have inherited the specific right. It is interesting that both this and the other mirror-based innovations are "owned" by the same residential segment.

Separated by only a few decades, the Kayapo of the Xingu groups already display some noticeable divergences in their material culture, divergences which can be partly explained by contacts with different "neighbouring" tribes which each of the groups maintained. Yet, these divergences become more accentuated when comparing the material culture of the three main Kayapo groups (Kayapo of the Xingu, Kayapo of the Araguaia and Kayapo Xikrin). In an even more general view, comparing the Kayapo material culture with that of other linguistically and culturally related tribes such as the Northern Gê, it can be said that the Kayapo display a much richer array of ornaments than these other tribes.

These observations can partially be understood and explained as a consequence of the Kayapo migration into a different cultural area: from a pre dominantly Gê area (along the Tocantins River) into a predominantly Tupi one (along the Xingu River). Yet, the Kayapo facility and capacity of assimilating elements of other cultures cannot be omitted in this regard. Few groups that undertook important migrations into another cultural area as did the Kayapo displayed the same capacity (or interest) in incorporating aspects of their "new neighbours". An interesting case is presented by the Kisedje (a closely related Northern Gê group). In the remote past (early nineteenth century?) a schism occurred in that tribe (Seeger 1981: 49-50). While the Eastern group moved to the upper Xingu area, making alternatively peaceful and inimical contact with the upper Xingu tribes and assimilating several aspects of these "neighbours", the Western group settled along the Arinos River (a tributary of the Tapayoz River and therefore near the Tupi Kawahib cultural area), assimilating very few aspects of these "neighbouring" tribes.

My point is that the institutional scheme of ritual privilege can be seen as one of the major impulses in Kayapo material culture. Ritual privileges embracing the majority of the ornaments are owned by residential segments and the use of these items is by definition restricted to specific individuals. This restrictive imposition in a way stimulates the search for new variations where the use of primary materials occupies an important place. And this search for innovations probably led the Kayapo to make occasional contact with neighbouring societies from which they could borrow new techniques, new ornaments, new materials and new ideas. When such initially peaceful contacts broke down, the Kayapo tried, by antagonism, to obtain the materials they had learned to appreciate and had incorporated in their material culture. Warfare, therefore, was an important factor in the process of intertribal acculturation.

An additional note should be added on the introduction of commodities: in 1939, the warriors brought back lots of hammocks, cloth and other tools. Shortly after this event, an epidemic (of influenza?) broke out, killing several Indians in a few days' time. The Mekranoti say that this epidemic originated from the booty obtained and they related it to the *kubẽdjudjy* ("sorcery of the non-Kayapo"). To be sure, this was probably not the only occasion when such drastic consequences followed the import of contaminated cloths. Posey (1981ms) demonstrates how cloths, pets, bird feathers, and so on, which were often traded with "unpacified" tribes, may have led to epidemics and a consequent decrease in population long before the tribe in question ever had direct contact with members of the national society.

It is highly probable that the incorporation of dogs has led to the appearance of several diseases or epidemics in the Mekranoti villages long before so called "pacification" in 1953-1957. The Mekranoti had very few dogs in the beginning of this century. Taken as booty from the Brazilian settlements, dogs were and still are the most prized of all domestic animals: they are esteemed for their hunting qualities and are valued for their function as watch dogs, alerting the population of approaching enemies. At the time of the "pacification", the Mekranoti already had numerous dogs, but this number has increased during the last years. In 1980, I estimated that some hundred and forty dogs lived in the village which had a population of about three hundred and twenty Indians. Men who frequently visit towns usually return with loads of commodities as well as one or two puppies.

4. THE ACQUISITION OF KNOWLEDGE ABOUT OTHER SOCIETIES

The presence of non-Kayapo individuals in Kayapo villages is related in mythology (Wilbert 1978: 104-106) and seems to have already existed in the early nineteenth century (App. B: 7). Individuals who have been taken captive from other societies are referred to as *kubẽkra* or "non-Kayapo children".

It is an indisputable fact that, in the twentieth century, the Mekranoti abducted members of all categories of their enemies. But this does not mean that captives were systematically taken from all the categories of enemies. It is, therefore, risky to conclude that taking captives invariably figures among the basic purposes of Mekranoti warfare. I therefore begin the following section with a quick review of the societies raided to seek correlations between enemies and the taking of captives (see table 6a).

In looking over the informants' accounts of the Mekranoti raids on Brazilian settlements, it appears that captives were only sporadically taken on such occasions. To be more precise, during the twenty-one raids I managed to document for the period from 1917 to 1960, only fourteen children were abducted: four boys and eleven girls, all of whom were between the age of approximatively two and twelve years. This low number is sustained by comparing the available data on Kokraimoro who, in the thirteen raids performed in the period from 1950 to 1957, captured only one boy. By raiding during the daytime and by the practice of stealthily pillaging the Brazilian settlements whenever possible, the Mekranoti avoided in a way any direct contact with the Brazilians. This shunning of confrontation with these usually well-armed local Brazilians resulted in the fact that relatively few Brazilian children were abducted. This occurred only on occasions when the targeted dwelling happened to be occupied at the moment of the arrival of the warriors and when, consequently, a direct confrontation was brought about. Despite the fact that on these rare occasions Brazilian children were taken captives, it is evident that this attitude cannot be generalized and that the abduction of children (or women) cannot be taken as a primary purpose of raids on Brazilian settlements.

During the Mekranoti attacks on the Panara in 1921 and 1925, at least ten girls and four boys were taken captive. Informants indicated the age of these Panara children roughly between two and twelve years. During the 1968 raid, five[8] Panara captives were taken: two boys, two girls and one woman. The latter was killed on the way back to the village since she "struggled too much" and was considered "really wild" ('àkrê kumrẽnhtx). One boy died shortly after the abduction, and one girl died in 1979 during childbirth. In sum, six boys, eleven girls and one women were abducted during the three Mekranoti attacks on Panara villages. The expression of some of the Mekranoti informants that they attacked the Panara "to bring back children" (krãjôkàr kra-o bôx kadjy) therefore seems to reflect a realistic aspect of these raids.

During the fifteen attacks on other Kayapo villages I was able to document, captives were taken on only four occasions. In total, six boys, eleven girls and three women were abducted.

During the two raids on the Yudja and the single raid on the Tapirape and on the Munduruku in the period from 1915 to 1960, the Mekranoti took two boys, six adolescent girls and one very young women with her son.

This condensed survey shows that, with the exception of raids on Brazilian settlers, the taking of captives undoubtedly was one of the main features of nearly all Mekranoti raids. The fact that Brazilian children were rarely abducted is not due to any selective pattern, but rather is the outcome of strategic practices where the Mekranoti eluded direct confrontation with the Brazilians (see further this Chapter) and this avoid-

8   Although Heelas (1979: 11) reported that eight Panara children were captured during the 1968 raid, the Mekranoti mentioned only five.

ance evidently led to a noticeable reduction in the abduction of Brazilian children.

In general, raids occurred after an "important man" (merax) had incited and convinced some members of their men's group to undertake such ventures. Field data indicate that, when a child was captured, it was usually given either to the instigator of the raid or to the chief who led the attack (both functions were often held by one and the same person), who adopted it for himself or gave it to a close kinsmen, such as a sister or a daughter[9].

The remark that Brazilian captives occasionally were used as emissaries for contacts with members of the national society is interesting. This is illustrated in the following examples:

— In 1936, the Gorotire split off from the Kubenkranken village and peacefully contacted the Brazilians who were living in Nova Olinda, a small settlement along the mid-Fresco River. Vicente, a boy who had been taken captive some time before, was used as a go-between to bring about this peaceful contact between the Indians and the local population;

— In 1942, Àkkajpry (a Brazilian girl captured in the early 1930s at the age of about ten years) was taken along on a raid. On arriving near a settlement, she was urged to yell in Portuguese to lure the inhabitants and to draw their attention. Since no one replied, the house was pillaged;

— In that same year, Tàpjêt and his men wanted to make friendly relations with the Brazilians living along the Jamanxim River. They took Irekàrênh along. Irekàrênh was a girl who had been captured by Tàpjêt in 1934 in that same area. When arriving at the opposite bank from the settlement, the Indians prompted Irekàrênh to go into the water and swim to the Brazilians to tell them about the peaceful mission. The Mekranoti men started yelling "friend, father" in Portuguese. Nonetheless, the Brazilians thought the Indians were mounting an attack and started shooting. The unsuccessful Mekranoti returned to their village.

By using the captives as emissaries, this procedure was obviously meant to be a means to inspire confidence in the Brazilians with whom contact was to be established. It also had linguistic grounds facilitating contact with the Brazilians.

In the literature on the Amerindians, the abduction of captives (and more specifically of female captives) is widely accepted as one of the

9   Of the thirty-one non-Kayapo captives I have data on, no less than twenty-two (seventy-one percent) were adopted by an "important man" (in ten, i.e., forty-five percent of these cases, the adoption was done by a chief); three (ten percent) were adopted by such a man's mother (i.e., as a sibling of the man); three (ten percent) were by such a man's sister; two (seven percent) by his daughter and one (three percent) by his son.

main motives for indigenous warfare. Or, as Clastres deduced:

> *We know that the capture of women is one of the most emphasized*
> *aims of warfare in all primitive societies: one attacks enemies to*
> *abduct their women. (Clastres 1980: 199)*

In view of this observation, it is interesting to see whether or not the Me-kranoti predominantly abducted female captives. Field data show that in the period 1915-1968, the Mekranoti took sixty-three captives, of whom forty-four (seventy percent) were female. These numbers are statistically significant. It can therefore be accepted that there is a certain preference in abducting females rather than males.

The fact that girls were more frequently abducted than adult women does not change the essence of the point. The Kayapo apparently had a preference for capturing young girls. This is due to the fact that, according to informants, adult captives frequently ran off to find their way back to their native villages. Likewise, adult women often offered considerable resistance to their capture and were killed before reaching the Kayapo village.

Sexual intercourse with a non-Kayapo female captive was only initi-ated once the girl/woman had "no more shame" (*arỳp piaàm ket kam*): i.e., after being integrated into the community. A certain time was there-fore given to the captive to allow her to adapt gradually to the new envi-ronment and to become integrated into the community. This integration is not only effected through adoption, but also and specifically through learning the Kayapo language. In other words, by the time the female captive had learned to speak Kayapo fluently, she was fully integrated into society and was considered ready for sexual intercourse.

Most warlike tribes of the Amazon area are polygynous societies[10] and the need for more women can in such cases be explained not only in the light of procreation but also likewise as a factor of prestige. Yet, the question can be raised why the monogamous Kayapo were in need of more females at the time of the capture. In monogamous societies, such as the Kayapo, an equilibrium in the sex ratio between adult men and women would represent what one might call a "normal" state of be-ing. Yet, Kayapo monogamy is more symbolic than factual. The Kayapo men are indeed married to only one woman (*prõ djwỳnh*, "real spouse") at a time but they also often have a "fiancée" (*prõ ka'àk*, "unreal spouse" or *krô-'ã prõ*, "substitute spouse"). And during the long post partum

---

10   The two Brazilian tribes that have received most attention regarding warfare are Tupinamba (Fernandes 1970; Moore 1978; Balée 1984) and Yanomami (Chagnon 1968, 1973; Lizot 1975, 1977; Harris 1977, 1979). Both tribes are polygynous.

restriction period (which, in pre-contact times, was often spread over periods of one year or more), the men go to live in the men's house and maintain sexual relations with "substitute spouses" who are *kupry* women (unmarried women with children). My reconstruction of the 1936 census reveals that at that time some thirty-two *kupry* women existed. Since all adult men were married, these thirty-two unmarried women were those who, due to the rule of monogamy, could not have husbands. The existence of the category of *kupry* women both in pre- and post-contact eras indicates that it is a normal pattern in Kayapo societies to have a surplus of mature women.

For the Mekranoti, the abduction of female captives therefore seems to be a guarantee for maintaining the category of *kupry* women, i.e., of supplementary "substitute spouses", since field data indicate that most captured females became *kupry* women[11]. The importance of women to the survival of any society is obvious. Their procreation capacity guarantees the biological and social reproduction of the society or, as Clastres wrote:

> *...femininity is maternity, first as a biological function, but above all as a sociological mastery exercised on the production of children; it depends entirely on women whether to have children or not. (Clastres 1980: 241)*

While the capturing of females improves the reproduction possibilities for the community itself, this phenomenon simultaneously reduces such reproduction possibilities for the enemies.

Yet procreation was not the only reason for the Mekranoti to take female captives. Young "non-Kayapo women" (*kubẽni-re*) were often captured to teach the Kayapo songs of their native tribes. The Mekranoti say they abducted female *kubẽkakrit* (non-Gê) "to learn the songs of their groups". This motive is explicitly mentioned in narrative 17 (Appendix B) where Mote-re insisted on raiding the Yudja to capture girls to teach Yudja songs. The Mekranoti, and through them, the other Kayapo of the Xingu groups, had learned to perform the Yudja *kwỳrỳkangô* ceremony from Kajngàràti, a young Mekranoti man who, after residing for years among the Yudja, in about 1895 (?) returned to his group. Informants stated that Kajwa and Kôkôpte, two very young Yudja women abducted in about 1915, taught them that same ceremony "more correctly", i.e., they corrected the songs and added some ritual expressions which Kajngàràti

---

11   I have specific data on only twenty-six of the thirty non-Kayapo females captured by the Mekranoti. Eleven (forty-two percent) of them died before reaching adulthood; of the other fifteen, only four (twenty-six percent) were married while eleven (seventy-four percent) remained *kupry*.

had misinterpreted or omitted. That is why some elder Mekranoti still know two versions of the *kwỳrỳkangô* ceremony: the one introduced by Kajngàràti and the other by Kajwa and Kôkôpte[12].

In 1947-1948, two Tapirape adolescent girls between fifteen and twenty years of age were taken captives. They taught the Mekranoti several Tapirape songs, some of which nowadays are incorporated in the *mebijôk* naming ceremony. Since no Panara women were brought into the village for reasons already mentioned, the Mekranoti never learned any Panara songs or ceremonies.

This phenomenon of incorporating songs and dances through female captives does not seem to be a recent one, since it is displayed in an event the Mekranoti relate to the period when they still lived along the Tocantins River (see App. B: 3): the Kayapo attacked the Krãjôkàr-re, capturing several children and adolescent girls. The latter introduced the *ôkrepôx* dance, part of the contemporary *mebijôk* naming ceremonies.

This process was an important aspect of intertribal acculturation and can be taken as a prolongation of the discussion regarding the taking of booty. While some songs and rituals were learned during more or less peaceful encounters with other tribes, the majority of non-Kayapo songs and dances which are nowadays performed and incorporated in ritual life, were obtained through young female captives. Sometimes, raids were undertaken with the specific goal of bringing back young women "to sing and dance". The impact of this procedure is noteworthy: four of the eleven naming ceremonies are said to have originated from other, non-Kayapo societies.

Yet, as mentioned earlier, the Kayapo basically made use of two ways of maintaining peaceful contact with other societies: "indirect contact" and "direct contact". The first one has been discussed in the preceding section and I will now turn to the strategy and implications of "direct contact" which, in pre-contact times, concerned especially the non-Gê tribes.

Numerous references by Mekranoti informants make clear that in several periods some of their ancestors occasionally visited neighbouring indigenous groups, sometimes remaining for months in the other village. Such instances were reported concerning the Tapirape (Wagley 1977: 29), the Xambioa (field notes) and the Yudja (Verswijver 1983). Although trading invariably took place during these visits, it is uncertain whether intermarriage resulted. It is known, however, that some Kayapo women

---

12   It was partly through the Mekranoti groups led by Karànhĩn and Ku'at which migrated to the Kubenkranken in 1942 and 1948, respectively, that the other Kayapo of the Xingu groups learned this second "improved" version of the *kwỳrỳkangô* ceremony.

remained to live in the Yudja village.

Direct exchange has to be taken as the most influential of all contacts between groups. Such exchanges had a great social and cultural impact on the Kayapo communities as these made possible a more profound approach, as well as cultural knowledge, between the two communities; members who frequently and lengthy visited other groups usually ended up learning the language, songs and even entire ceremonies or rituals of the other society. That is why frequent contact with other societies often led to the incorporation of new ceremonies: the Kayapo learned the *aruanã* ceremony — often called *bô kam me tor* — during such visits to the Xambioa; the initial version of the *kwỳrỳkangô* was learned from the Yudja by one Mekranoti man; and the *mebijôk* ceremonies are said to be composed of songs and dances adopted from several different groups.

In addition, the Mekranoti are in the process of incorporating the local Brazilian Saturday evening dances as a new (naming?) ceremony. Some Mekranoti men who have visited Brazilian towns have at several occasions witnessed the local Brazilian evening dances. In 1975, the Central Mekranoti started performing such dances as well. While tapping on empty tin cans to sketch out the rhythm, the young men sang in an unintelligible language, copying those songs they repeatedly had heard on the radios of FUNAI agents. All dressed up, girls and boys (as well as some mature men and women) would stand on opposite sides and the male participants then went to the girls, inviting them to dance in the Brazilian way. Invariably performed at night and often lasting up to three or four o'clock in the morning, the ceremony led to illicit sexual intercourse. This ceremony, called the "spinning dance" (*metorokajkep*), is frequently performed in the dry season, being the inactive season for most other ritual expressions. After a few performances, it gradually incorporated characteristics of Kayapo ritual life: a young couple proposed to sponsor the ceremony, thereby becoming responsible for the food supply and for serving coffee. Chiefs started to give speeches to open up the ceremony and there were talks of incorporating it as a naming ceremony. The procedure of the incorporation of these Brazilian dances and songs therefore parallel the erstwhile strategy of incorporating songs and even entire ceremonies through Kayapo men who visited other indigenous tribes.

In a way, this phenomenon still continues today. Right after the initial peaceful contacts with the national society, several Kayapo groups allowed the Brazilians to raise some of their boys (usually orphans), insisting that the boys return to the village of origin some years later — occasionally adolescents proposed to live with the Brazilians for a few years. The Kayapo wanted these boys to learn Portuguese and to learn to understand the Brazilian culture. Upon returning, the boys were to be the intermediaries between the Kayapo and the national society. The Central Mekranoti have allowed two such boys to be raised by Brazilians. Neither of them have returned though and whenever talking about it, the Indians often react detachedly. They really feel betrayed and often associate their lack of knowledge of Brazilian ways to the treachery of the local Brazilians who took the boys along. In several other Kayapo groups, however, the boys did return and eventually became a source of information on the Brazilian way of life and their views. I will return to the importance of these intermediaries in the Chapter 5.

But the fairly regular abduction of persons and the occasional (lengthy) visits of Kayapo men to non-Kayapo indigenous societies are but two examples of how the Kayapo acquired knowledge about other societies. There were indeed other ways through which such knowledge circulated between groups. One other way was the examination of the attacked sites; once in a while informants would describe how they thoroughly inspected the belongings as well as the slain bodies *in loco* after the attack. Likewise, the sporadic return of captives cannot be omitted: Banner (1975: 50) mentioned how both a captured Brazilian girl and a Yudja man managed to escape and return to their people; another Brazilian boy captured by the Mekranoti along the Araguaia returned to his kin in the mid-1950s. Such instances also occurred between Kayapo villages. Likewise, the occasional fusion of two Kayapo groups and the sporadic migration of individuals to other Kayapo communities were important vehicles in the circulation of knowledge on the weal and woe of other groups and their experience with other societies[13].

5. TACTICS

In this section I will discuss two phenomena which seem to be on par: the definition of the group of warriors that undertook the raids and how the raids were undertaken. These data will be presented separately for each of the four categories of enemies under consideration.

5.1 — The Brazilians

Analysing the data I obtained on eighteen of the twenty-one raids which

13   One particular Kayapo man, for instance, joined Mote-re in 1905 but returned to the Gorotire in about 1920. Later on, the same man joined with Tàpjêt to the Mekranoti in 1936 and returned to the Kubenkranken along with Karànhĩn in 1941.

the Mekranoti undertook in the period from 1917 to 1960 on Brazilian settlements, it appears that the informants identified the warriors in ten cases as members of the *menõrõny-re* age grade; in four cases as the majority of the men of a small group which temporarily had split off from the main village; in two cases as nearly all men (*menõrõny-re* and *mekra-re*) of a determined men's house; in one case as the senior men of the *mekrakramtĩ* age grade; and in one case as the men of one of the men's societies.

These data may appear confusing and inconsistent but, in fact, they are not: the frequent fluctuations and changes in political configurations within the Mekranoti communities have to be taken into consideration in order to evaluate the constitution of the group of warriors. In other words, the definitions as given by the informants reflect the specific political configuration at the time of the raid. A more general definition can therefore only be put forward when the informants' data are paralleled with the political configuration of that particular moment. As mentioned in Chapter 1, the Mekranoti ideal of maintaining a political division of the mature men according to two men's societies was not always realized. Indeed, this configuration based on men's societies was often realized either by arrangements where the men were seated according to age grades or age-sets or where they were divided over two men's houses (each of these with a disposition of "sitting places" according to age grades).

In evaluating the informants' data on war participation with the fluctuations in political configurations, we can accept that the groups of warriors usually were composed of either the *menõrõny-re* men, or one of the mature men's groups (whether a specific age grade, a men's society or, in one case, a men's house). Indeed, in not a single case was it evidenced that all of the then existing men's groups jointly participated in such a raid.

As a matter of comparison, in the period from 1942 to 1950, the Kubenkranken undertook no less than seventeen raids. Ten were undertaken by the *menõrõny-re* and seven by one of the existing men's societies. And the Kokraimoro, in the period from 1950 to 1957, undertook thirteen raids, nine by the *menõrõny-re*[14] and four by one of the two men's societies. These data on other Kayapo groups support the conclusion drawn from the (confusing) Mekranoti data, specifically that only one small group of men invariably undertook raids on Brazilian settlements.

---

14   If significantly more Kokraimoro raids were performed by the *menõrõny-re* then by married men, this can be explained by the fact that the majority of the men in that village belonged to this specific age grade.

Yet, the definitions used by the informants may not be taken ad litteram; when it is said that the *menõrõny-re* took off to raid, they were usually accompanied by a few *mekrakramtĩ* elders to guide and supervise them as well as to prepare the medicinal plants used on such occasions. Or, when informants stated that the men of a given men's society left on a raid, a few members of another men's society also went along. In conclusion, it can be said that the Mekranoti war parties leaving on a raid on Brazilian settlements were usually undertaken by a group of men who were members of one single "sitting place", since never did such various groups of men unite forces to jointly undertake such a raid.

The raided Brazilian settlements were usually very small, often only made up of one or two nuclear families, and a reconstruction of the groups of men that left on raids against Brazilian settlements reveals that an average war party numbered between ten and thirty men.

In general, the tactics of raids on Brazilian settlements can be described as follows: during their long venture, members of the war party sighted a settlement and a few men (i.e., scouts) were sent to spy on the dwelling in order to have an idea of the number of occupants, how well these were armed, and so on. On the return of these scouts, the *metemari* ("those who know [the medicinal plants]") immediately prepared a mixture of plants and centipedes[15] that was thrown in the direction of the Brazilians and which was believed to "remove the occupants from their dwelling" and "to weaken" them. The warriors then invaded the dwelling, killing the mature occupants, taking their children captives and pillaging the dwelling.

Raids were, therefore, not always undertaken at daybreak. To be sure, most raids on Brazilian settlements were undertaken during daytime. This rather uncommon tactic had its importance; since the local Brazilian population greatly feared attacks from the Kayapo, they adopted the custom that husband, wife and children go together into the forest to perform their daily tasks. Thus, during the daytime, their dwellings were often deserted. By raiding during daytime, the Kayapo in a way evaded the probability of direct and often violent confrontation with the usually well-armed Brazilians. This observation is sustained by the Kayapo use of plants which are believed to remove the inhabitants from the area.

The Mekranoti once told me how (that in about 1956?) they entered a deserted settlement along the Iriri River. Among the many trade goods,

---

15   Centipedes have the characteristic of curling up whenever menaced becoming, in this way, defenceless. Informants told me that centipedes were used in the mixture so as to "provoke the defenceless state of the enemy".

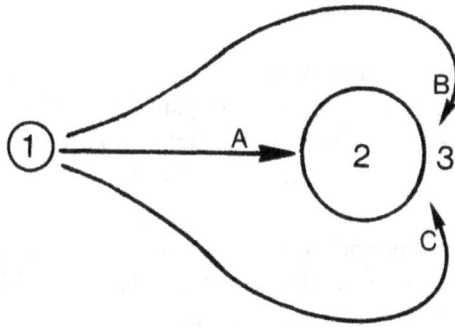

Figure 14 — Strategy used during attacks on Panara and on non-Gê Indian villages. (1) campsite of the Mekranoti warriors; (2) aimed enemy village; (3) battle-site. In case of an attack on the Panara: (A) the *menõrõny-re* men (less experienced warriors); (B) either the members of one men's society, or the *mekrany-re* (junior group of married men); (C) either the members of the other men's society, or the *mekrakramtĩ* (senior group of married men).
In case of an attack on a non-Gê Indian village: (A) the less experienced warriors; (B-C) two small groups of experienced warriors who await the fleeing enemies

a huge and heavy metal trunk was found. Since it was locked, they tried in vain to open it. After a while they heard the owners arriving in their canoes and returned to their campsite. The trunk was left at the site. This example illustrates that the Mekranoti men were not mainly concerned with facing the Brazilians, since they entered the dwelling in a quiet manner, and left when they heard the occupants arriving.

Firearms were often taken along during such raids, but they were not always used, as the avoidance of direct confrontations with Brazilians points out. Yet, this avoidance cannot be taken as signs of fear since, if the warriors noticed that the dwelling was occupied at the moment, the raid was not postponed nor cancelled: the warriors then "just ran into the settlement" (*tu 'yr prõt ne*). The mentioned evasion has to be taken as a strategic abatement of the risks of loss of lives on their side, and as an indication of the fact that neither the killing of Brazilians nor the abduction of children were the main motivations for such raids. Raided settlements were invariably pillaged and the booty obtained was taken back to their village. If the warriors noticed that the dwelling was (temporarily) deserted, they would not "run into the settlement", but rather approach it quietly and proceed to pillage.

5.2. Non-Gê Indian tribes

The formation of groups of men constituting a war party leaving on a raid on *kubẽkakrit* villages was usually similar to those undertaken on Brazilian settlements. In other words, such war parties usually consisted of a group of men who were members of a single "sitting place" within the men's house.

Yet, the tactics were not the same: while Brazilian settlements were frequently raided during the daytime, the *kubẽkakrit* villages were usually attacked in the early morning. The scouts usually returned from their venture in the late afternoon and the night was spent near a garden of the enemy village. According to the type of settlement of the enemy, different raiding tactics were adopted. In the case of the Yudja, who lived in small settlements of fifty or fewer Indians and built their villages on river islands in defence of Kayapo raids[16], the Kayapo attacks were limited to assaults either on groups of men on a hunt or on small groups of people working in the gardens. But as the Yudja men used firearms from the mid-nineteenth century on, attacks on hunting parties were avoided. Rather, family units which went working in their gardens on the mainland were targeted. Using mixtures of medicinal plants which are said to allure enemy families to go and work on their gardens (see App. B: 17), the adversaries were usually attacked in or near their gardens. This procedure simultaneously increased the possibility of abducting Yudja women, since fields are maintained by women. From a secure distance, the male Yudja tribesmen were killed (or chased away) with spears or arrows, then clubbed by the remainder of the participants of the war party. Finally, the surviving females and children were taken captives while the gardens were plundered.

In the case of the Tapirape, who lived in major villages accommodating hundred or more Indians, the small party of about ten to thirty warriors would divide into three groups. One group would scare off the enemy by yelling from one side of the village, while the other two groups would await the fleeing people on the other side (see figure 15). After the raid, the warriors entered the village often plundering it and burning down the houses.

So far as has been recorded, only one men's group went on raids on non-Gê Indian groups: out of the six cases (including the planned raid on the Kisedje in 1952), four times the *menõrõny-re* constituted the corps of

16   As a people inhabiting interfluvial areas, the Kayapo usually crossed big rivers on rafts and considered such main water-courses obstacles.

the "army", and twice the mature men with children.

The Mekranoti usually attacked *kubĕkakrit* in two phases and Vidal (1977: 155-156) noted the same for Xikrin attacks on the Asurini. On return of the first group of warriors (being the more mature and experienced warriors such as the *mekra-re* and the *menõrõny'ãtũm*), a second war party (of some elder men guiding the younger *menõrõny-re* and *me'ôk-re*) would set out to raid the same enemy. While the first raid was considered to be more exploratory, ambivalent and therefore a more dangerous venture, the second rather had the characteristic of less dangerous training; it was usually focused on pillaging rather than taking captives.

Raids on non-Gê Indian groups usually were undertaken making use of only the traditional weapons (spears, bows and arrows and, above all, clubs).

5.3 — The Panara (Kreen Akrore)

On all three occasions that the Mekranoti undertook an attack on the Panara (1921, 1925 and 1967), nearly all of the men in the village participated. The number of warriors varied between about seventy in 1921 and thirty-five in 1968. As occurred during the attacks on the *kubĕkakrit* tribes, scouts were sent ahead to spy on the enemy village and the attacks were invariably executed in the early morning.

The tactics were somewhat similar to the ones used during raids on the non-Gê Indian tribes. At the moment of the raid, the warriors divided into three groups; the unexperienced men (i.e., the *menõrõny-re*) invariably formed the centre group which would scare off the Panara by yelling. If the contemporary political configuration was based on age grades, the two other groups would be formed by distinct men's age-sets (*mekrany-re* and *mekrakramtĩ*). If the political configuration was based on men's societies (such as in 1921), each of the men's societies would form one group. Both these groups settled on the opposite side of the yelling *menõrõny-re*, awaiting the fleeing Panara (see figure 15).

Informants stated that during the 1968 attack, the village chief remained with the *menõrõny-re* and *me'ôk-re* youngsters in a nearby campsite while the mature men undertook the raid. It seems that the Panara had placed thorns in the paths, and most of the men had infected feet by the time they reached the village; only the bravest, experienced and hardened men proceeded to the attack. Based on the descriptions of the Panara, Heelas described this last Mekranoti attack as follows:

> *The Mekranoti party surrounded the village before dawn and attacked by firing guns into the houses. The Panara were taken total-*

ly unaware, only realizing the threat when they heard the whistles and imitation of bird calls of the attackers. Resistance was brief in the face of gunfire, with most of the inhabitants fleeing into the forest... The Mekranoti suffered no casualties. (Heelas 1979: 10-11)

It appears that in the 1921 attack, few firearms were used. In the period from 1923 to 1924 the Mekranoti markedly amplified their arsenal by raiding several Brazilian settlements. So, the 1925 attack was performed with considerably more firearms. Despite this fact, the Mekranoti say that the Panara — who didn't possess firearms at all — showed little or no fear of these weapons. In 1968, the Mekranoti asked the missionary who was active in their village to provide them with ammunition to facilitate a ceremonial hunt. But, rather than using the obtained ammunition for the hunt, they used it on the attack against the Panara. The fact that firearms were used during these attacks can probably be explained by the great losses the Mekranoti suffered in the Panara counter attack of 1922: first, a couple was killed, but then the Panara killed fourteen more Mekranoti near the Curua River. The Mekranoti had never suffered such major losses in their history. In fact, they had never been attacked in their village by non-Kayapo.

5.4 — The Kayapo

Attacks on other Kayapo villages were generally organized either by a combination of the majority of men from the attacking village, or by major men's groups. The number of warriors can be estimated as being between fifty and hundred men on each occasion.

As numerous references in the narratives of Appendix B show, tactics consisted of surrounding the enemy village in the early morning. A sign for the attack was given by imitating bird calls or by shaking rattle girdles (see also Wilbert & Simoneau 1984: 313-316).

The assaulted village plaza was the arena of the attack. The assailants often used firearms while charging into the village. While women and children tried to hide in the surrounding forest or bushes, the men fought hand-to-hand with their clubs on the plaza.

In sum, it can be said that the numerical composition of the "army" of Mekranoti warriors that set out for a raid was determined in function of a combination of two factors: the size of the enemy group to be raided, and the warlike strength and character of the enemy.

— The size of the enemy group: the targeted Brazilian settlements as well as most *kubēkakrit* villages usually were rather small, numbering between ten and hundred and fifty inhabitants. The size of the Panara and Kayapo villages was more important, since these villages numbered between hundred and fifty and over one thousand Indians.

— The warlike strength and character of the enemy or, in other words, the adversity that could be expected during and after the raid. Attacked Panara and Kayapo groups, for instance, offered great resistance and were very likely to pursue the assailants in order to drive them away. These Indians likewise often undertook counter-attacks against the Mekranoti. *Kubẽkakrit* groups were considered weak by the Mekranoti since these never offered much resistance during the raid and since these groups rarely counter-attacked. The Brazilians, on the other hand, were feared because of their resistance during raids and because of their punitive expeditions. But, like the *kubẽkakrit*, Brazilians rarely counterattacked in the Mekranoti villages. To be precise, field data shows that the Brazilians on only one occasion undertook a revenge action against the Mekranoti by invading the Northern Mekranoti village in 1948. The Indians noticed the arrival of the aggressors and managed to flee in time. The Brazilians therefore invaded a deserted village but still encountered many belongings of the Indians which had been left behind after the hasty retreat (Preihs 1952ms: 2).

Depending on these two factors, the war party was composed of either a single men's group (such as for raids on the Brazilians and on the *kubẽkakrit*) or nearly all the men of the village (for raids on the Panara and the Kayapo). The number of warriors, therefore, varied from ten to thirty in the first case, and from thirty to hundred in the latter.

Just as the numerical strength of the war party varied from enemy to enemy, strategy during raids was adapted for the targeted enemy. Distinctions can be made according to four raiding tactics:

1. "Running into the settlement", used during raids on inhabited Brazilian settlements;

2. "Quiet entrance of a settlement", used when a Brazilian settlement was unoccupied;

3. Dividing the army into three groups which encircled the enemy village. One group (the youngest and least experienced warriors) would start shouting to scare off the enemy while the other two groups would await the fleeing people on the opposite side of the village. This tactic was used for raids on Panara and *kubẽkakrit* villages and in such cases, the area around the enemy village was the arena of the fighting;

4. Encirclement of the enemy village and attack from all sides. This tactic was used for attacks on Kayapo villages and in such case, the village plaza was the arena of the fighting.

The attacks were usually undertaken in the early morning. By attacking at that time, it was more or less certain that the entire village population was present in the village. This strategy, therefore, eliminated the possibility of a surprise reaction by groups of men that returned to their village and that would unexpectedly attack the assailants from the rear. The tactic of approaching Brazilian settlements during daytime has been explained in light of avoiding direct confrontations with those settlers.

Most raids were undertaken making use of traditional Kayapo weapons such as clubs, spears and bows and arrows. While firearms were only occasionally used during raids on the *kubĕkakrit* and the Kayapo, such weapons were often used against the Brazilians — for obvious reasons of fighting on "equal terms" — and against the Panara.

6. ON BELLICOSITY

In addition to the specific attributes of Kayapo warfare presented in the preceding pages, there are two features which are common to Kayapo warfare in general: revenge and the display of male bellicosity. In this section, I will be mostly concerned with bellicosity, while revenge will be dealt with in the next section.

Exhibition of bravery, of fearlessness and of belligerence is, *de facto*, omni-present in Mekranoti warfare. Since booty was unimportant during attacks on Kayapo villages, I suggest that this particular type of warfare can best be understood in light of a demonstration of Kayapo male virtues. Kayapo males are educated in the spirit of strength (*tỳx*), of insensibility to pain and fatigue (*amakkre ket*)[17], and of courage (*uma ket*, "without fear"). To encourage, stimulate and instil these ideals, the Kayapo make use of a series of rigorous tests to harden the younger men. For example, the legs of the *menŏrŏny-re* adolescents are at times scraped with a scarificator to improve their agility during hunts; wasp nests are attacked with the bare hands to make the men insensible to serious pains; wrestling is promoted at ceremonial occasions to test the strength of the younger men; racing is organized to improve speed; foot-stamping fights are occasionally organized to improve agility and endure pain; traditional stick ball (or "hockey") games improve speed; and stick-throwing games improve agility as well as combat efficiency. Male virtues of strength and courage are also promoted during the daily orations, in which younger tribesmen are often referred to as weak and tame by the village elders, instigating

17   Literally "no ear-hole": i.e., with a covered ear and therefore "insensible" (Vidal 1977: 126).

these younger men to demonstrate their belligerence. Understanding these ideal virtues of Kayapo men is, therefore, unquestionably one of the basic principles of comprehending Kayapo warfare in general.

Although informants frequently mentioned revenge as a main motive of internecine (i.e., intervillage Kayapo) warfare, the display of bellicosity must also be taken into consideration. As an exhibition of combat assertiveness, bellicosity is the issue of the praised and roused ideal male virtues such as strength and courage, and is on a par with fearlessness. Belligerence is, therefore, often mentioned by the Mekranoti as one of the characteristics of important men such as chiefs, leaders and scouts, who are supposed to display exemplary (male) behaviour. Among the Kayapo, the image of ideal manhood is indeed that of the bellicose hunter/ warrior. Many narratives in Appendix B relate to the men's belligerence and fearlessness. Narrative 4, for example, relates how a village chief had the impression that the visiting men of another Kayapo village were about to kill him. Despite his sense of approaching death, he did not run away; rather, as a demonstration of his fearlessness, he asked his wife to embellish him so that he could die with dignity.

Since other Kayapo groups share the phenomenon of educating males in the spirit of bellicosity, it is of more esteem to kill a Kayapo man than to kill a "less important non-Kayapo" man. This way of thinking reflects a concept of self-valorisation: saying that one's equals are bellicose and fearless means as much as attributing these qualities to oneself.

The display of belligerent and valiant behaviour was one of the main inducements for raiding Kayapo villages. A war party was only considered successful when the belligerent performance of the warriors resulted in a display of supremacy over the raided group. The capturing of women and children (usually girls) was one way of demonstrating superiority. Women and girls were therefore not only taken for their procreative qualities, but likewise as an evidence of the enemy's vulnerability and weakness. The most esteemed demonstration of belligerence, however, seemed to be able to force the raided group to flee temporarily from its village. Such an accomplishment was taken as an outstanding and praiseworthy evidence of the supremacy of the assailants. Few explicit examples of this particular achievement exist in known Kayapo history, but all of these known cases are narrated circumstantially by the informants. After the split between the Gorotire and the Ira'amranh, for example, the Gorotire returned to raid their former friends, forcing the Ira'amranh to flee to the north. More recently, the numerically more important Kubenkranken were forced to flee from the raiding Kokraimoro in 1950. This Kokraimoro achievement is considered by both Kokraimoro and Mekranoti informants as a major expression of Kokraimoro belligerence as well as of Kubenkranken vulnerability.

It should be emphasized, however, that the goal of raids on Kayapo villages was never to achieve territorial conquest, a phenomenon which has often been mentioned as essential to indigenous warfare. Tornay (1979: 115) rightly said that "Territorial conquest... is a characteristic of sedentary peoples. For nomads, or semi-nomads, gaining free access to a place is more important than occupying it." Yet, ecological theorists have often used the argument of protein scarcity to explain band and village warfare. Lathrap (1968: 36) showed that tropical forest zones away from major rivers — such as the Kayapo habitats — have meagre game resources and that the fishing potential of smaller tributaries is limited. Living in such "interfluvial" habitats, where hunting rather than fishing must be relied on for the bulk of protein in the diet, would be incompatible to sedentary village life (Carneiro 1970: 245). In horticultural societies such as the Kayapo, who lived in interfluvial zones, protein scarcity would lead to the conquest of new hunting territories and to the inevitability of armed conflict. Recent research on primitive economies, however, indicates that such societies are not as limited by protein resources as portrayed. Concerning the Mekranoti, for example, Gross (1979) and Flowers (1982) have shown how these Indians obtain an abundant amount of calories with low agricultural effort, and Werner (1980) has noted that hunting provides ample protein.

It is clearly shown in Chapter 2 that, prior to the contact period from 1953 to 1957, the Mekranoti occupied a huge territory of approximatively sixty thousand square kilometres or more. Most villages were built on the savannah at the edge of the gallery forest or within the near vicinity of tropical forests. By moving from one village site to another, the exploitation of game was evened out over a range of hunting zones. Likewise, by alternatively exploiting different ecological zones, the depletion of game resources was less likely, even with a much higher population density as in the pre-contact era, when villages at times numbered seven hundred or more Indians.

In this century, the traditional Mekranoti area was located in a virtually unoccupied part of Central Brazil: their nearest neighbours were the Yudja (Juruna) and the Panara (at some hundred and twenty and hundred and fifty kilometres respectively of their main villages). The attack of these tribes, or the Tapirape who lived three hundred kilometres from the centre of Mekranoti territory, can hardly be attributed to the "conquest" of new hunting territories. Protein scarcity can, therefore, not be taken as a main motive for Mekranoti warfare.

Ethno-historical data show that raids on other Kayapo groups never resulted in the *permanent* removal of the raided Kayapo community. I emphasize the word permanent to make clear that *temporary* removals did indeed exist: field data indicate that it was not uncommon for a raided Kayapo community to temporarily seek refuge in the nearby vicinity of their village such as in the gardens[18], or to more distant sites such as ancient villages — and this either for a few weeks, or even a year or more. However, in all but one of the cases of removal caused by warfare, the groups always ended up returning to their traditional habitat. The sole exception seems to be when, after the Gorotire attacked the Mekranoti in the beginning of this century, the assailed Mekranoti moved permanently to the south. Yet, this Mekranoti southward migration from the village of *arerek-re* to the one of *rojkô-re* was due to historical coincidence: the Mekranoti had already planned their move to *rojkô-re* (they had already prepared the new village with corresponding gardens) and had only temporarily returned to *arerek-re* to collect garden products when the Gorotire attacked. After the attack, the Mekranoti moved to the area near *rojkô-re*. This event cannot be taken as an example of territorial conquest, nor as an expulsion of the Mekranoti for living "too close" to the Gorotire. It is, as such, no exception to the rule since the Mekranoti had already begun this southward movement.

Accordingly, no evidence could be found in the available field data to sustain the hypothesis that Kayapo communities definitively left their territories because of raids. Territorial conquest did not figure among the main motives of the type of Mekranoti warfare in discussion. The mentioned attempt to expel temporarily the enemy from its habitat can only be taken as a demonstration of the assailant's supremacy and the raided group's vulnerability.

The display of bravery was slightly different regarding attacks on the *kubẽkakrit* Indians. The Mekranoti greatly despised some *kubẽkakrit* tribes for their cannibalistic habits; they loathed the Yudja who kept skulls of their slain enemies or cut the body of their victims (see App. B: 15), and hated the Arara who took such war trophies as scalps, skulls and teeth, or the entire skin of their dead enemies (Nimuendajú 1946: 236). Although despised, these two as well as other *kubẽkakrit* tribes were not really feared; in a way, they were respected for certain cultural traits, but were simultaneously considered to be weak (*rerek*) and tame

18   Anderson and Posey (1984ms) explain that *apê-te* (literally "made" — a reference to "islands" of woody vegetation on the savannah) are created and maintained by the Kayapo. Such *apê-te* bring about a constant source of vegetal and animal resources and serve as a refuge during epidemics and warfare.

(*uabô*). The attribution of these characteristics can be understood by the apparent facility with which the Mekranoti say captives were taken, and by the pacific conduct of these Indians, who never or rarely counter-attacked. Likewise, according to the Mekranoti, these tribes offered little resistance and were easily driven out of their villages.

These reflections may explain why small groups of Mekranoti warriors turned to raid these enemies. If all warriors of a Mekranoti village would jointly confront such a *kubẽkakrit* tribe, the sum of Mekranoti warriors was likely to outnumber the sum of men of the usually small *kubẽkakrit* villages and, consequently, more captives could be taken, as well as more enemies killed. Yet, such a venture would not be esteemed as a really "dangerous" enterprise by the Mekranoti. This is probably one of the reasons why the Mekranoti often raided such villages in two stages, where at each phase a reduced number of Mekranoti warriors participated. By diminishing the number of warriors in a single war party, the risks involved increased. In addition, exposure to injuries also grew and the achievements were more highly valued. This occurred not only because the number of Mekranoti warriors was then equal or even inferior to the number of *kubẽkakrit* men, but also because the few participants had to be fearless to remain firm in the face of the natural and supernatural dangers they were likely to confront away from their homeland. The Mekranoti greatly fear supernatural dangers in distant, unknown territories, much in the same ways as they fear these dangers when they have to spend a night alone in the forest. The more people present, the more secure they feel. Thus, the handful of warriors who dared to take off for such distant sites was considered brave.

An additional danger existed: the small group of warriors could also suffer unexpected attacks from migrating or trekking enemies, as well as the risks of getting slaughtered by numerically stronger enemies when the war party was formed by only a few warriors. Such an unexpected confrontation occurred in 1948 when Kruma-re, a young Southern Mekranoti leader, left with only six other warriors to raid the Tapirape. On the way back to their village, the warriors came across a Xavante trekking group. A confrontation took place, and three Xavante women were killed. Fearing a Xavante counter-attack, the Southern Mekranoti then moved to join the Central Mekranoti.

These reflections lead us to the observation that the Kayapo term used for non-Kayapo groups should be understood in view of this less belligerent character of these Indians. Bellicosity is a praised Kayapo male value and those groups that are not bellicose are considered "less important people" (*kubẽkakrit*). The use of this term can therefore be understood as a paraphrase of saying as much as "inferior people", where bellicosity figures as a parameter of this distinction; those who lack the very important male value of bellicosity are taken as "inferior". The term *kubēkakrit* is, therefore, often used in a disapproving sense, and it is in view of this that both the Kayapo and the Panara[19] are the most respected enemies; they are put on an equal level since, as the Mekranoti, these two groups did not fear to undertake a counter-attack, and praised the same ideal of bellicosity. Due to these facts, the Mekranoti never include the other Kayapo or the Panara in the category of "less important people".

Since the Panara were considered among the most valiant of enemies, any confrontation with this group was a display of bravery per se. But there was an additional feature: that of the near vicinity of the Panara villages. This was often referred to by informants as a threat to the Mekranoti. The mere fact of remaining in the tribal territory can therefore be taken as yet another display of fearlessness. Indeed, in spite of the violent Panara counter-attacks, the Mekranoti did not permanently flee to settle at a greater distance from the Panara villages, which they easily could have done considering the enormous size of their traditional pre-contact tribal territory.

The Brazilians were not really considered brave, but were feared because of their use of firearms. The fact that small groups of Mekranoti warriors usually took off to raid these settlements can, once again, already be considered a display of male bravery because the risks of getting killed were higher and each member of the small "army" had to be brave to face the natural and supernatural dangers in distant territories. In this view, it is important to repeat that raids on Brazilian settlements were often conducted far beyond the traditional perambulation area at sites of up to six hundred kilometres distant from the Mekranoti villages.

7. DIFFERENT TYPES OF KAYAPO WARFARE

In sum, the previous analysis shows that not only a neat distinction can be drawn between the various incentives for the Kayapo to engage in warfare, but also that different military strategies were applied. The numerical strength of the "army" seemed to be adapted either to the circumstances of the raid, or to the category of enemy which was being confronted.

19   I am not sure whether the Kisedje (Suya) and the Xavante (two other Gê tribes) are put on a same level as the Panara.

Otterbein (1968) distinguishes between two types of warfare: "internal war" (warfare between culturally similar political communities) and "external war" (warfare between culturally different political communities). Regarding the Kayapo, applying Otterbein's distinction would boil down to the subsequent distinction: "internal war" is the one against other Kayapo groups and the Panara (who were assimilated to the category of Kayapo-like enemies) — these raids were undertaken mainly for vengeance and glory — and "external war" is the one against Brazilians and non-Gê Indian peoples.

Yet, this distinction seems too superficial. Certainly, the conspicuous nature of these differences indicates that it is unwarranted to consider the phenomenon of "Mekranoti Warfare" as one single entity. Yet what we have here is not merely a distinction between "internal" and "external war" for, as evidenced in the analysis of numerous Mekranoti raids, a distinction should be made regarding basic war related aspects such as ideology (related to specific motivations) and actual execution (related to strategy and tactics). This leads us to make a distinction between two types of "external war": warfare against Brazilians and warfare against non-Gê Indian groups. The basic *leitmotif* for the first type was the appropriation of firearms and manufactured goods; warfare with Brazilians was indeed primarily a form of circulation of commodities. Raids against non-Gê Indian peoples were conceived of as almost adventurous undertakings, aimed at capturing children to raise and acquiring exotic artifacts and ritual objects to add to the Kayapo repertoire of "ritual wealth" (*nêkrêx*).

In the following pages, I will occasionally return to this distinction between "internal war" and "external war" on the one hand, and between the two types of "external war" on the other.

8. REFLECTIONS ON THE IMPACT OF PRE-CONTACT WARFARE ON THE MEKRANOTI COMMUNITIES

The previous analysis on Mekranoti raiding patterns clearly shows that warfare often involves the display of those ideal male values which are stimulated and aroused in the sphere of the men's house. The exhibition of these male virtues, when confronting an adversary, has comprehensive repercussions on Mekranoti behaviour rules since it reflects both at the individual and the communal level of society. I will now discuss the importance and some consequences of warfare in Mekranoti society.

8.1 — The warrior's fortune

Before and during a raid, three categories of men stand out conspicuously for performing a specific war-related task. These three functions are scout, instigator and military leader.

I. the scouts (*meoprãr-re*)

Whenever it is decided to raid an enemy, two or three men are sent ahead of the rest of the warriors. These men have the specific task of going and spying on the enemy, and are referred to as *meoprãr-re* ("those who flatten", a term I freely translate as "scouts" — see Chapter 1). The scouts' task of spying on the enemy is considered a risky enterprise. They penetrate into territories well beyond the community's traditional area, where the natural and supernatural dangers are unknown and, consequently, greatly feared. Scouts also come face to face with the risks of being killed by the enemy, since their enterprise requires a close approximation to the enemy village in order to check on the village site and lay-out, on the size of the community, and on the location of the gardens near the village. Field data shows that many of the pre-contact Mekranoti chiefs had been a *meoprãr-re* while a *menõrõny 'ãtũm* or *mekrany-re* — i.e., before being formally installed in the office of chieftaincy. In all likelihood, they did so to display their male values of belligerence and, above all, fearlessness.

II. the instigator (*me kutã nojarêt djwỳnh*)

The idea of undertaking a given raid is often put forward by one particular man. These usually are "great" or "important men" (*merax*) such as chiefs, leaders or scouts. Either through oratory or through persuasion, the instigator provokes his fellow tribesmen to join him in the dangerous venture he proposes. After convincing a group of men to undertake a raid, it is this particular man who will perform the formal *nojarêt* (literally "to pull out the eye" — see Chapter 1) speech, as is expressed in the term "he who really stood (in front) to do the *nojarêt*" (*me kutã nojarêt djwỳnh*). The *nojarêt* is performed standing in front of the group of warriors, on the day of their departure. The instigator invariably participates in the raid and usually claims the adoption of captives, if any are captured. This was, for example, the case during the attack on the Panara in 1967. A senior man who had lost a close kinsman during an earlier confrontation with the Panara, launched the idea of an attack. On that occasion, he insisted on taking revenge and added that, since he had very few children, he wanted to capture a Panara child. The attack occurred and the instigator adopted one of the four captured children.

The way the instigator persuades his fellow tribesmen to participate in a raid leads to reflections on revenge. While in the case of external war (i.e., an attack on Brazilians or *kubẽkakrit*) the instigator is likely to argue for the prospect of acquiring booty or of capturing children, in the case of internal war (i.e., an attack on another Kayapo group or on the Panara) he usually argues by alluding to the victims of earlier conflicts with that particular enemy and by insisting that revenge should be taken. Though informants seldom mentioned revenge as a motive for raids on *kubẽkakrit* groups, this can be explained by the fact that very few or no Kayapo warriors were killed during these events. Vengeance was, however, often mentioned as a main issue for raiding groups where earlier confrontations had led to casualties: that is for raids against other Kayapo groups (cf. App. B: 7-8) and against the Panara (the most closely related non-Kayapo group).

Among the Tupinamba Indians of the Brazilian coast, revenge has no end, but also has no outset: it is a mnemotechnic, mobilized for the production of a future (Carneiro da Cunha & Viveiros de Castro 1985: 201-202). Things are different among the Kayapo, though, where, as expressed in several myths (Wilbert & Simoneau 1984: 366-368, 393-394, 405) and in the Kayapo term for revenge (*pãnh*, "payment", "compensation", "retaliation"), the taking of revenge is a conclusion: vengeance abolishes the infringement of the killing of a kinsman. This is true, at least, for individual revenge, though during the very act of raiding, other casualties are likely to occur which, in their turn, require revenge by the kinsmen of the new victims. Revenge therefore results in a sort of vendetta in which the emotional and symbolic aspects are emphasized rather than the materialistic ones.

III. the military leader (*mekurêdjwỳnh 'ỳr meobadjwỳnh*)

Formally installed chiefs (or, if they are too old to participate effectively, the younger chiefs of their men's society), or leaders (*meoba djwỳnh*) of the younger men's groups act as the military leader of the raid: i.e., as "he who really goes towards the enemy" (*mekurêdjwỳnh 'ỳr meobadjwỳnh*). This command over the war party is one of the specific functions of a chief. It involves the preparation and use of medicinal plants to influence the course of events, the performance of the *bẽn* ritual speech performed both on the day of the attack and on the arrival of the warriors back in the village, and often entails guidance over the *menõrõny-re* or less experienced warriors.

The regular performance of any of these three functions is conducive to individual political status within the community. Yet, despite the fact that all of three these war-related functions are invariably held by "important men", the acquisition of prestige through warfare is not limited to these already influential men. This is because the phenomenon of a reduced number of participating warriors in some raids can be understood as a means of increasing the value of the individual achievement of each of the warriors during the undertaking. An additional reflection should nevertheless be made. By analysing the composition of the groups of warriors that participated in the raids in question, my attention was drawn to the fact that the names of several men were almost constantly mentioned. These men (*meàkrê*, "bellicose men") were to be among the most warlike members of the community. In the late pre-contact era, when warfare was frequent, any Mekranoti village seemed to have several men that were more likely to engage in raiding than other men. And these men often seemed to form small units which, under the conduct of one particular chief or leader, usually took off as a corporate group. So, for example, in the period from 1937 to 1942, Tàpjêt was accompanied by a group of five to eight men who followed him in almost all raids. Kreti-re had such a unit of five or six men in the period from 1940 to 1950. The composition of these more warlike units did not necessarily correspond to the existing men's societies or to the corporate groupings according to particular age grades. Rather, these small units were "cliques"[20] *within* the political factions.

The "sitting place" (*krĩdjà*) led by Tàpjêt, for instance, numbered over twenty men, of whom only five to eight formed the warlike "clique" — and this while no other such "clique" existed within that same "sitting place". But, it was rare that only the men of such a "clique" engaged in warfare, since they were usually joined by several others, most commonly members of the same "sitting place". These additional men only sporadically and occasionally participated, as if they took turns in joining the nucleus of the more warlike "clique". Yet, these additional men did not always belong to the men's society of the warlike "clique". Informants stated that when men of other men's societies participated, these men would change membership by becoming members of the men's society with which they would join on raids. Warfare on *kubẽkakrit* villages and Brazilian settlements, therefore, played an important role in (re)defining the composition of men's societies. Such men's societies, thus, were not stationary political factions, since on each raid the composition of the

---

20   The question can be raised whether or not these "cliques" were homogenous. Although the relationship of ceremonial friends (*kràbdjwỳ*) seems involved, I failed to check on this important aspect.

members was likely to change. If chiefs often acted as instigators of such raids, this can be explained as being a way to gain new adherents to their men's society.

The men of such "cliques" were those who, due to individual propensity, most anxiously participated in any confrontation with adversaries. Field data show that it was these "cliques" which most arduously raided *kubĕkakrit* villages and Brazilian settlements. Clastres (1980: 212-213) refers to such "cliques" within warlike societies as "a minority of men who constantly make war" and adds that these men often proceed to make warfare on their own initiative, not necessarily corresponding to a collective, communal imperative.

Field data gathered in the Mekranoti villages sustains Clastres' distinction between "communal" and "individual warfare" which, in the case of the Kayapo, boils down to the distinction made earlier between internal and external war. Mekranoti history demonstrates that attacks on Kayapo and Panara villages usually arose when one or more "important men" managed to convince the entire community to join such a raid, using such arguments as revenge and bravery. The attack then became a communal matter and nearly all men participated in the dangerous event. Raids on *kubĕkakrit* villages and Brazilian settlements, on the other hand, looked more like individual initiatives of the more martial chiefs, who managed to convince their warlike "cliques" to participate. And it is not surprising that exactly the two types of raids which are conducted by small groups of warriors are simultaneously those types of warfare characterized by the achievement of booty.

Trade goods in general are referred to as *õ nêkrêx* ("one's wealth"). The term *õ nêkrêx*, however, is used in a stricter sense to refer to ornaments, or specific rights which are individually inherited. *Õ nêkrêx*, whether in the form of trade goods or of inherited rights, are highly esteemed and valued. They are invariably individual possessions. Items brought back from the enemy brought about the possibility of inventing new variations on ornaments which then became the ritual privilege of the inventor. Both the raids on Brazilian and *kubĕkakrit* settlements, therefore, imply a strong motivation for accumulating individual "wealth" (*õ nêkrêx*)[21].

Mekranoti warfare also had something of a pioneering character. Mekranoti history indicates the remarkable mobility of these Indians within

21   The world of the relations between ritual and politics — i.e., the very particular relation that the Kayapo have with the songs and ceremonies of their neighbours, their eagerness to incorporate supplementary ritual functions, their investment in ornaments and ritualization — are points to be developed in future research.

Table 6 — The ethnic identity of killers and victims of Mekranoti warfare.

(a) the captives taken by Mekrãgnoti warriors :

	Kubekryt Δ O		Yudja Δ O		Kuruaya Δ O		Munduruku Δ O		Tapirape Δ O		Panara Δ O		Kayapo Δ O		TOTAL Δ O	
1905-1935	3	4	1	2	1	1	0	2	0	0	4	10	0	7	9	26
1936-1952	1	6	0	0	0	0	0	0	1	2	0	0	6	7	8	15
1953-1966	0	0	0	0	0	0	0	0	0	0	0	0	0	0	0	0
1967-1981	0	0	0	0	0	0	0	0	0	0	2	3	0	0	2	3
Total	4	10	1	2	1	1	0	2	1	2	6	13	6	14	19	44
	14		3		2		2		3		19		20		63	

(b) the victims of Mekrãgnoti aggression :

(*) estimation based on the impact of the 1967 attack.

	Kubekryt Δ O		Yudja Δ O		Tapirape Δ O		Panara Δ O		Kayapo Δ O		TOTAL Δ O	
1905-1935	3	4	1	0	0	0	27*	3*	2	3	33	10
1936-1952	7	9	0	0	0	3	4	0	8	0	19	12
1953-1966	1	0	0	0	0	0	1	0	0	0	2	0
1967-1981	33	0	0	0	0	0	27	3	0	0	60	3
Total	44	13	1	0	0	3	59	6	10	3	114	25
	57		1		3		65		13		139	

(c) the ethnic identity of those who have killed Mekrãgnoti individuals :

	Kubekryt Δ O		Yudja Δ O		Panara Δ O		Kayapo Δ O		TOTAL Δ O	
1905-1935	5	0	2	0	9	7	4	1	20	8
1936-1952	24	4	0	0	4	4	13	4	41	12
1953-1966	5	0	0	0	3	2	10	2	18	4
1967-1981	1	0	0	0	0	0	0	0	1	0
Total	35	4	2	0	16	13	27	7	80	24
	39		2		29		34		104	

their tribal territory; the Mekranoti constantly moved inside in their tribal territory, occasionally moving to sites as far as hundred and fifty kilometres from the previously inhabited village. While this mobility permitted a constant control over their territory, the considerable mobility related to warfare undoubtedly led to a vast knowledge of huge parts of Central Brazil. Some groups of warriors remained out of the village for periods of over a year. Such groups were usually mainly composed of *menõrõnyre* who, due to their unmarried status, were not as yet burdened by the economic responsibilities of supporting a nuclear family. Going from one site to another, raiding or not, these groups often covered enormous distances, up to six hundred kilometres from the village.

This explorational sense was not limited to geographical discovery or the love of warfare, but also reflected a desire to learn about other cultures. Whether through direct or indirect contact, the Mekranoti have frequently maintained trading relations with several *kubẽkakrit* tribes, and also intended to do so with the Brazilians before "pacification" — e.g., the incident of 1942, when the Mekranoti tried to establish trading relationships with the Brazilians. By maintaining such contacts, they acquired primary materials or ornaments, obtained trade goods, and learned songs and dances. After some time of more or less peaceful contacts, however, these relations usually turned into overt hostility. Lévi-Strauss (1943: 138) referred to the relationship between exchange and hostility as follows:

> *...in South America, conflicts and economic exchanges not only constitute two types of coexisting relations, rather they are two opposed and indissoluble aspects of a single and identical process.*

Hostile relations would be the consequence of unfortunate trading transactions.

Whether through peaceful or hostile relations, the Mekranoti contemplated the achievement of the same elements of ritual importance: ornaments (or, more specifically, *õ nêkrêx*), songs and ritual expressions. All these elements were incorporated in Mekranoti ritual life, and became the property of that man who introduced the ornament/song/ceremony into the community. The *kwỳrỳkangô* naming ceremony, for example, was introduced by Kajngàrti (App. B: 14) in about 1895. In an initial stage, the right to sponsor this ceremony was restricted to his residential segment by birth. It was only in about 1915, when the performance of this ceremony was altered through suggestions of two Yudja female captives, that the right to sponsor this ceremony was extended to any and all residential segments.

Another individual achievement related to the participation in raids on Brazilian and *kubẽkakrit* settlements is that of becoming recognized as an esteemed warrior; in this way status and prestige increases within the community.

8.2 — The warrior's misfortune

In general, the number of warriors who died during a raid was not high, being rarely higher than one or two. Due, however, to repeated fighting in certain late pre-contact eras, the mortality rate of adult men was remarkably high and had important consequences for the demographic profile of the community (see table 6c). In the pre-1936 era, for example, sixty-three deaths were recorded among the adults, forty (sixty-three percent) of which were male[22]. Of these forty, no less than thirteen (thirty-two percent) deaths were directly related to warfare — whether during attacks or during counter-attacks. Similarly, in the period from 1936 to 1955, of the two hundred and two deaths that were recorded among the adults, hundred and twenty-nine (sixty-four percent) were male and forty-four (thirty-four percent) were due to warfare[23]. In both pre-contact periods, over thirty percent of the deaths of mature men was related to warfare. Participation in raids, therefore, involved considerable risks and simultaneously provoked violent counter-attacks. Both these war-related expressions led to an increased male mortality rate.

Yet, although participation in warfare was often used as an instrument to improve prestige, the individual accomplishment of effectively killing an enemy during aggressions did not necessarily lead to the acquisition of such a status. For, in warfare, the act of killing an enemy rarely becomes an individual achievement. It is a Kayapo custom for several warriors to "participate" in the killing of one single enemy. When, during an attack, a Kayapo man either succeeds in seriously injuring an enemy (e.g., with a spear or with a shot of his bow or firearm) or manages to knock down an enemy with strikes of his club, several other warriors join the man in beating the enemy to death with clubs. Other warriors, who are too distant from the scene at such a mo-

---

22   My data often lack specification on causes of death and I therefore considered it more appropriate to use Werner's data (1980: 49-50).

23   It is striking that in both these pre-contact periods nearly twice as many men are reported to have died than women. This higher male mortality rate cannot exclusively be attributed to the consequences of warfare. Rather, it is the result of the combined risks and dangers related to warfare *as well as* to other male activities such as hunting, trekking or fishing, where men are more frequently and more openly exposed to the dangers of the environment, to accidents and to sickness than women, whose activities are concentrated in or near the village.

ment, may later club the body of the already slain victim. The result of this procedure is that, as Banner (1961: 23) observed, the body of a victim of Kayapo aggression usually becomes mutilated due to the numerous strikes given with clubs, either during or after the killing. This particular way of accomplishment explains the following aspects of Mekranoti warfare:

— While discussing the killing of an enemy, informants usually paid no attention at all to who exactly was the "effective killer". This act is, indeed, of no importance to the Mekranoti since the victim is not killed by a single warrior, but rather by the corporate group of warriors, each of whom struck the victim with their club. The "effective killer" is, however, the man who appropriates the belongings of the victim;

— All, or nearly all of the Mekranoti warriors who participate in a raid are reckoned to have "killed", and this irrespective of the number of effective victims, since all warriors shared in the slaying of the victims;

— Informants stated that, regardless of whether having effectively killed an enemy or not, all warriors who had participated in a particular war received tattoo marks (*kwakbê*) during the post-war ritual (see Chapter 4). This reflects the informants' ideal conception that all men had participated in killing.

Killing an enemy during warfare is ideally conceived as a corporate group accomplishment and can therefore not really be employed as a means to improve personal prestige. Yet, the Kayapo do distinguish people who have killed a lot; these are referred to as *mebĩdjwỳnh*[24] *("real killers")*. The term is, however, used in a derogatory sense. "Real killers" are those men who have killed members of their own community, usually during club-fights. Since club-fights endanger the unity of the community, this kind of accomplishment is not always an instrument of improved status. Several older Mekranoti men were occasionally referred to as "real killers" by some informants, but all Mekranoti seemed to agree to the fact that Kôkôjàmti, Ku'at and Kenti, for example, were *mebĩdjwỳnh*; Kôkôjàmti was a young chief of one of the men's societies in the Gorotire village of 1935, and after having killed some men during internal village disputes, he was accused of sorcery (*udjy*) and eventually expelled from that village; Ku'at and Kenti were Mekranoti leaders in about 1940-1947, and after killing some men during internal strife, they were driven out of the village.

Some informants mentioned that Kenti, Ku'at and Kôkôjàmti were

---

24   A plural term in use is *meparidjwỳnh* ("the real killer"). *Pa-ri* is a plural form of (*ku*)*bĩ* and consequently refers to repeated killings.

"no real chiefs" (*bẽnjadjwỳr djwỳnh ket*), since they lacked the necessary training by an older village chief as well as formal installation in that office. Rather, they were considered leaders who occupied a strong position because they were feared by other people. The Kayapo refer to this as *uma kôt meoba*, literally "leading because feared".

Yet, Mekranoti history shows not only that some leaders were expelled, but also that several important chiefs such as Kubẽdjàgogo and Tàpjêt had been killed by tribesmen. This observation leads us to my earlier analysis on the ambiguity of the office of chieftaincy. On the one hand, chiefs are expected to be bellicose and aggressively affirmative to conduct their men's society, and on the other hand they are expected to act as appeasers to maintain the unity within their men's society as well as within the community as a whole. Most chiefs tend to specialize in one of these two roles. Kenti, Ku'at and Kôkôjàmti — whether "real chiefs" or not — are cases of leading men who were overly aggressive in conducting their position and winning respect.

These three men also had not only regularly fought the enemy, but had also often antagonized members of the opposing men's societies within the community. The result was that in these cases, the community expelled these leaders as well as those men who were inclined to follow them. Clastres (1980: 210) states that

> *War, no more than peace, does not allow a chief to act as a chief... if a chief tries to impose his own desire for war upon the community, he will be abandoned by the community. This, because the community wants to follow its own collective and free will, and does not want to submit itself to the law of a longing for power. In the best of the cases, one turns his back on a chief who wants to `act as a chief'; in the worst of the cases, he is killed.*

And it is in this view that the expulsion of Kenti, Ku'at and Kôkôjàmti can be understood. But field data gathered among the Mekranoti proves that these cases were not the only ones, or by far the most extreme: out of the twelve chiefs who died in the period from 1910 to 1955, no less than five were killed by tribesmen during club-fights or during particularly violent incidents where even firearms were used. Following Clastres' line of thought, these killings of chiefs can be explained as cases where the political leaders in question transgressed their conferred offices. Instead of personifying the social desire of the community to remain undivided by maintaining a social equilibrium between the various political factions, they provoked disharmony and disequilibrium by imposing their personal ambition for bravery through instigating disputes. Bellicosity is a highly praised male value, but those men who did not control their nervousness about fighting and who regularly antagonized tribesmen, were either killed or expelled from the community.

9. WARFARE AND VILLAGE STABILITY

In the course of this century, the Mekranoti have been extremely mobile, even by Kayapo standards. In the period from 1910 to 1956, an average of one move per year was recorded and the longest successive period the Mekranoti lived in one village was two and a half years.

Things were different in the nineteenth century. All contemporary Kayapo of the Xingu villages are descendant of *pykatôti*. This historic Kayapo village was located in the savannah east of the upper Riozinho River. Posey visited the site of the ancient *pykatôti* village. He estimated the diameter of the village circle of residential houses at one thousand and fifty meters (!) and concluded that at one time about three thousand seven hundred to five thousand four hundred Indians must have lived there (Posey 1979a: 56). At the time of his visit in 1979, the depth of paths in *pykatôti* at some places reached about fifteen centimetres. This is indicative of the long occupancy of this village — an observation which is confirmed in the ethno-historic survey (Chapter 2), where I mentioned that *pykatôti* must have been occupied from about 1870 (or earlier?) to about 1935. More important, however, is the observation that the Kayapo of the Xingu did not suffer any village schism in the period from around 1840 to 1905. Data on Mekranoti mobility and village schisms throughout this century are therefore not congruent with data available on *pykatôti*. In this section I will endeavour to analyse this phenomenon and will argue that warfare is at the basis of the noted dissimilarities. Accordingly, in this section I will be mainly concerned with the social implications of warfare to Kayapo society.

In the view of my proposed analysis, the period from 1943 to 1947 is of particular interest because it undoubtedly figures among the most tempestuous epochs in Mekranoti history. This period was ushered in by the assassination of Tàpjêt and ended with the permanent breakup of the village. The period was characterized by a constant succession of internal disputes, as well as by a frequent rearrangement of political factions. The men's societies seemed very unstable, since, during the five years in question, political factions were altered on four occasions. Out of fear of being killed, many men constantly changed membership in the men's groups, and a more or less definite arrangement of the men's associations came about only after 1947 and after that the more combative group (the

Northern Mekranoti, mainly composed of Tàpjêt's followers) was expelled. In this period, too, not a single raid was undertaken, in complete contrast with the preceding years. Similarly, in spite of the fact that the Kubenkranken-Kokraimoro almost continuously engaged in warfare in the period from 1940 to 1957, no wars were undertaken in 1949-1950 when internal disputes proved frequent. This lack of warfare is probably a direct consequence of the political instability, where the community's unity proved fragile.

In order to perceive what might have led to such a period of internal disputes, village instability and a total absence of raids, it is useful to focus on the occurrences preceding Tàpjêt's assassination. Or, in other words, what happened before Tàpjêt's death that might have led to social disorder?

I have mentioned earlier that Tàpjêt had revealed himself as an ardent war leader while still living among the Gorotire. Upon arriving among the Mekranoti, he continued raiding as he had done before. This led to a sudden increase in the number of raids undertaken by the Mekranoti. Indeed, during the five years that Tàpjêt was living among the Mekranoti (from 1937 to 1942), six attacks were mounted against the Brazilians and one against the Kubenkranken. In the five years preceding Tàpjêt's arrival, the Mekranoti had only undertaken a single attack, *in casu* against the Brazilians.

Tàpjêt's arrival thus led to a sudden increase in the number of raids undertaken by the Mekranoti. And this escalation of warfare has to be taken as one of the most immediate causes of village instability. A detailed survey of ethno-historical data on intragroup and intergroup conflicts and fissions indicates a strong correlation between warfare and intergroup cohesion; Mekranoti ethno-history shows that periods marked by the intensification of raids are usually followed by periods of internal conflicts which, in their turn, often lead to schisms in the community. This is not entirely congruous with the view of Clastres who said that "when war stops, then the heart of the primitive society stops beating" (Clastres 1980: 203). The increase in warfare greatly affected Kayapo village stability in the sense that intensification of warfare brought about the gradual segmentation of the community; escalation of intergroup conflict led to an increase of intragroup disputes. A high military activity therefore seemed inconsistent with village stability.

At this point, it is important to repeat that over sixty-five percent of all Mekranoti raids in the course of this century were carried out against Brazilians. In an earlier section, I have drawn attention to the fact that the acquisition of booty (or, more specifically, of firearms and ammunition)

192 — GUSTAAF VERSWIJVER

figured as the main goal of such raids. Yet, since attacks against Brazilians were only undertaken on a regular basis from the early twentieth century on, it is reasonable to assume that the escalation of Kayapo warfare is a recent phenomenon. Accordingly, the Kayapo were far less "warlike" in the nineteenth century and their villages were, consequently, more stable in periods before the early twentieth century.

Frequent raiding of Brazilian settlements therefore had a disruptive effect on Kayapo society. Surely, raids against other Kayapo groups (such as the Xikrin and the Ira'amranh) and against the *kubēkakrit* (non-Gê) Indians were undertaken before the early twentieth century, but were rather infrequent; this raiding pattern therefore didn't have the same disruptive effect. But there was an additional distinction, since internal war was characterized by a demonstration of social cohesion.

Considering the period from 1920 to 1955 for the Mekranoti, and the period from 1941 to 1955 for the Kokraimoro, we have data on eleven fusions between different Kayapo subgroups (see Appendix A). In six of these cases, the fusion was immediately followed by the performance of a major naming ceremony; in the five others, it was directly followed by a raid. Of these five raids, four were undertaken against other Kayapo groups or against the Panara; the fifth was against the Brazilians. What the performance of a major ceremony and the undertaking of an attack have in common is that they promote unity within the community. Murphy (1957: 1034) noted that warfare is "an especially effective means of promoting social cohesion in that it provides an occasion upon which the members of the society unite and submerge their factional differences in the vigorous pursuit of a common purpose". If fusions were often followed by raids against other Kayapo groups or against the Panara and not against the non-Gê tribes or the Brazilians, this can be explained by the fact that, in Kayapo society, the submersion of factional differences during warfare can only be effected during the raids on these two particular enemies since, it should be recalled, these are the sole instances when the several men's societies form an alliance to jointly meet the enemy.

But, in such cases of raids where nearly all men jointly participate, the unity between the several men's societies is not only expressed in the concerted participation in the venture, but likewise by the ritual performed before leaving the village. This ritual is usually referred to as *ngryk-'ã tor* ("dance to become angry") or as *kru-wa'ã tor* ("dance of the arrows")[25]. The social importance of dances and the successive attacks

---

25   Radcliffe-Brown (1933: 252-253) also viewed the social function of the pre-warfare dances in Andaman Island communities as an intensification of the collective

can be understood as promoting the social cohesion of the community.

In addition to these expressions of unity between the existing men's societies, there was another cause for attacking other Kayapo groups after a fusion: the integration of the fusing group. To explain this remark, it is important to look at the mechanism of village schisms and it is useful, at this point, to distinguish between two types of schisms: temporary and permanent ones.

At times, groups may leave to remain away from the main village for one or (many) more years. These temporary separations may be effected to diminish tension within the community, may occur when a splinter group desires to live closer to a *kubēkakrit* village, or may result when a splinter group flees out of fear for an enemy attack. The main characteristics of these peaceful temporary splits are that they are usually not the consequence of a collective club-fight and that the separated group usually returns to live in the main village after a certain period.

Permanent separations, however, are more drastic occurrences. As mentioned in Chapter 1, persistent disputes within a Kayapo community often result in collective club-fights where two men's associations or age-sets confront one another in physical combat. In some cases, tension in the village becomes so high that the group which is vanquished during a collective club-fight leaves the village and establishes a new independent village. Informants often relate such instances to disputes over adultery. This can be explained by the disruptive faculty of adulterous relations. Turner (1987ms: 29-30) states that one of the major threats to the internal harmony and peaceful relations between the men's associations of a given community is posed by the individual relations of their members to women and to particular nuclear families. Disputes over adultery may therefore threaten the balance between the domestic and communal institutional levels of Kayapo society.

Yet, adultery is a quite common feature in Kayapo communities, as are club-duels between two (or a few) men. The question can therefore be raised as to why in some cases such disputes did lead to collective club-fights, and not in others. Upon closer examination, ethno-historical data seem to indicate that several of the major schisms coincided with a far greater danger, one that was induced by forces alien to the community. Indeed, many major schisms coincided with periods where either contacts with members of the national society were approaching or where such contacts had been recently established. Numerous statements by in-

hatred against the enemy and as a stimulation of the community's unity in the spirit of each warrior.

formants demonstrate that the so-called "pacification" (i.e., the occasion when peaceful contact was made with Whites) was often followed by a period of severe tension within the community. The same was true when the Mekranoti entered into peaceful relations with the Yudja in the late nineteenth Century; on that occasion, the Mekranoti actually separated from the main Gorotire group, leading to a tenuous relationship between these two Kayapo groups.

Tension seemed particularly high, however, in the period *preceding* contact with the national society; several major village schisms[26] actually occurred in the period just before contact was established. It is evident that contact with the national society must have led to a tenuous situation, and this not only due to the startling prospect of making direct contact with someone who up to then was your enemy, but also to expectations on such an occasion. The tension in the community was probably magnified by an antagonism between those who were in favour of the contact and those who opposed it. Informants occasionally mentioned the dissension that arose between opponents and proponents to such contacts: opponents justified their attitude by referring to the great danger of diseases, while proponents did so by referring to the relative ease with which commodities could be obtained. This situation of incompatibility of interests was likely to lead to aggression and, in these circumstances, cases over adultery often developed into political issues.

Once a village suffered such a schism, the two groups continued to be reciprocally hostile; surprise attacks were then usually undertaken by the secessionist group that had been forced to leave, initiating in this way a process of occasional mutual attack. Instances where the separated group returned to live with the main group were observed but these were rather rare and usually resulted in a new separation some time later.

Ethno-historical data also show that small secessionist groups often preferred not to live apart, but rather to join another Kayapo group which lived on hostile terms with the one from whom they recently separated. This was particularly so when the split occurred along the lines of families rather than along the men's associations or age-sets, as was usually the case[27]. All the cases of fusions of two groups which had lived on hostile

26   I refer here to the following important schisms: between the Ira'amranh and Gorotire in about 1840; between the Central and Southern Mekranoti in 1953; and the breakdown of the main Gorotire village into four distinct communities (Gorotire, Kubenkranken, Kararaô and Menokanê) in 1935-1937.

27   The following were instances where Mekranoti secessionist groups were mainly composed of people from one or two families: the group led by Karànhĩn (mainly composed of Karànhĩn's affin and by the kin of Bàka'ê, a trainee by Karànhĩn

terms obviously led to a very tense situation. That is why it was common for members of the arriving group to participate actively in ceremonial life by co-sponsoring a naming ceremony[28] immediately after settling in the embracing community. In other cases, the arriving group often insisted on a joint attack against the group from which they had just separated: i.e., the group which had become their common enemy. Both performances were undertaken in order to secure their integration into the embracing community. Clastres refers to this relationship between warfare and internal stability in the following terms:

> To be able to think in the form of Us, the community has to be at one and the same time undivided (one) and independent (totality); the internal oneness and the external opposition are linked: each one is conditional upon the other. (Clastres 1980: 203)

This "union" was not always achieved since fusions between two groups didn't always work out: some instances are known where the fusions simply failed, others where the arriving group was not accepted. Of the three Mekranoti groups that returned to the Kubenkranken in 1941-1959, the ones led by Karànhĩn and Ku'at were at first integrated but left the Kubenkranken village again a few years later, giving origin to the Kokraimoro; the one led by Kremôr was almost entirely massacred. Likewise, the Mekranoti did not always accept approaching groups: the Kararaô wanted to join them but were chased away; the groups led by Tàpjêt and Kenti were accepted, but Kenti himself was banished.

To summarize these reflections, it can be said that, in contradistinction to the numerous centrifugal forces of Kayapo society, where the ties of solidarity are weak and easily surpassed by internal disputes, internal war (against the Kayapo and the Panara) is a means of assuring social cohesion. It is the type of warfare in which all adult men of a village participate and which involves a lot on the symbolic level. This observation fits the distinction made earlier in this Chapter between this type of warfare and external war, the one which aims at the acquisition of commodities, exotic artifacts and ritual objects, which involves only a small group of warriors and which, once escalated, had a disruptive effect on Kayapo society. Similarly, the prospect of direct contacts with non-Gê groups (whether Brazilians or *kubẽkakrit*) seems to have disrupted

---

into chieftaincy); the group led by Nhôjkrã (mainly composed by Nhôjkrã's kin); and the group led by Kremôr (mainly composed by Kremôr's kin).

28   In addition to the political aspect related to integration, this act of co-sponsoring a naming ceremony with members of the embracing group also brought about the integration of the arriving nuclear families in the extended families of the embracing group.

Kayapo society on some occasions.

And it is in view of these observations that I can explain village stability in periods prior to the early twentieth century. *Pykatôti* was the last village the Kayapo of the Xingu occupied before the arrival of the Brazilian colonists in the very first years of this century. It was, therefore, the last pre-contact village occupied before the escalation of raiding. It was, as such, also the last pre-contact village to be occupied for a great number of years.

CHAPTER IV

THE RITUAL OF THE RETURNING WARRIORS

"...the body, affirmed or negated, painted or perforated, pro-
tected or devoured, always tends to occupy a central position
in the vision the Indian societies have of the nature of the human being." (Seeger, Da Matta & Viveiros de Castro 1979:2)

Research on the relation between the body and the symbolism of body
ornamentation has been of continuing anthropological interest. Mauss
(1936:352) argued that the human body and its substances can be taken as
a man's primary "objet-technique" for expressing cultural values, while
Lévi-Strauss (1945), departing from a set of Caduveo body paintings and
tattoos, reconstructed the social and cultural context of such decorations
in that society. In a more broader perspective, Douglas (1966) and Victor
Turner (1967) argued that the ornaments of the body and its substances
are important symbol referents which, as Douglas demonstrated, may
reveal a close relation between the treatment of body and social structure.
The set of body ornaments used indeed defines a people as a group, i.e.
as a unity different from the "others".

More recently, several authors have discussed such body ornamentation as body paintings, lip-disks, earplugs, hairstyles and penis sheaths
of various Central Brazilian Gê groups: Müller (1976) on the Xavante;
Seeger (1975) on the Kisedje (Suya); Vidal (1978, 1981) on the Kayapo-
Xikrin and Terence Turner (1969, 1980) on the Kayapo in general. T.

Turner (1969:59) stated that

> Lip plug, earplugs, penis sheath, hairstyle, cotton leg and arm
> bands, and body painting make up a symbolic language that ex-
> presses a wide range of information about social status, sex, and
> age. As a language, however, it does more than merely communi-
> cate this information from one individual to another: at a deeper
> level, it establishes a channel of communication within the indi-
> vidual between the social and biological aspects of his personality.

Following this line of thought, I will discuss the ritual performed on the
occasion of the return of the Kayapo warriors. A return which is marked
not only by a set of various body ornamentations which distinguish the
different age grades and parallel the male developmental cycle, but also
by a specific restriction period. This Chapter is, as such, mainly concerned
with the construction of the individual as social actor. The following
analysis of the post-war restriction period not only allows us to clearly see
in the symbolic importance of warfare in Kayapo society, but also to approach several aspects of Kayapo social structure in a more detailed way.

To begin this Chapter, I will first furnish a description of the ritual
performed by the warriors upon returning to the village after an attack.
The following analysis deals with tattoo marks, body painting, hairstyle
and hair ornaments. In a final section, the relationship between the post-
war ritual and rituals performed on other occasions is provided.

1. THE RITUAL ON THE RETURN OF KAYAPO WARRIORS[1]

The returning warriors erect a forest camp (*adjôre*) at a distance of about
ten kilometres from the village. From there, two men are sent to go and
spy upon the village. Unseen, both men check upon village activities —
e.g., to see if any ceremony is being performed — and if the village is still
occupied. This act is called *meàpkàr-o tẽn* and on the men's return to their
fellows in the forest, they give an account of what they were able to record.

1.1 — The first day

The following day, early in the morning, the warriors leave the forest
camp to undertake the last stretch of their long and dangerous venture. In
their pierced earlobes, they wear some babassu (*Orbignia sp.*) palm seeds,
and a necklace (*õkretã*) of different types of strings around the neck. Ar-

---

1   As I never witnessed this ritual, the following section is based exclusively on
descriptions provided by a few senior informants.

riving near the village site, they dance the *mengre-re prõ-ne ba*, while singing the *mekurwỳk* song[2]. This song is sung in falsetto, allowing it to be heard at great distances. For each enemy, a specific *mekurwỳk* song exists and by singing the one corresponding to the enemy encountered, the villagers are notified whether the attack has been undertaken and whether the raid was successful or not. Upon hearing the *mekurwỳk*, the women go and meet the approaching men in order to take their load (*jêj*) and bring it to the village. This allows the returning men to continue their ritual entrance in the village merely carrying their weapons.

Near the village, the men set up a campsite outside the village circle and paint each other entirely black using charcoal. The motif is called *amĩtyk*. The men also put on a headband of dried palm leaves. The *me-mydjêny-re* — that is, those adolescents who have received their penis sheath during this particular expedition — are then sent to the village in order to hand over the babassu palm seeds they carry in their pierced earlobes to their "substitute spouse" (*krô-'ã prõ*).

When these boys return, the men take up their weapons as well as a particular type of club called *akêtêtyk*. Singing the *mekurwỳk*, they enter the village in a single file: the youngest (*me'ôk-re*) go in front, followed by the boys who just received their penis sheath (*memydjêny-re*), the *menõrõny-re* and finally the men with children in wedlock and the elder men. Upon reaching the men's house, they form a set of concentric circles (the youngest in the inner circle, the eldest in the outer one) and at the end of the song, the chief performs the ritual *bẽn*. The men then enter the men's house to meet those who have not joined them on their venture.

One by one, the women come to fetch their husbands, sons or brothers and lead them to their houses, where they proceed to the ritual wailing called *aben jabêj mu-wa* ("crying to each other in a questioning form"). During this wailing, the events that occurred during the warrior's absence are related. In an act of intimacy and intense social care, the women then start delousing (*ngô-re kanhã*) their arriving relatives.

By noon, the warriors take a bath to remove the black charcoal body paint and return to the house of their relatives to be painted slightly red all over with urucu (anatto). This body painting is called *ràràr*. In addition, the *memydjêny-re* have their face painted red by the *krô-'ã prõ* ("substitute spouse") to whom they gave the babassu palm seeds earlier that day.

Early in the afternoon, all warriors meet at the village plaza, in front

---

2   This song is also sung on a number of other occasions, such as the men's return from a trek in the forest or when a man returns to the village from a successful hunt. For each occasion, a specific song exists (Verswijver 1988: 15-20; 1989: 39, 46).

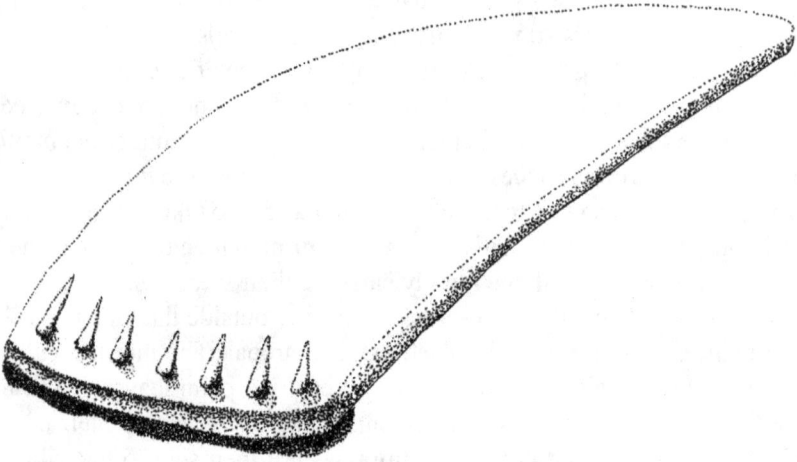

Figure 15 — A *tepdjua* scarificator: teeth of the piranha or another vora-
cious fresh-water fish glued in a gourd segment.

of the men's house, where the eldest of the participants recite the occurrences of their venture to those who had remained in the village. Meanwhile, one of the warriors takes a basket and goes from house to house
asking for food, which is then taken to the men's house.

When all are reassembled in the men's house, a specialist starts tat-
tooing the warriors. Regardless of whether the person has killed an enemy
or not, all warriors receive tattoo marks (*mekwakbê*) on their chest. These
consist of a series of short parallel lines, running horizontally from near the
shoulder unto the stomach at the side of the navel. The specialists use the
scarificator (*tepdjwa*, "fish teeth" — see figure 16) to make the incisions;
charcoal is rubbed on the wounds to leave permanent, fine black lines.

At sunset, the warriors gather in front on the men's house. Seated on
palm leaves, they sing the *mengre-re prõt ariba*. While singing, a few men
earlier designated as "really pitiful people" (*meuatĩdjwnh*)[3] come out of
the men's house, go to the easternmost house of the village circle and start
dancing towards a house on the opposite side. From there, they continue
dancing criss-cross around the village plaza, visiting all the houses. Upon

3   This ritual function is not transmitted, nor does it involve any form of training.
Informants stated that the ritual duty of the *meuatĩdjwỹnh* is always performed by a
man who, at the time of the performance and for one reason or another, is recognized as
passing a particularly unfavorable phase in his life, e.g. when temporarily unmarried or
when temporarily out of luck during hunting.

returning to the men's house, the men's singing stops.

That night, each warrior of the age grade of "men with children" (*mekra-re*) sleeps in his wife's house. The *menõrõny'ãtũm*, if already having a "real spouse" (*prõ djwỳnh*) may do so too; if not, they will sleep in the men's house, just like the younger boys (*me'ôk-re* and *memydjêny-re*) as well as the men whose wives are far advanced in pregnancy (*metujarô rax*) and the men whose wives have recently given birth (*mekrakarà-re*). The latter, as well as the *menõrõny'ãtũm*, may leave at night and have sexual intercourse with their "substitute spouses" (*krô-'ã prõ*).

1.2 — The second day

Early in the morning, before sunrise, the singing of the *mengre-re prõt ariba* is repeated outside the men's house. After this short ritual, the warriors go bathing together and, once more, apply the *amĩtyk* ("entirely black body") painting with charcoal. They each don a headband of dried palm leaves (*krãdjêjamy*, "headband with a tail") and have little white feather down glued on their hair (*krãjamĩ*).

Some men leave the men's house. They simply walk in front of the houses constituting the village circle: some walk clockwise, others counter clockwise. This is called "wandering next to the houses" (*kikre kabe-'ã ajkame*) and is performed in order to advise all men to unite in the men's house. Once united, an elderly man then selects two men to lead the following dance. Leaving the men's house, both the selected men dance side by side towards the house opposite the main entrance of the men's house. At intervals, pairs of men join them. Gradually, a long double file of dancers is constituted. The dancers visit all houses, proceeding crisscross around the village plaza.

After this *mengre-re prõt ariba* dance, all men gather in front of the men's house where, standing in concentric circles — once again, the youngest in the centre and the eldest at the periphery — they perform a brief dance called "the dance of the *tàkàk*" (*tàkàk-'ã tor*)[4]. The palm leaf headbands are then gathered, by the men who have inherited the specific right to do so, and are hung up on the poles of the men's house. After this dance, all dancers go to the river to bathe in order to remove the black body paint.

1.3 — The next three days

During two or three consecutive days, the warriors spend the daytime in

---

4   The dancing and the tune of the songs are identical to the ones song during the final phase of the *tàkàk* naming ceremony; the lyrics are, however, different.

their campsite outside the village circle. They observe severe food taboos and return to the village only at night to sleep.

1.4 — The sixth day

In the early morning, gathered in their campsites, the warriors say "now we can paint, as our tattoo is dry" and then go bathing to be newly painted.

The men first prepare the genipap dye in their campsite. Then, in single file, they go to the men's house. Carrying their weapons — guns, bows and arrows or clubs — and adorned with the colourful *meàkkà* head-dresses, they make a spiral around the men's house and finally stand in front of it, still in a single row, with their back to that house. This ritual is called "the dance for the *kakôkreti* painting" (*mekakôkreti kadjy ban tor*). After standing there for a while, immobile, the men disperse to have their body painted with the black genipap dye. This body painting, however, is applied in two phases: initially, i.e., at this particular stage, the *kakô'ôk* is applied. This painting consists of a black part from the neck down to the upper part of the chest and is applied by different categories of kins-women, and in different sites. The boys of the *me'ôk-re* age grade, the youngsters who have recently received their penis sheath (*memydjêny-re*) and the adolescents of the *menõrõny-re* age grade, first have their hair shaven by a kinswoman. They then go to the campsite to get painted with the genipap dye which has been prepared earlier that morning: the *menõrõny-re* paint each other, while the other boys get painted by their "substitute father" (*krô'ãbãm*). None of these boys or adolescents get facial paint. For those married men of the *mekra-re* age grade who have not killed an enemy during the raid, it is applied at their wife's house. These men also get an additional *inhykangã* painting on their cheeks. Those men who have killed an enemy have the painting applied by women who had a kinsman (*õbikwa*) killed by members of that specific inimical group which has just been raided.

When all warriors, duly painted, are gathered at the campsite again, the men of a given men's society once more perform the *mekakôkreti ban tor*. On their return, the members of the other men's society repeat the ritual.

Once all are reunited in the campsite, the *menõrõny'ãtũm* put on their *ità* ornament, while the women come to the campsite. It is only at this stage that the body painting of the warriors is completed. This completion is done by first painting the body entirely black with genipap dye — con-tinuing, as such, the already applied *kakô'ôk* — and then by removing with the finger nail a line on the chest. The painting is completed by the same person who earlier that day applied the upper part.

In addition, the senior *menõrõny 'ãtũm* glue the upper hair of the newly incorporated *menõrõny-re* and put it upright. This particular hairstyle is referred to as "the upper hair that stands upright" (*jô kàj-mã krãkàdja*) and is, as the Indians say, an imitation of the bird crest of a *Cracidae* species. All *menõrõny 'ãtũm* then have a painting on the cheeks which continues down to the lips (*inhy-'ã tepre 'i*) applied by kinswomen.

The newly introduced *memydjêny-re* get a black facial paint known as *ngôkraxkôkjêr*. It is applied by their "substitute father". This is, in fact, the last time the adolescent is painted by his "substitute father": this occasion is the rite of passage from the *me 'ôk-re* age grade to the one of the *menõrõny-re*. After the painting, the "substitute father" gives a short speech during which he states that the boys is big enough to paint himself now. The *me 'ôk-re* boys have a specific additional decoration in which the open spaced line on their chest is painted red with urucu. They also have a small red facial paint referred to as *py-'ã ajtẽnk* (see figure 17a). Concluding these facial and body paintings, all warriors have their feet painted red with urucu (*teino*, "red legs") and this is done once again by the person who has started painting the warrior.

Then the two men's societies and their affiliated youngsters will once again go to the village. They do so successively — one men's society after the other — while dancing and singing the *mekakôkreti ban tor*. Yet, this time they do not return to the campsite but rather enter the men's house where they join those men who have not gone along on the raid. Reunited, all men — warriors and others — collectively perform the *àkjêr-o prõt* dance. On this occasion, the men who had not joined the raid do not wear any specific painting or headdress.

About a week later, when the *kakôkreti* paint has disappeared, another painting with the black genipap dye is applied to the warriors: the *pàtjarape 'ôk* (see figure 17b) This occasion indicates the end of the restriction period for warriors returning from a raid.

2. BLOOD AND TATTOO MARKS

The day of the warriors' return to the village is characterized by a brief but conspicuous ritual during which all the warriors of the expedition gather in the men's house to receive tattoo marks (*kwakbê*). Making use of a scarificator, a male specialist applies two series of short, horizontal incisions on the warriors' chest: two rows running in the form of a V from the shoulders to the navel. The incisions may be superficial but are still deep enough to be painful and to bleed profusely. Charcoal is rubbed on the cuttings leaving fine, permanent scars across the chest when healed.

And so, still today, several of the older Mekranoti men present such tattoos. The application of this emblematic incision is evidently a distinctive mark for those men who have participated in one of the war expeditions; it marks his bravery and bellicosity. But there is more to it. I once witnessed the scraping of adolescents' thighs in the Mekranoti village. Before and after the application of the incisions on his fellow tribesmen, the specialist — an older man — went through a series of preparative and conclusive acts which struck me as markedly sacred. I was particularly impressed by the way the blood was dealt with.

Indeed, to the Kayapo, blood is a dangerous substance and dealing with blood requires specific attention. Several sorts of precautions are necessary and special handling codes are used by those who are (or have been) in close contact with it. The following examples illustrate the usage of such precautions and handling codes. After preparing and distributing the meat of a freshly slain animal, its blood is washed from the person's body as soon as possible, as the blood of a slain animal is seen to be not only dirty, but also to be an anti-social and perilous element, noxious when in contact with the human skin (T. Turner 1980:115). The hazards of such a situation are revealed in Kayapo mythology. One particular myth (Wilbert & Simoneau 1984:213) draws attention to this fact and relates how a man became berserk (*aibãn*)[5] after having had the blood of a tapir spilled on his skin. Running off into the forest, a metamorphosis took place with the man partly turning into a tapir and eventually having to be cured by a shaman who healed his skin with medicinal herbs.

As another example of the dangerous properties of blood, I vividly

5   Although often used in a mockingly and loose way to refer to people who intentionally or accidentally act foolishly, in a strict sense *aibãn* refers to a particular state of emotional and physical weakness. The most frequent cases of *aibãn* occur when a man suddenly becomes seriously ill, or after a prolonged illness, or again after some period of stress. The Kayapo say that the phenomenon becomes manifest through the person's incapacity to see clearly ("their eyes become fuzzy", *norã*). In it's most violent form a man may take his gun and start shooting wildly, sometimes even hitting someone. One Mekranoti man was injured in this fashion when his brother became *aibãn* and shot him in the face. After such moments of frenzy, a man usually runs off into the forest where he remains for a few days to return to the village "healed". Such an extreme case of "craziness" is referred to by the Kayapo as *ropkro-ri kam aibãn*, "the crazyness of the jaguar" (see also Moreira Neto 1965). Along with disease, death and the breaking of certain taboos, *aibãn* is conceived of as an improper form of eruption at the biological level of existence into the social, orderly level (T. Turner 1969:70).

recall an experience I had in the Central Mekranoti village in 1974, just a few weeks after arriving for the first time in the village. It was the kind of experience which, I imagine, many of my fieldwork colleagues share, because it involved a spontaneous reaction of the fieldworker to a situation in which tribal mores were unknowingly disrespected. A young girl, in the throes of giving birth, was unable to rid herself of the placenta causing a serious haemorrhage. Considering her as "almost dead"[6], no one paid any attention to the young mother. I was to visit the girl several times during the next days, giving her medicine and checking her constantly declining blood-pressure. This, although of little help, was accompanied by a daily bath which was all I could do: it would at least remove the blood and therefore diminish the heaps of flies and mosquitos surrounding the motionless body. When asked for help in these tasks, no one reacted; everyone stood around at a safe distance, observing and discussing my "courage". I went alone to cut fresh leaves for the girl to sleep on. Disappointed at the disinterest and lack of participation of the villagers, I was only later to perceive the Indians' acute aversion to blood: to the Kayapo, touching human blood is extremely risky. And this explains the Indians' "admiration" and astonishment towards my behaviour.

These examples show that different risks are involved according to the various degrees of human contact with blood. In a decreasing order of danger blood can be symbolically ingested, penetrate the body, be spilt on the skin and merely be touched. In addition, there is also a distinction between contact with human blood and contact with animal blood. Depending on a combination of these factors, contact may be more or less dangerous to a person's health. Carneiro da Cunha (1978:100-110) traces an excellent analysis between the interaction of the different levels of blood-related dangers as perceived in Krahô society — a closely related Gê group. She presents a chart showing the conditions under which contact with blood is to be regarded as a "transgression of limits", invariably leading to a subsequent and particular period of precautions. Carneiro da Cunha also shows that, in reference to Krahô society,

> ...the spilling of dangerous blood requires a restriction period but, due to the cases of illness, the reciprocal doesn't seem to be true: e.g., not all restriction periods are related to the spilling of blood. (ibid. 105)

These observations are equally valid for the Kayapo.

6   Although the mentioned Mekranoti girl died three days later, she was considered "already dead" by the other Indians. Such a person is placed outside society and is no longer given (medical) attention, save the attention which is given to the dead.

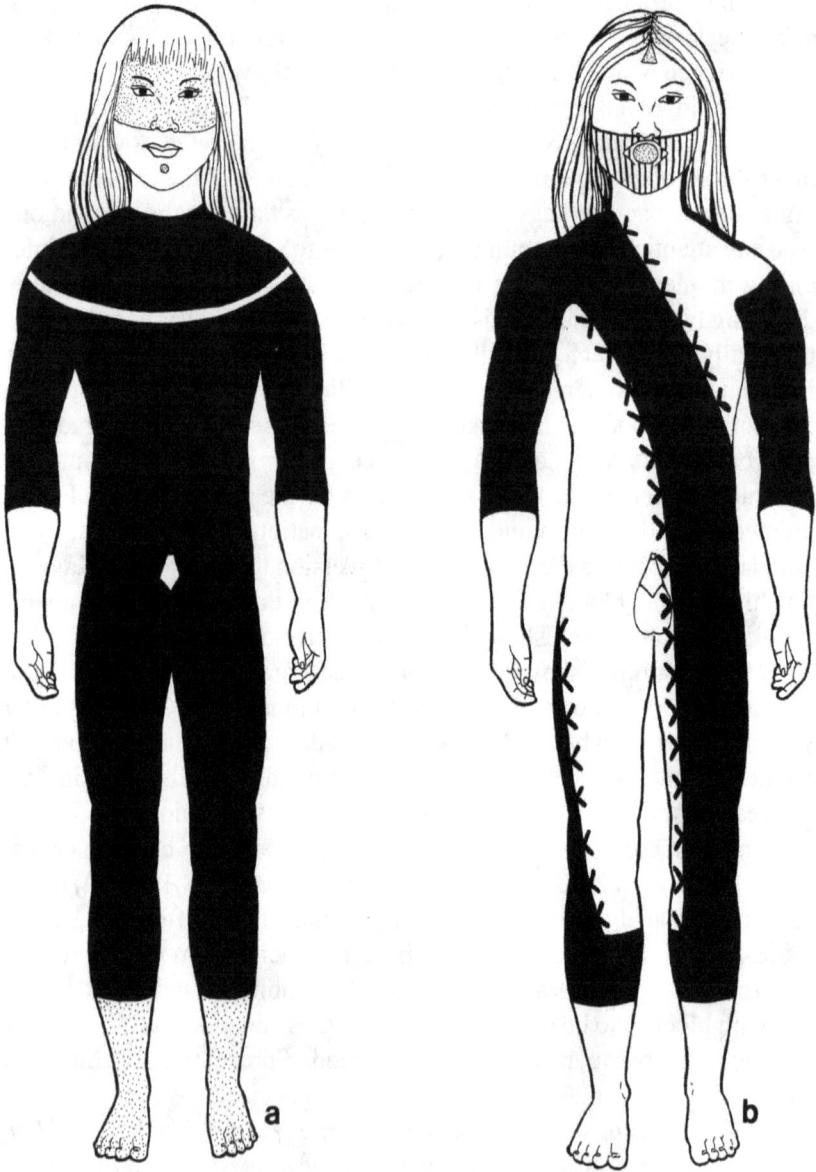

Figure 16 — Final phase of the reintegration process of the returning warriors. (a) a *me'ôk-re* boy (here symbollically wearing a penis sheath) with the black *kakôkreti* paint, and with reddened face and feet; (b) a *menõrõny'ãtũm* with the *pàtjarapê*, a handapplied "beautiful painting".

The relationship between ritual prohibitions dealing on one hand with human blood and, to a lesser degree, with animal blood on the other, is shown in various periods of restriction. Restriction (*jangri*, literally "to do restriction for") can be undertaken either as a prophylactic action to protect against certain influences, which a human being makes himself extremely vulnerable to in certain periods, or as a curative action. Depending on the cause which leads to such precautions, as well as the occasion and on the duration of the period of abstention, a restriction period may include food taboos, sexual taboos and the refraining from participation in ceremonies and other communal activities.

The restriction period which occurs after the "first menstruation" or "defloration" of a pubescent girl is, however, probably the most outstanding and explicit of them all. This event is called "the people's blood" (*mekamrô*)[7] and is performed when, upon awaking one early morning, a mother first discovers the blood of her daughter's menstrual effluvium. During the following three to six days, the girl and her "husband" remain under a mat of woven palm fibres, remaining motionless during the day[8]. Respecting severe food taboos, this ritual ends with a dance during which the husband is beautifully adorned and painted black in the *amĩtyk* design — typifying the conclusion of most restriction periods.

It is in this scheme of blood-related precautions and prohibitions that the post-war restrictions, as well as the application of tattoo marks, can be understood.

The particular precautions of returning Kayapo warriors in relation to human blood are illustrated in the following passage:

> ...back in the village... [the Xikrin] put stones in the middle of the village and each warrior seated himself in the sun, on one of these, leaning on a big stick. As such, the Indians say that they remained exposed to the sun to dry the blood of the [kubẽ] Indians, or to rid themselves of the blood of their enemies. (Vidal 1977:156)

In former times, the Xikrin also applied tattoos on their chest, although this custom has now disappeared. The relationship between the return of the warriors and a preoccupation with the enemy's blood, however, is indicative.

Although distinct in form and application procedures, the phenomenon of incising a warrior's body is widespread among the Central and Northern Gê groups: similar to the Kayapo, the Apinaye applied incisions to the

---

7   For a detailed description of the *mekamrô* ritual, see Banner (1961:11), Diniz (1962:25-26), Dreyfus (1963:55-56), T. Turner (1965:359-365) and Vidal (1977:160-161).
8   This ritual emphasizes the union of the couple. After copulating, the young man and woman are united by links of a common substance, blood.

warrior's chest (Nimuendajú 1956:97); the Krahô warriors scarified their arms and legs several times (Melatti 1978:124-126); the Xavante "killer bleeds himself making a series of lateral incisions across his chest and upper arms with the claw of an animal" (Maybury-Lewis 1974:282); and the Kisedje (Suya) warrior has his chest, back, legs and arms scraped with a sharpened tool (Seeger 1981:167). In all these variations, nevertheless, one central theme remains unchanged: the returning warrior — whether as an effective "killer" or not — has to bleed. It is indeed in the light of these Indians' notions on blood that the meaning of Kayapo *kwakbê* tattoos can be comprehended.

The Kayapo say that participants in war expeditions are affected or contaminated by the blood of their enemies — that is their victims — and that the tattoos are applied "to undo the strangers' blood" (*kubẽ kamrô apêx kadjy*) or, more specifically, "to undo the bad blood" (*kamrô punu apêx kadjy*). The scraping of the chest of Mekranoti warriors can thus be understood as a process similar to the one of drying the enemy's blood, as done by the Xikrin. Both procedures focus upon freeing the warrior from the enemy's "bad" blood, which is considered dangerous and which has to be removed since it establishes a tacit relationship between warrior and victim(s). As Da Matta (1976:87) stated, "...to purify and to equilibrate the killer, it is necessary to undo the social relationship established with the victim." And this purification of the warrior is obtained through the warrior ritual, as described above.

In sum: blood is dangerous since it may lead to skin disease and eventually to death. But another danger involved in contact with blood is the risk to incorporate any "surplus" of blood. It is, hence, the mixture of different bloods (human/animal or human/human) which is to be avoided at all costs (Carneiro da Cunha 1978:103).

The precautions taken when a man touches human blood are conspicuous during the process of application of the *kwakbê* tattoo marks. The scarificator used to apply the incisions is called "fish teeth" (*tepdjwa*) and consists of a triangular piece of gourd with sharp fish teeth inserted on one side. According to the Indians, the pain provoked by the scraping of the scarificator on the skin may be increased or diminished by alternating the size of the scarificator and the type of beeswax used to glue the teeth to the gourd in question. According to the age grade of the warrior, three different sizes of scarificators may be employed: a "small one" (*tepdjwa kry-re*) for the boys of the *me'ôk-re* age grade; a normal or "nearly big one" (*tepdjwa kàjbê rũnh*) for the adolescents of the *menõrõny-re* age grade; and a "big one" (*tepdjwa rũnh*) for mature men of the *mekra-re* age grade.

After scraping the chest with short and steady strokes, strips of inner bark of a tree (*bànhôr*) are rubbed onto the bleeding skin. These strips of bark or liber are said to have the capacity to "dry blood" (*kamrô ngrà kadjy*) or stop its flow and are likewise tied around the abdomen of women at childbirth. These strips are always buried outside the village circle in order to avoid accidental contact with the blood-stained liber, a custom that invariably goes for any material sullied or stained with blood and is particularly the case if the bloodstains are caused by the "bad" blood of a sick person, an enemy, and so on.

The fine black and permanent tattoo marking on the warriors' chest is made by rubbing charcoal on the incisions. For this purpose the charcoal is prepared by the specialist and is mixed with medicinal herbs which are believed to "strengthen" or "stimulate bravery" (*metỳx kadjy* or *meàkrê kadjy*). The seclusion of the warriors at their campsite outside the village circle lasts until the incisions have healed, in other words until the "bad blood" is definitively undone and the danger is past. It is only at this moment that the men are allowed to proceed with the final phase of their reintegration into the community.

Contrary to most other Gê warriors, the returning Kayapo warriors are allowed to maintain sexual relations. This indicates that the dangers involved by contact with enemy blood are of a strictly individual character, as is expressed in the fact that the kinsmen of the warriors do not have to follow food taboos.

The specialist who applies the *kwakbê* tattoo marks is known as "he who really knows the *kwakbê*" (*kute kwakbê ma-ri*). He is also known as "the genuine scraper" (*kubêdjwỳnh*). *Kubê* is a variant of the *kwakbê* tattoo marks. *Kubê* is a general term for the different categories of body scraping that are applied during many ritualistic or secular occasions. It can be used on children in extreme cases of disobedience or when they have undertaken something considered as a trespassing of acceptable limits (e.g., the killing of a good hunting dog); on youths considered to be too lazy by the village elders — in such a case, the application of incisions is limited to the thighs "to make them run faster" (*me mranh tỳx kadjy*)[9]; and on an adolescent who has forced a young girl into sexual intercourse — a case where the boy's father will invite the specialist to use the most "painful" of all scarificators.

The formal differences between the *kwakbê* and the *kubê* scrapings can thus be precised as follows: *kubê* is invariably applied to boys and young

9   To be in a normal physical state, a balanced blood count is necessary. Male ideals of lightness and speed cannot be achieved when the body is too heavy with blood. Women are often said to have too much blood, while elder men are said to have too little (hence their slowness).

men who are not yet incorporated in one of the mature men's associations. It is applied always on the arms or legs or, during certain occasions, simultaneously on both limbs. For the *kubê*, charcoal is not used and the scraping therefore does not leave permanent black marks. Nevertheless, whether intentionally or accidentally, the incisions are sometimes so profound that they heal very badly, thus leaving obvious scars.

Before applying the *kwakbê* or *kubê*, the specialist duly protects himself against the bleeding he is about to provoke. In his spouse's household he minutely and carefully prepares a delicate mixture of charcoal with medicinal plants said to contain "scaring" elements (*umadjà*). Taking some of this black compound on his forefinger, he rubs it onto his face in a design consisting of three stripes — two of them running from both corners of the mouth up to the earlobes, a third one dividing the forehead at the top of the nose bridge. The specialist also separates two tresses of the long hair covering his ears, knotting them together at the back of his head. Both the described hairstyle (*amĩ ô wajkatu-wa*, "pounding the hair in the front") and the facial painting are visual symbols indicating a state of fury[10] and are likewise applied by the warriors before and during a raid. The specialist therefore prepares for a symbolic war: he prepares to face something dangerous, *in casu*, human blood.

After applying the incisions — it takes a matter of seconds for each person to be scraped — the specialist rubs some of the herbs on the body of his fellow tribesman, once again to "strengthen" or "stimulate bravery".

3. BLACK BODY PAINTING OR THE VISUAL ORGANIZATION OF RITUAL

It should have become clear in the preceding description of post-war processes that alternatively applied black and red body and facial paintings play an important role in the visual organization of ritual. In an earlier paper, Vidal (1981) has presented a graphic sequence of body paintings in the Kayapo-Xikrin society and I will now proceed by testing this "model" (see table 7) and its relationship to the return of the men from war or raiding parties.

In the post-war sequence as such, however, it is first of all necessary to distinguish between two different levels of expression, the first one related

---

10   The black facial paint referred to is used exclusively in certain rituals of warlike character. The hairstyle described, on the other hand, is also applied on a secular basis. This occurs when, for one reason or another, a man wants to show his state of anger (see also App. B:7). When donned with that hairstyle, the man will not be spoken to or joked with until he unties his hair, indicating that his temper has calmed down.

to *body* painting whereby a graphic and ritualistic sequence dealing with the reintegration of the warrior is described, and a second level related to *facial* painting and adornments where a distinction is drawn between the different age grades. In this section, I am exclusively concerned with the analysis of the sequence of *body* painting as used throughout ritual.

3.1 — Body painting: colours and motifs

On arriving for the first time in a Kayapo village and after a first quick glimpse of the Indians surrounding the plane, one immediately feels admiration and appreciation for Kayapo body painting as a whole. Combinations of red and black dyes, traced to form either fine geometric motifs resembling dresses, or broad red and black lines across face and body, or again of narrow and brilliantly shiny lines to adorn a partly shaven head, it is indeed as rare to see the Kayapo unpainted as it is rare to see a newcomer untouched by such a fine mode of artistic expression.

But for the Kayapo, body painting means more than "merely" ornamenting the body: it is a medium of visual communication and consists of a series of codes reflecting on and informing status, life processes and social behaviour. Or, as Vidal has put it so rightly, "among the Kayapo to be, or better to make sense, is in a large measure to appear in a culturally appropriate manner. Body paintings and body ornamentation as a whole, must be seen as a code itself, internally patterned and itself a part of a large patterned universe" (Vidal 1981:291).

As several authors have given some details on this matter[11], it is not my intention to enter, at this point, into the intricate details of Kayapo body painting as an art expression. Yet, all Kayapo rituals are scrupulously linked to this form of visual expression. Since the process of reintegration of returning warriors is a proof of this relationship, I intend to give a short analysis of body painting in Kayapo society.

Body paintings are applied for ritual and daily living. Body painting involves a vast repertory and certainly constitutes the most elaborate of all Kayapo visual symbols. Making use of red, black and, to a much lesser extent, white pigments, through a variety of styles, a combination of graphic units is obtained — units which relate to a specific status or circumstance. Not being painted, for instance, implies a very precise and inherent social position and condition: it expresses an a-social state of being, such as sickness of the individual or one of his very close kin members, and therefore is directly connected to a specific behaviour, comprising food

11   See in particular Diniz (1963), Fuerst (1964), T. Turner (1969, 1980) and Vidal (1981, 1988).

Table 7 — Vidal's model of Xikrin body paintings applied during the final phase of a restriction period.

A ⟶ B ⟶ C ⟶ G 1/2/3/4/ ⟶ G₅			
	father only		
URUCU	URUCU, CHARCOAL	GENIPAPO	GENIPAPO
— Liminal position	— Reintegration into the men's council	— End of restrictions	— Normal position
— Severe restrictions	— Periphery → center	— Transition towards normality and reintegration into the community	— Full participation in communal life
— Domestic groups periphery	— Groomed by female formal friend and conducted to the center of the plaza by a male formal friend	— Specific designs indicating process of reintegration	— Specific designs for children (G_{5e}), female (G_{5f}) and male (G_{5m}) adults.
— Each one applies his own layer of urucu.	B : fresh hair shaving, ointed with babassu oil. Face dyed black with charcoal and body with urucu. Uses a large red wooden lip plug.	G_1 : *tepibê*, design consisting of parallel, vertical stripes, specific for new-born babies, applied with the fingers ; represents indiscriminately skin designs of young tapir deer or small fish. Recognizes the new-born as human and identifies him as a Kaiapo.	always painted by kin women.
	C : entire body and face blackened with charcoal.	G_2 : "*äkrekô*, first design for a new mother ; represents the design of a fish.	
		G_3 : *ropkro-ri*, usual female design indicating end of restriction period ; represents the skin of the jaguar.	
		G_4 : *metyk*, another variety indicating end of restriction period ; all black, female (G_{4f}) and male (G_{4m}) variety differ only for face design.	

taboos, refrainment from participation in communal activities, and so on.

The various colours have a specific and symbolic association to the different aspects of life. Red, for instance, is associated with notions of vitality and energy. The Kayapo obtain the red dye from seeds of the urucu (*Bixa orellana L*) shrub and often mix it with the oil of the babassu palm seeds to give it a shiny effect. White — obtained from clay and only applied during one specific and extremely rare ceremony — is associated with old age and ghosts, while black is associated with transformations between society and unsocialized nature (see also T. Turner 1980:121-124). There are two black colour dyes: the first is obtained by mixing the wild genipap (*Genipa americana L*) fruit kernel with ashes from inner bark plus water or saliva; and the second is made from charcoal mixed with water.

Of all colourings only the black genipap dye does not disappear after bathing, as the juice of this fruit, once in contact with human skin, becomes oxidized. The motifs applied in this fashion remain visible seven to ten days, sometimes even more, depending upon the ripeness of the fruit used in the mixture and likewise the amount of charcoal and water or saliva that is used. Genipap is the most commonly used dye for *body* painting. The black charcoal dye is used during those occasions that require the body painting to be easily removed in order to enable the application of a painting with another design the next day or so.

Referring to body painting in the strict sense of the word, two basic styles of patterns are to be distinguished: a first one applied with the fine stem of the central rib of a palm leaf, and a second one applied with the hand or with stamps (see table 8).

The first style consists of a series of motives made up of innumerable fine parallel lines resulting in geometric designs of striped lines. Patiently applied with the fine stem of the central rib of a palm leaf, this particular style is almost exclusive to children of both sexes (and this on a secular basis), and is used on adults and adolescents only on specific ritualistic occasions. Only women do this kind of painting: mothers use these delicate body-covering motives on their children while wives and sisters paint the bodies of their husbands and brothers.

The second type is applied with the hand and is generally made up of broad lines crossing the body, or of entire body parts painted with genipap dye or with charcoal. It is the most common type of body painting used by adolescents and adults of both sexes. When painting occurs in the village periphery — i.e. in or near the ring of residential houses — this type of painting is invariably applied by women: a man will then usually be painted by his spouse, his sister or his mother. The type in question is likewise applied by women during the regular body painting assemblies

Table 8 — Main categories of Mekrãnoti body painting.

TYPE OF BLACK BODY PAINTING		DESCRIPTION	APPLICATION			(on adults) DESIGN DETERMINATED BY
			BY	OCCASION		
				on CHILDREN	on ADOLESCENTS/ ADULTS	
applied with stem		fine geometric designs	O	daily	ritual occasions	sex + ritual position
hand-applied	"beautiful" body painting	broad lines or entire areas covering the body	Δ/O		daily	sex
	"specific" body painting				ritual occasion	sex + ritual occasion + specific status

during which women of the same women's society or age grade paint each other. A woman may, however, occasionally paint herself this manner at the end of a restriction period. In the village centre or during exclusive male forest treks, however, men may also use the black genipap or charcoal dye. On these occasions, men belonging to a specific men's society or age grade paint each other. Young boys of the *me'ôk-re* age grade are invariably painted by their "substitute fathers".

At this point, a distinction should be made between the "secular" and the "ritual" categories of hand-applied black body paintings (see also table 8). The "secular" one generally consists of broad lines covering parts of the body, arms and legs, alternated at times with spots applied to the body with the fingertips or with a stamp. The use of most of these designs is customarily defined by the sex of the bearer. These paintings carry names like "the design of the big gourd" (*ngôkônti-re 'ôk*) or "the design of the slot of the forest turtle" (*kaprãnpa'i 'ôk*). Following Kayapo custom, I will proceed by applying a single and all-embracing expression to this important and varied set of designs: "beautiful painting" ('*ôk mex*)[12].

The second or "ritual" category of hand-applied black paintings consists either of whole areas of the body being painted black (sometimes presenting fine straight or interrupted white lines, achieved by withdrawing part of the freshly applied paint with the fingernails), or, simply, of a few broad lines circling the knees and thighs, on the belly and on the upper arm, leaving wide spaces of the body unpainted. The use of this set of designs is not solely defined by the bearer's sex, but is also scrupulously related to specific rituals or rites de passage, to specific status or age grades. The use of these body paintings therefore usually presupposes a typical behaviour which — contrarily to moments when one of the above mentioned "beautiful designs" is applied — is not always considered "normal". This because it generally excludes the bearer from full participation in communal life. As each and every one of these designs implies a specific and precise condition of the bearer, no generalized designation for this category of hand-applied black designs exists. Rather, several of these motives receive names which refer to the particular condition of the bearer, such as "the design of the pregnant people" (*tyjarô'ôk*). But this is by no means a general rule since many of these designations merely are descriptive of the pattern or structure of the design — such as "entirely black body" (*amĩtyk*)

---

12   The meaning of the term "beautiful" (*mex*, also "good") has to be understood in the sense of the "normal" state of being of the bearer of such a design. In other words, it implies the regular social context in which the body painting has been applied and therefore means that the bearer is free(d) from any severe restriction and, in consequence, fully participates in communal life.

or "design with big spots" ('*ôk kroriti*). As a matter of convenience, I will proceed by referring to this category of designs by an arbitrarily chosen, illustrative term: "specific (hand-applied black) design".

The "ritual" category of hand-applied body paintings is by far the most richly informative of all painting categories: a great variety of the existing patterns are indeed only used on very specific occasions. Yet, a distinct difference exists between secular and ritualistic hand-applied black body painting, not only as regards usage but also likewise as regards form.

In general, hand-applied genipap or charcoal motifs — whether secular or ritual, i.e., "beautiful" or "specific" — are, thus, not only the most informative, but also the most varied of all Kayapo body paintings. They make clear distinctions among age, sex, status, behaviour and may, at times, reflect a unity whereby members of a socially defined and corporative group of men or women apply one, particular design.

3.2 — The visual organization of the ritual

Vidal's (1981) earlier mentioned model and analysis are based on the sequence of body painting pertaining to the ritual of the *pyte* or "red leg" which takes place at the birth of the first child of a young couple. A comparison between the rituals of *pyte* and of the return of the warriors is justified, since both forms revolve around one, common, central theme: the reintegration of members into the community, that is the transition from a period of severe restrictions to a state of normality.

Nevertheless, in order really to understand the social meaning of the designs in discussion, it seems not only useful to compare the presented data on the return of the warriors with Vidal's model — based, it should be reminded, on the Kayapo-Xikrin — but also to examine their relationship with other Kayapo-Mekranoti rituals. Indeed, not only do the black (genipap) body paintings as used by these two Kayapo groups often differ in nature and patterns, but it is also true that each group seems to make use of a different variety of designs, applying a set of designs and patterns unknown to the other.

With these notions in mind it should become apparent that in order to comprehend the real social significance of each of the designs in question, it is necessary to analyse body paintings in a comparative perspective: i.e., when and how each design is applied and used. This is why, before turning to an exact analyses of the paintings reproduced during the reintegration process of returning warriors, I begin with a short survey of some of the Mekranoti rituals focusing transition from a state of restrictions to full participation in communal activities[13].

I. the *pyte* ("red leg") ritual

From the birth of the first child of a young couple until the new-born's umbilical cord has fallen, the genitor remains unpainted — indicative of a position of extreme weakness, simultaneously referring to severe restrictions such as subjection to rigorous food taboos, and so on. The *pyte* ritual is one of a series of protective measures performed for the well-being of the new-born child, and generally referred to as "precautions for the child" (*krajangri*). The *pyte* marks the end of the genitor's severe restriction period and, ideally, also implies his rite of passage from the *menõrõny-re* age grade to the one of *mekra-re*. This is the moment in a man's life when he will join one of the senior men's groups, that is, one of the existing men's societies.

The core of the *pyte* ritual is scattered over a period of two or three days. Each day, the genitor and his brothers — real or fictitious, all being classificatory fathers of the new-born — walk around the village plaza with a huge, reddened buriti (*Mauritia flexuosa*) palm pole. Each day a different body painting is applied. At first the body is slightly reddened with urucu (the *ràràr* design) and the forehead blackened with charcoal (the "black forehead" or *nokretyk* design). Then, on the second day, the body as well as the face is blackened with charcoal in the "entirely black body" (*amĩtyk*) design. On the third and final day, all painting is done using the genipap dye: while the classificatory fathers apply any "beautiful design", the genitor is once again painted with the *amĩtyk* motif. In fact, the genitor continues with the *amĩtyk* paint until his child starts to walk. This event marks the moment at which he may return to sleep with his wife in her maternal house after having slept for months in the men's house. On this occasion, the genitor and those brothers of the *me'ôk-re* age grade or older have the sides of their bodies painted black with the genipap dye; white lines are drawn vertically within the black zone by removing the fresh paint with the fingernails or with a special wooden painting comb. This "specific design", called "striped body" (*amĩ-'ã kakênh*) is applied in the men's house by one of the older men. After this body painting has disappeared, the genitor will once again be painted together with the members of his men's society, now applying "beautiful designs".

---

13   This survey is far from complete, though it reflects some of the major restriction phases I have witnessed in fieldwork. I have solely concentrated upon male reintegration processes, the post-war process being primarily a masculine matter. Women's designs may vary considerably from those applied to men, but the structural ordering of patterns remains roughly the same as the one discussed here.

II. the *tàkàk* naming ceremony

Performed every five years or so, the *tàkàk* ceremony can last up to three months or more. It is during this ceremony that several boys and girls are honoured: the boys have their beautiful name with the *tàkàk* prefixes confirmed, while the girls — and, occasionally, one or more boys — have their beautiful name with the *nhàk* prefixes confirmed (Verswijver 1982a; 1983b). The end of this ceremony is marked by what is called "the precautions for all children" (*kra kunĩ jangri*). During this occasion, all the male dancers perform a major, all-night ritual with the *pyte* pole in their hands. They all are slightly painted red all over (the *ràràr* design). The following day, the participants have their bodies painted black with charcoal (the *amĩtyk* design). Those men whose children have entered the walking stage and who, therefore, have spent months with the *amĩtyk* design, will get their "striped body" (*amĩ-'ã kakênh*) design after which they return to sleep with their spouse and will, from then on, be painted with the same "beautiful designs" as the other members of their men's society.

III. the *meĩtyk-re* initiation

The initiation of the boys, called "the people with the black bracelets" (*mei 'ĩtyk-re*), is never performed separately but rather is always included in the *bep* or *tàkàk* naming ceremonies, or in the *ngô-re* fishing ritual. It implies a symbolic marriage — signifying "marriageability" — which is not a binding union in itself. During the *tàkàk* ceremony, the initiate boys also participate in the dances and, instead of holding a *pyte* pole, dance with a ceremonial stone axe, part of their specific ceremonial dress (Verswijver 1983c). After the major dance where they, too, are painted slightly red all over (*ràràr* design), these boys will spend a few days in a campsite outside the village circle. Upon their return, when they are integrated into the village centre or men's house, they are painted black with charcoal (the *amĩtyk* design) combined with a particular facial design. From the next day on, they are (again)[14] painted together with the boys of their age grade in the men's house.

IV. *bixjangri*: the death of a spouse or child

Immediately after the death of a spouse or a child, a man has his body painted black with charcoal. This design is called "body black up to the collar-bone" (*amĩ kakôx nhitep-'ã amĩtyk*) and is applied by his spouse

14   At certain events and for some boys, this *mei 'ĩtyk-re* initiation simultaneously implies and replaces the "painted people" (*me 'ôk*) rite of passage from the *mebôkti-re* age grade to the *me 'ôk-re* age grade.

(in the case of the death of his child) or by his mother or sister (in the case of the death of his spouse). This act initiates a long period during which the man remains unpainted, abstains from talking loudly and may not enter the men's house. After several months of severe restrictions, the same woman will then paint his body completely black (*amĩtyk*), enabling him to join his men's society again and to be painted together with his fellow members.

The various periods of restriction mentioned above allow us to outline the basic principles regarding the succession of body paintings used in diverse rituals focusing on the reintegration of single persons or groups of individuals into full participation in society. Just like Vidal (1981:292) has noted regarding the *pyte* ritual, these cases demonstrate that a specific structure or pattern, as well as a visible order of graphic units, is maintained throughout all of these rituals, with only a few alterations corresponding to specific contexts. Turning to the body paintings applied during the ritual of the returning warriors, the following order of designs can be observed:

First phase: the *ràràr* design (red urucu painting)
The day the warriors arrive in the village, their sphere of interactions is pre-eminently limited to the village periphery: they visit their kin peram-bulating between their maternal household and their spouse's house. This is characteristic of severe restriction periods as shown in the case of the "fathers" who undergo a period of restriction for their newborn children (*krajangri*) during the *pyte* and *tàkàk* rituals, or of the men who undergo such a period for their deceased child or spouse (*bixjangri*). In all these cases, the actors are excluded from corporate activities related to the vil-lage centre. In all these cases, too, the men in question have their body painted slightly red all over (*ràràr* design).

Second phase: the *amĩtyk* design (black charcoal painting)
From the second to the fifth day after their arrival, all warriors remain in a campsite outside the village circle. During this period, they have their bodies painted with the *amĩtyk* design. As seen in the *pyte* and *tàkàk* rituals as well as in the *bixjangri* process, the *amĩtyk* design is always applied under specific circumstances: the (re)integration into the men's house, which, as the centre of Kayapo society, opens the way to participa-tion in collective activities. It is interesting to note that in all the above-mentioned cases, the *ràràr* design is invariably followed by the *amĩtyk*.

Third phase: the "specific" design (black genipap painting)
Depending upon the occasion, a different and specific genipap design is

applied after the *amĩtyk* one: during the *pyte* and *tàkàk* rituals — both of which mark the end of restriction periods related to new-born children (*krajangri*) — the *amĩ-'ã kakênh* motif is used; during the post-war process, the *kakôkreti* design will be applied. Such hand-applied specific design marks the transition from charcoal painting to collective painting between fellow members in the men's associations. In other words, this phase marks the end of restrictions and symbolizes the transition towards reintegration into the community.

Fourth phase: the "beautiful" design (black genipap painting)
This last phase indicates a normal situation and full participation in communal life, the men now being painted in the same fashion as their fellow group members. Depending on the occasion, black genipap painting is applied either by their fellow members within the men's house or by a kinswoman in the village periphery — a point I will take up in more detail further-on.

Summarizing these reflections, I can now deduce some general characteristics concerning the colour of the dyes used — reflections which, it should be emphasized, correspond entirely with Vidal's findings:
  1. Red painting is generally applied to the peripheral parts of the body (face and feet). The urucu facial paint is most commonly applied to members of the junior age grades, reflecting their vitality on a secular basis, or to junior as well as senior age grades during rituals. In addition, red painting is likewise related to the village periphery or domestic sphere, to liminal position and isolation. The *ràràr* design is applied exclusively to men during a period of severe restriction: it marks their particular position during which they do not fully participate in communal village activities related to the village centre. If it is never applied to women, this can be explained by the fact that the village periphery constitutes their normal sphere of interaction.
  2. The black charcoal paintings combined, on some occasions, with urucu facial designs, relate to a transitional period and to the approaching reintegration into full participation in communal activities.
  3. The specific black genipap painting, on the other hand, indicates the end of restrictions and normal, full participation in social, communal life and corporate activities, when a "beautiful" design is used.
  The normal and theoretically most complete sequence of gradual integration into communal life is expressed in the following sequence: unpainted — red urucu paint — black charcoal paint — black genipap paint with "specific" design — black genipap paint with "beautiful" de-

sign. In practice, however, sequence is adapted to circumstance, as well as to the degree of gravity involved in the incident leading to an enduring restrictive period.

Genipap is feared since it is considered to be dangerous. That is why people who have been seriously ill, and who have therefore remained unpainted, first apply a urucu painting; urucu is to be used as it "makes the skin light" (*kà kajkrit kadjy*). The term "light skin" connotes recuperation and recovery, and is a term that may likewise be used after a successful application of injections or other beneficial medical treatment. Individuals who are painted black with genipap dye are therefore not only considered physically strong and healthy, but also socially in a normal position allowing them to participate in communal activities.

To conclude, I may say that the return process of the warriors displays structural similarities with several other rituals that deal with gradual reintegration of members of the society into that aspect of community life from which they were excluded.

3.3 — The act of painting

A few points should still be mentioned regarding the importance given to whoever actually does a body painting. Vidal (1981:295) states that in Xikrin society only women use black genipap dye for body painting, men going to their kinswomen — spouse, sister or mother — to get painted. In Mekranoti society, this is not a general rule. Elders usually act identical to their Xikrin congeners, but younger men may also use the genipap dye.

Once every ten days or so, all men have their bodies freshly painted with genipap. While the married men usually go to a kinswoman, the *menõrõny-re* unite in the men's house to have painting assemblies during which they paint each other with genipap applying a "beautiful" design. On a secular basis, boys of the *me'ôk-re* age grade are invariably painted by their "substitute father", a non-kin who is either a *menõrõny-re* or a *mekrany-re* man. And during forest treks when only men participate, all men paint each other with the genipap dye in the forest campsites. On some ritual occasions, the *menõrõny-re* may apply a "specific" design, while married men may be painted by non-kin.

During the process of the returning warriors, those men who have killed a foe are painted by the kinswomen of a person killed in previous skirmishes with the enemy in question, whether during a war expedition or during a counterattack. Yet, since Kayapo villages rarely suffered attacks, what is here referred to as a "victim" commonly implies on a Kayapo who has participated in one or another raiding expedition and who has been killed in battle. If a kinswoman of the killed person paints the man (or men) who has (have) killed a member of that specific adversary, this is to be seen as a social act compensating for the loss of their kin as well as social recognition of revenge.

4. HEAD ORNAMENTS

In the preceding pages I have shown that such ornaments as tattoo marks and painting, when applied on the *body*, are not merely to be taken as visual symbols reflecting a specific message, but are also to be understood as indicative of the various stages of reintegration into full participation in communal life.

However, earlier in this Chapter, I mentioned that a clear distinction between *body* and *head* paintings and ornaments had to be made. Indeed, the Kayapo body is related to the village periphery[15], while the head is directly related to the village centre: the precise sphere of corporate ceremonial, politic and economic activities in which a man is allowed to participate only when not observing any kind of restriction. It is therefore not surprising to observe that head ornaments and facial paintings are related to the gradual process of reaching sociological adulthood and maturity.

Mature manhood is only achieved when a man establishes a nuclear family of his own, that is when he initiates his attachment to his affinal household. The transitional stage between childhood — when the child or youngster still lives in his maternal household — and mature manhood is associated with residence in the men's house. How this process of sociological recognition is specifically related to war (or vice-versa) is what I intend to elaborate in the following pages. This part of my description therefore focuses upon themes such as head ornaments and rites of passage from childhood to manhood. It is, as such, closely related to conception and sexual maturity. This section offers more detail on rites of passage between puberty and mature manhood than those described in Chapter 1.

The sequence which will be established and used in the following discussion is based upon statements by Mekranoti elders who, one and

15   It is interesting at this point to analyze the Kayapo term *tikiai*. In relation to Kayapo cosmological views (Chapter 1) I have translated this term as "the sides", and have mentioned that it is used as a reference to north and south. *Tik* is the Kayapo word for belly; *ai* means "flank". Accordingly, a more literate translation of *tikiai* is "the sides of the belly".

all, actually participated in several war expeditions in the period from 1930 to 1955.

4.1 — First phase: the *me'ôk-re*

When the "substitute father" leaves with his fellow men's society members on a war expedition, the *me'ôk-re* boy may go along. But on the day of the actual attack the boy usually remains behind in the campsite which is erected a few kilometres distant from the enemy's village and from where the warriors leave, early in the morning, for the attack. Some elderly men will stay behind in the camp with the youngest *me'ôk-re* boys; the oldest among them — those aged about twelve or more and referred to as *mebêngàdjyti* — may take part in the attack, but even then their participation is limited to a position in the rear. The latter will, for this occasion, receive a penis sheath (*mydjê*). It consists of a small cone made of palm leaves, open at the top and bottom. With a fine stem taken from the central rib of a palm leaf, the prepuce is introduced into the sheath so that the emerged skin slightly holds the sheath over the glans penis — the only part of the genitals it keeps covered. The *mydjê* is the only Kayapo form of "clothing". The bestowal of a penis sheath on *me'ôk-re* boys before a raid is considered temporary as the sheath will be withdrawn after the raid: it is indeed solely conferred because, during an attack, no man exhibits himself naked: i.e., without a penis sheath. That is why the sheath conferred at this occasion is referred to as an "unreal penis sheath" (*mydjê kajgo*).

Back in the village and at the conclusion of the post-war restrictions, it is, as usual, the "substitute father" who paints the boy. The design applied is the *kakôkreti'ôk*, the same as for the older participants. The boy also gets a red facial paint; a red stripe is applied, with the forefinger, from the corners of the mouth up to the ears. This red design is applied by senior men and is the distinctive mark of the boys of this particular age grade for the occasion in question.

4.2 — Second phase: the *memydjêny-re*

A few years later, when the boy is between fourteen and sixteen, he once again accompanies his "substitute father" on a war expedition. In the forest, on the day or a few days before the actual attack, an older man bestows the penis sheath on the boy. The young man will participate in the attack in training to eventually become a full-fledged warrior. At this stage, the penis sheath is no longer removed after the attack: the boy is now referred to as *memydjêny-re* ("person with a newly received penis sheath"), some-one about to become a member of the *menõrõny-re* age grade.

After the attack he wears a specific ornamentation consisting of a few babassu palm seeds wrapped up in dried palm leaves and inserted in his pierced earlobes. Upon nearing the village, the warriors are met by the women who take their assets (*jêj*) with the exception of the men's weapons. The *memydjêny-re* give their load to their "real spouse" (*prõ djwỳnh*) — ideally the girl he ritually married during the earlier celebrated *mei 'ĩtyk-re* initiation — or, if the girl is too young (which is usually the case), to her mother.

After this the mature men send the *memydjêny-re* to the village to deliver the palm seeds they carry in their earlobes to their "substitute spouses" (*krô'ãprõ*) — girls about their age whom they are courting. Mixing the babassu palm seeds brought along by the adolescent boy, the girl will apply a special facial paint the boy. This painting is called "split half-gourd" (*ngôkraxkôkjêr*) and consists of an almost triangular shaped reddening of the face and forehead, starting from the top of the crown and continuing up to the cheeks and neck (figure 18a).

Upon the sixth day after the warriors' return and during the already mentioned painting session, it is the boy's "substitute mother" — the wife of his "substitute father" — who prepares the black genipap dye for his body painting. This is done while his real mother or sister shaves his hair in the hairstyle called *jôkàr* (see further).

Back in the campsite his "substitute father" will then paint him with the black *kakôkreti* design, removing with his fingernail the part on the boy's collar-bone: this area will then be filled with the red colour dye. When he finishes painting, the "substitute father" stands in front of the boy who, with head lowered in shame, listens to his ritual father's speech:

> *"Bep-pe[16], it was I who painted you. Through me you became strong. I painted you with charcoal and watched you being painted with genipap and urucu. It is through me that you became strong."*

This short ritual of painting and formal speech represents the final phase of rite of passage from the *me'ôk-re* age grade to the one of *menõrõny-re* — the first one being the actual bestowal of the penis sheath. The ritual in question is called "the end of the painting" (*ôk oinore-re*) and, as the name suggests, consists of the last time the "substitute father" paints the boy. From then on, the responsibilities of the "substitute father" have ended and the boy will sit in the men's house together with the adolescents of

---

16   *Bep-pe* is a teknonyme for boys and men who have their "beautiful" *bep* name ritually confirmed during the appropriate naming ceremony.

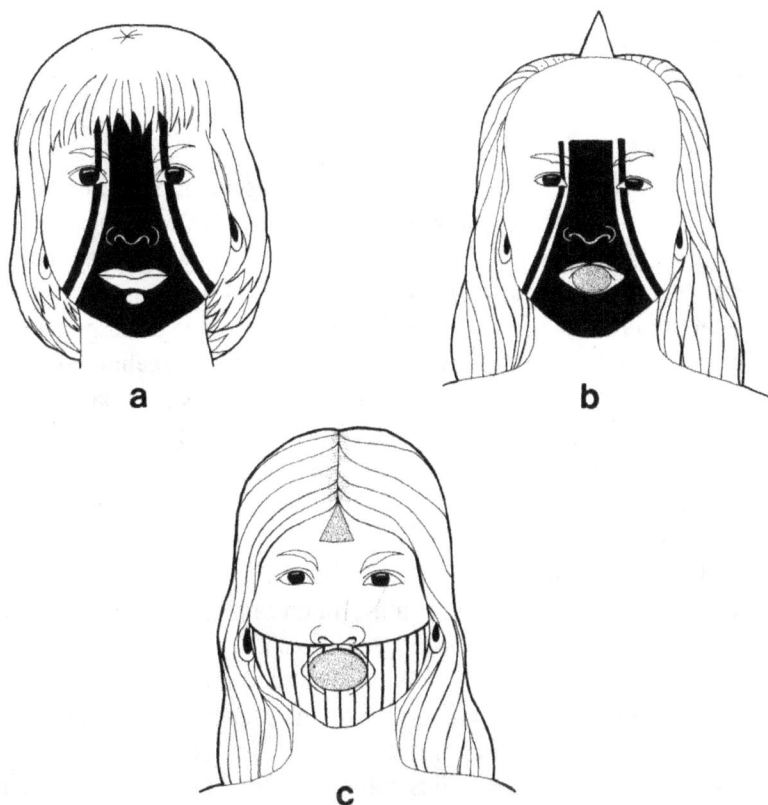

Figure 17 — Facial paintings as used during the final phase of the re-integration process of the returning warriors. (a) the *ngôkraxkôkjêr* facial paint of a *memydjêny-re* boy; (b) the *ngôkraxkôkjêr* facial paint, the small lip disc and the *krãkàtyk* upstanding hair of a *memydjê'ãtũm*; (c) the i*nhy'ãtepre'i* facial paint, the lip disc and the *ità* head ornament of a *menõrõny'ãtũm* warrior

his age grade or, as the Kayapo say, "he then sits with the *menõrõny-re*" (*aryp nõrõny-re kam krî*).

The preceding section is endowed with a particular complexity. I therefore consider it crucial, at this point, to go into detail on each one of the above-mentioned symbolic and ritual representations.

I. the bestowal of the penis sheath

The penis sheath is bestowed on pubescents who have reached biological maturity. Before receiving the penis sheath, boys are not supposed to have sexual relations — there are, of course, exceptions to the rule — and the bestowal of this conic sheath expresses a symbolic affirmation of physiological maturity. It therefore symbolises, as T. Turner (1980:119) has put it, "the collective appropriation of male powers of sexual reproduction for the purpose of sexual reproduction".

Once officially bestowed, a man is seldom seen in public without his penis sheath. On the rare occasions when he does not wear the sheath, he may tie his foreskin with a string, thus keeping the glans penis covered or may secure the foreskin under a string around the waist. To show an uncovered penis — that is, for the Kayapo, to expose the glans penis — is considered highly humiliating involving strong feelings of shame (*piaàm*). This is why the oldest *me'ôk-re*, when allowed to participate in an attack, temporarily receive a penis sheath. As explicitly revealed in narrative 17 of the Appendix B, the Kayapo are well aware of the distinct notions of shame in different societies and will, as such, avoid revealing their "nakedness" to an outsider.

It should be emphasized, however, that the category of *memydjêny-re* does not constitute an age grade in itself but, rather, has to be considered as a distinctive designation for the transitional stage between the *me'ôk-re* and *menõrõny-re* age grades. It is, in other words, a term referring to the junior members of the *menõrõny-re* age grade. But the bestowal of the penis sheath is *not* in and of itself the rite of passage between the two mentioned age grades. Rather, it is only a first phase in a process which terminates when the "substitute father" paints the youngster for the last time.

II. on "real" and "substitute spouses"

As mentioned earlier, the important *mei'ĩtyk-re* rite simultaneously involves an initiation and a ritual marriage. For this purpose the boy's parents arrange a "spouse" for their son. His parents usually combine with mutual friends — non-kin who are members of the category of *meba'itêm*, "people outside my own people" — who are willing to give their daughter in marriage. During this time, the boy generally belongs to the *me'ôk-re* age grade. Terence Turner (1966:164) states that in the Kayapo-Gorotire village "it is normal but not mandatory to receive a penis sheath before initiation". Mekranoti informants, however, explicitly state that a boy initiate has not, as yet, received his penis sheath, a statement confirmed by my own personal observations during the *mei'ĩtyk-re* rite I witnessed in 1974-1975 at which five boys were honoured, four of whom were still *mebôkti-re* and one who was a *me'ôk-re* (Verswijver 1981:111).

During the *mei'ĩtyk-re* initiation, the "spouse" is usually only three or four years old and is, consequently, much younger than the boy. Although it seldom occurs, a couple may even engage their unborn daughter in a symbolic "marriage" which may, of course, never actually occur if no daughter is born in due time. But the main point here is that the age difference between boy and "spouse" is generally quite large.

This ritual marriage is not a binding one. Rather than an effective bond it is a symbolic act, indicating the state of marriageability and certifying the readiness of the boy for marriage. Admitting that the boy has a certain right to the girl, and although he readily refers to her as his "real spouse" (*prõ djwỳnh*), few boys wait long enough to get married when the girl in question has become sexually mature. If, however, the boy does wait until his "real spouse" has attained the proper age to engage in marriage, the ritual marriage may be consummated. This is regarded by the Kayapo as "beautiful". Not only because the ritual marriage has indeed taken place, but also because it consequently implies that he has "waited a long time": i.e., that he has become a biological *and* sociological mature man, having attained the status of "old *menõrõny-re*" (*menõrõny'ãtũm*).

The age difference between the boy and his ritually arranged "spouse" is usually considerable. That is why, upon becoming *memydjêny-re*, the majority of these boys already have a girlfriend considerably older than the "real spouse". Upon receiving the penis sheath, they will commence sexual relations with this girlfriend. The latter is referred to as a "substitute spouse" (*krô'ãprõ*) and may eventually, if the relationship becomes permanent, turn into his "real spouse" and lead to marriage[17].

III. The delivery of palm seeds and assets

To the Kayapo, babassu palm seeds are important since their oil is mixed with the red urucu dye during painting or may be rubbed on a person's hair to give it a shiny effect. Just as delousing may be taken as one of the most intimate acts between a man and his wife, body painting and the oiling of hair are, likewise, expressions of affection. Thus when the *memydjêny-re* deliver babassu palm seeds to their "substitute spouse", it is an indication of his affection. In other words, through this act, the *memydjêny-re* — now allowed to carry on sexual relations — make known their choice of sexual partners. As long the "real spouse" is still too young

---

17   *Menõrõny-re* often change fiancées but they eventually "settle down" and maintain a more permanent relation with the girl of their choice. This may — as I witnessed in the field — preoccupy the mother of the "real spouse" who may then pressure the boy's mother. She does so by insisting that her son should delay such a fixed liaison, and that he should wait for his "real spouse" to reach the proper age for marriage. In all of the cases I was able to observe, after a certain amount of time the boy proceeded according to his personal choice.

for sexual intercourse, her mother will accept such behaviour but expects to receive the boy's packs upon his return from a war, and this is taken as a token of future compromise. This transaction is typical of the period a boy spends in the men's house. Upon entering the men's house after the *me'ôk* ritual, and through the ritual marriage related to the *mei'ĩtyk-re* initiation, the sphere of influence from his kin weakens in intensity: a process of relationships starts to take place beyond the sphere of his kin relations where upon the boy gradually initiates his social and economic attachment to his affines. This process is symbolized through the conferral of meat. Being allowed to use clubs — a further sign of their physical maturity since clubs are weapons of adult men — the *memydjêny-re* boy may occasionally start to hunt. When returning from a successful hunt he will give a piece of meat to his "mother-in-law", that is to the mother of his "real spouse". He may also offer meat to his mother, his sister(s), his "substitute mother", and what is left over to his girlfriend.

4.3 — Third phase: the *memydjê'ãtũm* or *menõrõny-re*

The *menõrõny-re* are sociologically defined as marriageable and sexually active. They have their proper "sitting place" (*krĩdjà*) in the men's house, separate from the men's societies' sitting places which are exclusively for married men with children in wedlock. Young men of the *menõrõny-re* age grade are supposed to be the most energetically active partakers in communal activities such as ceremonies, and may undertake long hunting and raiding expeditions on their own. They also regularly hold painting assemblies where they paint each other's bodies with the black genipap dye. After returning from a new war expedition and having his head shaven *jôkàr* by his kinswomen, fellow age grade members will paint his body in the *kakôkreti* design and his face with the *ngôkraxkôkjêr* (figure 18b). The boy is now considered to be a "person who long ago received a penis sheath" (*memydjê'ãtũm*) — a paraphrase of a "person who really is a *menõrõny-re*" (*menõrõny-re kumrẽnhtx*).

4.4 — Fourth phase: the *menõrõny-re*

After going on yet another war expedition the young men will, for the last time during the post-war rituals, be given the *ngôkraxkôkjêr* facial paint. The Mekranoti relate this to the "end of the shaving of the head" (*jôkàr oinorer kadjy*). The little tuft of hair which is left at the crown is kept upright by covering it with the hardened resin of the jatoba (*Rymenaea courbaril L*) tree mixed with a little urucu dye — a mixture which is called *ràp*. The young man will have his hair cut semi-short so that it reaches his collar-bone: this is the typical hairstyle of the *menõrõny-re*.

4.5 — Fifth phase: the *menõrõny'ãtũm*

Having reached the age of about twenty or more, the *menõrõny-re* are referred to as *menõrõny'ãtũm* ("persons who are *menõrõny-re* for a long time"). These young men have usually already established a fixed relationship with one particular girl — either the one arranged through ritual marriage, or a girl of his own choice — and may already have moved into his wife's house, no longer returning to the men's house before dawn. Yet it would be incorrect to describe these men as married men without children as most of them have already engendered children either with a girl they were either unwilling to marry or with an unmarried older woman. It seems therefore more appropriate to refer to the *menõrõny'ãtũm* as married men without children in wedlock. Although they may reside in their wife's house, they still belong to the *menõrõny-re* age grade and have not yet joined one of the men's societies. Living with a girl means that this girl is recognized as his "real spouse" and, as a recognition of such, that a new nuclear family is soon to be established.

On returning from a war expedition as a *menõrõny'ãtũm*, the young man will be painted with the *kakôkreti* design by a kinswoman: mother, sister or spouse if she is old enough and practised in the art of body painting. This kinswoman will also apply his special facial genipap design, applied with a palm rib stylet and called "the little fish bones on the upper lip" (*inhy-'ã tepre'i*) — see figure 18c. It consists of a series of parallel, vertical lines, running uninterrupted from one ear to the other over cheeks and chin. It should be noted that, in earlier times, at this stage of a man's life, the man had already adopted a large lip-disk, thus the painting continued on the expanded part of his lower lip.

The lip-disk (*akàkakô*, "lower lip plug") is a typical Kayapo male ornament and consists of a saucer-like, light wooden disk which is inserted in a hole perforating the lower lip. A few days after birth, male children get their lower lip perforated and a small cotton string is inserted to prevent the wound from healing. Boys may wear a small pendant with glass beads strung through the little hole in the lower lip. Upon induction to the men's house, a little wooden plug is inserted taking the place of the bead pendant. This plug is gradually replaced by other ones, progressively bigger in size and the disk may reach a maximum size of about ten centimetres in diameter when a man reaches the age grade of "father of many children" (*mekrakramtĩ*). Both Seeger (1975:216-218; 1981:230-233) and T. Turner (1980:120-121) have analysed the lip-disk as a portrayal of male belligerence and bellicosity, which are correlates of masculine self-assertion and public oratory: the modes of expression essential for political power. The lip-disk, thus, is to be seen as a physical expression of the oral assertiveness of mature men.

4.6 — Sixth phase: the *mekra-re*

The Mekranoti informants state that, upon participation in yet another war expedition, most *menõrõny'ãtũm* will have already consummated marriage, that is, they will have engendered children in wedlock.

When a *mekra-re* leaves on a war expedition he does so with the members of his men's society. On his return, his spouse will paint his body with the black *kakôkreti* design and his face with the *ajtẽnk* design. The latter is applied to the cheeks with a palm rib stylet and usually consists of two symmetrical and rectangular-shaped motives. This set of body and facial paintings will be repeated each time the man returns from a war expedition.

5. ON HAIRSTYLE

There is a social distinction related to hairstyle in Kayapo society. A "suckling person" (*mekarà*) has long hair. This is because, while a child is nursing, it is still considered to be an extension of the biological being of its parents, who also have long hair. Weaning is an important point marking the beginning of a person's life as a separate biological and social being. The hair of boys of the *meprĩ-re*, *mebôkti-re* and *me'ôk-re* age grades is cut short. This is because they have not as yet developed their own bio-sexual powers. The moment that a person has developed his own biological powers or, as T. Turner (1980:118) has put it, the moment when these powers "become strong enough to be socially extended, through sexual intercourse and procreation, as the basis of a new family", the hair is allowed to grow to full length. It is the moment a boy receives his penis sheath and becomes a member of the *menõrõny-re* age grade. From then on, a person's hair is kept long, except while mourning the death of close kin. In such a case, death marks the breaking off of a biological relationship: parents cut their hair at the death of a child because it severs the common physical substance they share through conception; spouses do so because death severs their sexual relationship which is seen as part of a "natural" procreative, libidinal community (*ibid*.: 117).

The typical Kayapo tribal coiffure consists of shaving the hair with a razor-blade above the forehead to its crown, while leaving the hair at its appropriate length (long or cut short) on both sides and at the back. This hairstyle is called a *jôkàr* ("shaven head"). Children of the *meprĩ-re* and, to a lesser extent, of the *mebôkti-re* age grade often have their hair shaved this way on a secular basis. From the moment a person is associated with the men's house (i.e., *me'ôk-re* and older), the *jôkàr* hairstyle is only done on specific ritual occasions. In addition, a little tuft of hair is left at the crown. The latter is particular to all men (*me'ôk-re* and older) whenever they have their head shaved in the *jôkàr* fashion. Informants told me that this little and almost triangular shaped tress of hair is the symbol of the female vagina, thus highlighting the relationship between hairstyle and bio-sexual powers.

During the post-war ritual as described earlier, for instance, junior warriors without children (that is, the boys of the *me'ôk-re* age grade as well as the adolescents of the *menõrõny-re* age grade) are shaved in this fashion. On this occasion, too, the little tuft of hair which is left at the crown of the *menõrõny-re* is kept upright by covering it with the hardened resin of the jatoba tree mixed with a little urucu dye — a mixture which is called *ràp*. This hair adornment (*krãkàtyk*, "black head-skin" — see figure 18b) is said by the Indians to resemble the black crown feathers of the jacú (a *Cracidae* species) bird which stands upright.

The *menõrõny'ãtũm* — being those who are recognized as men with children (*in casu*, out of wedlock) — do not have their hair shaved in the *jôkàr* fashion. Instead, their hair at the crown is separated and little white down feathers are glued with resin into the parting. On the forehead, a small triangular piece of red cloth is glued. This ornament is called *ità* and was copied from the neighbouring Yudja (Juruna) at the end of the last century (Verswijver 1983b). The *ità* is most commonly used by the *menõrõny'ãtũm* and, to a lesser extent, by the *mekrany-re* ("fathers with new children") — since the *menõrõny'ãtũm* have usually already procreated children out of wedlock, these two categories de facto refer to all men with "few children".

During the *mengre-re prõt ariba* dance of the post-war ritual, all returning warriors have little white feather down of vultures or eagles glued to their hair (*krãjamĩ*). This particular adornment is also applied to all dancers during the final phase of several major ceremonies such as the corn festival and the *mebijôk* naming ceremonies. On these occasions, it is combined with the breast plumage of macaws and parrots which is glued to the body, covering the earlier applied body paint. This ornamentation is called *djwỳnhngwỳnh*. The combination of the two feather ornaments glued on the body and hair constitutes what might be called the most prestigious form of ritual costume. At the conclusion of the major ceremony, the white down on the hair is covered with the red colour dye of the urucu by a ceremonial friend (*kràbdjwỳ*)[18]. This hair ornamentation with white feather down is also applied to a deceased person, but then the down is not painted red with urucu: this is because, in this case, the "passage" is a conclusive one.

The ritual that is performed on the occasion of a death is a concise one. While the corpse of the deceased is being painted, donned with several ornaments as well as feather down, a dance is performed on the village plaza if the deceased was a "beautiful person" (*memêx*): i.e., someone "honoured" during his youth in one of the major ceremonies. The dance is a commemorative one and is said to "drive away the ghost" (*mekarõ mũm kujatê kadjy*). Only men dance for a dead man, and only women dance for a dead woman. The dance and accompanying songs are taken from the ceremonies in which he or she had been "honoured".

Deceased persons are buried in a special site located in the surrounding *atyk-mã*, not too distant from the village circle. The corpse is placed in a circular grave on its back with the knees drawn up to fit the hole. The head is pointed to the east because the village of the dead is located in that direction. Many of the belongings of the deceased are cast into the grave for his spirit not to molest the living. Poles are placed across the mouth of the grave and they are covered with the mats in which the corpse was carried to the graveyard. The earth from the grave is then heaped over the mats into a conical mound, called a *pykakrã* ("earth head"). The hair of the spouse or, if a child of the parents, is hung up on a pole near the grave. A small fire is lit near the grave: it is kept alive for weeks so that the deceased should not feel cold and return to the village. The latter symbolizes the fear the Kayapo have for the spirit of the dead.

Mekranoti informants state that bodies of enemies killed near the Mekranoti village were not buried. They also state that Mekranoti warriors killed during combat were buried, whenever possible: if the attack occurred near the Mekranoti village, the people would take the bodies to the village and bury them in the appropriate manner; if the attack occurred in an enemy village, they would take the bodies and bury them in the forest. The latter was not always possible, though, as the warriors sometimes had to leave the bodies and run off — leaving, as the informants stated, the

18   One of the most important functions of ceremonial friends is the one of mediator in the final phase of a rite of passage.

bodies lying there to be eaten by vultures. When warriors were buried in the distant forest, no dancing was done. This lack of the prescribed ritual features can be explained by the actual distance between the burial site and the proper village: the ghosts of the deceased warriors were left too far away from the village to find their way back to their kin. In addition, no specific adornments were applied on the bodies of the deceased. But then, the Mekranoti informants insist that, in addition to a series of other ornaments, warriors put the *krãjamĩ* head ornament on their hair before any attack. As such, the warriors were ideally donned with the same ornaments applied on a person buried in the appropriate manner near the village.

If, then, informants stated that a group of men donned the *krãjamĩ* on their hair before going on a visit to an inimical Kayapo group (see App. B:9), it is evident that the *krãjamĩ* hair ornament is put on ideally before any occasion involving eminent danger of being killed (e.g., before an attack or a visit to enemy group). And if the *krãjamĩ* ornament is also put on to all warriors in the final phase of the post-war ritual, this no longer involves the same connotations of danger: rather, it is related to the earlier mentioned occasions where the ornament in question is applied at the final phase of several major rituals, often related to a rite of passage.

6. CONCLUSION

The complete "cycle" as presented by the Mekranoti informants relates to six consecutive phases, each of these being associated with successive war expeditions. Each phase is also associated with a different age grade or sub-category of this age grade. It should, nevertheless, be emphasized that field data indicate a certain discrepancy between theory and the practical obedience of such cycles. The cycle as such and as presented by the elders reflects an idealized concept of reality since most elders questioned had participated in only three to five war expeditions during the age grades in consideration. Furthermore, some men had participated in two or three war expeditions during one particular age grade and none while a member of the next age grade.

But, as the Kayapo have tried to make clear, between early puberty and the moment a man engenders his first child in wedlock, a young man should, ideally, participate in several war expeditions. In the idealized sequence, the informants seem to assume that with each participation, a youth will pass from one age grade or sub-category of one age grade to another and, by doing this, will be gradually and formally recognized as a mature man. At each phase or passage, some change in his adornment

— whether painting or some other form of adornment — is introduced. Whether through the bestowal of the penis sheath and the ensuing rite manifested by the "last painting" applied to his body by his "substitute father", or through a change in hairstyle, or again through accentuating the lip-disk, some aspect of his biological and social development is always emphasized. It can therefore be assumed that the Kayapo perceive warfare to be an inherent part of a man's development.

But this aspect is not only emphasized in the final day of the post-war rite, it is also — although in a less expressive and more symbolic manner — present during the actual return of the warriors, when they carry two emblems which distinguish the carrier's age grade: the club and the necklace.

— The war club (*kôjaka*, "white round club") is left by the warriors at the site of the attack. Right after the attack and in order to return "armed" to the village, the warriors make a club called *akêtêtyk* (after the type of wood) or *abêrdjà* ("hitting thing"). It is made from a long piece of wood cut from a tree or bush near the enemy village. No decoration whatsoever is applied to this club of which three types exist according to the size: young men carry big *akêtêtyk* clubs, senior men smaller ones[19].

— The necklace called *õkretã* ("throat pendant") is made from cotton or fibre strings which are tied around the neck so that numerous strings hang loosely onto the person's back. Distinction is made as to which type of string is used: the one of the young boys is made of *djy-djêdjêti* (a type of bark fibre used to make bow-strings), and the one of the adolescents and of senior men is made of "cotton from the non-Kayapo" (*kubêkadjàt*). Since only a few of the *me'ôk-re* boys actually participate in the attack, the informants' data can be paraphrased as actual participants in the war are donned with cotton taken from the enemy village, while the young boys who remained in the last campsite are donned with bark fibre. A distinction is, therefore, made at this point between actual partakers and those who remained in a rear position.

7. HUMAN ENEMIES, WASPS AND JAGUARS

The ritual of the wasps (*amjy-'ã tor*, "dance of the wasps")[20] and the one

---

19   If the senior warriors carry smaller clubs, the Kayapo explain this by pointing out the fact that such men also have to carry other weapons such as a bow and arrows and, occasionally, a rifle.

20   The ritual of the wasps is performed whenever a group of boys or men performs a ritual attack on a wasp nest. Such an attack is performed when a wasp nest

performed after killing a jaguar show similarities with the post-war ritual. Since I never actually saw the wasp ritual, I will here only be concerned with a comparison of the components displayed in the latter two rituals.

7.1 — The "dance of the jaguar"

After killing a jaguar, the hunter brings it to the village singing the appropriate *mekurwỳk* song (see footnote 2 p. 199). Upon entering the village, he throws the animal in front of the men's house, where it remains for an hour or so attached to a pole. All people (both male and female) who have been "honoured" during the *tàkàk* naming ceremony stand in a semi-circle behind the jaguar. The other men gather inside the men's house: they stand in a semi-circle behind the ritual leader who, holding a rattle, sings a brief song. Then the boys of the *me'ôk-re* age grade carry the animal to a place outside the village circle. Often assisted by one or two senior tribesmen (including the hunter), they skin the jaguar. They then roast it on a fire and eat it. In the early evening the men gather in front of the men's house or, if it rains, inside that house. Seated on palm leaves, a man starts to deliver the "speech of the non-Kayapo people" (*kubẽkakrit kabẽn*). Following the speech, the men perform in low pitch the "song of the jaguar" (*rop-'ã ngre-re*) which lasts about twenty minutes.The next morning, all men gather in the men's house. A senior man selects two men to lead the *mengre-re prõt ariba* dance. The two men leave the men's house shouting and start singing the "songs of the jaguar" (*rop-'ã ngre-re*). Gradually, other pairs of dancers join them. The singing is in falsetto. The double row of dancers criss-cross around the village plaza, visiting all houses in a random sequence. Occasionally, a senior woman joins in the dancing, carrying a young grandson who is still a member of the *meprĩ-re* age grade. The *mengre-re prõt ariba* dance is interrupted on one occasion, when the men line up in front of the men's house to perform the *tàkàk-'ã tor* dance while standing in concentric circles.After the dance, all men gather

has been found at a site not too far from the village. The man who discovers the nest informs the men in his men's society of his find. As a corporate group, the latter men challenge another group of men or boys to attack the nest. The decision as to which group is challenged depends on the size of the nest: if the nest is not too big, the boys of the *me'ôk-re* will be challenged; if it is a big one, the young men of the *menõrõny-re* age grade or the men of the opposing men's society will be challenged. Most commonly, the *me'ôk-re* or the *menõrõny-re* are challenged, as such an attack is to be seen as one of the several rigorous tests which harden the younger men.

in the men's house and a specialist applies the *kwakbê* scarification to the chest of all the *me'ôk-re* boys. In the early evening, the men gather once again in front of the men's house to sing the *rop-'ã ngre-re*. In the afternoon of the next day, after bathing, all men receive a "beautiful" black painting, *in casu* the *pàtjarapê'ôk*, which concludes the ritual.

Ideally, the "dance of the jaguar" (*rop-'ã tor*) should be performed whenever a jaguar is killed. In practice, however, I only saw it accomplished when a young man killed his first jaguar or when a particularly "fierce" jaguar had been killed — e.g., one that had killed chickens near the village and which, as such, became an actual menace to the safety of the people in the village. In addition, the ritual was performed only when the killed jaguar was brought to the village, never when it was killed during a forest trek.

7.2 — Comparison with the post-war ritual

As should be clear, the ritual costume, the sequence of body painting, the application of *kwakbê* scarification on the body, and the performance of the *mengre-re prõt ariba* dance interrupted by the *tàkàk-'ã tor* dance are elements equally found in the post-war ritual. In addition, other aspects stand out as particular or as distinct from the ones described for the post-war ritual.

Whereas the returning warriors act as *dramatis personae* during the post-war ritual, the hunter who killed the jaguar has no specific role in the jaguar ritual. This can be explained by the fact that the ritual of the jaguar is a corporate activity emphasizing communal values rather than individual ones. The hunter does keep the skin of the slain animal and makes a hunting bag (*ropkà*, "jaguar skin") of it: carrying such a bag identifies all men who have killed a jaguar[21].

The hunter brings the slain jaguar to the village centre, where it remains attached to a pole for all people to see it. Such a procedure is also mentioned in a tale (App. B:4) where the scouts brought to the village specimens of people, plants, snakes and jaguars which they had encountered during their exploration. In all cases, the specimen brought to the village was related either to something unknown to the scouts, or to something dangerous. Hence, in all cases it was something "wild" (natural), alien, and therefore "unsocialized" which was withdrawn from the natural environment, the anti-social domain. While in this tale it is said that the

---

21   This custom is no longer practiced, as all jaguar skins are sold through FUNAI agents and as the traditional hunting bags have been replaced by plastic or leather ones.

people in the village beat the "natural" element, I never saw this happen with a slain jaguar. Instead, the people gathered around the animal and vividly commented on its physical power.

The performance of a "blessing song" by ritual leaders (*mengrenhõdjwỳnh*) is always prescribed at the first harvest of a newly ripened crop in the gardens or, in other words, before the crop can be eaten. Similarly, the intervention by the ritual leaders during the jaguar ritual is an act of "blessing" the jaguar before it can be eaten. "Blessing" is necessary in particular contexts in order to socialize a "wild" and "natural" element.

In the final phase of the *tàkàk* naming ceremony, the "honoured" children are "attacked" by a man embodying the jaguar. Holding the jaws of wild pigs in his hands, the "jaguar" symbolically scrapes the body of all honoured children as well as those of the accompanying ceremonial friends. That is why, as the Kayapo explain, the honoured children are extremely weak during that phase of the naming ceremony in question. In that ceremony, the jaguar is not killed but after the dance ritual specialists sing brief songs while facing the honoured children. These songs are said to "undo" the effects of the scrapings. After the killing of a jaguar, then, and while the ritual leader sings his "blessing song", all *me bê tàkàk* ("the tàkàk people") and *me bê nhàk* ("the *nhàk* people") gather around the slain jaguar. This is done to solemnize the killing of the jaguar who "has previously scraped them".

Before the singing of the "song of the jaguar" begins, a man delivers an improvised talk in a peculiar mocking tone of voice. It is called the "speech of the non-Kayapo people" (*kubẽkakrit kabẽn*) and is a humorous imitation of the language of the non-Kayapo who, as *kubẽ* ("strangers") and therefore less important people, are said to speak a nonsensical language. The incorporation of this ridiculing of the language of non-Kayapo people in the jaguar ritual can be explained by the fact that the jaguar lives in the same domain as the non-Kayapo people. It is the "natural" and anti-social area in which, as mentioned in Chapter 1, people may be transformed into animals or spirits, or where unknown, animal-like humans may live.

The *mengre-re prõt ariba* dance is performed in the early morning and is identical to the one described during the post-war ritual. When the dancers pass in front of a house who has lost a member to a (human) enemy, a kinswoman carrying a child or occasionally a grandchild of the victim on her shoulders, joins the group. This act can be compared to the one where, during the post-war ritual, kinswomen of victims of earlier attacks paint the returning warriors — an act explained as a social recognition of revenge. The *mengre-re prõt ariba* dance is briefly interrupted by another one called "the dance of the *tàkàk*" (*tàkàk-'ã tor*) — an allusion to the *tàkàk* naming ceremony during which, as mentioned earlier, the "honoured" children are symbolically "attacked" by a man embodying the jaguar.

The ritual costume which is worn during the *mengre-re prõt ariba* dance is identical to the one worn during the same dance in the post-war ritual: the bodies of the dancers are painted black all over (*amĩtyk* design) with charcoal, white feather down is glued to their hair with resin, and headbands of dried palm leaves (*krãdjêjamy*) are donned. Fibre or bark strips are twisted around their wrists and inserted in their armbands. The palm leaf headbands as well as the fibre or bark strips are gathered and hung up on the poles of the men's house.

After the dancing, a specialist applies the *kwakbê* scarification on the chest of all *me'ôk-re* boys; they are the ones who have eaten (or, at least, were allowed to eat)[22] the jaguar. On this occasion, however — and this is in contradistinction to the *kwakbê* applied during the post-war ritual — no charcoal is rubbed on the incisions and the scarification therefore leaves no permanent black lines on the body. As in the case during the post-war ritual, the *kwakbê* is applied to those who have been in touch with the blood of the victim and, as mentioned earlier, is meant to "undo the bad blood".

This brief analysis points out a remarkable structural similarity between the post-war ritual and the one performed on the occasion of the killing of a jaguar. And this is done not only in ritual expressions, but also, and above all, in ideological terms. This can be explained by the fact that jaguars (*rop*) are viewed by the Kayapo as "real enemies" (*kurêdjwỳnh*). The same being true for wasps (*amjy, Polybia sp.*): jaguars and wasps are renowned for their fierceness and fearlessness. As such, both the post-war and jaguar rituals are performed following the killing of an enemy. Therefore, in spite of differences in accentuation, the collective activities performed on both the occasions in question revolve around one central theme: the socialization of the killing of an enemy or, in other words, of someone or something considered dangerous to the community and, at the same time, "wild" and part of the "natural" domain.

---

22   The chest of all *me'ôk-re* is scarified on this occasion, even those who do not eat the jaguar meat.

CHAPTER V

RECENT ADAPTATIONS AND CONTEMPORARY WARFARE

During the last two decades, the Central Mekranoti and all other Kayapo groups have suffered important changes. Many of these changes came about because of their peaceful relations with the national society. At first, the Kayapo viewed these relations as a positive phenomenon, but it soon turned out that the price they had to pay for them far exceeded their expectations. In this Chapter, I will be mainly concerned with the changes on a socio-political level, as well as with the shift in frequency of warfare.

1. RECENT CHANGES: THE DIMINISHING OF THE OCCURRENCE OF WARFARE AND ITS CONSEQUENCES

By using the past tense whenever referring to the described Mekranoti raiding patterns, I have dealt with Mekranoti wars as if these were phenomena which are no longer practised. And, indeed, to a certain degree, this is true. Frequent and often peaceful contacts with certain groups or members of Western European and South American society have to be taken as the main reasons for this recent change. Basically, however, not only has warfare been affected by these recent contacts with the Brazilian society, since important alterations have been noted on several distinct levels, such as changes in the succession of chieftaincy, in the economy, and in the attitude of the younger men.

1.1 — Population increase: its causes and consequences

One of the most striking occurrences in recent Mekranoti history is the remarkable populational growth. The causes of this phenomenon and its consequences are what I will discuss in this section. In the following pages, I will provide a brief analysis of the available demographic data

GOT

GOT

GOT/KKK

KKK

KKK

±1905

±1906

1936

1941

(Ku'at)

1948

(Ku'at)
51 (9/10)

1941

(Nhõjkrã)
18 (6/3)

1947

northern mekranoti
(Angme'ê, Kênti)

(Angme'ê, Kênti)

(Angme'ê)
143 (15/22)

1947

1948

1957

(Bâti)
12 (4/2)

(Kênti)
68 (1/12)

(Tãpjêt)
150 (25/9)

(Karãnhin)
103 (13/14)

central mekranoti
(Kreti-re, Bepgogoti)
397 (41/47)

1955-1956

mekranoti
(Mote-re)
±100

mekranoti ±1906
(Mote-re)

±1906 (Õket, Pãnhkĩ, Karãnhin)
±90

mekranoti
(Mote-re,
Pãnhkĩ...)
190 (25/30)

1936

mekranoti
(Mote-re,
Pãnhkĩ...)
520 (56/61)

mekranoti

1947

mekranoti

1947

mekranoti

1947

mekranoti

southern mekranoti
(Kremõr...)
120 (9/18)

KEY

(...)   name of chief or leading man/men

26 (3/1)

⇡ ⇡ ⇡   number of adult men (*me kra-re* and *me bêngêt*)
           number of bachelors (*menõrõny-re*)
           total population

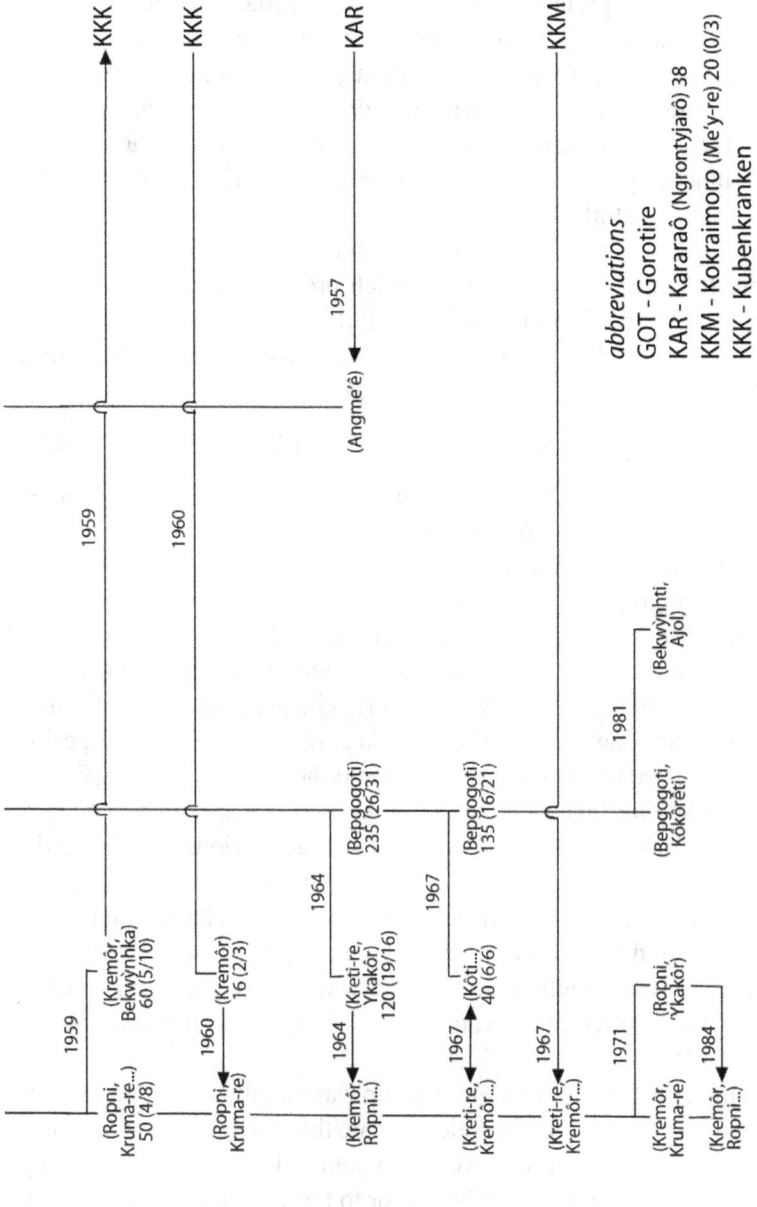

Figure 18 — Schematic representation of the main schisms and fusions of Mekranoti groups and their corresponding population size (until 1988)

on the Mekranoti groups. This analysis is important because several of the recent changes in Mekranoti society are, in one way or another, due to the favourable demographic evolution and vice versa.

Since this Chapter deals with *recent* adaptations, discussions here mainly focus on the period from 1967 to 1989. This period has not been chosen randomly: 1967 is the year when missionaries for the first time settled in the Central Mekranoti village, thus initiating the period of permanent contact between these Indians and agents of the Western civilization. It is also the first year on which precise demographic data are available. Instead of describing in detail the manifold aspects involved, I will often proceed by commenting on the data displayed in the form of graphics and tables.

I. the demographic evolution in the period from 1905 to 1967

First of all, it is interesting to focus upon the demographic aspects of Mekranoti population prior to 1967 by examining data on the demographic evolution of the Mekranoti population throughout this century. These data are displayed graphically in figure 18, a schematic presentation which is based upon a detailed analysis of the complex genealogical data gathered during fieldwork terms, and upon data provided by informants when discussing the composition of several historic villages. Yet, a note of caution is in order: although seemingly quite accurate, data regarding periods prior to 1967 are to be taken as estimates rather than as unerring figures. For the following investigation, I will present the data and ensuing reflections according to the two main pre-contact periods as discussed in Chapter 2: the period from 1905 to 1936 and the one from 1937 to 1953. A third part focuses upon the period from 1954 to 1967, the contact period.

In the period from 1906 to 1936, population increased from hundred and ninety to five hundred and twenty, which represents an annual increase of 3.4%. Three causes can be cited which elucidate this favourable development:

— first, in 1906 the Mekranoti group was mainly composed of young couples. Data gathered in the field indicate that the village of 1906 numbered fifty-five men, thirty-seven of whom belonged either to the age grade of the bachelors (*menõrõny-re*) or to the one of the young married men (*mekrany-re*). This explains why genealogical data evidence that many children were born in the first few years after the Mekranoti separated from the Gorotire. As a consequence, it is reasonable to assume that many of the children born in the first decade after the Mekranoti-Gorotire schism had become mature by the early 1930s: they had, as such, consummated marriage and this must have led, once again, to the birth of many children in the 1930s;

— second, table 6c shows that "only" twenty-eight people died either during attacks undertaken or during attacks suffered during this period. This relatively low death rate in comparison to later eras parallels the relatively few raids undertaken by the Mekranoti in that period;

— third, it is important to emphasize that not one Indian was reported to have died due to internal conflicts in that same period.

The year of 1937 was marked by the historically momentous fusion between the Mekranoti and the Menokanê, a dissident Gorotire group which was led by Tàpjêt and which numbered about hundred and fifty followers. The Mekranoti village therefore suddenly grew to about six hundred and seventy Indians. In the early contact period (1953-1957), the total Mekranoti population was about seven hundred and fifty Indians, divided over four communities. Yet, in the view of an analysis on population growth, this is quite an abstract number for, as I have stated earlier, two minor Mekranoti groups led by Karànhĩn and Ku'at had separated and had joined the Kubenkranken in that period. The combined population of these two secessionist groups was about hundred and fifty Indians. That is why, for reasons of comparability, I will here hypothetically assume that the total 1953 Mekranoti population numbered about nine hundred Indians — being the sum of the earlier mentioned figures. If so, the annual increase was about 1.9%, which is distinctly lower than in the preceding period. This relatively "low" growth can be ascribed to three causes:

— first, the high mortality rate due to warfare: of the two hundred and nineteen deaths recorded by Werner (1980:49-50) in the 1937-1953 period, no less than sixty-five (thirty percent) were related to warfare. In Chapter 3 I have already explained that this increase in war-related casualties was related to the escalation of the number of raids (especially on Brazilian settlements);

— second, the equally high mortality rate due to internal conflicts: Werner (ibid.:52-53) mentions nineteen deaths due to "homicide". I would like to add two remarks to Werner's data. First, it is unfortunate that Werner doesn't distinguish here between intragroup conflict and conflicts with other Kayapo groups: he uses the term "homicide" as a reference to both types of conflict. Second, in Chapter 3 I have already referred to the incongruity between Werner's data and my own. At this point, it is important to mention that Werner refers to a total of five hundred and ninety-seven deaths in the period from 1905 to 1977, whereas my genealogical data refer to no less than eight hundred and twenty-nine deaths in the same period. The only cause of death which I really investigated in

AGE	NUMBER of INDIV.	▲	●	NUMBER of INDIV.
75–79	–		a	–
70–74	–			1
65–69	1			1
60–64	1			2
55–59	2			1
50–54	3			4
45–49	7			10
40–44	11			4
35–39	6			4
30–34	5			5
25–29	5			6
20–24	11	1953 ⟶		23
15–19	9	1958 ⟶		10
10–14	7	1961 ⟶		10
5–9	15	1968 ⟶		12
0–4	28			34

AGE	NUMBER of INDIV.	▲	●	NUMBER of INDIV.
80–84	1		b	–
75–79	1			–
70–74	2			–
65–69	3			3
60–64	5			7
55–59	9			4
50–54	4			4
45–49	5			6
40–44	5			6
35–39	11			20
30–34	9			10
25–29	7			8
20–24	14			14
15–19	27			29
10–14	29			40
5–9	39			37
0–4	53			52

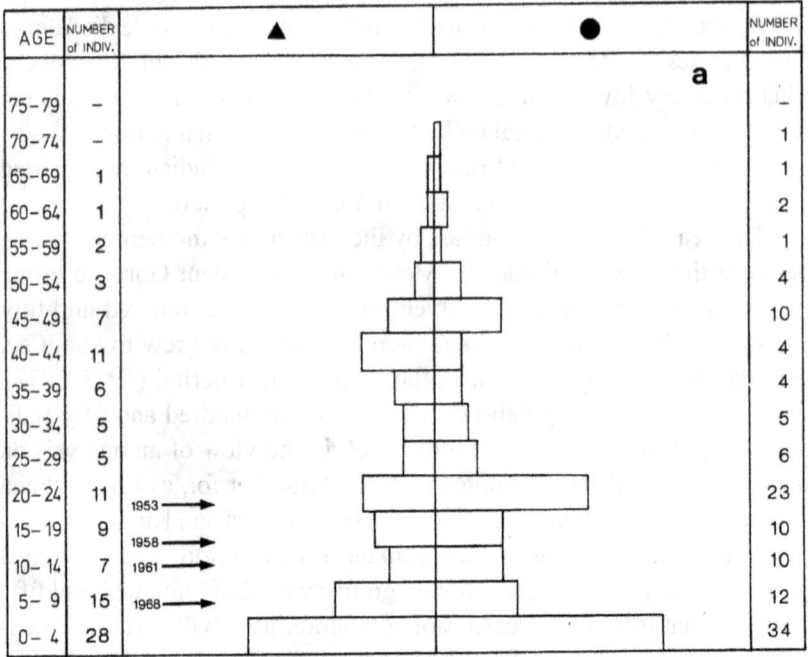

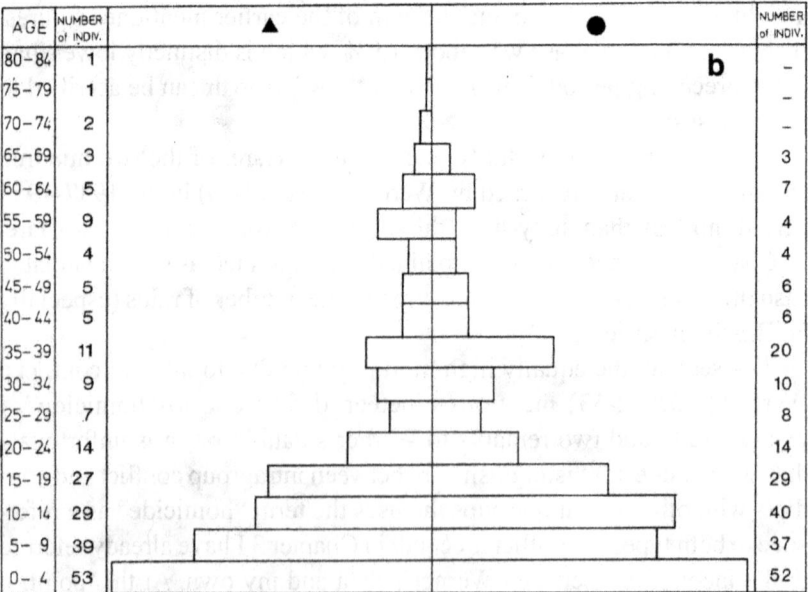

Figure 19 — Age pyramids of the population at the Central Mekranoti village. (a) situation in 1974; (b) situation in 1989

the field was victims due to warfare and of which hundred and four Indians died (see table 6c). Of the remaining seven hundred and twenty-five casualties, I have specific data on death causes for only three hundred and sixty-nine (fifty-one percent) persons: nineteen (three percent) died of old age; forty-four (six percent) died of numerous causes such as accidents, general weakness, childbirth, and so on; two hundred and forty-seven (thirty-four percent) died of disease; and fifty-one (seven percent) during intragroup conflicts; an additional eight (one percent) Indians were said to be lost and never found again. As such, I found at least forty-one (!) deaths related to intragroup conflict in the period 1937-1953. This number is significantly higher than the nineteen suggested by Werner.

The period from 1954 to 1967 was marked by "pacification" and by the ensuing contact diseases. The number of victims of diseases such as measles, whooping cough, influenza and common colds was extremely high. Werner (1980:49-50) reports that, in these turbulent years, ninety-nine (forty-six percent) of the two hundred and fourteen casualties among the Mekranoti were due to disease. I take the view that many more Indians have died of disease and I do, therefore, cast doubt upon the actual number of victims which, according to Werner, have died due to contact diseases. This discrepancy between Werner's data and mine can be a consequence of the above-mentioned difference in data regarding the total number of deaths recorded regarding the 1905-1977 period: my data refers to thirty-eight percent more casualties than that mentioned by Werner. To provide evidence that ninety-nine casualties due to contact diseases must be an underestimation, it suffices to have a look at the case of the Northern Mekranoti: this group — the smallest of all three Mekranoti groups — numbered about hundred and sixty Indians in 1957 and was joined by thirty-eight Kararaô Indians that same year. Yet, despite this fusion, only fifty survived in 1967, twenty of whom were living in other Mekranoti villages. I consequently assume that the number of casualties due to disease among the Northern Mekranoti alone would be at least eighty or so. Similarly, the Central Mekranoti suffered greatly from contact diseases: after "pacification" along the Jarina River in 1953, they moved to the Iriri-Curua River area where on three occasions the governmental Indian agency tried to settle these Indians near newly established posts. In vain, however, since the Indians always retreated to their former habitat. Whenever discussing these movements with the informants, they insisted over and over again that many had died (especially children and older people) near each of these posts. It is therefore rather ironic that the Central Mekranoti, who departed from the traditional Jarina River area to flee from the diseases and from the "inadequate" medical assistance, suffered more from contact diseases than the Southern Mekranoti who remained in the Jarina area. Indeed, the Southern Mekranoti probably were those Mekranoti to have suffered the least from contact diseases. T. Turner (1987ms:89) mentions that "Metuktire [Southern Mekranoti] losses from contact epidemic diseases did not amount to an aggregate total of more than ten percent". This less dramatic death rate was partly due to the better medical assistance provided by the Villas Bôas brothers, and partly due to the fact that no post was erected near the Southern Mekranoti village during these critical years; contact with outsiders was, as such, limited to the very minimum. Things were entirely different during the three earlier mentioned attempts to attract the Central Mekranoti, where medical assistance was often rendered impossible due to the lack of financial means and where national colonists moved in (or very near) the newly erected Indian posts.

In all, thus, the effect of contact diseases was tremendous, and the original 1953 population of about seven hundred and fifty Mekranoti had dwindled to about four hundred and thirty Indians in 1967, divided as follows: two hundred and six Central Mekranoti; some hundred and ninety Southern Mekranoti; and less than thirty Northern Mekranoti. It should be mentioned, though, that about fifty-five Southern Mekranoti joined the Kubenkranken in 1959, of whom some fifteen eventually returned. In addition to the sixty-five (thirty percent) casualties resulting from war-related activities, Werner (1980:49-50) also mentions that seven (three percent) died of accidents, ten (four percent) of old age and eighty-three (thirty-eight percent) of other causes.

If, for reasons of comparability, I hypothetically assume that the total 1967 Mekranoti population numbered about four hundred and eighty-five Indians — being the sum of the above-mentioned 1967 population of four hundred and thirty Indians and the fifty-five or so Southern Mekranoti that joined the Kubenkranken — the average annual *decrease* was about 3.0%.

The devastating effect of the high mortality rate due to contact diseases is clearly visible in figure 19a where the population pyramid is "squeezed" for the age periods five to twenty. These are people who were born during the contact years.

II. recent population growth (1969-1989): its causes

One of the most striking changes I was able to observe in Mekranoti society in the period from 1974 to 1981 was the earlier attachment of young men to the affinal household, that is to the village periphery. There was, as a matter of fact, a tendency in which emphasis is shifting from the village centre to the village periphery. This tendency was noticeable in the following four recent developments: the anticipated marriage of young men; the process of spending less time in the men's house by the young men; the emergence of a new and periphery-oriented form of leadership; and emphasis on ceremonies organized along the lines of kinship. I will now discuss these phenomena consecutively, and will also show how these recent developments influence the village community life.

III. the anticipated marriage of young men

Since most of the following discussions involve the Central Mekranoti, I will here only be concerned with an examination of the recent demographic evolution of that particular group. The data on which the following interpretations are based are displayed in tables 9a-c.

Reviewing the period of twenty years under consideration, the first aspect that draws attention is the marked population growth. Indeed, in the period from 1969 to 1989, the average annual population increase was about 5.6% which is strikingly higher than for any of the above-mentioned pre-contact periods. This phenomenon can partly be explained by the improved medical assistance. As mentioned earlier, missionaries first settled among the Central Mekranoti in 1967 and this event marked the introduction of adequate medical assistance: at first, it was provided only on an irregular basis (1967-1970), and an epidemic of malaria with complications killed about forty Indians in 1968 — an occasion during which the missionary and his family also nearly died. But from then on, medical assistance was provided quite consistently first by missionaries of the Summer Institute of Linguistics (from 1971 on) and later by agents from FUNAI (from 1973 on).

Such factors as the introduction of "miracle drugs", a quite effective vaccination program coupled with the occasional visits of medical teams to the community, and the transportation by plane of severely sick people to small hospitals in interior towns such as Altamira or Itaituba, all greatly improved the health situation in the community and severely cut down the number of casualties. Yet, improved medication alone cannot account for the astounding population increase. Indeed, it looks as if in the contemporary Mekranoti villages, the acceleration of the boy's developmental cycle is stimulated, if not provoked, by the elders.

When asking a mature Mekranoti approximately when a boy has his penis sheath (*mydjê*) bestowed, he will answer that the decision depends on the elder men in the men's house and will immediately add that in former times, penis sheaths were bestowed on much older boys than today. To be more specific, informants often insisted that the penis sheath used

Table 9 — Demographic evolution of Central Mekranoti population in the period 1969-1989. (+) immigrants and (-) emigrants in the preceding system; (*) for the 1969 calculation, the small group of men that followed Kreti-re to *porori* and returned shortly afterwards, has been included.

	1969*	1970-1974			1975-1979			1980-1984			1985-1989		
AGE	TTL	+	−	TTL	+	−	TTL	+	−	TTL	+	−	TTL
80-84													1
75-79										1			1
70-74							1			1			2
65-69				1			1			2			3
60-64	1			1			2			3		2	5
55-59	1			2			3			7		2	9
50-54	2			3			7			11			4
45-49	3			7			11	1	1	4		1	5
40-44	6	1		11			5			6		1	5
35-39	10	2		6			5			6			11
30-34	6	1		5			5	2		11		1	9
25-29	4	1		5			12		1	10		1	7
20-24	4	1	1	11	2		8	3	1	8			14
15-19	10	3		9			7	1		15		3	27
10-14	8	2		7	1		15			30		2	29
5-9	7			15			28	4		31	1	2	39
0-4	15			28			34	1		42		1	53
Total	79	11	1	112	3	0	144	12	3	188	1	16	224

Caption row: MALE POPULATION

	1969*	1970-1974			1975-1979			1980-1984			1985-1989		
AGE	TTL	+	−	TTL	+	−	TTL	+	−	TTL	+	−	TTL
80-84										1			
75-79							1						
70-74				1									
65-69	1	1		1									3
60-64				2			1			3		1	7
55-59	2			1			4	1		9	1		4
50-54	1	1		4	1		11			3			4
45-49	3			10			3	1		4			6
40-44	10	I		4			4	1		6			6
35-39	5		1	4			5			6		4	20
30-34	5			5			6	2		25	1		10
25-29	5	2		6			23	1	1	9			8
20-24	4	1		23			10			8		1	14
15-19	23		1	10			9	3		15			29
10-14	12	1		10			12			29		4	40
5-9	9	1		12			33	4	2	44		5	37
0-4	11			34		1	47	3		43		2	52
Total	91	8	2	127	1	1	169	15	4	207	2	17	240

Caption row: FEMALE POPULATION

AGE	TOTAL CENTRAL MEKRANOTI POPULATION												
	1969	1970-1974			1975-1979			1980-1984			1985-1989		
	TTL	+	−	TTL	+	−	TTL	+	−	TTL	+	−	TTL
80-84										1			1
75-79							1			1			1
70-74				1			1			1			2
65-69	1	1		2			1			2			6
60-64	1			3			3			6		3	12
55-59	3			3			7		1	16	1	2	13
50-54	3	1		7	1		18	1	1	14			8
45-49	6	2	1	17			14	1		8		1	11
40-44	16	2		15			9	2		12		1	11
35-39	15	1	2	10			10	1		12		4	31
30-34	11	1		10			11	2	1	36	1	1	19
25-29	9	3		11	1		35	4	2	19		1	15
20-24	8	4		34			18	1		16		1	28
15-19	33	1	1	19			16	3		30		3	56
10-14	20	2		17			27	4		59		6	69
5-9	16	1		27			61	5	2	75		7	76
0-4	26			62		1	81	3		85		3	105
Total	170	19	4	239	2	1	313	27	7	395	2	33	464

to be bestowed when the boy "already had pubic hair" (*arỳp ngre 'ô kam*) that is, at the age of about fifteen. I initially considered such a statement as an idealized reflection on the past, "when things were better" and "when the Kayapo customs were truly followed", until I saw a picture taken by Fritz Krause in 1909 in an Irã'ãmranhre village. The picture shows an adolescent boy without a penis sheath, at an age any contemporary Mekranoti boy would already have had his penis sheath for years.

Field data show that most mature Mekranoti men of some forty years or older had received their penis sheath at the age of fifteen to eighteen or more[1]. Currently, the penis sheath is being bestowed on boys of some eleven to fourteen years. The "age" when young men consummate marriage becomes even more conspicuous: today this occurs at the age of fifteen to eighteen years, while the oral tradition on earlier times indicates twenty-five to thirty years. Disregarding the few exceptions which exist both in pre- and post-contact eras, a boy generally used to remain a member of the *me 'ôk-re* age grade for about eight to fourteen years; nowadays this period under ritual tutelage by a "substitute father" is limited to four

---

1   The referred "ages" were obtained by trying to localize the period when a given person was born, when he received his penis sheath and when he consummated marriage. I used the dates I obtained through the group's ethno-history (Appendix A).

or five years. This phenomenon is even more accentuated for the period a young man belongs to the *menõrõny-re* age grade: nine to fifteen years in pre-contact period, three to five years in these days.

Although it has to be emphasized that the transition from one age grade to another is measured in terms of the physical development of the person, it cannot be denied that the acceleration of the male developmental process is factual and this may lead to some interesting reflections.

The most immediate consequence of early marriage is that nowadays hardly any young man reaches the status of *menõrõny'ãtũm*. This status has always been idealized: the Mekranoti consider such men to be strong and insensible to pain — both highly appreciated male virtues. To marry soon was continually taken as a sign of weakness: it was avoided since this would lead to a premature incorporation into the *mekrakramtĩ* age grade. *Mekrakramtĩ* are senior men who may give formal orations and who, as T. Turner (1965:333) has put it, "are cast in the more dynamic role of the political leaders of the community". It was, therefore, considered undesirable to become a *mekrakramtĩ*, if a man had not yet acquired a solid basis of experience and prestige.

Yet, in the Central Mekranoti village of 1981, three men had already become a *mekrakramtĩ* at a fairly young age; by 1989, there were no less than nine of them. Given the current young marriage age, the tendency is for this phenomenon to become more and more generalized. As the older Mekranoti disapprovingly allude, "the young men just got their penis sheath and they already have a child".

In ancient Mekranoti villages, such as *krãnhmrõpryjaka*, a numerical balance almost existed between the *menõrõny-re* and *mekra-re* age grades — *in casu* sixty-two *menõrõny-re* and sixty-five *mekra-re* and *mebêngêt*. The Mekranoti consider such a situation desirable and this may be explained not only in the light of the apparent population increase which such a position implies, but likewise as the accomplishment of an ideal form of formal opposition between the *menõrõny-re* and *mekra-re* age grades — opposition which is expressed in certain ritual contexts[2].

In 1980, the Central Mekranoti village numbered thirteen *menõrõny-re* and only two *menõrõny'ãtũm*. This while there were no less than fifty-eight *mekra-re* and *mebêngêt*. And although this disequilibrium might partially be explained by the result of severe epidemics which killed many children between 1953 and 1963 (see figure 19a), the anticipated

---

2   Including sexual relations since an institutional pattern of sexual rivalry exists between these two age grades (T. Turner 1965:280-285): the wives of the *mekra-re* prefer the *menõrõny-re* as lovers, and in turn the *mekra-re* have sexual intercourse with the wives of the *menõrõny-re* (cf. App. B:11-12).

marriage of the young men unquestionably is more important a factor in determining this phenomenon.

Since the bestowal of the penis sheath is invariably attributed to the decision of the elder men, by bestowing the penis sheath, these senior men — representing the community's decision — formally recognize the sexual maturity of the boys and consequently acknowledge the boys' readiness for procreation.

This observation is congruous with "recent" Mekranoti philosophy. Many formal orations I witnessed in the 1974-1979 period included direct stimulus towards the young men to procreate. Similar assertions were invariably associated with such positive factors as the permanent medical assistance they received from the Brazilians, the abundance of natural resources in the area, the lack of the possibility of being attacked by enemies and, above all, the "good mutual understanding" (*uma-ri mex kam*) within the community: between 1973 and 1983, only one club-fight took place in that particular village and major ceremonies succeeded each other at a steady rhythm of two or three performances each year. It therefore seems as if the Mekranoti intentionally reduced the period a young man spends in the men's house on behalf of a swift demographic increase or, as they perpetually say, "to have a village as large as before". The earlier bestowal of the penis sheath and the accelerated process of consummating marriage are therefore consequences of the eagerness to exploit the current propitious circumstances.

In a way, this acceleration process is also related to the current lack of warfare. In pre-contact eras, the young men (i.e. the *menõrõny-re* and, to a lesser extent, the *mekrany-re*) figured among the most active warriors. Warfare was a time-consuming matter, since the warriors often spent months in a row away from the village. Combined with the high male mortality rate in warfare, this absence of warriors led to the phenomenon that, in pre-contact eras, women spent nearly fifty-two percent of their reproductive years without a husband (Werner 1983:242). Using the techniques described by Bogue and Bogue (1970), Werner calculated that the fertility rate in that period was 6.5, meaning that a woman who survived to age fifty could expect to give birth 6.5 times. Things have changed drastically in the last years. Long war-expeditions are practically non-existent, while the length of major treks is nowadays reduced to the very minimum (see the next section). Young men therefore spend much less time away from the village, with the result that women were single for only thirty-three percent of their reproductive years in the period from 1965 to 1977 (Werner 1983:242). As a result, the fertility rate has soared to 8.5 in recent years.

1.2 — The process of spending less time in the men's house by the young men

In addition to the anticipated marriage of young men, yet another change has recently taken place: not only has the period which the young men spend in the men's house been severely reduced due to early marriage, but also these younger men equally adopted the custom of not sleeping in the men's house. Instead, they sleep in their maternal household or, as sometimes occurs, in the house of a fiancée. To be more precise, since about 1977 only some married men with new-born children (*mekrakarà-re*) still occasionally reside in the men's house[3].

Even during the daytime, however, the *me'ôk-re* and *menõrõny-re* started showing up less frequently in the men's house. When this tendency became more and more accentuated, some friction resulted: in 1978, the mature men openly started commenting upon this trend. Jokingly, the young men were designated as *metekrekamprêtx* ("people with itchy bottoms") by the older ones. This designation referred to the apparent impossibility of remaining seated for some time and obviously alluded to the younger men's actions in the men's house.

About a year later, during the final phase of a major ceremony, the frictions between the more "traditional" men (those who continued going to the men's house and generally belonging to the *mekrakramtî* and *mebêngêt* age grades) and those who didn't regularly spend some time with their fellow tribesmen (generally of the *me'ôk-re*, *menõrõny-re* and *mekrany-re* age grades) reached a high point. A ceremonial trek of about one month was planned and it was decided that only the men would go on this trek, leaving the women and children in the village to obtain medical assistance. A discussion arose. Although the debate apparently focused upon which *direction* to take for the ceremonial trek, the essence of the discussion turned around the *duration* of the trek[4]: moving to the east (as the elders wanted) would take a longer time but more meat and palm straw could be obtained. The younger men preferred trekking to the west, hoping to remain less time out of the village. The discussion was left unsettled when the more "traditional" group took off to the east, the direction they had opted for. This, while the others stayed behind in the

3   But even this aspect of the post-partum restriction period has been cut: it ideally spreads over a period of one to two years and is nowadays reduced to six months or, at times, merely a few weeks.
4   It should be emphasized that at this occasion some elder men took sides with the *mekrany-re*, openly defending and even supporting the young men's idea as to which direction should be taken.

village "to remain close to their spouses" (*prõ kôt ikwã kadjy*). This was viewed with contempt by the other group.

During that ceremonial trek, which was reduced to two weeks, a general feeling of depression seemed to have stricken the men. Almost every night the conversation was concentrated on the recently developed crisis. No enthusiasm seemed to prevail during the hunting and moving to the next campsite. I often heard the men say that they "no longer had a good mutual understanding" (*arỳp uma-ri punu*) within the village and that a "split was about to occur" (*aben owajki-ja 'ỳr*). One young leader then suggested a change in the sitting places in the men's house; he proposed that the *mekrany-re* and the *menõrõny-re* would all occupy a single sitting place (thus forming one men's group), while the older men would occupy a second sitting place (forming, as such, the second men's group). The re-ordering of the men's societies and the composition of the "sitting places" frequently happened in Mekranoti history: just like temporary schisms, these rearrangements often were carried into effect as an attempt to reduce existing tension within the community.

As he explained to me later, the young leader wanted to reunite both these younger men's groups since "there are too few *menõrõny-re*" — or, as the Mekranoti say, "there are no *menõrõny-re*" (*menõrõny-re ne ket*) — in the hope that reuniting them with the *mekrany-re*[5] would stimulate these younger men to come and stay more often in the men's house instead of staying in the residential houses. According to him, the younger men's lack of attachment to the men's house was the essence of the disagreement. This phenomenon can, once again, be partly explained by the abatement of warfare: during the often lengthy war expeditions, the younger men were taught such things as endurance and bellicosity, but also male solidarity. Now that warfare was no longer regularly undertaken, this solidarity was fading among the youngsters. Instead, their aspirations were directed towards the village periphery — a point which I will return to later in this Chapter.

Although the idea of rearranging the men's groups seemed to receive the approval of those who had participated in the trek, things changed upon returning to the village. Several older men, among them the main village chief, resisted the idea by arguing that there were enough men to maintain the two men's societies and that they preferred it this way. The discussion then slowly died out.

---

5   As mentioned earlier, in 1980, the Central Mekranoti village numbered seventeen *mekrany-re* and fifteen *menõrõny-re*, as opposed to forty-one *mekrakramtĩ* and *mebêngêt*.

1.3 — The emergence of a new and periphery-oriented form of leadership

About two decades ago, a new type leadership emerged in the Gorotire village. From there, it spread to most of the other Kayapo villages. I refer to the function of what the Kayapo nowadays call *"delegado"* (the Portuguese term for police officer). Similar to Brazilian pattern, these *"delegados"* lead the "police". A Kayapo police-corps consists of several men but does not constitute a separate men's society. Rather, the police-corps is formed by members of the various men's societies. Membership in the police-corps is free to any man who is willing to join it. Generally, only *menõrõny-re* or *mekrany-re* men seem to join the *krã kam ngônh* ("people with pans on their heads" or police). The activities of the *delegado* and his adherents are pre-eminently related to the sphere of the village periphery. All dressed up in hats, shirts, a pair of trousers, socks and shoes, and carrying the indispensable revolver, these men are said to prevent stealing and adulterous relations, to see to it that the people work well and that the people dance "nicely", to prevent confusion at the arrival of an airplane and to expel the "bad Brazilians" (*kubẽ punu bõm kumê* i.e. "to throw out the bad non-Kayapo"). In PI Mekranoti, however, these functions are more symbolic than effective: no prison exists[6], nor have I ever seen the police-corps act against intruders (such action still being organized by men's societies). Nowadays, however, several police-men are present during any major communal activity.

The police-corps never assembles in the men's house, as is the case for the men's societies. Rather, they assemble in the house of the *delegado*. Coffee and some food is given to the police-men during their short, nearly daily meetings.

In 1978, the police-corps organized a short "engagement" ritual. One evening, all police-men gathered in front of the house of the *delegado*. Seated on mats or tree-trunks, they formed a ring, encircling a group of about ten *menõrõny-re* boys. Some elderly women (among which the *benjadjwỳrỳni*, the female chief) were seated outside the ring of police-men. The *delegado* then asked a boy which girl he was courting, if he would maintain her as fiancée and eventually marry her. The boy said the name of his girl-friend and the *delegado* then went to the elderly women to consult them on whether such a relationship was allowed and/ or desired. The *delegado* proceeded like that, consulting boy after boy. Never did the elderly women object to the choices made, but on one

6   In 1974-1975 such a small prison existed in PI Gorotire.

occasion there was some hesitation on the part of the *delegado* when a boy mentioned the name of a *kupry* woman who had already procreated two children. The ritual was concluded by a short speech, in which the *delegado* proclaimed the values of monogamous relationships "just as Brazilians do" (*kubenkryt kôt*) and where he stated the duty of the policemen to prevent adultery in the village.

This "engagement" ritual was not a traditional Kayapo one. The *delegado* informed me that he had set up this meeting to obtain a definition of the composition of the young couples and in order to, in this way, avoid the occasional frictions between these young men over girls.

I only saw this ritual performed once, and about a year later many of the boys already had changed fiancées. Yet, the interesting point of the ritual is that marriage — a kin-based matter and, therefore, one of the basic principles of domestic group organization — proved to be the focus of the ritual. It clearly was a Kayapo adaptation of the Brazilian marriage ritual, which the *delegado* had seen during one of his visits to interior towns.

The police-corps represents one of the elements which the Kayapo took over from other, non-Kayapo societies. It constitutes a progressive force within the community. The Mekranoti police-corps is composed mostly of younger men who prove to be the most susceptible to adopting Brazilian customs. Being organized as a corporate group, these progressive men are introducing some small changes in rules of behaviour: they are visiting houses they normally would never enter, and are occasionally censuring other tribesmen.

During my stays in PI Mekranoti, centre-oriented traditional chieftaincy (*benjadjwỳr*) was not combined with the periphery-oriented function of *delegado* in the sense that one man never held both these political functions at the same time. Rather, one "important man" (such as a man who had been trained in chieftaincy or who had proven his capacity as a potential young leader) held the function of *delegado*. When being indicated as a "real chief" (*benjadjwỳr kumrenhtx*), the *delegado* indicates his successor and leaves the police-corps to lead his men's society.

Several of the recently appointed Kayapo chiefs, such as Tôtô'i (in PI Gorotire), Kôkôrêti and Ajol (in the Central Mekranoti village) have been a *delegado* before becoming chief of a men's society. The institution of head of the police-corps has, therefore, turned into one of the possible means of consolidating one's future appointment as a chief; it can thus be taken as a newly emerged variation of being leader (*meobadjwỳnh*) of the junior men in the men's house.

This new form of leadership has been severely condemned by the

Southern Mekranoti, numerically the sole important Kayapo of the Xingu group not to have any form of police-corps. The more conservative Southern Mekranoti argue that the Kayapo should not imitate similar Brazilian political institutions, but rather should maintain and limit themselves to the proper, traditional Kayapo organizations. To be sure, the Southern Mekranoti are currently to be considered among the most warlike of all Kayapo groups. This factor, as well as the one that the posts near these villages are run by tribesmen, may explain the rejection of excessive Brazilian influence.

1.4 — Emphasis on ceremonies organized along the lines of kinship

In pre-contact eras, the numerous trekking groups reunited in the ancestral villages to carry out the elaborate ceremonial activities (Gross 1979:330; Posey 1981ms). Ceremonialism seems to atrophy in the current small villages as a direct consequence of a reduced village population. Many Kayapo ceremonies are characterized by the participation of individuals who have inherited the right to perform a specific ritual act or to carry out a specific ritual function. The participation of such individuals is seen as an essential part of the performance of the ceremonies. Smaller villages who lack the necessary number of men to fulfil the many ritual privileges, as well as the necessary holders of each of these related privileges, are confronted with the impossibility of performing such ceremonies.

In Chapter 1, I drew attention to the distinction between "specific naming ceremonies" and "comprehensive naming ceremonies". "Specific naming ceremonies" such as *bep*, *kôkô*, *ire*, and so on, are sponsored by members of different residential segments — i.e., of different families and therefore not necessarily by siblings. This while all four of the "comprehensive naming ceremonies" — *memybijôk, menibijôk, krwỳrỳkangô* and *bô kam me tor* — have the specific feature that all sponsors are invariably parallel-sex siblings. Comprehensive naming ceremonies therefore accentuate kinship relations which are the basis of the organization of the village periphery: emphasis in these ceremonies is, accordingly, put on periphery-oriented organization.

The category of specific naming ceremonies seems to be the most easily affected by such populational fluctuations. These ceremonies are among the first to no longer be performed. In fact, forty-eight (seventy percent) of the total number of sixty-eight naming ceremonies performed prior to the contact period (1953-1957) were comprehensive naming ceremonies; after the contact period, no less than forty-one (seventy-seven

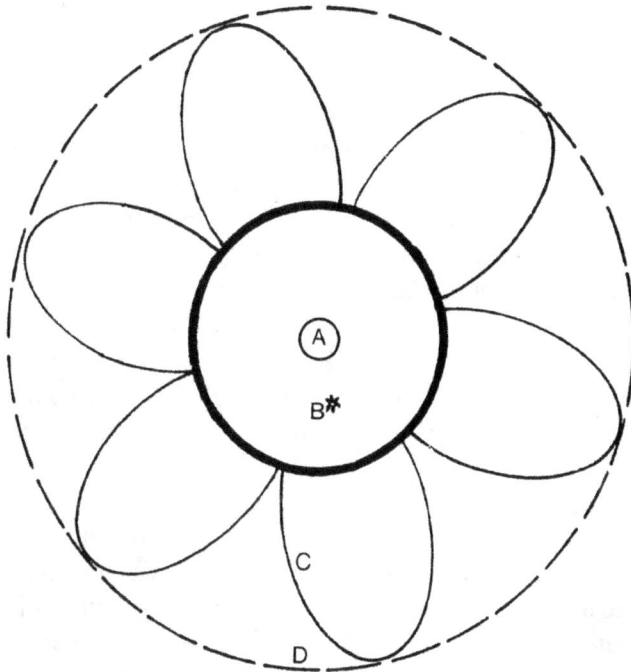

Figure 20 — Model of exploitation of natural resources around a village by alternatively undertaking circular treks in different directions. (A) village; (B) *kutakênhtxdjà* area of daily hunting; (C) *õntomõr* (circular trekking); (D) area exploited

percent) of the fifty-three[7] naming ceremonies performed were of the comprehensive type. More strikingly, however, is the observation that all twelve naming ceremonies performed by groups on the occasion of a temporary village schism were of the comprehensive type. This, as well as the increase in the number of comprehensive naming ceremonies performed in recent years, seems partly due to demographic reasons. Indeed, specific naming ceremonies are particularly complex in the sense of requiring numerous holders of specific privileges. Referring to the functioning of communal political groups, T. Turner (1965:79) mentioned that "the 'critical mass' of population for the effective functioning of the com-

7   These numbers include the naming ceremonies performed by the Southern Mekranoti in the period between 1964 and 1969 and which are not displayed in the Appendix A.

munal institutions is probably between hundred and twenty and hundred and fifty". I suggest that the same is true for the effective functioning of ceremonial life. Yet, the number and variation of residential segments in a village are more indicative than references to overall village population: two villages with the same population are not necessarily able to perform the same gamma of ceremonies, nor the same variety of ceremonies. The ritual privileges being held by residential segments, those villages which lack the owing segments (and, consequently, the individuals who have inherited the specific rights related to these segments) of the privileges that are related to the ceremony, are unable to perform that ritual. The most dramatic restriction is the one on villages lacking the residential segment which owns the ritual function of ceremonial leader (*ngrenhõdjwỳnh*). The presence of a man with that ritual function is imperative in all specific naming ceremonies.

"Comprehensive naming ceremonies", on the other hand, are not characterized by the necessary participation of a great number of such individuals with specific privileges. These ceremonies are, therefore, often the sole naming ceremonies which smaller villages still can perform. Still, in these cases, a minimum of participant dancers is required. I suggest that with a population of less than ten mature men or women (representing a minimum village population of forty to sixty Indians), naming ceremonies would cease to be celebrated.

There is, nevertheless, nowadays a tendency for smaller villages to join other villages in order to celebrate the important naming ceremonies. In this way, in 1980, the Southern Mekranoti of PI Kretire managed to perform a *bep* (specific) naming ceremony by inviting the men of PI Jarina as well as two of the three ritual specialists (*ngrenhõdjwỳnh*) of PI Mekranoti. Likewise, in PI Bau, a comprehensive naming ceremony was performed during a visit of some Central Mekranoti families in 1980: it was the first naming ceremony performed in that group in the last fifteen years.

In sum, these recent changes seem to indicate that it is not really ceremonialism which is necessarily profoundly affected, but rather the centre-related political groupings. In addition, this diminishing emphasis on centre-related political groupings seems to be a consequence of the lack of a continuous state of warfare.

2. THE 1980 VILLAGE SCHISM

In spite of the fact that internal peace has prevailed in the Central Mekranoti village since 1973, a village schism did occur. During this schism,

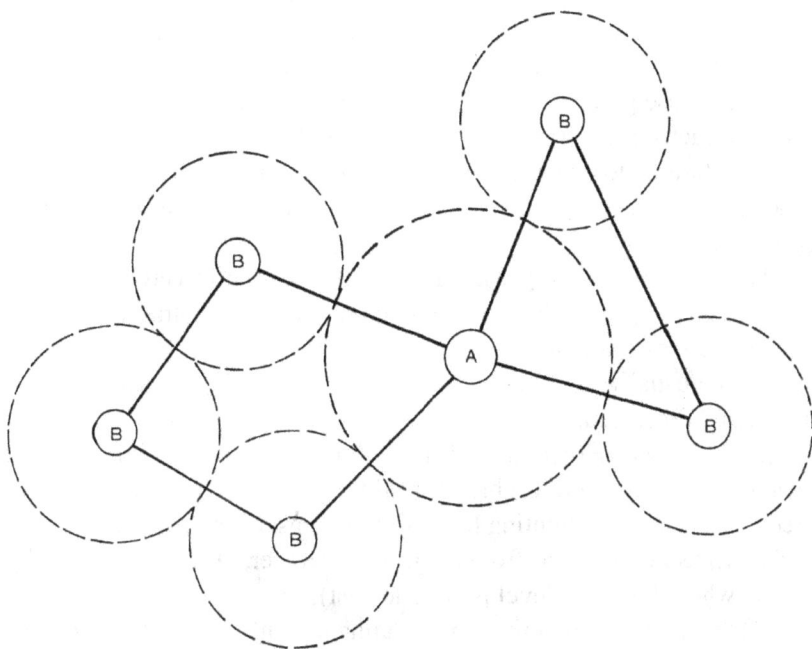

Figure 21 — Model of Mekranoti trekking pattern in recent pre-contact periods. (A) base village; (B) surrounding villages.

a small group of men moved with their families to the Iriri River, the FUNAI post near the village was named PI Pukanu. The motives for this village schism can be found in tension which emerged on a political level (see next section) and the economic adaptation which involves village sedentarism. To understand the mechanism of this village schism and the move of the main Central Mekranoti group to the Iriri Novo River, it is useful to first look at the extent of the recent economic adaptation.

2.1 — The economic pressure

Prior to the so-called "pacification" in 1953-1957, the Mekranoti occupied extensive interfluvial areas of Central Brazil. Numerous villages were built between the Xingu and Jamanxim Rivers. Dispersed over the tribal territory, these villages were, nevertheless, often not occupied for periods exceeding one or two years. Rather, the population tended to move constantly from one village to another. Such migrations, during which often relatively important distances were covered (ranging, at times, over hundred and fifty kilometres), had important economic foundations and consequences. Residing in a given village, the Mekranoti exploited those gardens which had been laid out during a previous stay, while on each occasion new gardens were laid out. The continuous procedure of returning to villages which had been occupied beforehand resulted in a constant regeneration of available gardens spread over the almost entire tribal territory.

This constant moving was undoubtedly related to ceremonial life. Most major rituals, such as naming ceremonies, are characterized by a fixed pattern of four phases:

(1) the usually long period of preparations, during which songs are taught and rehearsed;

(2) the *õntomõr* (ceremonial trek), during which large quantities of meat or fish are gathered. This is usually done either by collecting hundreds of tortoises, by hunting herds of wild pigs, or by using the timbó[8] (a fishing technique used from August to October, at the end of the dry season when the water-level is at its lowest);

(3) the preparation of the food, relating not only to the obtained meat or fish, but also to the harvesting and preparation of vast amounts of manioc or corn flour;

(4) the climax of the ceremony, usually accompanied by a major all-night dance, interrupted on one or two occasions when most of the prepared food is consumed.

Unless simplified by a stroke of luck when a herd of wild pigs was encountered exactly at the planned conclusive phase of the ceremony, the second phase invariably required a ceremonial trek. Such *õntomõr* ("to go away for a few nights") was undertaken either to a major river to fish, or into the forest to collect tortoises. The third phase, on the other hand, demanded the harvest of large quantities of manioc or corn from the sponsors' gardens.

Yet, two types of treks are to be distinguished:

(1) the *õntomõr* which I refer to as "circular trekking": during such treks, the participants leave the village, make a circular movement on one side of the settlement, and return to that same village to conclude the ceremony;

(2) the *mey* which I refer to as "linear trekking": during such treks, the people leave the village to go slowly to another site where the people

---

8   Timbó is a generic term referring to drugs found in tropical lianas and roots throughout the Amazon basin.

either spend some time, or erect a new village.

Ethno-historical data show that many ceremonial treks were undertaken as *mey* (linear treks): the people all migrated to another village where they moved in and where they concluded the ceremony, making use of the existing gardens at that site to satisfy the needs of a large quantity of manioc or corn.

The option for one or the other of these types seems to have depended on a number of factors, such as the available quantity of manioc and corn in the inhabited village, the duration of occupation in the inhabited village, and the direction of the trek. The tendency was to proceed to circular trekking during one or two years, alternatively covering each direction surrounding the village (see figure 20) and then to shift to a linear trek. On this occasion, the community moved to another village in order to exploit the gardens laid out there beforehand. Regarding the productivity of gardens, Posey says that

> *Kayapo 'new fields' peak in production of principal cultivators in two or three years but continue to bear domesticated plant products for many years (sweet potatoes for four to five years, yams and taro for five to six years, manioc for four to six years, and papaya for five or more years). Some banana varieties continue to bear fruit for fifteen to twenty years, 'urucu' for twenty-five years and 'cupá' (cissus gongylodes) for forty years. Cupá is an important Kayapo domesticate, little known outside the Indian area. (Posey 1984:114)*

Most migrations from one village site to another were, therefore, undertaken as linear ceremonial treks, coinciding in this way with the cycle of rituals. Yet, a few base villages seem to have existed. I refer to such villages as *krãnhmrôpryjaka, rojkô-re, adytirekreky* and so on, which were all located on the savannah between the Jarina and Iriri Novo Rivers, and to which the Mekranoti usually returned after spending some two to five years in other, surrounding villages. Figure 21 displays a model of this complex traditional Mekranoti trekking pattern.

The constant moving around of the Mekranoti groups, as shown in the proposed model, led to the following features: the control over tribal territory was improved; in case of being attacked, these Indians always had villages to flee to, where the existing gardens guaranteed the necessary crops to continue life on the same basis; and the amount of proteins in the diet increased. The latter was effected through the regular movement between savannah and tropical forest, movements during which the natural resources not only of different areas, but also of different ecological zones, were exploited. The possibility of depleting the resources in the

Table 10 — Demographic evolution of Central Mekranoti population according to age categories (1969-1989).

AGE CATEGORY	ANNO	1969			1974			1979			1984			1989		
		Δ	O	TTL	Δ	O	TTL	Δ	O	TTL	Δ	O	TTL	Δ	O	TTL
– 12 YEARS	N	27	27	54	47	49	96	74	89	163	97	107	204	103	111	214
	%	15.9	15.9	31.8	19.7	20.5	40.2	23.6	28.4	52.0	24.6	27.1	51.7	22.2	23.9	46.1
+ 12 YEARS	N	52	64	116	65	78	143	70	80	150	91	100	191	121	129	250
	%	30.6	37.6	68.2	27.2	32.6	59.8	22.4	25.6	48.0	23.0	25.3	48.3	26.1	27.8	53.9
TOTAL	N	79	91	170	112	127	239	144	169	313	188	207	395	224	240	464
	%	46.5	53.5	100.0	46.9	53.1	100.0	46.0	54.0	100.0	47.6	52.4	100.0	48.3	51.7	100.0

relatively poor interfluvial areas was, in this way, reduced. In this regard, Carneiro (1970:245) mentioned that not fishing but "hunting... must be relied on for, the bulk of protein in diet" and that protein scarcity "is of special significance for settlement pattern since heavy reliance on hunting is incompatible with sedentary village life".

Contrary to this pre-contact migration process, where villages were not occupied for long periods, several contemporary Kayapo villages have not moved for over twenty or thirty years. As such, ceremonial trekking is nowadays invariably of the circular type, while seasonal treks still are of the linear type. Seasonal treks are undertaken in the dry season and by trekking groups which take off to areas rich in specific resources such as fruits, fish, meat, palm trees, bamboo cane, etc. And while linear (seasonal) treks can be undertaken to very distant sites such as the ones the Central Mekranoti undertake to the Northern Mekranoti village at PI Bau, the area covered during contemporary ceremonial trekking is limited to the near vicinity of the permanent village setting. This phenomenon can be explained in the light of the medical assistance provided at the village post. Ceremonial treks are undertaken in the rainy season, when all kinds of diseases are much more frequent. That is why, whenever women and children participate in the ceremonial trek, the Mekranoti avoid going too far from the village and its post where medical assistance can be provided. It becomes more frequent, though, that only the men leave on a trek, while the women and children remain in the village and enjoy permanent medical care. Yet, in such cases, the men often tend to avoid staying too long away from their families, limiting as such the duration (and hence, the distance covered) during the treks.

Two important changes have, therefore, recently emerged: the contemporary sedentary village life; and the limitations on trekking patterns. Both these alterations can equally be attributed to the location of missionary or governmental posts. These posts require a complex infrastructure of houses, installation of radios, the construction of a small airstrip and the supply of medicines. They are, therefore, not easily moved. Serving as attraction points for the Indians (where trade goods are obtained, where medical assistance is provided and where radios as well as visitors may bring news of other Kayapo villages), the contemporary Kayapo villages are less likely to be moved.

In the 1970s, the last Kayapo village still to be located at an interfluvial location was the one at PI Mekranoti. While in the 1953-1967 period the Central Mekranoti had often moved to other village sites, from 1967 on these Indians maintained a more sedentary village pattern. Still, the sedentary village life in the interfluvial area led to a gradual depletion of

Table 11 — Migrational trends between the Central Mekranoti and other Kayapo villages (1969-1989). (+) immigrants;(-) emigrants; (S) Southern Mekranoti; (N) Northern Mekranoti; (G) Gorotire (PI Gorotire or PI Kikretum); (J) Jamanxim river area.

TOTAL CENTRAL MEKRÃGNOTI POPULATION

AGE	1969-1974 +Δ	+O	−Δ	−O	TTL	1974-1979 +Δ	+O	−Δ	−O	TTL	1979-1984 +Δ	+O	−Δ	−O	TTL	1984-1989 +Δ	+O	−Δ	−O	TTL
65-69		1N			+1													2G	1S	−3
60-64																	1J	1S1G		−1
55-59		1S			+1															
50-54							1G			+1				1G	−1			1G		−1
45-49		1N			+1													1N		−1
40-44	1S				+1						1S	1N	1N		+1				2N2G	−4
35-39	1S1N				+2							1S			+1		1J	1N		0
30-34	1N			1S	0						1S1G	2N			+4			1S		−1
25-29	1S	2S	1S		+2							1S	1S	1N	−1				1N	−1
20-24	1S	1N		1N	+1	1S1N				+2	1S2N		1N		+2			2S1N		−3
15-19	3S				+3						1N	1S2N			+4			2N	4N	−6
10-14	2S	1N			+3	1S				+1	2S2N	2S2N		2N	+6			1G	1S3N1G	−6
5-9		1N			+1				1N	−1	1N	2S1N			+4	1N		1N1G	1N1G	−3
0-4																				
Total	+11	+8	−1	−2	+16	+3	+1	0	−1	+3	+12	+15	−3	−4	+20	+1	+2	−16	−17	−30

available meat. Fishing treks to the Xixê River (some forty kilometres to the east of the village) became more frequent. Gardens were laid out along that river as well as half-way, to serve as points of support for travelling families or trekking groups, and several seasonal treks were undertaken to these points.

But after living over ten years on the same site, protein scarcity became a problem. This phenomenon was exacerbated by the remarkable population growth: in 1978, more than fifty-two percent of the village population was less than twelve years old! By that time, things had started to change. While the earlier mentioned friction arose during the preparation for a forest trek, those couples with many children started complaining that their children had no meat to eat[9]. These families also put forward the idea of moving the village to a point near the Xixê River. Bepgogoti, the old village chief, as well as most village elders disagreed with the plan. They argued that people were more likely to catch diseases living along major rivers, as they had discovered to their detriment in the period from 1953 to 1961. The majority of the village population decided to remain in the established village when, in 1980, eighteen men took off to set up a village along the Iriri River. These men were led by the young leaders Ajol and Bekwỳnhti, and by Pykati-re, the sole Central Mekranoti man to speak and understand Portuguese reasonably well. The FUNAI post near this new village was designated PI Pukanu (*pykany* is a Kayapo term meaning "new land").

Animated by the news of the visiting men of the new village who proved enthusiastic about the abundance of meat and fish, another group set off in 1983 to settle along the Iriri Novo River, upstream of PI Pukanu. The Iriri Novo site was chosen so that it satisfied the requisites of both the groups residing at PI Pukanu and PI Mekranoti: it is located near a river abounding in fish (pleasing, as such, the people of PI Pukanu); and the Iriri Novo River is a relatively small water-course, contenting in this way Bepgogoti and the other village elders who refused to live near a big stream. Furthermore, the site is located closer to the traditional savannah area, where Bepgogoti and most other village elders were born.

By choosing this strategical site to build this village, Kute'ê (Bepgogoti's oldest son) and Kôkôrêti (the chief of the Iriri Novo village) hoped that the groups of PI Pukanu and PI Mekranoti would move into his village, reuniting all Central Mekranoti once again in a single, im-

---

9   It should be emphasized that the schedule of schools maintained by FUNAI and the various tasks the Indians were asked to do for FUNAI also reduced the time available for hunting in the late 1970s.

portant village.

A fusion with the people of PI Pukanu never occurred, but Bepgogoti and his people did move into the Iriri Novo village in 1984. A new FUNAI post was established and named PI Kubenkokre (after Kubẽkàk-re, one of Bepgogoti's names).

The move to the virtually unexplored area near PI Kubenkokre had a positive effect on the population profile. Upon close inspection, it appears that the above-mentioned average annual population increase of 5.6% in the 1969-1989 period was not evenly spread over the period of twenty years in consideration. This "irregular" course of events is above all conspicuous if we consider the annual increase not taking into account the effects of migrants, both emigrants and immigrants (see table 11). From a high point in the 1974-1979 period (7%), it reached its lowest in the 1979-1984 period (3.7%). This lowest point coincides with the period of moving to a new village and follows the period where people complained about the lack of meat. After settling in the new area, the average annual increase soared again to 4.6%.

2.2 — The instigators of the 1980 schism

In addition to the economic pressure, the motives , r the 1980 village schism are partly to be found in the emergence of serious tensions at the political level. I have already briefly referred to this tension in an earlier section where I examined how the younger men were reluctant to depart on a long ceremonial trek, and where I explained how a young leader suggested the rearrangement of the men's groups in the men's house. This event did lead, however, to serious consequences on a political level. Two men stand out as the main provokers of the 1980 schism. These two men were Pykati-re and Ajol. Each of these men had his own motives for urging a group of men to separate. I will now discuss these two motives separately.

I. Pykati-re and his role as interlocutor

As mentioned earlier, Pykati-re was — and still is — the sole Central Mekranoti man who understands and speaks Portuguese with a certain amount of fluency. As such, most visitors to the community (FUNAI agents, members of medical teams, newly-arriving missionaries and anthropologists, and others) greatly depended upon Pykati-re to communicate with the people. This particular monopoly made him into a rather indispensable man in the community. Pykati-re is an ambitious man and due to a series of circumstances; there was a time when he felt that he could not achieve the status in the community he had hoped for and left the village. To understand Pykati-re's motives for leaving the village, it is necessary to examine the circumstances which made him feel that way. This analysis leads us to an examination of the distribution of commodities.

Due to the fairly recent date of the so-called "pacification", most of the current senior Kayapo chiefs were already adult men when peaceful contacts were established with the Brazilians. As such, they are now among the oldest members of the community and hardly speak any Portuguese. Those who were younger at the times of these contacts, however, spent more time with the Brazilians and acquired some fluency in speaking Portuguese. Most visitors being entirely dependent on such interlocutors, these young men are now in a privileged position: frequently acting as mediators, they often enjoy the confidence of the visitors and, as a result, they usually end up receiving more commodities than many other tribesmen. At times, they are even invited to distribute large quantities of commodities. In this way, their prestige within the community increases. Considering the importance attached to the peaceful understanding with the Brazilians, these men eventually gain political status and thus become important competitors to already established chiefs or to young leaders.

In an extreme case, however, the repeated offerings of gifts may even influence the succession of chiefs. This actually occurred in several Kayapo villages where men who demonstrated a certain affinity with the visitors, frequently received commodities for distribution. Such men were not necessarily considered by the community to be a potential chief (lacking, for example, the specific training by an elder chief). Yet, as status is gained by distributing commodities, these men managed to gain support of a group of men, eventually forming their own nucleus of followers and becoming a leader or a chief.

Among the Central Mekranoti, only one man is fluent in Portuguese. This can be explained by the fact that, up to a few years ago, these Indians had very little contact with the national society. In the period from 1967 to 1973 — being the first years when members of Western civilization settled in the village — contact was limited to missionaries who already had acquired some fluency in the Kayapo language, having spent some time in other Kayapo villages. A translator was, therefore, not really indispensable. But things changed more recently, with the ever increasing number of all kinds of visitors. Moreover, an interlocutor became of vital importance during the economic transactions with FUNAI. Since the Central Mekranoti often mistrusted FUNAI agents, they relied upon Pykati-re to handle and to control these transactions. Pykati-re was often called upon, especially whenever money was involved.

That is how Pykati-re played a prominent role in the distribution of the payment in compensation for the nearly annual Brazil nut collecting. His role, however, led to a series of conflicts with his tribesmen. It is, at this point, interesting to see how Pykati-re's prestige within the community diminished while his economic role increased.

Months after the nearly annual communal labour of collecting Brazil nuts, FUNAI proceeded to pay the Indians. In the period from 1973 to 1975, Pykati-re was invariably chosen by the Indians to travel with the FUNAI agents to town to buy the commodities the community wanted. Returning to the village with the payment, he handed the commodities to the two chiefs who then proceeded with the distribution. Yet, this distribution process displeased many men since the earnings were not always in accordance with their efforts: some men had worked for weeks and received few items, while other men had not participated in the labour and received lots of commodities.

In 1976, the matter was openly discussed in the men's house. It was then decided to put aside the existing random distribution and to pay the participants in accordance with the quantity of Brazil nuts each man had collected: FUNAI agents accompanied the men during the Brazil nut collecting and kept track of the individual contributions of each man. Once again, Pykati-re was requested to do the buying. For weeks he would record and discuss the amount and quality of commodities each of the participants requested.

By that time, Pykati-re had become an indispensable person to the community. Aware of his growing status, Pykati-re thought it to be the appropriate moment for him to confirm his position. Wanting to become a leader, he asked Bepgogoti — chief of the major men's society — to train him in traditional lore, a training which is given to adolescents in preparation of possible future leadership. The old chief refused, alleging that Pykati-re, being a married man with children, was too old to be taught these skills. Pykati-re was disappointed. He told me that he expected this reaction from Bepgogoti, but he had somehow hoped for some official recognition from Bepgogoti that he could become a chief. In answer to my questions in relation to this event, Bepgogoti merely referred to the fact that Pykati-re was known in the village as one of the most promiscuous men, a situation which had already led to denouncements and at times nearly developed into overt antagonism in the community.

In 1978-1979, Bõti-re (one of Bepgogoti's sons and at that time considered as the possible successor to his father) and Kôkôrêti (chief of the smaller men's society) accompanied Pykati-re during the buyings. It should be mentioned here that from 1975 on, Central Mekranoti men showed a great interest in learning how to handle money, making efforts to learn how to count and invariably asking the price of commodities. By 1978-1979, some men already had a basic notion of the general values of commodities, thus ending Pykati-re's monopoly regarding financial transactions.

By that time, a rumour had been spread where Pykati-re was accused of withholding part of the payment. In addition, a venereal disease had reached the community and Pykati-re was being held responsible for having introduced it to the community. Neither of these accusations were ever proven[10], but they seriously affected Pykati-re's demeanour: the otherwise very animated man felt betrayed and didn't hide his disappointment. He then told me that his real ambition was to become a FUNAI agent, just like Payakãn in PI Aukre, Bepdjaj in PI Kretire and Puju in PI Jarina.

In early 1980, a quarrel arose over one of Pykati-re's adulterous relationships. Both Pykati-re and the cuckolded husband belonged to the major men's society, and the latter challenged Pykati-re to a club-fight. Bepgogoti successfully intervened by calming both parties. Although overt action was avoided, Pykati-re felt ashamed about this event. Realizing that this incident seriously undermined his political career in that village, he left the village and moved to the Northern Mekranoti village, hundred and seventy kilometres to the northeast. Both Bepgogoti and Kôkôrêti then spoke with Pykati-re by radio, urging him to come back. He returned only when the members of the smaller men's society asked him to join their group[11]. He returned to the village and became one of the main instigators of a village split which occurred only a few months later. Pykati-re hoped to be able to build up his political career in the new village, which he eventually did: no FUNAI agent was sent to work in the village at PI Pukanu, and Pykati-re eventually became the man responsible for the application of medicinal treatment and for the radio-communication with Altamira and Belem. Later, he was officially recognized by FUNAI as head of the post and, as such, receives a salary.

II. Ajol, the disappointed young leader

Unlike his brother Bekwỳnhti (who had been trained by Kreti-re), Ajol

10   FUNAI agents later found out that, a few months before the disease broke out, a rather young Central Mekranoti woman had had sexual intercourse with a Brazilian man while spending a few weeks in the town of Altamira.

11   Discussing this phase with Pykati-re and other men, all agreed that Kôkôrêti (the chief of the smaller men's society), "out of respect for Bepgogoti", would never have asked Pykati-re to join his men's society being, therefore, Kôkôrêti's men who made the request to which Kôkôrêti agreed.

was never trained in traditional lore to become a chief. As a young man, however, he was respected for his enthusiasm displayed when participating in communal activities, his intelligence and his capacity for decision-taking. He also displayed a great interest in traditional culture: this, while simultaneously being one of the men who maintained the most frequent contact with the agents of Western civilization (FUNAI agents and missionaries).

As such, Ajol had developed into one of the leaders (*meobadjwỳnh*) of the *meõtotikry-re* (the junior men of the *meõtoti* men's society). He was, more precisely, the leader of the communal works and of certain treks. Two other young leaders existed within that same men's group: his close friend Bepkũm and the earlier mentioned Bõti-re. The latter two were primarily recognized as possible successors to their father Bepgogoti, mainly because they both had been trained in the specific knowledge of chieftaincy by their father. Interesting, at this point, is the suggestion made by Werner (1982) that Mekranoti leadership inheritance was enhanced, in a rather subtle fashion, by contact. This is because outsiders often rely on the chief and his close kin when dealing with the community. As a result, members of the chief's family not only become "culture-brokers" but also are among those who can most easily acquire knowledge of civilized ways.

During the earlier mentioned 1978 crisis, it was Ajol who suggested the rearrangement of the men's groups. This was an important and radical proposal which had important implications for Ajol's future: not only because the proposal was being rejected, but mainly because Bepgogoti (the chief of the *meõtoti* men's society) disagreed with the idea. This drastically weakened Ajol's position in the group. In 1979, Kôkôrêti was appointed chief (*benjadjwỳr*) of the *mepa'ãkadjàt* men's society. He therefore had to resign from his earlier position of *delegado*. Ajol soon developed into the new *delegado*.

Many of Ajol's age-mates were among those who most resolutely insisted that the village should be moved to the Iriri River. And when Pykati-re said he wanted to move to that area, Ajol was one of the first to join in. Ajol and his brother Bekwỳnhti eventually became the two chiefs of the new village at PI Pukanu.

3. INTERGROUP RELATIONS AND THE CESSATION OF "TRADITIONAL" WARFARE

The recent occurrences in other Kayapo villages and the common struggle of all Kayapo groups to preserve their tribal territory have greatly influenced the intergroup (read: inter-Kayapo) relationships. But this is not an isolated phenomenon, since relationships with other, non-Gê societies have also been altered. The causes and consequences of these changes are what I will examine in the following pages.

3.1 — The recent increase in commodities

In the 1970s, the Central Mekranoti had relatively little access to commodities. The most important source of income for these Indians was the cash-crop production of Brazil nuts. Programmed to occur annually, this project often failed due to the precarious logistic assistance offered by FUNAI. The sale of handicrafts — such as weapons, feather crowns and baskets — continued on a regular basis. Although the sale of handicrafts was a profitable matter, many Indians displayed little enthusiasm for this kind of transaction because the Indians occasionally discovered that some FUNAI agents cheated them by not paying them at all or by paying them less than was promised. Accordingly, the sale of handicrafts did not amount to important sums of money. Things improved when more and more Indians were flown to the cities. Instead of sending the handicrafts through FUNAI agents, the Indians preferred to hand the artefacts to their fellow tribesmen, entrusting them with the sale and with the purchase of the required commodities.

In all, however, commodities were hard to obtain. But things changed by 1982, when the Kayapo communities of PI Kikretum and, later, of PI Gorotire suddenly acquired large amounts of money and started sending commodities to their kin at the Central Mekranoti village. To understand the effects of this increased introduction of commodities, it seems useful to first observe the causes which allowed these two Kayapo communities to send gifts to the Central Mekranoti (and other Kayapo groups).

Already in the 1960s, gold had been found in the southern part of the State of Pará, but the late 1970s marked the beginning of a major gold rush in Brazil. Soon, tens of thousands of gold seekers penetrated the most remote areas of the State of Pará. Of all the ensuing gold mines, Serra Pelada is probably the most famous.

The Kayapo Indian Reserve (the habitat of the Gorotire, Kubenkranken and Kokraimoro) is located fairly close to Serra Pelada. Consequently, the effects of the gold rush soon reached these Kayapo Indians. In fact, the two most easterly located Kayapo villages (PI Kikretum and PI Gorotire) suddenly had to face the problem of invasion into their reserve which, at the time, still had to cope with serious problems: although officially recognized, the area still wasn't completely demarcated.

The first Kayapo group to deal with the gold seekers was PI Kikretum. Gold seekers had illegally penetrated the extreme north-eastern part of the Indian reserve. Initially, the Indians were not aware of this invasion, but then their attention was drawn to the numerous small airplanes that could constantly be heard flying, landing and taking off in that border area. By mid-1980, chief Tut (also called Colonel Pombo) invaded the Garimpo Batéia with thirty-five of his warriors. Without use of violence, all three hundred gold seekers were expelled: the gold seekers were terrified by the arrival of the Indian warriors.

Tut, however, didn't really want to paralyse the works definitively. Rather, he wanted to gain control over the cause of the invasion into Indian territory, and simultaneously hand over the benefits of the mining to his community. To achieve this goal, Tut faced a period of years of negotiating with private mining companies and with local groups of independent gold seekers who were eager to exploit his area. This went on while FUNAI tried to manoeuvre the situation so that the mining would be state-controlled. In 1981, the two gold mines in the area were operative again and were called Kikretum (ex-Batéia) and Nova Olinda.

Tut signed an agreement which not only limited the number of gold seekers allowed into the area, but also specified that five percent of the profits would be handed over to the Indian community in the form of royalties. A few of Tut's warriors checked upon the production but it soon appeared that the Indians were being cheated: they did get some money, but large quantities of gold were perpetually being smuggled out of the area (e.g., by hiding the precious metal in soap). Soon a situation of mistrust grew. Meanwhile, Tut and his people spent much of the earnings by constantly travelling back and forth to other Kayapo villages in hired planes loaded with gifts. They also made huge debts in the nearby settlement of Tucumã, where they bought lots of commodities and where several men often spent weeks in the local hotel.

Things changed by 1983, when FUNAI offered efficient aid to control the two gold mines. Due to the improved control, the debts could be paid and new money became available. In order to cut down their expenses at Tucumã, the Indians also bought a small hotel in that small settlement.

In the meantime, the people at PI Gorotire faced similar problems. By 1980, thousands of gold seekers overwhelmed the area of Fazenda Cumaru, just outside the Reserve boundaries. This eventually led to an invasion of the Indian Reserve. That same year, the Gorotire visited the site called Espadilha, where Brazilians were deforesting in preparation for the establishment of a huge farm. A conflict arose and sixteen Brazilians were killed.

Not far from there, gold seekers invaded the Reserve and reached a point located no more than fifteen kilometres from the Gorotire village. Three gold mines appeared within Reserve boundaries: Tarzan, Maria Bonita and Cumaruzinho. In 1981 and 1982, the annual production of these mines reached nearly two tons of gold. While the mines near PI Kikretum remained in the hands of private mining companies, those near PI Gorotire were state-controlled. Due to efficient control (first by FU-NAI, and later by the Indians themselves) the Gorotire suddenly started receiving huge amounts of money.

In early 1985, however, the Gorotire suddenly stopped receiving money, while the mining continued uninterrupted. Two hundred men from the villages of PI Gorotire and PI Kikretum then invaded Maria Bonita which, with nearly five thousand gold seekers, was the largest of all three gold mines. The warriors occupied the mine and threatened to paralyse all the other mines in the area unless the following four claims were conceded: the payment of the royalties; an increase of the production royalties from 0.1% to 1%; a reduction of the number of gold seekers; and the effective demarcation of their Reserve (which had been postponed already for years). After occupying the mines for several weeks, the government finally gave in. The Gorotire now control all the mining within their Reserve, earning about two million dollars a year. With this money, they bought a small plane and installed video equipment (camera, TV-screen and generator) in the Kayapo villages at PI Gorotire, PI Kikretum and PI Metuktire. They also bought a truck and a car, as well as a house in the city of Belem. The money also allowed the Indians to hire teachers for the local schools and a pilot to fly the plane, and to install electricity as well as water-pumps in the village[12]. Finally, the money was also used to finance the transport of hundreds of Kayapo Indians to major cities such as Belem and Brasilia on a number of occasions (a point I will discuss in more detail in a later section of this Chapter).

The financial potential of the two Gorotire groups, of PI Kikretum and PI Gorotire, have greatly influenced the Central Mekranoti in recent years. In the 1970s, an average of four to ten planes landed annually in the village. This number suddenly increased from 1982 on: in the period from 1982 to 1985, planes landed at least once every ten days or so. These planes were hired by the Kayapo community of PI Kikretum. Tut and his people often visited the Central Mekranoti village as well as all the other

12   Mercury is being used in the gold mine located fifteen kilometers upriver from the village. As a result, the water near PI Gorotire is highly polluted.

Kayapo villages. When the Gorotire bought their own plane in 1985, the number of flights to the Central Mekranoti village increased even more: nowadays, planes land there every three days or so.

These planes allow people to go frequently and visit their kinsmen in other Kayapo villages. The planes also often bring commodities which the people of PI Gorotire and PI Kikretum send as gifts to their Central Mekranoti kinsmen. This all led to major consequences: the increased flux of migrations; the more frequent visits (and sojourns) in interior towns; and the fact that the Central Mekranoti envy the Gorotire groups.

In a way, the Central Mekranoti envy the Gorotire groups who are in a position to acquire large amounts of money. The Central Mekranoti also want to have this and that is why, on two occasions, they have encouraged the invasion of gold seekers into tribal territory. Yet, on each occasion, the gold seekers left after a short period of time, since the exploitation of gold didn't seem to be feasible. Similarly, the Central Mekranoti have in vain tried to attract timber-cutters in their area, as the problems related to the transportation of the cut wood kept the company from exploitation in the rather isolated Central Mekranoti area. But things are likely to change within a few years: the colonization is approaching these Indians' area at a fast and steady pace, and it can be predicted that the exploitation of timber in the Central Mekranoti area will soon become a profitable matter in the very near future[13].

A second effect of the numerous planes visiting the Central Mekranoti village is the sudden increase of Indians going back and forth to small interior towns such as Altamira, Conceição do Araguaia and, above all, Redenção. It is young men who most frequently go to such towns, often spending several weeks there in the company of men from other Kayapo villages. This constant visiting has led to the continuous importation of diseases to the Central Mekranoti village.

Last, but not least, the facilities of travelling to other Kayapo villages has led to an increase in the number of migrations. At this point, it is interesting to examine this phenomenon in the Central Mekranoti group in the period from 1969 to 1989. Table 11 shows a fairly high number of (Southern Mekranoti) immigrants in the period from 1969 to 1974. This period corresponds with the construction of the BR 080 road and the conflicts following the removal of the Southern Mekranoti land from the

---

13   In 1989-1990, a rudimentary road was built by lumbermen, connecting the village of PI Kokraimoro and PI Pukanu. From 1990 on, timber will be cut in the vicinity of PI Pukanu and will be transported via the new road to PI Kokraimoro, where it will be shipped to São Felix do Xingu and then further to Belem.

Xingu National Park. At that time, several Southern Mekranoti families preferred to move to the Central Mekranoti village where no such tension existed. The flow of migrations almost disappeared in the period from 1974 to 1979, only to increase again five years later when two Southern Mekranoti families and one big Northern Mekranoti family immigrated.

More recently, things have gone just the other way: since 1984, an important number of people started leaving the Central Mekranoti village, moving to the Northern Mekranoti, the Southern Mekranoti and the two Gorotire groups (PI Kikretum and PI Gorotire). This emigration is a consequence of the relative ease with which people can now move from one village to another. Several people moved to the Gorotire villages: this represents a new tendency in recent Mekranoti history and can partly be explained in terms of kin relations. In addition, it is sure that the Central Mekranoti are attracted to these two villages because of the facility with which commodities can be obtained there.

One striking tendency regarding the recent migration process is that, relatively speaking, many senior Central Mekranoti tribesmen seem to emigrate. Indeed, no less than six men and one woman aged over forty years have left the Central Mekranoti village during the last five years.

3.2 — Recent warfare

The recent "pacification" of the Mekranoti (or Kayapo in general) by the Brazilians has greatly influenced both the intergroup and intertribal relationships. In fact, through this state of peaceful relations with Brazilians, friendly — or at least pacified — relations are maintained with any Kayapo or non-Kayapo Indian group. Such recent developments have resulted in the cessation of all four types of pre-contact warfare which I described in Chapter 3. It is nevertheless not so that the objectives which lie at the basis of these pre-contact raids have disappeared, or that the interests in such objects have diminished. Rather, these same objects are nowadays attained through peaceful transactions.

I have already shown that the acquisition of commodities (evidenced as the main goal of pre-contact raids on Brazilian settlements) is nowadays obtained on a peaceful basis. Whether through trading, as gifts, as compensation for executed works, as payment for the sale of handicrafts or of collected Brazil nuts, or through massive purchases, commodities are appearing in ever increasing quantities in Kayapo villages.

Warfare with other Indian tribes has almost been suppressed, the rare exceptions being a Central Mekranoti attack on the Kreen Akrore in 1967, and a Xikrin attack on a Parakanã group in 1977 (Aspelim & Coelho dos

Santos 1982:5). *Kubĕkakrit* tribes are now peacefully visited. The pre-contact aim of obtaining primary materials or ornaments from such tribes is currently achieved through an intricate network of trading transactions. Songs and ceremonies can be learned from these tribes by mutual visitations. One of the most striking cases in this respect is that Ropni, a renown Southern Mekranoti leader, has been an apprentice of Takumã (a famous Kamaiura shaman) and has learned some of Takumã's skills. The frequent peaceful contacts with non-Gê tribes have also led to some intermarriage between the Southern Mekranoti and such tribes as the Trumai, Kamaiura and Suia (all inhabitants of the Xingu National Park).

The Kreen Akrore were contacted by the Villas Bôas brothers in 1973 and nowadays live within the boundaries of the Xingu National Park, where they are close neighbours of the Southern Mekranoti; some intermarriage has resulted. In addition, two Kreen Akrore adolescents have recently moved to the Central Mekranoti village. During one of his recent visits to the Xingu National Park, a senior Central Mekranoti man received a beautiful feather headdress from a Kreen Akrore friend. The Central Mekranoti man told me that he considers this headdress as his ritual privilege (*õ nêkrêx*) and that he will eventually transmit the right to don it to one of his grandchildren.

Although the various types of pre-contact war seem to have disappeared, this does not mean that the Kayapo no longer practice any form of warfare; since "pacification", a new type of Kayapo warfare has emerged against intruders into tribal territory. Such intruders usually are back-woodsmen who work for farmers or great landholders, and invariably are referred to by the Kayapo as *kubĕkryt* (literally, "light coloured non-Kayapo"). The main motive of these recent raids is territorial defence. Still, it should be emphasized that the Kayapo are not defending the entire territory they consider as *mebêngôkre nhõ pyka* ("Kayapo land" — see Chapter 1). Rather, each community defends a given area around the village, including the necessary space for trekking, as well as certain sites where specific primary materials, fruits, types of game and fish are abundant. These are, to be sure, the territories each community considers as the minimum to survive and guarantee their future, and it can be predicted that these Indians will never cease in their demands for the legal adjudication of these territories.

The present military strategy consists of visiting the site where the Brazilians trespassed the boundaries of tribal territory. Since several Kayapo men nowadays speak Portuguese, the Indians do not attack on the first visit. Rather, they warn the intruders that they are on Indian land and that they have to leave. If the intruders refuse to comply with the warning, a raid may be mounted, during which all settlers are killed and their possessions taken as booty. Only traditional weapons (particularly the *kô* round clubs) are used during the attacks. Usually the majority of the men in a village participate in a raid. This is a significant change compared with the earlier discussed pattern of pre-contact raids on Brazilian settlements. But this change can be explained by a shift in the aim of the raid: whereas pre-contact warfare against Brazilians aimed at the acquisition of commodities (an individual motive), the newly emerged type of warfare against Brazilians aims at the protection of tribal territory (a communal motive). As such, recent warfare against Brazilians is characterized by communal values and this explains why it no longer has the characteristics of "individual warfare", but rather of "communal warfare".

Yet, not always do intrusions lead to such raids. In some recent cases, the Indians took some hostages to their village. Under the realistic threat of killing these hostages, the Indians pressure the FUNAI officials to send federal police to expel the intruders. Such more moderate behaviour is undoubtedly a consequence of not willing to provoke a break in the peaceful relations with certain groups of Brazilians, such as FUNAI agents and missionaries.

Since the contemporary Central Mekranoti suffer no potential danger from being attacked, and since they haven't really suffered any invasion in their territory, some male virtues such as strength (*tỳx*), bravery and bellicosity (*àkrê*), and insensibility to pain (*amakkreket*), *although still accentuated and praised*, have decreased in importance. As mentioned earlier, the *me'ôk-re* and *menõrõny-re* — who in earlier times were gradually educated in this spirit of warfare within the sphere of the men's house — nowadays become involved in the mechanism of seeking the suitable partner for marriage. At a much earlier stage than in preceding times, they have to attach themselves to the affinal household and all this seems to be achieved at the expense of their full-time adheration to the men's house.

The young men who now beget children at an early age in wedlock, and who therefore are liable to become *mekrakramtĩ* at a premature stage of maturity, are presented with two opposite tendencies which exert pressure on their conduct. One consists of an internal, institutional influence where the senior tribesmen — probably more persistently than in earlier times — tease the younger men by challenging them to display their bellicose abilities and, therefore, provoking them to leave on a war party. The young men thoroughly sense the absence of the prestige which is linked and gained through warfare and the senior men do not allow any opportunity go by without drawing the young men's attention to this (whether through continuous references in formal speeches or through continuous condemnations). Yet, it is exactly this group of young men that has the strongest attachments to the Brazilians. And the elder men recognize the necessity of this attachment to retain the agents who provide medical assistance and acquire commodities. Therefore, as a vindication against the senior men's pressure, the young men often allude that warfare is of the past and that the effective preoccupation of the community should be focused on seeking or maintaining peaceful relations with the Brazilians.

Thus, when the Mekranoti elders say that the young men (both the *menõrõny-re* and *mekrany-re*) are weak (*rerek*) and tame (*uabô*), this not only reflects the young men's (unintended) lack of experience in warfare (through which prestige was gained and proof of bellicosity was exhibited), but also because of their early attachment to the affinal household which has always been considered to be a sign of feebleness.

But, notwithstanding this reaction, the *menõrõny-re* and *mekrany-re* still represent the group who, under the current circumstances, are the most likely to depart on a war expedition. Although the Central Mekranoti have not undertaken any significant raid in the last twenty years, I did observe on several occasions that the younger men prepared to do so, only being stopped when FUNAI agents intervened and discouraged them from going on a raid.

4. THE EMERGENCE OF COLLECTIVE SELF-CONFIDENCE

One of the most important recent changes concerns the approximation of Kayapo groups. Some tension between historically more distant Kayapo groups continued up to the early 1970s: e.g., between the Gorotire and Xikrin, between the Mekranoti and Kubenkranken, and between the Northern and Central Mekranoti. These antagonisms recently have turned into a peaceful approximation. Recent developments, such as the possibilities of talking with kinsmen of other Kayapo groups using FUNAI radios, the ease of visiting other Kayapo groups using air transport, and the occasional reunions promoted between the Kayapo chiefs in the last few years, have undoubtedly brought about a sense of unity between the many Kayapo communities.

The common difficulties encountered by each Kayapo group in their struggle to resist all sorts of pressures from the national society have led to the emergence of a new level of social and political self-consciousness. The Kayapo have always been a proud and headstrong people, and this has led to important achievements over the past few years, such as the occasions during which some Kayapo groups managed to win fundamental rights from the Brazilian government (e.g., having some of their reserves enlarged). This relative success in the struggle against pressures from the national society for assimilation have resulted in a strengthening of collective self-confidence.

In addition, this strengthened self-confidence radiates a dynamism which now seems to affect other, non-Kayapo Indian groups. In the 1970s, most Indians who went to the cities cut their hair in the Brazilian style and refrained from donning traditional ornaments; they tried to imitate the Brazilian as much as possible. This was because they didn't want to be too conspicuous and shunned being pointed at and ridiculed. Things are different nowadays; when going to town, Kayapo often are painted and wear coloured feather headdresses.

Ropni, a Southern Mekranoti leader, has played a prominent part in this process of self-confidence. This man, who retained his tribal lip-plug and hairstyle, became a national figure through his many visits in major cities. Through the years, he has received great coverage from the press whenever he undertook actions against the pressures from the national society. This is not only due to his impressive appearance, but also to the way he comments on most aspects of Brazilian society, culture and politics. He not only treats these aspects with derision, but also does it so eloquently that it enchants the spectators. In fact, the lucidity with which the Kayapo deal with problems related to their struggle for survival has made them into the foremost spokesmen of the Brazilian Indian societies.

In addition to Ropni, another young Kayapo man, Pajakãn, has developed into an international figure. He is the son of Txikiri, the senior chief in the Kubenkranken village of PI Aukre. Speaking Portuguese well, he had played an important role in the struggle of the Gorotire to achieve royalties from the mining on their territory. He was also one of the organizers of a delegation of over two hundred Kayapo men in the capital of Brasilia on the occasion of the final voting over the status of the Indians in the new Constitution. Vindicating their rights, the warriors danced in front of parliament. They also promoted important assemblies to illuminate and discuss the significance of the matter. This event received great press coverage and was successful.

But Pajakãn's role as a leading spokesman only became apparent when he and Kubẽ'i, a Gorotire man, were invited to participate at a symposium titled "Tropical Rainforests: Strategies for Wise Management". The symposium was held at the end of January, 1988, at the University of Florida with anthropologist Darrell Posey acting as interpreter. During the speech, both Kayapo men expressed their profound concern at the alarming increase in deforestation, mining, lumbering, water pollution and large-scale development projects near their area. Specific attention was drawn to the planned construction of enormous hydroelectric dams which would flood part of Kayapo land. Payakãn and Kubẽ'i were invited to go to Washington to plead their case directly to representatives of the World Bank and to members of the US Congress.

As a result, the World Bank temporarily postponed any loans to energy projects in Brazil. Upon returning, the two Kayapo men and Dr. Darrell Posey were threatened with criminal action for having "criticized Brazilian Indian policy, denigrating the country's image abroad". All three faced one to three years in prison and could then be expelled from the country. This was the first time that Brazilian Indians have ever been prosecuted as "foreigners". In October 1988, Kubẽ'i was called for a hearing in court. He came with more than four hundred Kayapo warriors, all dressed in ceremonial attire. Fifty shock troops of the military police confronted them at the door of the federal court. While the warriors danced — once again, under the eye of millions of spectators since the press was present — the judge refused to let Kubẽ'i in court unless he dressed in "white man's clothes": the judge considered the Indian's dress "a sign of disrespect". Kubẽ'i refused to comply and the hearing was suspended. Due, among other reasons, to the enormous repercussions of the case, both within Brazil and worldwide, the case was finally dropped in the beginning of 1989.

By that time, Pajakãn had undertaken a second and more important tour through the European countries and the US. Talking with heads of governments, bank directors and the press, the Kayapo struggle against the building of six hydroelectric dams along the Xingu River became world-news. During his tour, Pajakãn declared that a major meeting was to be held at Altamira, a small town along the lower Xingu River where the first dams were to be built.

The meeting in Altamira (February, 1989) was a protest against the construction of the dams. It was entirely organized by the Kayapo themselves and is the apogee of the Kayapo achievements of the last few years. Over seven hundred Indians attended the meeting, including about five hundred and fifty Kayapo from all fifteen villages, and representatives of many other Brazilian Indian tribes. Under the skilful conduct of Pajakãn, Indians, Brazilian and foreign governmental officials, as well as a director of Eletrobras (the governmental institution charged with the construction of the dams) took turns explaining their point of view on the matter. The press gave worldwide coverage to this impressive conference[14].

14   Media coverage was great during the manifestation. See, among others, the

In Altamira, the Kayapo managed to associate the indigenous claims with the growing worldwide ecological awareness. During the Altamira meeting, also, Ropni and popstar Sting hatched the plan for another worldwide tour during which both would raise funds for the effective demarcation of the Central and Northern Mekranoti Reserve. This tour was held in May 1989.

In all, the Kayapo have become popular on TV and in the newspapers. Yet, since large-scale colonization is only now reaching the Kayapo habitat, their fight against the pressures from the national society has not ended yet. It can be predicted that we will see and hear more of the Kayapo in the near future.

film "The Green Puzzle of Altamira" (prod. Lode Cafmeyer; 1990 - Variafilm, Antwerp - 52 min.) for a good synopsis of the inducement and the consequences of the meeting.

APPENDIX A

Mekranoti Ethno-History (1900-1989)

As shown in the Chapter 2, the recent pre-contact history of the Kayapo — and, more particularly, of the Mekranoti — is unusually complex. This is due to the many migrations, schisms and regroupings which took place during the period of eighty years or so which I have endeavored to analyze. The present Appendix deals with the history of the Mekranoti in this century. A substantial part of Chapter 2 is in fact a narrative version of the more important passages displayed in this Appendix.

Yet, it is important to warn the reader to regard the following parts with a certain amount of caution. Indeed, upon reading the following account, the reader may get the strong impression that Kayapo (Mekranoti) history is made up of a long series of raids, attacks and internal strife, and that their history is dominated by such events. *My selection of events puts a strong over-emphasis on this facet in view of the topic of this book!*

The diachronic aspect of the history utilized in this Appendix is maintained by presenting the happenings according to the seasons in which they took place. The dry season, from May to October, is referred to as "dry", the rainy season, from November to April, is referred to by the term "rain". January to April has therefore been included in the rainy season of the preceding year. For each season, main events such as raids, ceremonies, migrations, schisms, fusions and club-fights are mentioned. If I have insisted upon stressing *when* a major ceremony was performed, I did so considering this fact to be important to any future analysis of internal tensions manifested within Kayapo communities.

Since numerous club-fights occurred during the historical period considered, only those which led to major consequences such as homicides, schisms or reorganizations of political groupings within the men's house(s) have been mentioned in this account.

Names of places where villages were built (such as *pykatôti, rojkô-re,* and so on) are invariably mentioned. This is done to enable the reader to situate the geographical location of these sites on map 9 and to follow migration tendencies. They have also been included in order to allow the reader to perceive the distances which separate one village from another. Localization of the ancient villages on the map was obtained by combining informants' descriptions of the geographical aspects of the site, the distance between villages and the type of vegetation, and by localization of a few of these sites while personally flying over the area. The localizations as presented on the map are therefore not really accurate but, rather, indicative.

The greatest problem encountered in the reconstruction of Mekranoti history can be said to be its chronological sequence and, subsequently, the chronological sequence of events to be presented. This chronology remains the least reliable aspect of the following presentation. Still, the few bibliographic references found seem to confirm the dates presented in this Appendix. Dates, in general, should be considered mainly as a way of facilitating descriptive passages and should therefore be taken on a purely informative basis; rather than to conform to dates in the strict sense of the term, these are used throughout this book to consolidate the diachronic aspect of the account and are applied, in particular, to facilitate references to events mentioned.

Since the following account is solely based on data provided by the Mekranoti, bibliographic references are mentioned in footnotes.

1. THE GOROTIRE - MEKRANOTI SCHISM (1900-1934)

At the end of the nineteenth century, the Kayapo of the Xingu (the Gorotire) occupied a major village called *pykatôti*. It was located in the open grasslands (*cerrado* in Portuguese) along a tributary of the upper Riozinho River. Although several Gorotire bands occasionally left *pykatôti* to live temporarily in smaller villages in the surrounding forest, these bands always returned to the main village.

¤ rain about 1905   After having lived separately at *krã'ãbõm* for several years, Mote-re and his followers rejoined the Gorotire village of *pykatôti*, where he and his men were members of the western men's house. Mote-re had been a married man with two children, but by the time he moved back to the Gorotire he had separated from his wife and, consequently, had rejoined the younger men's group of his men's house. The reunion of both groups occurred during the rainy season and, right after that, a naming ceremony was performed. Betoroti (one of Mote-re's "fathers" through fictive kinship and a member of the eastern men's house) and his wife Pãnhtxwỳ were the sponsors. When the men left to the forest for the ceremonial migration õntomõr, Mote-re stayed behind and had adulterous sexual relations with Pãnhtxwỳ (see App. B:15). Betoroti was notified and a series of club-fights broke out between the two men. Tension grew in the village and this resulted in a collective club-fight. A schism became inevitable: Mote-re and his followers left the village again and moved to the west. They crossed the Xingu River and built a small village at a site called *arerek-re*, an area of open grassland (*cerrado*) between the Xingu and Iriri Rivers. The village numbered about hundred Indians, and the single men's house was called *mekrãgnoti*. Since no gardens existed there, the people lived on meat, palm, wild sweet potatoes, and so on.

¤ about 1906   Tension continued in Gorotire and, one year after the separation of the Mekranoti, another schism occurred: the men of another men's society belonging to the western men's house were afraid of being killed out of revenge for their taking sides with Mote-re the year before. They left and joined the Mekranoti. This second group also numbered some hundred Indians, and was led by the chiefs Pãnhmoti, Ôket and Karànhĩn.

¤ 1907-1917   Some two or three years later, during the dry season, Kruwaprêkti (a young Mekranoti leader) went to the Iriri River with his group of men. There they raided a small Brazilian settlement, took a boy captive after having killed the boy's parents, and brought back a firearm and some ammunition. Immediately after their return to the village, Mote-re set out towards that same area along the Iriri River, subsequently killing a Brazilian. About two years later, once again during the dry season, Mote-re and the men of the senior men's group attacked the Juruna (Yudja) tribe — then living along the upper Xingu River, near the Cachoeira Von Martius. One Yudja man and a boy were killed, while a woman and her son were taken captives (see App. B:16). A few months later, still during the same season, Mote-re returned to the Yudja. This time he went with the men of the younger men's group and killed one Yudja man.

By that time, the Mekranoti had large gardens and they moved south to a bigger area of open grassland located between the Jarina and Iriri Novo Rivers. There they built a village at a place called *rojkô-re*. During this period, some Mekranoti men still visited the Gorotire from time to time. Around 1912-1913, the Mekranoti moved to *arerek-re* once again to collect garden products. The village had one men's house with two men's societies. While living in *arerek-re*, Mote-re went to visit his brother Xwak-re who lived in the Gorotire village. Xwak-re was not around since he was out with a group of men visiting the Ira'amranh. Mote-re returned, bringing along five Gorotire visitors. A few months later, when the visitors had already left, Xwak-re and two other men arrived with their families and settled in the Mekranoti village. By that time, the Mekranoti possessed only a few dogs which they had taken from the Brazilians during their raids. One day, during a ceremonial trek, Bep'ô hit Karema's dog with a stick. The owner got upset and a club-duel arose between the two men. Defeated, Bep'ô and three other men and their families left and moved back to the Gorotire. Only a few months later, the Gorotire attacked the Mekranoti, killing a woman and her son. The Mekranoti then moved back to the south, to their village at *rojkô-re*. A year later, the Mekranoti took revenge by counterattacking the Gorotire[1]. The younger men's group of that village was out hunting parrots and the aggressors killed four Gorotire women as well as Wakõnkra, chief of the eastern men's house. They also captured seven girls, of whom one returned. A short time later, the Gorotire launched a counterattack, killing three Mekranoti men.

¤ RAIN 1918   After this series of attacks, the Mekranoti split into two groups. One group, almost exclusively composed of married men and their families, moved to the forest near the upper Iriri River, where they wandered around building temporary shelters. The other group, led by Mote-re and composed of members of the younger men's group, went to the north. The latter built a small village at a place called *krôdjãm-re*, to the west of the mid Iriri River. The men of this group attacked a Brazilian settlement near the Curuaes River and captured two girls and a boy[2], after having first killed their parents.

¤ DRY 1919   Mote-re's group went to fetch food at the gardens near the deserted village at *arerek-re*.

¤ RAIN 1919

¤ DRY 1920   Both Mote-re's and the other group reunited and

1   The informants added that, on this occasion, the Mekranoti had made several canoes. This is a rather uncommon feature as the Kayapo usually built rudimentary rafts to cross major rivers. This important crossing of the Xingu didn't remain unnoticed by the local Brazilian population, and that is why Nimuendajú (1932: 555) reported that a Kayapo group had crossed the Xingu River in March 1917.

2   A Kayapo attack in the area of the upper Iriri was reported in June 1918. During the attack, a Brazilian man and woman were killed (Nimuendajú 1932:555). It is reasonable to assume that this is the attack referred to by the Mekranoti informants. The captured boy was named Bemoti-re and still lives in the Central Mekranoti village of PI Kubenkokre.

built a new village near *rojkô-re*. The new village site was named *krãn-htykti* and many gardens were laid out.

¤ RAIN 1920   *bô kam me tor* naming ceremony.

¤ DRY 1921   Pãnhmoti, the oldest village chief, led a group of men to the Xingu River and attacked the Yudja. They took many garden products and killed one man. This was the last Mekranoti aggression towards the already decimated Yudja tribe[3].

¤ RAIN 1921   A group of Mekranoti men discovered the presence of an unknown tribe to the west of their village. They initially referred to this tribe as *mebêkôkrãti-re* ("people with big-headed clubs"). A few Mekranoti men were sent out to go and spy and, upon their return, it was decided to attack this tribe which they afterwards called *krãjôkàr*[4] ("shaven heads"). During the massive raid, some Panara children were taken captive, including a boy of about twelve years of age. Since the language of the Panara is related to Kayapo, the Mekranoti learned from the boy that several Panara villages existed, which were referred to as *mekrã-ne* ("head people"), *mekry-re* ("little people") and *metykti-re* ("big black people").

¤ DRY 1922   On the return of the warriors, the village split up into two groups: Mote-re settled at *ngrwakre-re*, about sixty kilometers distant from *krãnhtykti*; Pãnhmoti led his group to the Iriri Novo River, where they wandered around building temporary shelters.

¤ RAIN 1922   *kwỳrỳkangô* naming ceremony in Mote-re's group.

kwỳrỳkangô naming ceremony in Pãnhmoti's group.

The group led by Pãnhmoti raided a Brazilian settlement near the Curua River. The booty consisted of two firearms, some ammunition and tools. After that, both groups reunited at *ngrwakre-re*, i.e. Mote-re's village.

¤ DRY 1923   *tàkàk* naming ceremony.

During the performance of the ceremony, the Panara attacked and a Mekranoti couple was killed. The Mekranoti fled to the north, to a place near the Curua River, but their assailants pursued them and attacked again: this time eight boys and men as well as six girls and women were killed. The Mekranoti then returned to *krôdjãm-re*, where they reestablished their village.

---

3   The Gorotire and Kubenkranken continued raiding the Yudja in more recent periods.

4   The name of this Gê tribe is commonly spelled Kreen Akrore or Kranhacarore, respectively in English and Portuguese literature. As mentioned in the introduction of this book, I here use the term Panara, the selfdesignation of the tribe in question.

¤ RAIN 1923   Several raids were undertaken on Brazilian settlements along the Iriri, Curua, Xinxim and Ipixuna Rivers. The reason
for this series of attacks was to achieve many firearms and ammunition
as possible in order to better resist any further Panara attack. The booty
met their expectations.

¤ DRY 1924   Those men who had firearms and a sufficient
amount of ammunition returned to the fields near *krãnhtykti* to fetch food.
By then, some men insisted on counterattacking the Panara. A group of
men went, but near the village they saw signs of a bad omen and returned.
After that, a group of Mekranoti returned to live in *krãnhtykti*. Others,
still fearing a Panara attack, remained at *krôdjãm-re*.

¤ RAIN 1924   *kwỳrỳkangô* naming ceremony at *krãnhtykti*.

¤ DRY 1925   All Mekranoti reunited at *krãnhtykti*. Once more
it was decided to attack the Panara. Most men participated and during the
massive assault many Panara were killed but, exceptionally, no captives
were taken.

¤ RAIN 1925   Fearing a Panara counterattack, all the Mekranoti moved to *arerek-re*, about hundred and twenty kilometers northeast of
krãnhtykti. In *arerek-re*, they set up a big village with two men's houses.
Mote-re was the main leader in the eastern men's house, which housed
only men of the younger men's groups. Pãnhmoti, Ôket and Karànhĩn
were the chiefs in the western men's house, the senior men's group. Following Panara tradition, the eastern men's house was called *metykti-re*
and the western one *mekry-re*.

memybijôk naming ceremony.

All Mekranoti returned to *krãnhtykti*.

¤ DRY 1926   *bep* naming ceremony.

¤ RAIN 1926   After a short migration to *rikrekô-re*, they built
a new village at *adytirekrekỳ*.

kôkô naming ceremony.

¤ DRY 1927   A series of gardens were laid out.

¤ RAIN 1927   *pãnh-te* naming ceremony.

memybijôk naming ceremony.

After these two ceremonies, some men spotted recent traces of some
members of the Panara. Fearing an attack, they returned to *rikrekô-re*.

¤ DRY 1928   *bep* naming ceremony.

¤ RAIN 1928   The Mekranoti all moved to *krãnhkrax*, in the
forest, where they built a new village with two men's houses. The men of
the eastern men's house went out to raid Brazilian settlers near the Curua
River. One young Mekranoti man got killed and the warriors returned
having achieved nothing.

kwỳrỳkangô naming ceremony.

¤ DRY 1929   *kwỳrỳkangô* naming ceremony.

¤ RAIN 1929   *kôkô* naming ceremony.

¤ DRY 1930   *tàkàk* naming ceremony.

¤ RAIN 1930   *memybijôk* naming ceremony.

¤ DRY 1931   Some men had noticed the presence of a group of Gorotire men near the Iriri River. The Mekranoti attacked and killed one man. After that, they moved to *adytirekrekỳ*.

memybijôk naming ceremony.

¤ RAIN 1931   *kôkô* naming ceremony.

¤ DRY 1932   *bep* naming ceremony.

¤ RAIN 1932   *kwỳrỳkangô* naming ceremony.

¤ DRY 1933   *tàkàk* naming ceremony.

A quarrel arose over an adulterous relationship.

¤ RAIN 1933   The tension following the adulterous relationship led to some club-fights and a schism occurred. The *mekry-re*, the men of the western men's house, went to the north and built a village at *pykakrãkumex*, in the forest. The *metykti-re*, the men of the eastern men's house, went to *ropkakô*, a short distance due south from *adytirekrekỳ*.

kwỳrỳkangô naming ceremony in the *mekry-re* group.

memybijôk naming ceremony in the *metykti-re* group.

¤ DRY 1934   The *mekry-re* men went to the Jamanxim River. They raided a Brazilian settlement and captured a boy after having killed his parents. At their return, the people of *pykakrãkumex* reunited with the *metykti-re* at *ropkakô*.

tàkàk naming ceremony.

¤ RAIN 1934   All the Mekranoti moved to *adytirekrekỳ* where two men's houses were built again.

kwỳrỳkangô naming ceremony.

2. THE MENOKANÊ JOIN THE MEKRANOTI AND SEPARATE AGAIN (1935-1947)

¤ DRY 1935   After moving to *rikrekô-re*, in the forest, two groups of men left the village: while the men of the western men's house went to the Curua River to raid Brazilian settlements, those of the eastern men's house went to the Xingu River. The latter group met the Kararaô who, led by Kôkôjàmti, had just separated from the main Gorotire village. Both groups stayed together for one day. Kôkôjàmti expressed his wish to join the Mekranoti, but he was killed by a Mekranoti man that same night. The next day, the Kararaô fled to the north, while some of the young women stayed with the Mekranoti and moved to the village. After reuniting at *rikrekô-re*, all the Mekranoti moved to *pykakrãkumex*, where a village with only one men's house was built.

¤ RAIN 1935   Most men went out to attack the Gorotire. Before reaching the village, though, they sighted signs of a bad omen and returned.

kwỳrỳkangô naming ceremony.

The younger men's group went to the Jamanxim River and the senior men's group to the Curua River. No Brazilians were killed, but some firearms and ammunition were brought back.

¤ DRY 1936   On their return, they set off once again to the Curua and Jamanxim Rivers. The group that ventured near the Curua River met a group of Gorotire men, led by Tàpjêt. These men were on their way back from a raid along the Jamanxim River. Tàpjêt had captured a Brazilian girl (which they named Irekàrênh) after having killed her parents. The two groups stayed together for a few days and one Mekranoti man (Kopo'yr) joined Tàpjêt to the Gorotire village.

¤ RAIN 1936   Back in the village, the Mekranoti men went to attack the Gorotire, but once again the raid was not realized. At their return, all moved to *ropkakô*.

memybijôk naming ceremony.

After the ceremony, they moved to a place called *krãnhmrôpryjaka*.

¤ DRY 1937   *bep* naming ceremony.

During this ceremony, Kopo'yr arrived in the village bringing Tàpjêt and some hundred and twenty Indians along. This was the *menokanê* society which had separated from the Gorotire village and had decided to join the Mekranoti. Most of Tàpjêt's followers were men of the younger men's group (*menõrõny-re*) with their young wives of the *mekrajtyk* age grade. Including Tàpjêt's group, the Mekranoti population reached about six hundred and seventy Indians[5]. A new village was built to receive the newcomers. It had one big men's house with two men's societies and three "sitting places" for the younger men's groups.

¤ RAIN 1937   *kwỳrỳkangô* naming ceremony.

The ceremony was interrupted when Tàpjêt insisted on attacking *pykatôti* where, at that time, only the Kubenkranken remained[6]. Nearly

5   By that time, the Mekranoti village numbered sixty-one adult men as well as fifty-six *menõrõny-re*. Tàpjêt's group numbered nine *mekra-re* and twenty-five *menõrõny-re*.

6   In 1936, about half of the population had left *pykatôti*. This secessionist group became known in the literature by the name Gorotire.

all the Mekranoti men left: some Kubenkranken men were killed and six boys as well as seven girls were taken captives. After having returned to the village and finishing the *kwỳrỳkangô* ceremony, the younger men's group led by Ku'at and Pãnhkê went to raid Brazilian settlers along the Jamanxim, Curua and Iriri Rivers. Somewhere along the Jamanxim, a quarrel broke out between the men and during a club-fight, three men were killed.

¤ DRY 1938   *bep* naming ceremony.

Tàpjêt and his men decided to join the group led by Ku'at and Pãnhkê which had still not returned. Both groups met near the Jamanxim River and from there continued their venture up to the Tapayoz River[7]. There, they raided some settlements, captured two girls and proceeded their long venture to the Iriri River.

¤ RAIN 1938   The people who had stayed behind in the village moved to *akranhĩnkrô*.

kôkô naming ceremony.

Tàpjêt and the other men arrived when the ceremony had almost ended. The women of one of the two women's societies went to the Iriri Novo River to fetch palm nuts.

¤ DRY 1939   *kwỳrỳkangô* naming ceremony.

During the ceremony, the men of the *menhakrekroti* men's society left on the *õntomõr* (ceremonial trek), while the *menokà-re* went to the Curua River to raid Brazilian settlements. The latter brought back a great amount of hammocks, cloth and tools. On their return, all moved to *pyka-bãr* where a series of skirmishes arose, followed by several club-duels and club-fights[8].

¤ RAIN 1939   The younger men's group crossed the Xingu River to hunt parrots at a site called *kapôtninõr* (an area of open grass-land between the Xingu and Liberdade Rivers). In *pykabãr* an epidemic of influenza (?) broke out: within a few days, five women and girls died, and still others died later on. Leaving the "contaminated site"[9], all moved to *krãnhmrôpryjaka*. From there, Tàpjêt set off with his men to attack the

---

7   Nimuendajú (1952:433) mentioned that the Kayapo had expanded their perambulation area to the lower Tapayoz River by 1939.

8   The expression the Indians used here was *kô-o nhy* ("to sit with the clubs"), which is a reference to the continuous state of alertness for fighting.

9   During an epidemic of influenza in the Central Mekranoti village in 1978, six Indians died within a week and the people considered moving to another site. This phenomenon of leaving "contaminated" village sites is associated with the many spirits (*karõ*) that haunt the site after a series of deaths. In such cases, the Kayapo say that "the land has turned bad" (*arỳp pyka punu*) and they leave the village.

Kubenkranken.

¤ DRY 1940   Tàpjêt returned and all settled at *akranhĩnkrô*.
ngô-re fishing ceremony.

¤ RAIN 1940   When the younger men's group returned from
the hunting at *kapôtninõr*, all moved back to *pykabãr*. From there, Tàpjêt
set out once again to raid Brazilian settlements.
tàkàk naming ceremony.

¤ DRY 1941   All reunited at *pykabãr*.
kukryt-te tapir ceremony.

A series of disputes broke out during the ceremony[10]. All moved to
krãnhmrôpryjaka again and after a club-fight, Karànhĩn (by then an old
chief), left the village with twenty-six men and their families (hundred
and three Indians in all), mostly kinsmen. They built a temporary village
near the Iriri and Xinxim Rivers while the remaining Mekranoti population moved back to *pykabãr*.

kwỳrỳkangô naming ceremony in Karànhĩn's small village.
kwỳrỳkangô naming ceremony in *pykabãr*.

After the ceremony, Tàpjêt went raiding Brazilian settlers along the
Iriri River. He entered Karànhĩn's village, managing to convince ten
women, six young girls and one senior man to return with him to the
main village. As many women had left his group, Karànhĩn feared an
attack from the main Mekranoti group: he and his people then fled to the
Kubenkranken village where they moved in.

memybijôk naming ceremony in *pykabãr*.

¤ DRY 1942   At the end of the ceremony a collective *aben bê
paamỳ* ritual (institutionalized exchange of sexual partners) was held.
This led to frictions and it was decided to reestablish the two men's
houses. Once more, the eastern men's house was called *metykti-re* and
the western one *mekry-re*. Then the Kubenkranken attacked: three women
were taken captives and one man killed. In pursuit, four Kubenkranken
men were killed but again three Mekranoti women and a man were killed.
After this attack, Tàpjêt took the younger men's group of his men's house
to the Iriri River. Using Àkkajpry — a Brazilian girl he had taken captive
along the Itacaiunas River years before — the men approached a single,

---

10   *Kukryt-te* is a highly ritualized form of tapir hunting. It involves a series of
competitive events organized along the lines of the existing men's societies. Informants
stated that it is not uncommon for serious club-fights to arise during this particular
ceremony. In the Central Mekranoti village of PI Mekranoti, no club-duels had been
recorded in the period from 1971 to 1982. This interval ended when an important club-
fight arose between the men of the two men's societies during the performance of the
kukryt-te ceremony in 1982.

empty house. They took all they could get and on their way back they noticed a Brazilian man working in the forest. They killed him and took his gun. Meanwhile, Katàmkrãmex had taken his men to the upper Iriri River to hunt parrots, and a group of women had gone to the Curua River to fetch palm oil. Then all reunited in *pykabãr*.

¤ RAIN 1942   *memybijôk* naming ceremony.

Another *aben bê paamỳ* was held: the *mekry-re* men took the wives of the *metykti-re* men. After this ritual, they all moved to the north and settled at *krôdjãm-re*. From there, Kreti-re (Mote-re's son and leader of a group of young men in the western men's house) left with his men off raid Brazilian settlers along the Iriri and Curua Rivers. This group was away from the village for more than a year. Tàpjêt and a few of his *mekry-re* men went to Cachimbo — a small Brazilian settlement near the upper Curuaes River — and then proceeded to the Jamanxim River. Some *metykti-re* men as well as some young women went along. Among them was Irekàrênh, the Brazilian girl Tàpjêt had captured along the Jamanxim River in 1936. When the warriors sighted a large Brazilian settlement on the opposite side of the river, they decided to "pacify" these Brazilians in the hope of receiving firearms and ammunition. They threw Irekàrênh in the water, urging her to swim across, and yelled "Compadre! Papai!" ("Friend! Father!"), Portuguese words they had learned from Irekàrênh. The Brazilians probably thought it was an attack and started shooting. Tàpjêt got hit in the arm and the Indians retreated. On the way back, a dispute broke out between the men and, when arriving near the Xixê River, Ngôryti (one of the accompanying *metykti-re* men) killed Tàpjêt.

¤ DRY 1943   When the warriors arrived at the village, all inhabitants moved to *pykabãr* again. Passing by the old village site of *rojkô-re*, though, they noticed that the Panara had taken food from their gardens. A temporary Panara shelter was found at a nearby creek and the Mekranoti then called that site *krãjôkàrànôr* ("the sleeping place of the Panara"). Arriving at *pykabãr*, the village was reconstructed with only one men's house. Then, the Kubenkranken attacked, killing a Mekranoti couple. During a revenge skirmish, two Kubenkranken and one more Mekranoti men were killed. This was the last skirmish between these two Kayapo groups.

¤ RAIN 1943   They moved to *krãnhmrôpryjaka*.
     kwỳrỳkangô naming ceremony.

¤ DRY 1944   *tàkàk* naming ceremony.

Kreti-re and his young *mekry-re* men returned from their long venture. In revenge for the killing of Tàpjêt, they killed Ngôryti, Tàpjêt's killer.

kwỳrỳkangô naming ceremony.

Immediately after the ceremony, Katàmkrãmex, one of the *metykti-re* chiefs, as well as another *metykti-re* man were killed by Kreti-re and his followers. These killings led to a collective club-fight and a schism followed: Kreti-re and Bepkamati took the *mekry-re* to *krôdjãm-re*, while Kremôr and Bepgogoti took the *metykti-re* to *kapôtninôr*, a small area of open grassland on the right bank of the Xingu River. The *metykti-re* group then designated the *mekry-re* by the name *meatxweti* ("very false people"). Besides these two main groups, two small bands also separated: Pyrô took some twenty kinsmen and moved to the north[11].

¤ RAIN 1944   In the *mekry-re* village, club-fights kept going on. Ku'at (one of the leaders) left the village with twenty-four men and their families (some sixty-nine Indians in all) and moved towards the Tapayoz River, where this small group remained for years.

Kwỳrỳkangô naming ceremony in the *metykti-re* village.

¤ DRY 1945   The *metykti-re* moved back to the left bank of the Xingu River and settled at *rõntinôr*, where they were attacked by the Panara: one man and a girl got killed, and three Panara men were slain in revenge.

kwỳrỳkangô naming ceremony in the *metykti-re* village.

kwỳrỳkangô naming ceremony in the *mekry-re* village.

¤ RAIN 1945   A quarrel arose in the *metykti-re* village. Bepgogoti[12] left with a group of his followers and went to the Iriri Novo River where a temporary village was built. They raided some Brazilian settlements, taking many clothes and tools as booty. Back at *rõntinôr*, the Panara attacked once again: three Mekranoti girls, a boy and one Panara man were killed. Bepgogoti and his people then left *rõntinôr* and decided to proceed to *krôdjãm-re*, the *mekry-re* village. On their way, a disease

11   A few years after separating from the Mekranoti group, a quarrel arose between Pyro and Byriryti. The latter then separated with his wife and children and moved to the west, where they entered into conflict with Angme'ê's group. During one particular conflict, Byriryti killed one of Angme'ê's men and lost one of his sons in revenge. Byriryti and his family were contacted in 1968 and were settled in the Northern Mekranoti village near PI Bau. A year later, all but one boy died of measles. The boy, Ka'ênhtx, was taken along by a Brazilian family who promised to raise the child as "a good Brazilian" and to return the child afterwards. The boy never returned. The other part of the secessionist group, composed of two men (Pyro and Mongêt) and their families, still lives isolated in the forest near the mid Iriri River, without any known peaceful contacts with Brazilians or other Indian groups.

12   Bepgogoti was a leader who had originally been a *metykti-re* (before 1936). Between 1938 and 1942 he joined the *mekry-re* but during the last split, he joined the *metykti-re* once again.

(flu?) broke out, killing several children and two elder men. Meanwhile, Kreti-re had taken his men to the Formador do Curua River, leaving Bepkamati with a few men and the women and children in the village. Bepgogoti and his followers moved into *krôdjãm-re*. Yet, enmity got the upper hand again and Bepgogoti's men killed one man and four women of the *mekry-re* in revenge for the killing of Katàmkrãmex. Bepgogoti then left with his group and returned to the upper Iriri River. Meanwhile, in the *metykti-re* village, Kremôr had taken his men to raid Brazilian settlements along the mid Xingu River: two Brazilians were killed and several firearms were obtained. When Kreti-re returned to *krôdjãm-re* after his venture, he and Bepkamati moved their group south and joined the *metykti-re* at *rõntinôr* where, sometime later, Bepgogoti also arrived. A big village with one men's house was built.

menibijôk naming ceremony.

¤ DRY 1946   *kwỳrỳkangô* naming ceremony.

A disease (flu?) broke out in the village, killing several Indians, including two adult men. Ngrenhma-ri, a young *metykti-re* leader, left with some men for the Xingu River. The Brazilians killed one Mekranoti and the men then returned.

¤ RAIN 1946   The Mekranoti set off to *arerek-re* for a few weeks to fetch food at the old gardens where Êngri (a *mekry-re*) had adulterous relations with Ngrenhma-ri's wife. At night, both men fought with burning sticks and the next day Kenti (Êngri's brother and also a *mekry-re*) had a club-duel with Ngrenhma-ri. All then moved back to *rõntinôr* where two men's houses were built: the eastern one was called *metykti-re* and the western one *mekry-re*.

bàyjangri corn ceremony.

¤ DRY 1947   *memybijôk* naming ceremony.

For the ceremonial trek, the men divided into two groups[13]: the *mekry-re* went to hunt in the forest to the north of the village, while the *metykti-re* did so in the open grasslands to the south. Kreti-re, Bepgogoti and some men stayed behind in the village with the women and children. The *mekry-re* men came back earlier than agreed[14] and waited for the *metykti-re* near a garden. When the latter approached, some *mekry-re*

13   It is an highly unusual procedure for the men to be organized along the men's society's lines during ceremonial treks, since it is customary for all the participating men to be organized in teams working for the sponsors of the naming ceremony.

14   Whenever groups make an appointment to meet, they keep track of the time either by the moon, or by indicating the number of days on a stick. Each mark on the stick then corresponds to a day. Each group takes a similar stick along with an equal number of marks.

started shooting and Ngrenhma-ri was hit. Two *mekry-re* men and one girl (all kinsmen of Êngri) were killed in revenge. Back in the village, Kenti killed two *metykti-re* men and a woman. Despite the many club-fights which ensued, the naming ceremony was celebrated all the way through.

bep naming ceremony.

Kenti and his followers killed another *metykti-re* man, as well as his wife and young son. Tension was high in the village and, afraid of being killed, Kremôr left with twenty-two men (the *menõrõny-re* of the *metykti-re* men's house) and their families (about hundred and seventy Indians) and settled at *kapôtninõr*. Frictions continued in the main village and during a collective club-fight, the group led by Bepkamati, Angme'ê and Kenti was defeated and left the village. This *mekry-re* group numbered thirty-three men and their families (some two hundred Indians) and settled at *krôdjãm-re*. Kreti-re's group of twenty-nine men and the one of Bepgogoti of seventeen men (some two hundred and twenty and hundred and sixty Indians, respectively) stayed behind but also separated: both groups went north and wandered in the forest. Bepkamati's group attacked Kreti-re's small settlement[15] and two men and a boy were killed. Kreti-re then reunited with Bepgogoti's group and together they moved to *rõntinõr*, where one men's house was built. A group of fifteen *mekra-re* and *mebêngêt* separated with their families from *rõntinõr* and joined Kremôr's village on the other side of the Xingu River.

3. THE RECENT HISTORY OF THE NORTHERN MEKRANOTI (1947-1981)

¤ DRY 1947   When Bepkamati, Angme'ê and Kenti separated from the main Mekranoti village at *rõntinõr*, the group numbered about two hundred and ten Indians. These Northern Mekranoti went to the north, following the Iriri River. During this migration, some men returned to attack Kreti-re's village, killing two men and a boy. Frictions continued in Bepkamati's group though, and after a club-fight, a small group of six men — including the only *metykti-re* man who had joined this Northern Mekranoti group — and their families moved south and joined the community of Kreti-re and Bepgogoti at *rõntinõr*.

¤ RAIN 1947   The Northern Mekranoti settled at *krôdjãm-re* where a village with one men's house was built.

kwỳrỳkangô naming ceremony.

15   This attack was probably a retaliation for Kreti-re (a *mekry-re*), because he did not support Bepkamati and Angme'ê in the earlier collective club-fight.

At the end of the ceremony, they migrated to *bày*, passing through *kenpoti*. There they met up with and absorbed a small group of nine men and their families: the newcomers were a group that had split off from Ku'at's group which, at that time, still wandered in the forests near the Tapayoz River.

¤ DRY 1948   All moved to *rõn'ôkrĩdjà*.

¤ RAIN 1948   All moved to *kwỳrỳdjỳti*.

   memybijôk naming ceremony.

A collective club-fight arose before the conclusion of the ceremony. One man was killed and this led to a new schism. Bepkamati and Angme'ê left with some hundred and forty Indians and left for *rõn'ôkrĩdjà*. Kenti, on the other hand, went with the remaining group of about seventy Indians to the Teles Pires River, where they wandered about in the forest without building a permanent village. Shortly after this separation, Kenti and his men returned to attack Bepkamati's village: Bepkamati as well as Tàkàkpê (a young leader) were killed. Angme'ê then took his followers (thirty-seven men and their families) to *ngôkamrêkti*, near the old gardens of a deserted Brazilian settlement.

   ¤ DRY 1949   Angme'ê's men went to raid Kenti's group, but returned having achieved nothing.

   ¤ RAIN 1949   *Ngôkamrêkti* was abandoned and the people moved back to *kenpoti*. Kenti's group was attacked by local Brazilians living along the Curua River. During the skirmishes, two Brazilians were killed[16].

   ¤ DRY 1950   Once again, Angme'ê's people went to attack Kenti's group. But, by coincidence, they met up with Kenti and his men who were on their way to attack Angme'ê's village. Kenti's men fled, being pursued by those of Angme'ê. Some shooting[17] occurred but no-one got killed. Angme'ê's men kept pursuing the others who fled to their village. Two men, two women and one child (including Kenti's wife and child) were killed at Kenti's village somewhere between the Teles Pires and Jamanxim Rivers. On their return to the village, Angme'ê's men

16   Preihs (1952ms:2) reports how eighteen local Brazilians tried in vain to attack twice one of the Northern Mekranoti groups. During the first attempt, a campsite was located but the Indians managed to flee. A few days later, the same assailants reached the main village of the Kayapo group: once again, the Indians managed to escape. Two Brazilians were killed and in the confusion, the Brazilians managed to abduct a Brazilian female captive.

17   Informants stated that this was one of the rare occasions that firearms were used in clashes between Kayapo groups.

raided a series of settlements along the Jamanxim and Curua Rivers[18]. No Brazilians were killed, but lots of ammunition, many firearms, tools and a large quantity of manioc flour were taken.

¤ RAIN 1950   Angme'ê's group moved to *krãnhkaê*.

In Kenti's group, a fight broke out and one man was killed.

kwỳrỳkangô naming ceremony in Angme'ê's group[19].

After the ceremony, the main group left for *krôdjãm-re*.

¤ DRY 1951   Angme'ê's group separated into two groups. The schism was not due to internal strife, but was rather due to the decision of the younger men to raid some settlements along the Iriri River, while the senior men preferred to return to the old garden sites. So, Angme'ê and the elder men took their families to the Curua River where they stayed near the gardens without building a real village. Ykakôr, a young leader, took his followers to the Iriri River, where a small temporary village was built. From there, the men raided some Brazilian settlements along that river, killing two Brazilians. They then decided to attack the Mekranoti led by Kreti-re. Not knowing that this group had reunited with the ones of Bepgogoti and Kremôr, and that these *metykti-re* were wandering in the forest at a considerable distance to the north, Ykakôr only found a deserted village. After he left, the *metykti-re* returned to their gardens and noticed the recent passage of Ykakôr's group. An attack was immediately mounted and six of Ykakôr's men were killed. Ykakôr then returned with his reduced group, by means of the Iriri River, to join Angme'ê's village.

¤ RAIN 1951   *bô kam me tor* naming ceremony.

They built a new village at *krãnhnĩnõ*.

¤ DRY 1952   Gardens were laid out.

¤ RAIN 1952   *kwỳrỳkangô* naming ceremony.

bàyjangri corn festival.

¤ DRY 1953   They raided a few settlements along the Jamanxim River, killing four Brazilians and bringing along several firearms and tools.

¤ RAIN 1953   The men returned from their ventures.

---

18   An SPI report mentions that a large Brazilian settlement of some four hundred people existed near the confluence of the Curua and Bau Rivers, and that it had to be abandoned in 1947 due to the incessant Kayapo aggression in the area (Preihs 1952ms:1). In September 1950, the Kayapo surrounded the agglomeration of Bomfim. The Indians yelled "*atxwe-re*" (false, shameless) and discharged their arms in the direction of the houses but no-one was killed (*ibid*.:2). Both these Kayapo "attacks" along the Curua and the simulated attack on Bomfim probably were performed by the Northern Mekranoti led by Angme'ê to scare away those Brazilians who were living extremely close to Angme'ê's village.

19   No ceremony was ever celebrated in Kenti's group!

bô kam me tor naming ceremony.

¤ DRY 1954   The men left once again to the Iriri River. No one was killed, but lots of commodities were brought back.

¤ RAIN 1954   *bô kam me tor* naming ceremony.

¤ DRY 1955

¤ RAIN 1955   *menibijôk* naming ceremony.

¤ DRY 1956   The men noticed an important group of Brazilians in the proximity of their village. Fearing a massive attack, they fled into the forest where new gardens were laid out.

¤ RAIN 1956   The men left to the nearby Jamanxim River. Half-way, they noticed traces of the recent passage of Kenti's group and returned, afraid that the village would be attacked during their absence. They waited for some time and since no more signs of an attack were noticed, they went once again to raid Kenti's group. Two men (including Êngri, Kenti's brother), two women and a boy were killed, while three boys were taken captives.

¤ DRY 1957   Once again, they noticed that a big group of Brazilians was approaching their village. Scouts were sent to spy. These men brought back the news that the approaching Brazilians were accompanied by numerous Kayapo. This time, the Northern Mekranoti did not flee. In June 1957 the SPI team of thirty-five men (including some Gorotire and Kararaô men as guides and interpreters and led by Francisco Meirelles), arrived at the village, establishing peaceful relations with these Indians. The population was estimated to be about hundred and fifty Northern Mekranoti (Meirelles 1962:8 and Arnaud & Alves 1974:4). Meirelles convinced these Indians to settle along the Curua River where a post was to be established to supply medical care and the provision of commodities. The post was named Pôsto Curua and was built on the left bank of the Curua River, opposite Bom Futuro, a small Brazilian community. The SPI also settled some thirty-eight Kararaô Indians near that post. These Kararaô had been contacted by Meirelles' team a few months before. The village then totaled a little less than two hundred Indians.

¤ RAIN 1957   *kwỳrỳkangô* naming ceremony.

The ceremony was not totally celebrated since diseases killed nearly one fourth of the village population, including chief Angme'ê[20]. Meirelles asked the Indians to collect Brazil nuts and to gather rubber in exchange for commodities[21].

---

20   In a radio message dated February 12, 1958 and sent to the SPI office at Belém, Meirelles asked for an additional supply of medicines for flu and dysentery (SPI radio).

21   In that period, the Northern Mekranoti produced six hundred boxes of Brazil

¤ DRY 1958   Most of the men were asked to join Francisco Meirelles on his next expedition to contact the Central Mekranoti.

¤ RAIN 1958   After the expedition, the men returned to their village at Pôsto Curua and, upon seeing the numerous deaths, they complained to Meirelles about the inadequate medical assistance. Meirelles attested that he would find a solution in the very near future. Meanwhile, contact diseases imported through the inhabitants of Bom Futuro continued to decimate the village...

¤ 1960-1961   The Northern Mekranoti were moved further upriver, near the confluence of the Bau and Curua Rivers. A new post was built and called Pôsto Juscelino Kubitschek.

¤ 1967-1968   The post was renamed PI Bau.

4. THE PACIFICATION AND THE SEPARATION OF THE CENTRAL AND SOUTHERN MEKRANOTI (1947-1956)

¤ DRY 1947   Kreti-re, Bepgogoti and twenty-six other men lived with their families at *rõntinõr*, while Kremôr and thirty-six men lived with their families at *kapôtninõr*, to the east of the Xingu River. From this last village, some men went to the east where, along the lower Tapirape River — a tributary of the upper Araguaia — they raided the Tapirape tribe, burning down the village and killing three women. Two girls and one boy were captured[22].

¤ RAIN 1947   *kwỳrỳkangô* naming ceremony in the village at *rõntinõr*.

   kwỳrỳkangô naming ceremony in *kapôtninõr*.

   kukryt-te tapir ceremony in *kapôtninõr*.

---

nuts and 2.5 tons of rubber. In that same period, the Gorotire collected eight hundred boxes of Brazil nuts and six tons of rubber; the Kubenkranken collected two thousand boxes of Brazil nuts and eight tons of rubber (SPI report dated June 20, 1959).

22   Bibliographic data confirm this period of Mekranoti oral tradition, relating the devastating consequences of this raid on the small group of some sixty Tapirape Indians (Baldus 1970:78,142). The attack occurred in November 1947. Lelong (1952:65) wrote that "All the (Tapirape) men and the young people had all left to fish `tucunare', when the (Kayapo) warriors attacked the village by surprise. They killed three women and captured one women, a young girl and a boy... The population fled after the Gorotire had burnt down two houses, and took refuge near one of the Christian settlements". Lelong (*ibid.*:108) said that the name of the oldest captured girl was Iparenahi. This woman still lives in the main Central Mekranoti village at PI Kubenkokre; the captured Tapirape boy lives in the Southern Mekranoti village and the woman was abducted by the Xavante in 1948. Although both Lelong and Baldus took the Gorotire to be responsible for this raid, it was unquestionably executed by the Mekranoti.

¤ DRY 1948   Kruma-re, a young leader in Kremôr's village, left with six other men to raid the Tapirape tribe. Since the village was abandoned after the earlier attack, the seven men attacked a small Brazilian settlement along the Araguaia River. No one was killed, but on their retreat these Mekranoti men came across an important Xavante village[23]. A skirmish took place: armed with bows and arrows, the seven Kayapo confronted the Xavante, killing three women. The Xavante warriors, on the other hand, abducted the Tapirape woman.

¤ RAIN 1948   After this venture and fearing a massive Xavante counterattack, Kremôr's group retreated to the west of the Xingu River. Somewhere in the forest to the northwest of the lower Jarina, this Mekranoti group reunited with the one led by Kreti-re and Bepgogoti. Once reunited, the groups settled at *rojkô-re*, where one men's house was built.

bô kam me tor naming ceremony.

memybijôk naming ceremony.

¤ DRY 1949   *bep* naming ceremony.

While Bepgogoti remained with a few men and all the women and children in the village at *rojkô-re*, Kreti-re and Kremôr led a group of men to sack small Brazilian settlements along the Curua River. The men returned in time to participate in the final phase of the naming ceremony.

¤ RAIN 1949   *kwỳrỳkangô* naming ceremony.

A new village was built at *tekàdjỳtidjãm*, to the south of the open grasslands, where the ceremony was ended.

¤ DRY 1950   *tàkàk* naming ceremony.

All moved back to *rojkô-re* again.

menibijôk naming ceremony.

The ceremony was ended in the forest, northwest of the village site. Kreti-re and Kremôr went once again with a group of men to attack Brazilians along the Curua.

¤ RAIN 1950   *kukryt-te* tapir ceremony.

¤ DRY 1951   On their way back to *rojkô-re*, these Mekranoti sighted the recent passage of a group of Northern Mekranoti men. An attack was mounted and six Northern Mekranoti men were killed (see earlier).

¤ RAIN 1951   *kwỳrỳkangô* naming ceremony.

¤ DRY 1952   *bep* naming ceremony.

¤ RAIN 1952   *memybijôk* naming ceremony.

Pakyx, leader of the younger men's group, left with some of his fol-

23   The Xavante group in question was probably the one named *marãwasede* which was still "unpacified" in 1948 (Maybury-Lewis 1974:1, map).

lowers and set out to the south with the intention of attacking the Kisedje (Suya) tribe. At the mouth of the Suiá Missu River, where the Kisedje used to live, the warriors sighted a small, recently built Brazilian settlement[24]. The warriors wandered around that neighborhood for a few days until, struck by hunger, they decided to return to their village. On their way back, they met a group of Yudja men near the mouth of the Manissaua Missu River. During this brief encounter, some conversation took place[25] and the Yudja led the Mekranoti men to their village. In exchange for bows and arrows, the Yudja smothered the visitors with knives and glass beads which the Villas Bôas brothers had left there for that particular purpose[26]. The Yudja made it clear to the Mekranoti whom the gifts came from and that these *kubẽmex* ("good strangers") would certainly return one day to visit them and bring along even more gifts. The Mekranoti warriors then returned to their village.

    kwỳrỳkangô naming ceremony.

    kwỳrỳkangô naming ceremony.

    During the next few months, three groups of Mekranoti men went successively to the Yudja to obtain more gifts. Then, one day, two Yudja men arrived at *rojkô-re* to announce the approaching arrival of the Villas Bôas brothers. Immediately after the Yudja left, a fire broke out in the village, burning down many houses. Tension was high and a case of adultery led to a collective club-fight. A schism followed: the Central Mekranoti group of sixty men and their families and led by Kreti-re and Bepgogoti remained and rebuilt the village; the Southern Mekranoti group of thirty-

24   This settlement was Pôsto Diauarum, set up by the members of the FBC (Central Brazilian Foundation) in 1952. At the time, this foundation was sending out expeditions with the specific aim of laying out a series of small airstrips throughout Central Brazil. This was in preparation for a future network of airlines and with the idea of eventually linking these airstrips by roads. This was all done for the eventual opening of the interior of the country for development. The expedition in the area between the Araguaia and Tapayoz Rivers was led by the Villas Bôas brothers. The expedition members mentioned the presence of Kayapo Indians near the post (Villas Bôas 1954:80), probably referring to this Mekranoti venture in 1952.

25   Some elderly Mekranoti men still speak some Yudja, just as a few elderly Yudja men still speak some Kayapo (field notes). It was said that Mote-re and some other men of his generation spoke Yudja quite well (see App. B:15).

26   The Villas Bôas brothers had made contact with the Yudja by 1947 and estimated that it was through this tribe that they could most easily contact the Kayapo of that area. In their report, the Villas Bôas brothers referred to these contacts between the Kayapo and the Yudja (Villas Bôas 1954:81-82) and Cowell (1960:177) wrote that "the Txukarramãe (Mekranoti) entered the Yudja village for the first time in peace. On this momentous occasion, they exchanged some arrows for knives and tools left there by the Villas Bôas."

eight men and their families, led by Kremôr left and settled at *ngôrãrãnk*, a site near the Cachoeira Von Martius rapids. From this last village, seven men (including chief Kremôr) went to Pôsto Diauarum and eventually to Pôsto Vasconcellos[27], visiting several upper Xingu tribes. Shortly afterwards, Claudio and Orlando Villas Bôas, accompanied by two other Brazilians, visited the Southern Mekranoti. At that time, some Central Mekranoti men were visiting Kremôr's village and the Brazilian party also set out to contact the main village at *rojkô-re* as well[28]. This event, therefore, was the first peaceful contact these two Mekranoti groups had with the Brazilians. On their way back, the Villas Bôas brothers took five of Kremôr's men along (including Kruma-re) to visit Pôsto Vasconcellos.

¤ DRY 1953   The Central Mekranoti moved to a site called *pi'ydjãm*, between the Xixê and upper Curua Rivers, only to return to *rojkô-re* a few months later. Kremôr moved his group to *tekàdjỳtidjãm*.

¤ RAIN 1953   The Villas Bôas brothers returned with three Kajabi men and managed to convince both Mekranoti communities to reunite at *rõntinõr*. While the other visitors left, Claudio Villas Bôas remained with the Mekranoti in order to assist in the making of an airstrip near the village. After a long delay, the airplane came. It did not land but packages were dropped and Claudio then returned to Pôsto Vasconcellos.

¤ DRY 1954   An epidemic of flu or cold (*nharop*) broke out and *rõntinõr* was abandoned: while the Southern Mekranoti returned to *tekàdjỳtidjãm*, the Central Mekranoti first went to *djwỳkapĩdjà* to move later-on to *rojkô-re*.

tàkàk naming ceremony at *tekàdjỳtidjãm*.

¤ RAIN 1954   The Southern Mekranoti moved to *ngôrãrãnk*, where many died of contact diseases.

¤ DRY 1955   Both groups reunited at *rojkô-re*. Once again a fire broke out in the village. While rebuilding the village, a quarrel broke out between members of the younger men's group and their senior tribesmen. After a collective club-fight, Pakyx (a young leader), left the village with a group of twenty men (mostly members of the younger men's group) and moved towards the Tapayoz River, only to turn around almost immediately and eventually settle at *pi'ydjãm*, a site between the Xixê and Curuaes Rivers.

¤ RAIN 1955   A few months later, Kreti-re also left the village at *rojkô-re*. He was fleeing from the diseases and led an important

27   See Villas Bôas (1954:82), where this visit of the Mekranoti men to Pôsto Vasconcellos is mentioned. Upon the creation of the Xingu National Park in 1961, Pôsto Vasconcellos was renamed Pôsto Leonardo Villas Bôas.
28   See also Villas Bôas (1954:83) where this passage is mentioned.

group of forty men to join Pakyx's small community. While Kremôr and Kruma-re went with a small group to the gardens at *ngôrãrãnk*, Bepgogoti took his followers to *tepakàjtyk*, near *kũmjêkô*. On this occasion, many of Kremôr's followers (about fifteen men and their families) joined Bepgogoti's group.

¤ DRY 1956   When Bepgogoti's wife also succumbed to the flu, he eventually led his group to the northwest and moved in with his fellow tribesmen at *pi'ydjãm*, turning that particular village into the most important of all Kayapo villages at the time in terms of population: it numbered nearly four hundred Indians.

5. THE RECENT HISTORY OF THE CENTRAL MEKRANOTI (1956-1989)

¤ RAIN 1956   The Central Mekranoti lived in *pi'ydjãm*, where a village with one men's house was built, housing eighty-eight men.

kwỳrỳkangô naming ceremony.

tàkàk naming ceremony.

A group of men raided the Southern Mekranoti village at *ngôrãrãnk*, killing four men.

¤ DRY 1957   Nearly all of them moved to the Formador do Curua River to collect palm leaves and palm oil. In that area, they met up with and absorbed Kenti's small Northern Mekranoti group[29] of some seventy Indians and moved back to *pi'ydjãm*.

¤ RAIN 1957   A few men went to raid two small Brazilian settlements along the mid Iriri River[30]. In the meanwhile, the Central Mekranoti decided to kill Kenti in revenge for the many killings that had occurred more than a decade before and for which Kenti was considered to be one of those responsible. But fearing his powers as a sorcerer as well as his bravery, Kenti's brother was killed instead, while Kenti himself

---

29   From 1948 to 1957, Kenti and his group had sporadic contacts with gold-seekers in the area along the Jamanxim and along tributaries of the Tapayoz. During some of these contacts, the Brazilians gave the Indians some ammunition and other commodities.

30   In his report, SPI inspector Francisco Meirelles (1962:9) referred to these attacks which involved the settlements named Limeira and Trempes. During the attacks, one rubber tapper was killed. Meirelles described this passage as follows: "At a site called Entre Rios (Between Rivers), we heard that the Indians had attacked a rubber gatherer at a place called Limeira and that another one had been killed at Trempes... Upon arriving [in Limeira] I went to visit the wounded man. He had been shot in the back, at the height of his right omoplate. He was groaning and had high fever. His clothes and his hammock were soaked with blood."

managed to flee with his young pregnant wife to the west[31].

memybijôk naming ceremony.

¤ DRY 1958   Kreti-re led a group of men to the Iriri River, where a small Brazilian settlement was raided: one Brazilian and one Indian were killed, while another Brazilian was seriously hurt[32]. A short time later, Francisco Meirelles arrived with his "pacification" team, consisting of nineteen Brazilians and twenty-two Kayapo Indians (including some Northern Mekranoti men). The team built a post along the mid Iriri River, near the mouth of the Candoca tributary. This post was called Pôsto Candoca and from there, five SPI agents and nearly all the Indian guides were sent to *pi'ydjãm* to announce Meirelles' presence and to inform them of the peaceful character of the mission. While Bepgogoti remained in the village with the women and children, Kreti-re and his men went to Pôsto Candoca for a few weeks to contact the Brazilians and to acquire the firearms and ammunition which the SPI team had brought along for that purpose. Along with a host of other gifts, the Indians got thirty rifles, while each chief received a Winchester[33].

¤ RAIN 1958   *kukryt-te* tapir ceremony in *pi'ydjãm*, after Kreti-re's return.

kwỳrỳkangô naming ceremony.

¤ DRY 1959   Bepgogoti once again remained in the village while Kreti-re and his men left the village to go to the Bau River to collect palm leaves and palm oil. From there, this group continued downriver to Pôsto Curua. Many of the Northern Mekranoti there had already died of contact diseases and Kreti-re managed to convince six men and three women to join him and move into *pi'ydjãm*.

¤ RAIN 1959   The Panara approached the Central Mekranoti village and, near a garden, killed a young girl and two boys, and captured

31   Kenti died in the late 1960s. His wife and daughter (Irekà and Nhàkkamrêkti, respectively) roamed alone in the forests between the Jamanxim and Tapayoz Rivers until 1988, when they were contacted by gold-seekers who took them to Itaituba, the major town in the area. A few months later, they were flown to the Central Mekranoti village at PI Kubenkokre, where they still reside.

32   "We were told that the (Kayapo) Indians had just attacked a settlement called Laranjeira... killing a rubber gatherer and two other settlers. The situation was one of panic: it appears that the settlers and the rubber gatherers living along this river — in all, about five hundred including children — were abandoning the area and were heading towards Altamira. This, because they were terrified with the successive Indians attacks on rubber gatherers, fishermen and other settlers." (Meirelles 1962:10)

33   According to Meirelles (1962:12), the group was led by chief Kreti-re and by the young leaders Ngàjremy and Bekwỳnhti. Meirelles also mentioned Kute'ê (Bepgogoti's son) and Mànma-ri as young leaders. Based upon Meirelles' notes, Moreiro Neto (1959:58) estimated the Central Mekranoti population at some six hundred Indians.

another boy. A counterattack was immediately mounted. The Mekranoti men pursued the Panara warriors and killed one of them. Fearing another Panara attack, though, the Central Mekranoti immediately left the area and moved to Pôsto Candoca. Some SPI agents still resided in that post and in payment for tools and ammunition, the Indians collected large amounts of Brazil nuts for the SPI. Yet, since no medicines were available at the post, many children and elderly people soon died. The Indians then called the site *teprãndjànhõpyka* ("the land of the worms")[34].

¤ DRY 1960   Due to the many victims to the diseases, all returned to *pi'ydjãm.*

        bep naming ceremony.

¤ RAIN 1960   A small group — mostly composed of Kenti's followers — stayed at *pi'ydjãm,* while Kreti-re and Bepgogoti moved with the majority to *kũmjêkô,* in the area of open grassland between the Iriri Novo and Jarina Rivers. Those who left did so in the hope of obtaining better medical care near the Xingu than what they had received near Pôsto Candoca.

¤ DRY 1961   Some families of *pi'ydjãm* visited Pôsto Kubitschek (the newly established post near the Northern Mekranoti village). Half of the Central Mekranoti who visited Pôsto Kubitschek on this occasion were Kenti's former followers. In revenge for the killing of a kinsman about a decade before, one of the Northern Mekranoti man challenged one of Kenti's ex-followers to a club-duel. Tension grew and a collective club-fight broke out after a quarrel over an adulterous relationship. On that same night, Ngrõntyjarô, the Kararaô chief living in the Northern Mekranoti village, was killed. The aggressor, a Central Mekranoti man, was shot to death in revenge. These events led to new tensions between both Mekranoti groups. Fearing that the Central Mekranoti would start raiding Brazilian settlements again, the SPI sent out a new expedition to the area[35].

¤ RAIN 1961   *kwỳrỳkangô* naming ceremony in *kũmjêkô.*

¤ DRY 1962   Meirelles arrived to try to make peace in the area. He and his SPI team arrived via the Curuaes River, which he called Pitiatia. A new post was built and was called Pôsto Pitiatia. It was located some fifty kilometers south of Pôsto Kubitschek. Fearing new conflicts

---

34   Informants stated that many Indians died due to problems related to worms. Still today, the Mekranoti have an distinctive fear of intestinal worms.

35   A radio message sent by the SPI agent at Pôsto Kubitschek in February 1962 mentions that the visiting Central Mekranoti had returned to their traditional village site and that they had decided to live according to old customs again. The agent feared new attacks on both the Northern Mekranoti and local Brazilian settlers (SPI radio).

in the area, the SPI had indeed decided not to try to join both Mekranoti groups in a single village. Meirelles hoped that the Central Mekranoti would eventually settle near Pôsto Pitiatia, where fluvial access was much easier than at *pi'ydjãm*. In that period, not more than hundred Indians were living at *pi'ydjãm*. Meirelles urged the people to go and fetch the others to acquire the many tools, clothing, firearms and ammunition he had brought along. Bepgogoti's sons then set out for *kũmjêkô*. Meanwhile, in that village several Central Mekranoti had died of diseases. Kreti-re and Bepgogoti therefore decided to return to *pi'ydjãm*. They were already on their way back when they met Bepgogoti's sons who notified them of the presence of SPI agents near the Curuaes. By the time the main Central Mekranoti group arrived at Pôsto Pitiatia, Meirelles had already left but some of his agents had remained to distribute the gifts and to try to convince the Indians to settle near the post. The Indians, however, refused to live there and one SPI agent then decided to follow them to *pi'ydjãm* for a while in order to provide medical assistance in loco.

¤ RAIN 1962   A few months later, a temporary split occurred: Bepgogoti went with his followers to Pôsto Kubitschek and joined the Northern Mekranoti while Kreti-re stayed in *pi'ydjãm*[36].

kwỳrỳkangô naming ceremony in Pôsto Kubitschek.

kwỳrỳkangô naming ceremony in *pi'ydjãm*.

menibijôk naming ceremony in *pi'ydjãm*.

¤ DRY 1963   Bepgogoti returned with his followers to *pi'ydjãm*. Ykakôr — the Northern Mekranoti leader who, just like Bepgogoti, was displeased about the lack of medical assistance in Pôsto Kubitschek — and his family joined the Central Mekranoti and moved to *pi'ydjãm*.

¤ RAIN 1963   Three Central Mekranoti men and their families went for a short visit to *porori*, the new Southern Mekranoti village. Ropni — a young leader in that small community — accompanied them on their return and stayed for a few weeks at *pi'ydjãm*, trying to convince both Kreti-re and Bepgogoti to move to *porori*. Kreti-re accepted, on the grounds that better medical assistance was being provided there. Bepgogoti, however, refused. This was not only because he feared new tensions between him and Kremôr, but also because he had come to dislike living near main rivers for fear of epidemics[37]. When Ropni returned

36   In a SPI radio dated May 18, 1963, Hilmar Kluck mentions that Bepgogoti's people had approached the Northern Mekranoti village and that he hoped Kreti-re's people would eventually follow.

37   This reflection has to be understood in the light of the bad experiences related to living near main rivers such as the Xingu, Iriri and Curuaes where many of his fellow

to *porori*, Kreti-re once again set out towards the Curuaes River in order to collect palm leaves and palm oil, which are rather scarce in the Xingu area. Bepgogoti stayed behind in the village with the SPI agent who left some time later when all the Central Mekranoti reunited at *kapôtjaka-re*, a small area of open grassland some twenty kilometers northwest of *pi'ydjãm*.

> *pãnh-te* naming ceremony in *pi'ydjãm*.
> *kôkô* naming ceremony.
> *memybijôk* naming ceremony.

¤ DRY 1964   Once again, four Central Mekranoti men went for a short visit to *porori*.

> *bep* naming ceremony in *pi'ydjãm*.

Meanwhile, an epidemic of kanê (flu?) broke out at *pi'ydjãm* and several children died.

¤ RAIN 1964   Kreti-re, Ykakôr and fourteen other Central Mekranoti men and their families moved to *porori*, where they arrived in October of that year[38]. This group was not really composed of Kreti-re's followers, but rather by all those men who preferred to move to *porori* in search of better assistance (medical and otherwise). Bepgogoti and most of the thirty men who had remained in *pi'ydjãm* moved to Pôsto Kubitschek, in the hope of receiving the same assistance over there as in *porori*. Only a few families — mostly Kenti's ex-followers — remained in *pi'ydjãm*.

> *kwỳrỳkangô* naming ceremony in Pôsto Kubitschek.
> *menibijôk* naming ceremony in Pôsto Kubitschek.

¤ DRY 1965   Once again a club-fight broke out in Pôsto Kubitschek and Bepgogoti and his followers moved back to their base village at *pi'ydjãm*.

> *menibijôk* naming ceremony.

¤ RAIN 1965   Most men left to the Iriri River to gather jaguar and ocelot skins for which they received payment from the SPI agents at Pôsto Kubitschek.

¤ DRY 1966

¤ RAIN 1966   *memybijôk* naming ceremony.

The Panara killed two women near the Central Mekranoti gardens.

¤ DRY 1967   Dale Snyder, a missionary of Unevangelized Field Mission (UFM) arrived for a short visit from Pôsto Kubitschek (by

---

tribesmen and kinsmen had died in the period from 1953 to 1963.

38   In his superb photo book, King Leopold of Belgium (1974:83) renders an historic picture of the arrival of the Central Mekranoti at *porori*. See also Plates 29-30.

then called PI Bau). He asked the Central Mekranoti to lay out an airstrip in order to facilitate the supply of medicines and commodities. Most men worked non-stop on this clearing, while some others went skin-gathering.

¤ RAIN 1967   An SPI inspector by the name of Antônio Soares Cotrim arrived in the village. The Indians strongly emphasized their discontent about the lack of SPI assistance[39]. Sometime later, Dale Snyder and his family settled in the Central Mekranoti village. They had come by boat via PI Bau and then by land to *pi'ydjãm*. Once the airstrip was finished, a small missionary plane arrived, bringing medicines, tools and ammunition.

memybijôk naming ceremony.

After the ceremony, Pakyx instigated the men to attack the Panara in revenge for the numerous victims they had caused. In a massive attack, some thirty Panara were killed; one woman and four children were taken captives[40].

menibijôk naming ceremony.

A few weeks after the raid, Claudio Villas Bôas arrived with ATV film-producer Adrian Cowell to ask the Indians about the exact location of the Panara villages.

¤ DRY 1968   *kwỳrỳkangô* naming ceremony.

While Dale Snyder goes on a furlough, he was temporarily replaced by Horace Banner of the UFM who at the time continued to work among the Gorotire.

¤ RAIN 1968   *menibijôk* naming ceremony.

¤ DRY 1969   A disease broke out in the village[41]. Over forty Indians died and most of the survivors dispersed into the forest. At the time, Kreti-re arrived from *porori*. In vain, the missionary tried to persuade Kreti-re to turn back immediately, so as not to catch the disease: Kreti-re, tarried for a few weeks. Upon hearing of Kreti-re's visit, all the people returned to the village and Kreti-re tried to convince Bepgogoti to move to *porori*. Bepgogoti hesitated since he still feared squabbles with Kremôr. However, partly because Kreti-re's presence was seen as some guarantee of preventing skirmishes with Kremôr, and partly because

---

39   See Cotrim (1968ms:4).
40   The Central Mekranoti attack on the Panara occurred in the beginning of December 1967 (Adrian Cowell 1973:94-95).
41   According to information gathered in the field, the disease in question was malaria (*plasmodium falciparum*) with serious complications. Although malaria was not uncommon in the area, it had never appeared in the form of a massive disease and this explains why the Indians often told me that "Dale brought *kanê* (fever) to the village, and when he left, the disease ended."

Dale Snyder was about to leave the village and he did not know whether any FUNAI agent or missionary would come to the village, Bepgogoti finally agreed to move to *porori*. He was to come a year later, in this way allowing the Southern Mekranoti to prepare the necessary gardens in order to facilitate the settlement of the newcomers. Accompanied by some ten Central Mekranoti men and their families, Kreti-re left the village. During the trip back to *porori*, he died of the disease he had caught and some of Bepgogoti's followers immediately returned. After hearing the news, Bepgogoti decided not to move to *porori* after all where he and his people were likely to be accused of sorcery. Bepgogoti and his followers remained in their village.

    ¤ RAIN 1969   Dale Snyder left and a FUNAI agent settled in the village.

    ¤ DRY 1970   The FUNAI agent left and a few months later two SIL missionaries (Ruth Thomson and Mickey Stout) arrived in the village[42].

    ¤ RAIN 1970

    ¤ DRY 1971   *menibijôk* naming ceremony.

The Highway BR 165 was being built, connecting the cities of Cuyaba and Santarem. The Central Mekranoti ventured to that area and killed a few road-workers in an ambush.

    ¤ RAIN 1971   *kwỳrỳkangô* naming ceremony.

    ¤ DRY 1972   *bep* naming ceremony.

A Canadian film team spent a few weeks among the Central Mekranoti[43].

    ¤ RAIN 1972   *kwỳrỳkangô* naming ceremony.

The Central Mekranoti killed seven skin-hunters who were venturing in their area.

    ¤ DRY 1973   *menibijôk* naming ceremony.

    ¤ RAIN 1973   *memybijôk* naming ceremony.

The FUNAI officially creates PI Mekranoti and sends two agents to the area, of whom only one regularly spends sometime in the field. The FUNAI agents take most men to the area near PI Bau in order to collect large amounts of Brazil nuts to be sold by the FUNAI in Belém. During their stay in the area, a Central Mekranoti killed a Brazilian man who was leading a solitary life along the Curua River[44].

---

42   In the period from 1964 to 1969, these two missionaries had already worked for some time with the Southern Mekranoti at *porori*.

43   The team was led by François Flocquet and the resulting film was entitled "Ces hommes qui viennent du ciel" (60 min).

44   The Indians told me they killed this man as they feared he was a predecessor

¤ DRY 1974   *kwỳrỳkangô* naming ceremony.

SIL missionary Mickey Stout left the area to start working in other Kayapo villages (Gorotire and Kokraimoro). She was replaced by Kathleen Jefferson.

¤ RAIN 1974   *memybijôk* naming ceremony.

Most of the men left for the area near PI Bau in order to collect Brazil nuts to be sold to FUNAI. In the meantime, the author arrived for the first time in the village in December 1974: the village numbered two hundred and thirty-nine Indians.

   pãnh-te naming ceremony.

   tàkàk naming ceremony.

¤ DRY 1975   *kwỳrỳkangô* naming ceremony.

¤ RAIN 1975

¤ DRY 1976   FUNAI agents permanently settle in the post near the village. A new and larger airstrip is built by the Indians in order to allow planes of the FAB (Brazilian Air Force) to land regularly at PI Mekranoti[45].

¤ RAIN 1976   *menibijôk* naming ceremony.

   kôkô naming ceremony.

Friction arose between the Northern and Central Mekranoti over the organization of the nearly annual Brazil nut collecting. PI Bau being located near a major river, the Northern Mekranoti obtained logistical support (tools and ammunition) for their tasks from the FUNAI in October. They were able to start working immediately. In the meantime, the Indians of PI Mekranoti were anxiously awaiting their logistical support which had to come by plane. The plane arrived in January and by that time, the people of PI Bau had already collected all the Brazil nuts on their sites as well as on several others "owned"[46] by the Central Mekranoti. The FUNAI agent who brought the tools and other materials arrived in the Central Mekranoti village after a stopover at PI Bau. He brought the message that Màntino (son of Tàpjêt and the Northern Mekranoti chief) didn't want the Central Mekranoti to come and collect Brazil nuts that

of a more important and permanent settlement within the tribal area.

45   The Central Mekranoti continually complained about the lack of communication with the outside world. The FUNAI had made contact with the FAB and informed the Indians that the air force considered a new flight connecting the air base of Cachimbo with PI Mekranoti, PI Kubenkranken, PI Gorotire and Belém. The flights never took place.

46   During the migrations through the forest, Kayapo men occasionally plant Brazil nut trees. Such trees are "owned" by the man who planted them and by his descendants. The Kayapo often say they plant Brazil nut trees "for their grandchildren to eat" — it takes at least twenty years before such a tree bears fruit.

year as "all was already being collected by the Northern Mekranoti". Upon hearing this, Bepgogoti was upset and refused to discuss the matter any further. The FUNAI agent somehow understood the gravity of the situation and asked Bepgogoti to go and parley with Màntino, but Bepgogoti didn't want to pursue the matter any further. He delegated one of his sons who was taken by FUNAI plane to PI Bau. Upon returning two days later, he was upset with the relentless position of Màntino. Bepgogoti then examined the matter with Kôkôrêti, the second chief in PI Mekranoti and a son of Angme'ê, former major chief of the Northern Mekranoti. It was then judged for the better that Kôkôrêti would go to PI Bau at any rate in order to try to settle the matter. So, Kôkôrêti left with only twelve of his followers to collect Brazil nuts in the area along the Bau River. But the situation continued tense in the area and a few months later, the FUNAI opened up a new post. It was called Pôsto Candoca[47] and was erected near the confluence of the Iriri and Candoca Rivers, exactly at the spot where Francisco Meirelles had attracted the Central Mekranoti some twenty years before. The idea was to avoid having the Central Mekranoti to go to PI Bau each year by instigating them to collect Brazil nuts in the area of PI Candoca. The Central Mekranoti weren't very satisfied with this proposal[48].

¤ DRY 1977   *memybijôk* naming ceremony.

¤ RAIN 1977   Many men went to Pôsto Candoca to collect Brazil nuts for FUNAI.

¤ DRY 1978   An epidemic of flu broke out in the village. Within a week, three adults and three children died. Tension grew in the village and the FUNAI nurse was almost killed. FUNAI then evacuated several of the most seriously ill people to the small hospital at Itaituba. To make matters worse, about half of the village burned down about a month after the epidemic. Serious discussions followed and many Indians started talking about leaving the contaminated area in order to move to a new site. The FUNAI took advantage of the situation and suggested that the Indians move to Pôsto Candoca but, once again, the proposal was

47   Since no Indians lived there on a permanent basis, the post was not referred to as a *Pôsto Indígena*, but rather as *Pôsto*.
48   The FUNAI didn't realize the importance of the individual "owning" of Brazil nut trees. As the Central Mekranoti had never really lived near Pôsto Candoca, the question was raised as to who the owners of the numerous Brazil nut trees were. In addition, the area near the Bau and Curua Rivers are extremely rich in babassu (*Orbignya*) palm trees. Every two years or so, a group of Central Mekranoti families went to that area to collect palm leaves and to extract palm oil. No such concentrations of palm leaves exist near Pôsto Candoca.

received with little enthusiasm and the village was rebuilt on the same site.

In this turbulent period, a dispute broke out in the Northern Mekranoti village near PI Bau and chief Màntino got involved in a club-duel. During one of the radio contacts a few days later, some Northern Mekranoti men insisted that Kôkôrêti (son of former chief Angme'ê) come to the village and settle the conflict. Kôkôrêti left with seven other men and their families (thirty-eight Indians in total) to spend a few months in the village near PI Bau. The small group consisted of a few of Kôkôrêti's followers and others who had close kin in PI Bau.

¤ RAIN 1978   Kôkôrêti's small group participated in the Brazil nut collecting along the Bau River and assisted in the performance of a *menibijôk* naming ceremony. It was the first major ceremony performed in that village since 1965! Some men in the village insisted that Kôkôrêti stay as chief of the village. Kôkôrêti, however, refused and returned with the others to the village at PI Mekranoti.

bàyjangri corn ceremony.

During the last phase of the ceremony, a dispute broke out between the men regarding the direction to be chosen for the final ceremonial hunt. As a result, the men divided into two groups to go and collect the meat for the final dances. Several other men refused to participate and remained in the village. After the ceremony, a series of discussions ensued in the men's house and, for the first time in many years, the Indians said that "the good relations [within the community] had ended" (*arỳp uma-ri punu*).

menibijôk naming ceremony.

¤ DRY 1979

¤ RAIN 1979   *memybijôk* naming ceremony.

Many men went to the area near PI Bau in order to collect Brazil nuts. During a rather peaceful visit, the Central Mekranoti convinced the few Brazilians still residing in the nearby mining camp to leave the area[49].

---

49   By 1978 the mining company, which since 1973 had operated in and around the perambulation area of the Northern Mekranoti, had almost stopped its activities. The company's small base camp was located eight kilometers south of the village. Yet the idea grew among the Northern Mekranoti to expel the few Brazilian laborers who still resided in the base camp of the mining company. A discussion arose in the village: the advocates of the expulsion argued that these Brazilians were constantly hunting and fishing within their territory, therefore decreasing the outcome of their own hunting and fishing activities; the opponents of the expulsion argued that the presence of these Brazilians was their only source of constant supply of a significant amount of commodities, and that the expulsion might threaten their good relations with the Brazilians in general. The matter was settled at the end of 1979 when a group of Central Mekranoti men were in

The camp was sacked and the acquired trade goods were divided among the Northern Mekranoti.

   pãnh-te naming ceremony.

¤ DRY 1980   *kwỳrỳkangô* naming ceremony.

In the period from 1969 to 1980, internal peace prevailed in the Central Mekranoti village. Naming ceremonies followed at a steady rhythm of one to three performances a year and no club-fights occurred in the period from 1972 to 1983. Both phenomena are indicative of the internal village peace and undoubtedly were stimulated by Bepgogoti's mediation: this remarkable old chief has gained the reputation of a successful appeaser within the community. The ensuing political stability led to an ever increasing influx of immigrants: in recent years, over forty Northern and Southern Mekranoti Indians have migrated to *pi'ydjãm*. Due to this tendency, and due to the adequate medical assistance, the Central Mekranoti population has increased at a fast and steady rate: in 1968, the village numbered only hundred and seventy Indians; six years later it numbered two hundred and thirty-nine people and in 1980, the population had increased to three hundred and forty! But this favorable demographic situation also produced pressure on the village economy, since by 1980 over fifty-five percent of the village population was under fifteen years of age. Led by Bekwỳnhti (trained by Kreti-re to become a chief) and his brother Ayol, a group of eighteen men left with their families and moved to the lower Xixê River, building a new village. It was a peaceful separation. Nearly all these men were *mekrakramtĩ* ("men with many children") who decided to move to an area abounding in fish. FUNAI agents visited the area and insisted that the village be built further downriver, along the Iriri River, which would allow for easier fluvial access. The Indians then started building another village near the confluence of the Iriri and Xinxim Rivers, at a short distance from the site where Karànhĩn had lived in 1940 and where the Kokraimoro had lived the first year after their separation from the Kubenkranken in 1950. The Indians called the village *pykany* ("new land"). A FUNAI post was erected and called PI Pukanu. No FUNAI agents ever settled there and the post was run by Pykati-re, the sole Central Mekranoti man who spoke Portuguese.

¤ RAIN 1980   *memybijôk* naming ceremony in *pi'ydjãm*.

¤ DRY 1981

¤ RAIN 1981   *kwỳrỳkangô* naming ceremony in *pi'ydjãm*.

The people at PI Mekranoti envied those of PI Pukanu because of the

---

the area to collect Brazil nuts for FUNAI: the Northern Mekranoti managed to persuade these men to execute the expulsion.

profusion of meat in their newly occupied area and because of the ease of catching plenty of fish in the main river. Many Indians started talking about moving, but the village elders (including old chief Bepgogoti) said they would never go and live near a big river where, according to their experience, people could become sick very easily. Instead, these same elders considered moving to a site closer to the area of open grasslands between the Iriri and Jarina Rivers. After all, that was the core of tradi- tional Mekranoti area. They feared, however, that the FUNAI wouldn't agree with the site and that it therefore wouldn't provide the necessary support. What the Indians wanted was, in addition to the continuation of medical assistance in the village at PI Mekranoti, another nurse who would join the group that would set out to prepare the new habitat. The Indians asked me to take the matter to the high FUNAI officials, which I eventually did.

¤ RAIN 1982   Kute'ê (Bepgogoti's oldest son) and three other men set out for the upper Iriri River to select the site for the new village. They discovered a small Brazilian settlement near the confluence of the Iriri and Iriri Novo Rivers. It was the beginning of a base camp for a large farm and already had a short airstrip. Kute'ê and his companions returned to PI Mekranoti, only to backtrack a few weeks later with about a dozen men. When an airplane landed on the strip, the Indians stripped the Brazilians of all their clothes and sent them all naked back to town. They then started building a new village on that site.

¤ DRY 1983   Led by Kôkôrêti, about hundred and sixty In- dians moved to the Iriri Novo River. A new FUNAI post was erected and was named PI Kubenkokre (after Kubenkàk-re, one of Bepgogoti's names). Kôkôrêti hoped that both groups of PI Pukanu and PI Mekranoti would eventually join him.

¤ DRY 1985   Bepgogoti moved with all the people of PI Me- kranoti to the new village at PI Kubenkokre. The people of PI Pukanu, however, did not join.

¤ 1989   The current population is about three hundred and ninety Indians at PI Kubenkokre and ninety at PI Pukanu.

6. THE RECENT HISTORY OF THE SOUTHERN MEKRANOTI (1956-1989)

¤ RAIN 1956   Still another epidemic of *kanê* (flu?) broke out in *ngôrãrãnk*, the Southern Mekranoti village. Several children died and, in this difficult period, the village was raided by a group of Central Mekranoti men: four of Kremôr's followers were killed.

¤ DRY 1957   The group moved to *rõntinõr*.

tàkàk naming ceremony.

After the ceremony, the people moved back to *kapôtninõr*, to the east of the Xingu River.

¤ RAIN 1957   *kwỳrỳkangô* naming ceremony.

¤ DRY 1958   *menibijôk* naming ceremony.

During this ceremony, four Kubenkranken men briefly visited the Southern Mekranoti. The visitors were taken to Pôsto Vasconcellos and then returned to their village at the Riozinho River.

¤ RAIN 1958   Claudio Villas Bôas and reporter Adrian Cowell visit the small village between the Xingu and Liberdade Rivers.

¤ DRY 1959   Three Southern Mekranoti men went to the Xixê River, where they killed a Central Mekranoti man.

¤ RAIN 1959   A dispute broke out between Bekwỳnhka (a close kinsman of Kremôr) and Kruma-re (a young leader). Bekwỳnhka left the village with fourteen men and their families, including chief Kremôr. They moved to the Kubenkranken village at *krã'ãbõm* where they participated in two naming ceremonies. Only twelve men, including Kruma-re and his classificatory brother Ropni, remained in *kapôtninõr*.

¤ DRY 1960   The SPI took Ngroj-re, one of the main Kubenkranken chiefs, for a visit to the city of Belém. The chief died there and this led to serious conflicts in the Kubenkranken village. The Mekranoti newcomers were accused of sorcery and the Kubenkranken then decided to kill them all. A dozen of Kremôr's followers were killed in an ambush and eight others managed to escape to the Gorotire village with an airplane of the Brazilian Air Force[50]. Kremôr managed to flee by land and, accompanied by one of his followers as well as two Kubenkranken kinsmen[51] and their families, returned to *kapôtninõr*.

¤ RAIN 1960   Gardens ware laid out at *kapôtninõr*. Claudio Villas Bôas and a few other Brazilians visited the village. On Claudio's request the group moved back to the area of open grassland between the Jarina and Iriri Novo Rivers. An airstrip was made at *ràràtikô*, near the village of *rojkô-re*, and a plane arrived with many tools and other gifts. The Indians then temporarily moved back to *kapôtninõr* to collect garden

---

50   At the time, a more or less regular schedule of FAB (Brazilian Air Force) planes connected both the Kubenkranken and Gorotire villages with the city of Belém (T. Turner 1965:73-74).

51   Both were men members of Karànhĩn's group who had joined the Kubenkranken and later the Kokraimoro. After the "pacification" of the Kokraimoro, they had joined the Kubenkranken again.

products.

◻ DRY 1961   Back at *rojkô-re*, the men laid out a new airstrip, about fifteen kilometres from the village location. Several Brazilians (including the Villas Bôas brothers) assisted in the construction.

◻ RAIN 1961   The Southern Mekranoti laid out gardens near the airstrip and the Brazilians left. After a long wait, a plane finally landed and shortly afterwards, some parachutists were dropped. These brought a message from the Villas Bôas brothers, requesting the Indians to move their village to a site along the Xingu River, upstream of the mouth of the Jarina River[52].

◻ DRY 1962   Kremôr moved his followers to the south and built a new village at a site near a creek called *porori* ("red earth") by the Yudja who had lived in that area some decades before. The small village numbered only about sixty-five Indians (eighteen men and their families).

◻ RAIN 1962   Gardens were laid out.

◻ DRY 1963   The Southern Mekranoti went to the Yudja to get manioc flour.

◻ RAIN 1963   Three Central Mekranoti men and their families came over from *pi'ydjãm* for a visit. The visitors stayed only for a few months and eventually returned to their village. Ropni joined them in order personally to invite Kreti-re and Bepgogoti to settle at *porori*. Kreti-re accepted and it was decided that he would come with a group next year.

◻ DRY 1964   Once again, four Central Mekranoti men came for a short visit to *porori* and Ropni insisted that Bepgogoti should also come and live at *porori*, where an airstrip had been built and where good medical assistance was offered.

◻ RAIN 1964   Kreti-re, Ykakôr and fourteen other men and their families (some hundred Indians in total) arrived from *pi'ydjãm*. *Porori* was rebuilt at the same site, but with a greater village circle allowing shelter for the newcomers.

◻ 1984-5   All the Southern Mekranoti reunited in a single village, located near the former village of *ngôrãrãnk*. A post was established and named PI Metuktire.

◻ 1989   Current Southern Mekranoti population is about three hundred and sixty hundred Indians.

---

52   The Xingu National Park had officially been created on April 14, 1961. The Southern Mekranoti village of *rojkô-re* being outside Park limits, the Indians were asked to move south, within Park boundaries.

7. THE KOKRAIMORO OR THE MEKRANOTI WHO JOINED THE KUBENKRANKEN (1941-1958)

The present section on the Kokraimoro — a non-Mekranoti Kayapo group — can partly be justified by the fact that the history of the Kokraimoro is intimately related to the history of the Mekranoti. This is because the dissident Mekranoti groups led by Karànhĩn and Ku'at (with a population of hundred and three and fifty-one Indians, respectively) fled to the Kubenkranken. Later-on, these Mekranoti groups were the base of the separation of the Kokraimoro from the Kubenkranken.

The available literature provides little detail on the history of the Kokraimoro (T. Turner 1965; Moreiro Neto 1959; Dreyfus 1963). When trying to understand clearly the history of this Kayapo group, I was surprised by the number of raids and attacks the Kokraimoro had undertaken. Fuerst (pers. com.) and Moreiro Neto (1959:52) had mentioned that before the so-called "pacification" in 1957, the Kokraimoro have to be made responsible for the majority, if not all of the attacks on Brazilians in the area of the Xingu and Iriri Rivers in the period from 1950 to 1960. And rightly so. Although some raids are to be attributed to the Mekranoti and the Kubenkranken, there is no doubt that, in the decade in question, no other Kayapo group brought about the withdrawal of pioneering settlers in the area of Central Brazil as much as the Kokraimoro. Furthermore, no history of any other Kayapo group is marked by such a great number of homicides as that of the Kokraimoro.

Unlike the rest of this Appendix, for which every section has been worked on with several informants, I only had the opportunity to work with one single informant in reconstructing the Kokraimoro history. Meyre, the man in question, was born Mekranoti. He had joined with Karànhĩn to the Kubenkranken in 1941 and later the Kokraimoro where he became a leader. He returned to the Southern Mekranoti in 1967, where I met him at the village near PI Jarina in 1981. He is the oldest Kokraimoro man alive. While working with him, I repeated the Kokraimoro history several times. Each time, he proved to be consistent in his statements.

¤ RAIN 1941 　　　Karànhĩn and his group of hundred and two followers arrived in the Kubenkranken village at *krã'ãbõm*, located along the Riozinho River, a few kilometers south of the Cachoeira da Fumaça. After the reunion, the Kubenkranken village had one big men's house, with three men's societies, led by Ôket, Ngroj-re and Mànma-ri (one of Karànhĩn's followers). The younger men were divided along four separate "sitting places", led by Akruwa'êtyk, Ngôti-re, Bepkô and Kôkôrêti (also one of Karànhĩn's men).

kwỳrỳkangô naming ceremony.

A few months after the arrival of Karànhĩn's small Mekranoti group, a quarrel arose between the groups led by Ôket and Kôkôrêti. Three of Ôket's followers were killed, and eleven men and three women of Kôkôrêti's group were killed in revenge. Kôkôrêti and his followers then temporarily left the village. They settled in a forest camp, only to return to the Kubenkranken village a few months later.

¤ DRY 1942   *tàkàk* naming ceremony.

A group of Kubenkranken, led by Ôket and Ngôti-re, went to attack the Mekranoti, then living at *pykabãr*. Three Mekranoti women were captured and one man was killed. The Mekranoti then pursued the assailants and managed to kill four Kubenkranken men but, again, lost one man and three women. While Ôket was venturing near the Mekranoti village, two other groups of men had left the village to raid Brazilian settlements in order to obtain as many firearms and as much ammunition as possible: Ngroj-re led his men's society to the Iriri River, and Kôkôrêti had taken off to the west, to the Araguaia River. Kôkôrêti's group was the only one that managed to bring back some firearms.

¤ RAIN 1942   All three groups returned to the Kubenkranken village at *krã'ãbõm*.

kôkô naming ceremony.

¤ DRY 1943   Again, two raiding parties set out: one led by Kôkôrêti (once again to the Araguaia River, where one Brazilian was killed) and the other led by Ôket. The latter went to the Xingu and Iriri Rivers, but on their way back, these men decided to attack the Mekranoti. One Mekranoti man and one woman were killed, but the raided group reacted by killing two of Ôket's men. During this counterattack, however, one more Mekranoti man was killed.

¤ RAIN 1943   All reunited in the village at *krã'ãbõm*.

menibijôk naming ceremony.

¤ DRY 1944   *tàkàk* naming ceremony[53].

¤ RAIN 1944   Some Kubenkranken men set out to visit their kinsmen from the Gorotire. At that time, the Gorotire lived near the upper Fresco River, where an SPI post as well as a missionary post had been

---

53   Moreiro Neto (1959:52) mentions that nine Kokraimoro were killed by rubber-tappers along the Xingu River. The informant did not mention this important event. I am therefore inclined to suggest that the mentioned attack is the one suffered by the Kokraimoro in the dry season of 1957 (see further). In any case, it is impossible that the Kokraimoro could have suffered such an attack in 1944 since this group only separated from the Kubenkranken in 1950.

built near the village.

¤ DRY 1945   After the return of the visitors, the men's societies led by Ôket and Ngroj-re left jointly to raid Brazilian settlements near
the Jamanxim River.

¤ RAIN 1945   Upon the return of the raiding parties, new tensions arose in the village. Ôket's followers killed three men and two
women of Kôkôrêti's group, and the men of that group took revenge by
killing one of Ôket's men. Later, still another man of Kôkôrêti's group
was killed. Kôkôrêti and chief Mànma-ri — both Karànhĩn's ex-followers
— then left with their followers and built a new village to the south, near
the ancient village of *pykatôti*. This village probably numbered some hundred and fifty Indians. After the schism, the tension in the Kubenkranken
village diminished.

¤ DRY 1946   *bô kam me tor* naming ceremony at *krã'ãbõm*.
     kwỳrỳkangô naming ceremony at *krã'ãbõm*.

¤ RAIN 1946   *memybijôk* naming ceremony at *krã'ãbõm*.

¤ DRY 1947   Five men's groups left the Kubenkranken village
to raid Brazilian settlements at different sites. No data are available as
to the booty obtained nor the possible number of victims, but mention is
made of two Kubenkranken men who were killed by Brazilians along the
Xingu River. All groups returned to the village during the dry season.

¤ RAIN 1947   *tàkàk* naming ceremony at *krã'ãbõm*.
     menibijôk naming ceremony at *krã'ãbõm*.

¤ DRY 1948   *bekwỳnh* naming ceremony at *krã'ãbõm*.
     ngrenh-ri naming ceremony at *krã'ãbõm*.

Some men went to raid Brazilian settlements along the Xingu River,
but returned after a few days since they had noticed signs of a bad omen
on their way.

¤ RAIN 1948   *bàyjangri* corn festival at *krã'ãbõm*.
During the corn festival, Ku'at and his fifty followers arrived. They had
separated from the Mekranoti in 1944 and had wandered in the forest
for several years. Ku'at was eager to retaliate against the Mekranoti for
the killing of Tàpjêt. Immediately after his arrival in the Kubenkranken
village, he instigated Ôket to attack Kôkôrêti's village which was mainly
composed of Mekranoti men (i.e., Karànhĩn's followers). The attack took
place and one of Kôkôrêti's followers as well as one of Ôket's men were
killed.

¤ DRY 1949   Krã'ãkop had joined with Karànhĩn to the
Kubenkranken where he became a leader of a younger men's group. Ôket
and Ku'at were angry with Krã'ãkop because he had not joined them on
their raid against Kôkôrêti's people. When Krã'ãkop left the village with

a handful of his men to raid a Brazilian settlement along the Xingu River, one of his followers was killed by Ôket's men. On his return, Krã'ãkop killed a member of Ôket's men's society and he immediately went with his group to join the small village led by Kôkôrêti and Mànma-ri.

¤ RAIN 1949   The people of the small southern village returned to join the main group at *krã'ãbõm*, and the situation became rather tense again.

¤ DRY 1950   Just as in the dry season three years before, several groups of men went to raid Brazilian settlements near the Xingu River. When all of the groups had returned, Ôket and Ku'at insisted on joining forces to attack the Mekranoti in order to revenge the killing of Tàpjêt. But Bepnox and Kokraimoro, two new young leaders of the younger men's groups, left with their followers to attack Brazilian settlements along the Iriri River, undermining, in this way, Ku'at's plans. During their absence, Ôket's followers revenged Tàpjêt's death by killing six Mekranoti men who had joined the Kubenkranken village in 1941 as part of Karànhĩn's group. On their return, the men of Bepnox and Kokraimoro took revenge by killing six of Ôket's men. The two young leaders and their followers then separated from the main village. They settled in a temporary camp near the Xingu River: the separation had become definite and the formation of the Kokraimoro group was realized.

In the Kokraimoro village[54], one men's house was built with two men's societies and three separate sitting places for the younger men's groups. Jakuri and Moj'y-re were the chiefs of the men's societies, while Bepnox, Kàxwakre and Kokraimoro[55] along with Mey-re were the leaders of the three younger men's groups. According to my reconstruction of Kokraimoro "sitting places", the groups consisted of forty-three married men with children and seventy-nine *menõrõny-re*. Except for Ku'at and two of his followers, all of the surviving Mekranoti men — both of Karànhĩn's and Ku'at's groups — had joined the Kokraimoro. As such,

54   This dissident group is the one which is currently known as Kokraimoro. I calculate that the original Kokraimoro population was about three hundred Indians. Yet, this calculation — based on the fact that hundred and twenty-two men formed this village — is probably a low estimation: the informant repeatedly insisted that the original Kokraimoro village was nearly as big as *krãnhmrôpryjaka*, a Mekranoti village which in 1936 numbered some five hundred and twenty Indians...

55   It is not uncommon for Kayapo groups to refer to other Kayapo groups by "X *kam*" ("the place of X", where X stands for the name of a known chief or leader). This way of referring to other groups is usually done when the name(s) of the other village's men's societies are unknown. In this way also, the few small, still isolated Kayapo groups are referred to by the name of the oldest man (or leader) of the groups, i.e. Pyro, Ngramra-ri and Pitujarô.

the Mekranoti made up for about one fourth of the Kokraimoro population.

◻ RAIN 1950   The Kokraimoro raided the Kubenkranken who fled into the forest to the east of *krã'ãbõm*. The Kokraimoro managed to capture several Kubenkranken women and kept pursuing the fleeing group. In this pursuit, three Kubenkranken men and three women got killed near *ràptinõr*[56]. While the Kokraimoro returned to the Iriri River, Ngroj-re took refuge in the Gorotire village[57]. Ôket, on the other hand, was afraid of being killed by the Gorotire: he avoided coming anywhere near that village and returned immediately to *krã'ãbõm*. Sometime later, the great majority of the Kubenkranken reunited in their village, while a few families remained in the Gorotire village.

◻ DRY 1951   The Kokraimoro built a village near *kendjãm*, close to the site where Karànhĩn had built his small village a decade before. New gardens were laid out[58].

◻ RAIN 1951   *kwỳrỳkangô* naming ceremony.

After the ceremony, four Kokraimoro groups of men went to the Xingu and Iriri Rivers to raid Brazilian settlements to obtain new firearms and ammunition. Four Brazilians were killed along the Iriri, and five along the Xingu River. The booty was satisfying since many firearms and lots of ammunition were obtained.

bàyjangri corn festival.

◻ DRY 1952   An attack was planned on the Kubenkranken. On the way, somewhere near the Xingu River, the Brazilians killed one of the warriors. The others then returned to the village, having achieved nothing.

tàkàk naming ceremony.

◻ RAIN 1952   Once again four men's groups went to the Xingu and Iriri Rivers to obtain ammunition and firearms. Some Brazilians were killed along the Xingu River and several firearms and plenty of ammunition were brought back.

kôkô naming ceremony.

---

56   The informant specified that *ràptinõr* was the site of an ancient Kayapo village. Located along the Fresco River, it is said to have been occupied before *pykatôti* was ever built.

57   Cícero Cavalcanti, the SPI agent at the Gorotire village, gave a warm welcome to the Kubenkranken visitors. Chief Ngroj-re and Cavalcanti then agreed that the latter would come to visit the Kubenkranken village in a year's time, bringing lots of presents. This event marked the "pacification" of the Kubenkranken in 1952.

58   The informant added that the people were still able to collect some products from the old gardens laid out by Karànhĩn and his men a decade before.

¤ DRY 1953   While the married men with children stayed in the village in order to lay out new gardens, the young men of the *menõrõny-re* age grade went to the Tapayoz River to raid Brazilian settlements. Three Brazilians were killed and some ammunition was brought back.

¤ RAIN 1953   The *menõrõny-re* returned to *kendjãm*.
memybijôk naming ceremony.

After the ceremony, a quarrel arose and Kàxwakre — one of the *menõrõny-re* leaders — killed Krã'ãkop and still another man of Bepnox's group. This eventually led to a schism in the village: Jakuri, Moj'y-re, Kàxwakre and Mey-re stayed behind in *kendjãm*, while a small group — mainly consisting of *menõrõny-re* and led by Bepnox and Kokraimoro — left the village and took refuge in a temporary camp south of *kendjãm*. Moj'y-re pursued the dissident group southward and killed Kokraimoro.

¤ DRY 1954   All were reunited in Bepnox's camp. Kàxwakre and one of his followers were killed in revenge for the killing of Kokraimoro. This temporarily settled the tense situation, but not for long: when all had resettled in *kendjãm*, a new series of disputes broke out. Many club-fights took place and several men, belonging to all the men's groups, were killed.

¤ RAIN 1954   Moj'y-re suggested an attack on the Mekranoti. Yet, a club-fight arose over an adulterous relationship, and the ever growing tension led to a schism: Jakuri and Moj'y-re stayed behind in the village at *kendjãm*, while Bepnox, Mey-re, Karànhĩn and many others (including the majority of Mekranoti men) moved with their families to the south. They settled at *ngônhõngôkrô*, along the upper Xinxim River[59]. Bepnox immediately set out for an attack on the Northern Kokraimoro village and killed three of Jakuri's followers. On his return, Mey-re also went to the northern village and killed thirteen men and women.

¤ DRY 1955   While Karànhĩn and the elder men stayed behind in the village to lay out new gardens, Bepnox once again led his men on an attack against the Northern Kokraimoro. Five of Jakuri's men were killed, including chief Moj'y-re.

¤ RAIN 1955   *kwỳrỳkangô* naming ceremony in *ngônhõngôkrô* (Bepnox's group).

¤ DRY 1956   From the Southern Kokraimoro village, Bepnox took his men to raid Brazilians along the Xingu River, while Mey-re

59   This division remained in effect for some years, and in order to facilitate references, I will refer to Jakuri's group by the term Northern Kokraimoro, and to Bepnox's group by the term Southern Kokraimoro.

ventured along the Iriri River. Five Brazilians were killed, but very little ammunition was taken. All the men returned at the very end of the dry season.

¤ RAIN 1956   Mey-re took his group of *menõrõny-re* to the Xingu River, raiding a Brazilian settlement[60].

¤ DRY 1957   The SPI sent out an expedition to the Curua and Iriri Rivers to contact the hostile Kayapo groups which hampered the exploration and the colonization of the Brazilian interior. The expedition, led by Francisco Meirelles, set out in the beginning of 1957 and contacted first a small Kararaô group as well as the Northern Mekranoti village at the Curua River (see above). In April 1957, the SPI contacted the Northern Kokraimoro led by Jakuri. This contact took place near a site called Lageira, along the Iriri River, where these Indians had just raided a settlement called Empresa, killing one Brazilian. Jakuri's group numbered ninety-seven Indians (Meirelles 1958ms). At that time, Bepnox had left the main village with his men to raid Brazilian settlers along the Xingu River. They reached the settlement of Constantino Viana, a Brazilian with whom the Kubenkranken occasionally maintained peaceful contacts in 1939-1940 (Nimuendajú 1952:432,439-441). Bepnox made peace with Viana and the Brazilians asked the Indians to dance. While performing part of the *kwỳrỳkangô* naming ceremony, the Brazilians undertook a surprise attack: seven Kokraimoro men were killed and a young boy was taken captive. Bepnox and his men then returned to the village at *ngônhõngôkrô*.

¤ RAIN 1957   In November, the SPI team led by Raimundo Pinto (one of Meirelles' assistants) sailed up the Xingu River and up the tributary called Igarapé do Pôrto Seguro, where Bepnox's village was located. The first contact did not occur without any difficulty since the SPI team included Jakuri and his men. A fight almost broke out between the two Kokraimoro groups (Meirelles 1958ms:10) but after some parleying, the hundred and thirty-seven Indians of Bepnox's group were peacefully contacted.

¤ DRY 1958   The SPI reunited both Kokraimoro groups and decided to transfer them to a place along the mid Xingu River, more exactly near the Riozinho do Icatã and near the mountain ridge called Serra Encontrada. This site was located two day's distance from the small town of São Felix do Xingu. Many Indians died during the transfer; of

60   Meirelles (1958:9) mentions that just before so-called "pacification", the Kokraimoro attacked a local Brazilian settlement along the confluence of the Xingu and the Igarapé Pôrto Seguro. During the attack, three Brazilians were killed and one boy (named Pedro) was captured.

the original two hundred and thirty-four Kokraimoro Indians contacted a few months before, no more than hundred and seventeen reached the new site (thirty-nine of Jakuri's group, and seventy-eight of Bepnox's). Bad hygienic circumstances in the new village site, food shortages, contacts with the local settlers and lack of medicines during an epidemic of flu resulted in the fact that about one year after the arrival at the Xingu River, the Kokraimoro population had dwindled to about seventy survivors.

Appendix B

NARRATIVES[1]

During the course of my field work terms, senior informants occasionally narrated myths, memorates, legends and personal experience narratives in order to elucidate a specific topic of my inquiry. As I began to record some of these narratives on tape, those informants who were at the same time reputed storytellers seemed particularly encouraged. They started narrating even more, often insisting that their accounts be recorded. Once recorded, the people in the village repeatedly requested to hear these tapes over and over again — often to the point where I had no more batteries left to meet their requests.

Except for the one rendered under number 6, all of the narratives were done in the Kayapo language and were, subsequently, transcribed and translated with the help of a few young informants. In the present appendix, only brief abstracts are given; the unabridged versions of these and other narratives will be rendered in Volume II of this Series. The narratives 3 and 4 have already been published, without specific commentaries, in *Folk Literature of the Gê Indians*, Volume Two (Wilbert & Simoneau, eds., 1984).

The narratives which are presented here were narrated by six male informants, equally divided among the Central and Southern Mekranoti villages. The informants and their approximate year of birth were: Bepgogoti (° 1905), senior chief in the village at PI Mekranoti; Nikàiti (° 1933), second eldest son of Bepgogoti and trained as a *ngrenhõdjwỳnh* (ritual leader); Bemoti-re (° 1915), white man taken captive by the Mekranoti in about 1918; Ropni (° 1930), chief in the Southern Mekranoti village at PI Kretire; Kruma-re (° 1928), one of the leading men in the village at PI Jarina; and Krwỳnh'ê 'Mutum' (° 1930), a renown storyteller

---

1   The full version of these narratives will be published in Volume II of the cuirrent series, *Amazon Indians Monographs.*

in the village at PI Jarina.

1. ON THE OLD DAYS

This narrative is in fact a summary of narratives 2-6 of this appendix. It starts in the mythological past, when the Kayapo couldn't "see" things yet, and continues with relating how several socio-political features were introduced. Finally, mention is made of the beginning of the fragmentation of the ancestral Kayapo village into different groups.

2. THE ORIGIN OF THE *MEBIJÔK* NAMING CEREMONY.

This narrative relates how the women introduced the *mebijôk*, one of the most commonly performed naming ceremonies. It describes how the women started the ceremony playing around, putting flowers on their head to dance. The men then started to celebrate the *mebijôk* too.

3. THE ORIGIN OF THE *ÕKREPÔX* DANCE

The events in this narrative are said to have occurred while the Kayapo still lived along the *kôkati* river. It relates how the *õkrepôx* dance — part of the *mebijôk* naming ceremony — was introduced through captives of Krãjôkàr-re. They lived in acircular villages with two men's houses and with many logs laying scattered around the village plaza. The logs were used during log-races, a renowned ritualized competitive event in most Gê groups. According to the Mekranoti, the Krãjôkàr-re lived east of the *kôkati* river; the hairstyle of both the Kreen Akrore (*Krãjôkàr*) and the Krãjôkàr-re is said to be identical. All these and other cultural and linguistical features may well lead us to identify these Krãjôkàr-re as the Southern Kayapo.

4. PAPRETI AND KWỲRER, OR THE SEPARATION OF THE POREKRÔ AND THE GOROTI KUMRENHTX

Kwỳrer and Papreti, the two chiefs of the huge ancestral Kayapo village, led their respective groups on a journey together until Kwỳrer, stung by some offense, broke away to found a separate village. Papreti's group undertook a long and dangerous venture to the "area of the perpetual night", and eventually returned to live near Kwỳrer's group. Some of Kwỳrer's men visited the other group. Papreti suspected that they planned to kill him and he prepared for his own death. Soon after he was killed, Kwỳrer also died. Both Kayapo groups then moved to the west.

Informants stated that the huge ancestral Kayapo group was called Goroti Kumrẽnhtx. Kwỳrer's group is referred to by the same name; it gave origin to the Gorotire and to the extinct Ira'amranh. Papreti's group is referred to as the Porekrô; it gave origin to the Purukarwỳt [Xikrin] and the extinct Kôkôrekre and Djo-re.

5. THE FIRST CONTACTS WITH THE *KUBEKRYT* [BRAZILIANS] — (1)

The Brazilians and their Krahô allies approached the Goroti Kumrẽnhtx who, by that time, already occupied two separate villages. The invaders took many women and children captives. One Kayapo man, named Kenngà-re, went to fetch back his wife, his sister-in-law and her daughter. Fearing the well-armed Brazilians, all of the Goroti Kumrẽnhtx then moved due west. Bibliographic research has shown that this event occurred around 1810-1820.

6. THE FIRST CONTACTS WITH THE *KUBEKRYT* — (2)

A narrative collected by Louis Necker, director of the Ethnographic Museum at Geneva (1981-2003), during his field-work in the Xingu National Park. The narrative was told in Portuguese.

7. MYDJÊ-RE, OR THE STORY OF INTERNAL FIGHTS

Mydjê-re, a man of the Ira'amranh, went to the Gorotire in order to fetch his ceremonial friend. Through astute sleuthing, he managed to bring along several Gorotire men who were then all killed by the Ira'amranh. The latter undertook a massive revenge attack.

8. BEPRÃNTI, OR THE STORY OF THE GIANT BOY

A Gorotire man was killed by the Ira'amranh. Later on, the man's son — called Beprãnti and said to be a giant boy — was to be initiated during the *bep* ceremony. He went to the Ira'amranh in order to fetch a specific type of feathers which constituted his ritual privilege. After the ceremony, the Gorotire attacked the Ira'amranh in order to revenge the killing of the boy's father.

9. THE KILLING OF 'O-JORE

The *menõrõny-re* of the Ira'amranh village are instigated to attack the Gorotire. During the massive assault, 'O-jore — the main Gorotire chief — got killed and his followers then moved to the west, crossing the *kôkati* river.

10. THE SEPARATION OF THE GOROTIRE AND IRA'AMRANH — (1)

Friction in the huge village led to a separation along the two men's houses: the Gorotire left the ancestral village and moved due west, while the Ira'amranh remained behind.

The historic events related in this narrative probably occurred around 1840-1860.

11. THE SEPARATION OF THE GOROTIRE AND IRA'AMRANH — (2)

This is another version of the frictions between the members of the two men's houses which led to the separation of the Gorotire and the Ira'amranh.

12. THE SEPARATION OF THE GOROTIRE AND IRA'AMRANH — (3)

Yet another version of narratives 10 and 11.

13. FRICTIONS BETWEEN THE YUDJA AND THE KAYAPO

The Kayapo visited the Yudja (Juruna) in order to get glass beads, and killed a tribesman who resided among the Yudja.

14. KAJNGÀRÀTI INTRODUCES THE *KWŶRŶKANGÔ* CEREMONY TO THE MEKRANOTI

The Mekranoti, led by Mote-re, had temporarily separated from the main

Gorotire village in order to live closer to the Yudja Indians. At that time, a young Mekranoti man lived for years among the Yudja and, upon returning, introduced the *kwỳrỳkangô* ceremony which later spread among all of the other Kayapo groups. The events of this narrative occurred probably in the period between 1880-1900.

15. FRICTIONS BETWEEN THE YUDJA AND THE GOROTIRE

The Mekranoti lived close to the Yudja with whom they maintained peaceful relations. The Gorotire had a clash with the Yudja, after which the Mekranoti returned to live with the Gorotire.

16. THE SCHISM BETWEEN THE MEKRANOTI AND THE GOROTIRE

Immediately following the incident related in the former narrative, friction arose in the big Gorotire village. Chief Mote-re got involved in a case of adultery. After a series of individual and collective club-fights, he left with his followers and moved to the west, crossing the Xingu River. This was the definitive separation of the Mekranoti, an event that occurred around 1905.

17. THE MEKRANOTI ATTACK THE YUDJA

By 1910, the Yudja had moved from the area along the mid Xingu River to the Cachoeira von Martius, at the upper course of that river. A shaman told the Mote-re, one of the Mekranoti chiefs, where the Yudja had moved to. An attack was mounted during which a Yudja woman and her son were captured. She taught the Mekranoti new songs of the *kwỳrỳkangô* ceremony. The events of this narrative occurred around 1905-1915.

18. THE SPLIT BETWEEN THE NORTHERN, CENTRAL AND SOUTHERN MEKRANOTI

This narrative is a brief synopsis of the events that occurred in the period from 1946 to 1956. In that period, a series of internal strives led to the definitive separation of the Northern Mekranoti. The Southern and Central Mekranoti kept separating and reuniting several times until, not long after "pacification" in 1953, the separation became permanent.

Bibliography

ADALBERT, Prinz von Preussen, 1847. *Aus meine Tagebuch (1842-1843)*. Berlin.

ALMEIDA, Cândido Mendes de, 1852. *A Carolina ou a definitiva fixação de limites entre as províncias do Maranhão e Goyáz*. Rio de Janeiro.

ANDERSON, Andrew & Darrell POSEY, 1984. *Manejo de cerrado pelos índios Kayapó*. Unpublished manuscript, 18p.

ARNAUD, Expedíto, 1971. A ação indigenista no Sul do Pará (1940-1970). *Boletim do Museu Paraénse Emílio Goeldi*, Antropologia (nova série), n°49 (49p.)

ARNAUD, Expedito & Ana Rita ALVES, 1974. A extinção dos índios Kararaô (Kayapó) - baixo Xingu, Pará. *Boletim do Museu Paraense Emílio Goeldi*, Antropologia (nova série), n°53 (19p).

ASPELIM, P.L. & Sílvio COELHO DOS SANTOS, 1982. Áreas indígenas ameaçadas por projêtos hidrelétricas no Brasil. *Anais do Museu de Antropologia da Universidade Federal de Santa Catarina*, Ano XI-XIV, n°12-15:5-27.

AUDRIN, J.M., 1946. *Entre Sertanejos e Índios do Norte*. Rio de Janeiro.

BALDUS, Herbert, 1970. *Tapirapé, tribo tupí no Brasil Central*. São Paulo (Cia Ed. Nacional).

BALÉE, William, 1984. The Ecology of Ancient Tupi Warfare. *Warfare, Culture, and Environment* (R. Brian Ferguson, *ed.*). Orlando, San Diego: Academic Press, pp.241-265.

BAMBERGER, Joan, 1976ms. *Kayapó Age Grades: a Case of Political Development in Central Brazil*. Paper presented to the symposium "Age and generation: hierarchical relations in Lowland South America" at the 75th Annual Meeting of the American Anthropological Association (9p).

——, 1979. Exit and Voice: the Politics of Flight in Kayapó Society. *Dialectical Societies: the Gê and Bororo of Central Brazil* (Maybury-Lewis, *ed.*), pp.130-146.

BANNER, Horace, 1961. O índio Kayapó em seu acampamento. Boletim do *Museu*

Paraense Emílio Goeldi, Antropologia (nova série), n°13 (31p).

——, 1963. *Long Climb on the Xingu. Sequel to the Three Freds and After.* London, Melbourne, Bala-Cynwyd: Unevangelised Fields Mission.

——, 1975. *The Three Freds and After! Yield Xingu. A Sequel to "The Three Freds" Martyred Pioneers for Christ in Brazil.* London, Melbourne, Bala-Cynwyd: Unevangelised Fields Mission, 6th ed.

BOGUE,D.J. and E.J. BOGUE, 1970. *Techniques of Pregnancy History Analysis.* University of Chicago: Community and Family Study Center.

CARNEIRO, Robert, 1970. The Transition from Hunting to Horticulture in the Amazon Basin. *Eighth Congress of Anthropological and Ethnological Sciences*, Tokyo (Science Council of Japan), pp.244-248.

CARNEIRO DA CUNHA, Manuela, 1978. *Os Mortos e os outros.* São Paulo (Hucitec).

CARNEIRO DA CUNHA, Manuela (*ed.*), 1992. *História dos Índios no Brasil.* São Paulo (Companhia das Letras, Secretaria Municipal de Cultura, FAPESP).

CARNEIRO DA CUNHA, Manuela & Eduardo B. VIVEIROS DE CASTRO, 1985. Vingança e temporalidade: os Tupinamba. *Journal de la Société des Américanistes*, Paris, vol. 71:191-208.

CARON, Père Raymond, 1971. *Curé d'Indiens.* Paris (Union Générale d'Éditions).

CARVALHO FRANCO, F.A. de, 1953. *Dicionário de bandeirantes e sertanistas do Brasil.* São Paulo (Commissão do IV Centenário de São Paulo).

CASTELNAU, Francis de, 1850-1851. *Expéditions dans les parties centrales de l'Amérique du Sud, de Rio de Janeiro à Lima, et de Lima au Pará.* Paris (6 vols).

CAVALCANTI, Cícero, 1981. Doze anos convivendo com os Kayapó. *Revista da Atualidade Indígena*, n°21:18-23.

CHAGNON, Napoleon, 1968. Yanomamo Social Organization and Warfare. *War: the Anthropology of Armed Conflict and Aggression* (Fried, Harris & Murphy, *eds.*). Garden City, N.Y. Natural History P. for the American Museum of Natural History, pp.109-159.

——, 1973. The Culture-Ecology of Shifting (Pioneering) Cultivation among the Yanomamo Indians. *Peoples and Cultures in Native South America: an Anthropological Reader* (Gross, *ed.*). Garden City, N.Y.: Published for the American Museum of Natural History by Natural History Press, pp.126-142.

CHAUMEIL, Jean-Pierre, 1985. Échange d'énergie: guerre, identité et reproduction sociale chez les Yagua de l'Amazonie Péruvienne. *Journal de la Société des Américanistes*, Paris, vol. 71:143-157.

CHAVES, Carlos Eduardo, 2012. *Nas trilhas Irã Ãmrãnh: sobre história e cultura material Mebêngôkre.* Unpublished PhD dissertation, Universidade Federal do Pará (176 p.).

CLASTRES, Pierre, 1980. *Recherches d'anthropologie politique.* Paris (Éditions du Seuil).

COTRIM, Antônio Soares, 1968.ms *Relatório de viagem aos Kayapó-Mekrãnoty (apresentado ao SPI)*. Unpublished manuscript (8p).

COUDREAU, Henri, 1897a. *Voyage au Xingú, 30 mai 1896 – 23 octobre 1896*. Paris.

――――, 1897b. *Voyage au Tocantins-Araguaya: 31 décembre 1896-23 mai 1897*. Paris.

COWELL, Adrian, 1960. *The Heart of the Forest*. London: Travel Book Club, 238 p.

CUNHA MATTOS, Raymundo José da, 1874. Chorographia historico da Província de Goyáz (1824). *Revista trimestral do Instituto Histórico, Geografico e Ethnographico do Brasil*, vols. 37(1):213-398 and 38(1):5-150.

DA MATTA, Roberto, 1976. *Um mundo dividido: a estrutura social dos índios Apinayé*. Petrópolis (Editora Vozes).

DINIZ, Edson Soares, 1962. Os Kayapó-Gorotíre. Aspectos sócio-culturais no momento atual. *Boletim do Museu Paraense Emílio Goeldi, Antropologia*, nova série, n°18 (40p).

――――, 1963. Convívio enterétnico e aglutinação intergrupal. *Revista do Museu Paulista*, nova série, vol. 14:213-220.

DREYFUS, Simone, 1963. *Les Kayapó du Nord, État de Pará - Brésil: contribution à l'étude des Indiens Gé*. Paris et La Haye: Mouton & Co, 213 p.

DOUGLAS, Mary, 1966. *Purity and Danger*. London: Routledge & Kegan Paul.

EBNER, Carlos Borromeu, 1942. Erste Nachrichten über die Duludy-Indianer in Nord-Brasilien. *Anthropos*, vol. 35-36 (1940-1941), heft 1:363-368.

EHRENREICH, Paul, 1891. Die Einteilung und Verbreitung der Völkerstamme Brasiliens nach dem gegenwärtigen Stande unserer Kenntnisse. *Dr. A. Petermanns Mitteilungen au Justus Perthes' Geographischer Anstalt*, Gotha, vol.37:81-89, 114-124.

EMBER, Melvin and Carol R. EMBER, 1971. The Conditions Favoring Matrilocal versus Patrilocal Residence. *American Anthropologist*, vol. 73:571-594.

ERIKSON, Philippe, 1986. Alterité, tatouage et anthropophagie chez les Pano: la belliqueuse quête du soi. *Journal de la Société des Américanistes*, Paris, vol. 72:195-210.

Fernandes, Florestan, 1970. *A função social da guerra na sociedade Tupinambá*. São Paulo: Editora da USP. Re-edition of 1952.

FLOWERS, Nancy, Daniel GROSS, Madelein RITTER & Dennis WERNER, 1982. Variation in Swidden Practices in Four Central Brazilian Indian Sociaties. *Human Ecology*, vol. 10(2):203-217.

FUERST, René, 1964. La peinture collective des femmes Xikrin. *Völkerkundliche Abhandlungen, Beitrage zur Völkerkunde Sudamerikas*, Hannover, Band I:117-138.

———, 1966. Dissemblances matérielles chez les Indiens Kayapó du Brésil Central. *Bulletin de la Société Suisse des Américanistes*, vol. 31:17-34.

FUKUI, Katsuyoshi & David TURTON, 1979. Introduction. *Warfare among East African Herders* (Fukui K. & D. Turnton, *eds.*), Senri Ethnological Studies, vol. 3:3-13.

GALLAIS, Estevão-Maria, 1902. *Une Catéchèse chez les Indiens de l'Araguaya.* Toulouse: Imprimerie Vialelle et Perry.

———, 1942. *O apóstolo do Araguaia Frei Gil Vilanova, missionário dominicano. Rio de Janeiro*: Prelazia de Conceição do Araguaia.

GOLDSCHMIDT, Walter, 1988. Inducement to Military Participation in Tribal Societies. *The Social Dynamics of Peace and Conflict: Culture in International Security* (Rubinstein & LeCron Foster, *eds.*), pp. 47-65.

GROSS, Daniel, 1979. A New Approach to Central Brazilian Social Organization. *Brazil: Anthropological Perspectives* (Margolis & Carter, *eds.*), pp. 321-342.

GROSS, Daniel, George EITEN, Francesca LEOI, Madelein RITTER & Dennis WERNER, 1979. Ecology and Acculturation in Central Brazil. *Science*, vol. 206:1043-1050.

HARRIS, Marvin, 1977. *Cannibals and Kings: the Origins of Cultures.* New York: Random House.

———, 1979. The Yanomamo and the Causes of War in Band and Village Societies. *Brazil: Anthropological Perscpectives* (Margolis and Carter, *eds.*), pp. 121-132.

———, 1980. *Culture, People, Nature: an Introduction to General Anthropology.* New York: Harper & Row, 3rd ed.

HARTMANN, Gunther, 1982. Bei den Mekubenokré-Kayapo, Brasilien: Aus den Tagebugblattern Wilhelm Kissenberths. *Zeitschrift für Ethnologie*, Band 107(1):153-162.

HEATH, E.G. & Vilma CHIARA, 1977. *Brazilian Indian Archery.* Manchester: Simon Archery Foundation.

HEELAS, Richard, 1979. *The Social Organization of the Panara, a Gê Tribe of Central Brazil.* Unpublished PhD dissertation, University of Oxford (384p).

HEMMING, John, 1978. *Red Gold: the Conquest of the Brazilian Indians.* Southhampton: The Camelot Press Ltd.

HENLEY, Paul, 1996. Recent themes in the anthropology of Amazonia: history, exchange, alterity. *Bulletin Latin American Research*, vol. 15(2): 213-245.

HORTON, Donald, 1948. The Mundurucú. *Handbook of South American Indians* (Steward, *ed.*), vol. 3:271-281.

HONIGMANN, John J. (*ed.*), 1973. *Handbook of Social and Cultural Anthropology.* Chicago: Rand McNally & Cy.

IANNI, Octávio, 1979. *A luta pela terra.* Petrópolis: Editora Vozes.

KRÄUTLER, Eurico, 1979. *Sangue nas Pedras*. São Paulo: Coleção Perspectivas:10 — Edições Paulinas.

KRAUSE, Fritz, 1911. *In den Wildnissen Brasiliens. Bericht und Ergebnisse der Leipziger Araguaya-Expedition 1908*. Leipzig: R. Voigtländer Verlag, 512 p..

LATHRAP, Donald, 1968. The 'Hunting' Economics in the Tropical Forest Zone of South America: an Attempt at Historical Perspective. *Man the Hunter* (Lee and DeVore, *eds.*). Chicago: Aldine, pp. 23-29

LEA, Vanessa, 1986. *Nomes e nekrets Kayapó: uma concepção de riqueza*. Unpublished PhD dissertation, Universidade Federal do Rio de Janeiro (564p.).

— — , 2012. *Riquezas Intangiveis de pessoas partiveis. Os Mebêngôkre (Kayapó) do Brasil central*. São Paulo (Edusp, Fapesp), 495 p.

LELONG, Maurice H., 1952. *Les Indiens qui meurent*. Paris: René Juliard, 233 p.

LEOPOLD III OF BELGIUM, 1967. *La fête indienne. Souvenirs d'un voyage chez les Indiens du Haut-Xingú*. Paris: Hachette.

— — , 1974. *Indian Enchantment. Memories of a Sojourn among the Indians of the Upper-Xingu*. Los Angeles: Gateway Publishers.

LÉVI-STRAUSS, Claude, 1943. Guerre et commerce chez les Indiens de l'Amérique du Sud. *Renaissance*, vol. 1:122-139.

— — , 1945. Le dédoublement de la représentation dans les arts de l'Asie et de l'Amérique. *Renaissance*, vol. 2-3:168-186.

LIZOT, Jacques, 1975. Économie ou société: les Yanomami. *Éléments d'ethnologie* (Creswell, *ed.*), vol. 1:128-165.

— — , 1977. Population, Resources and Warfare among the Yanomami. *Man*, new series, vol. 12(3/4):497-517.

LOWIE, Robert, 1946. The Southern Cayapó. *Handbook of South American Indians* (Steward, *ed.*), vol. 3:519-520.

MAGALHÃES, Couto de, 1863. *Viagem ao Araguaya*. Goyaz: Typ. Provincial.

MALINOWSKI, Bronislaw, 1927 1929. *The Sexual Life of Savages in Northwestern Melanesia*. 2 vols. New York: H. Liveright; London: G. Routledge & sons, Ltd.

MARGOLIS, Maxine L. & William E. CARTER (*eds.*), 1979. *Brazil: Anthropological Perspectives; Essays in Honor of Charles Wagley*. New York: Columbia Universty Press.

MARIANO, Michelle Carlesso, 2014. *Da borduna às redes sociais: uma mostra do cotidiano Mebêngôkre Metyktire*. Unpublished PhD dissertation, Universidade Federal de Mato Grosso (241 p.).

MAUSS, Marcel, 1968. *Sociologie et Anthropologie*. Paris: Presses Universitaires de France. Re-edition of 1952.

MAYBURY-LEWIS, David, 1974. *Akwe-Shavante Society*. Oxford: University Press.

Re-edition of 1967.

MAYBURY-LEWIS, David (ed.), 1979. *Dialectical Societies: the Gê and Bororo of Central Brazil.* Massachusets: Harvard University Press.

MEIRELLES, Fransisco, 1958ms. *Relatório de trabalhos realizados em 1957 no Pará (região Xinguana) pelo Sr. Inspetor F. Furtado Soares de Meirelles - chefe da IR. 2- e incumbido do Plano Econômico de Valorização da Amazônia.* Unpublished manuscript (11 p).

———, 1962. Meirelles fala sobre os Kayapó: seus primeiros e últimos contatos com elementos civilizados. *Boletim interno do SPI*, n°56: 3-18.

MELATTI, Júlio Cézar, 1979. The Relationship System of the Krahô. *Dialectical Societies: the Gê and Bororo of Central Brazil* (Maybury-Lewis, ed.), pp. 83-129.

MISSÕES DOMINICANOS, 1933-1942. *Nossas Catequeses. Mensageiro do Santo Rosário.* Conceição do Araguaia.

MOORE, Alexander, 1978. *Cultural Anthropology.* New York: Harper & Row, Publishers.

MORÃES, Padre José de, 1860. *História da Companhia de Jesus na extincta Provincia do Maranhão e Pará. Memória para a história do extincto Estado do Maranhão (Almeida).* Rio de Janeiro: Typographia do Commercio, de Brito & Braga.

MOREIRA NETO, Carlos de Araújo, 1959. Relatório sobre a situação atual dos Índios Kayapó. *Revista de Antropologia*, vol. 7:49-64.

———, 1965. O estado de rop-króre kam aibãn entre os índios Kayapó. *América Indígena*, vol. 25(4):393-408.

MÜLLER, Regina P., 1976. *A pintura de corpo e os ornamentos Xavante: arte visual e comunicação social.* Unpublished Masters dissertation, Universidade Estadual de Campinas.

MURPHY, Robert F., 1957. Intergroup Hostility and Social Cohesion. *American Anthropologist*, vol. 59(6):1018-1035.

NEME, Mário, 1969. Dados para a história dos índios Cayapó. *Anais do Museu Paulista*, vol. 23:103-147.

NIMUENDAJÚ, Curt Unkel, 1932. Idiomas indígenas del Brasil. *Revista del Instituto de Etnologia*, vol. 2:543-618

———, 1939. *The Apinayé.* Washington (The Catholic University of America), Anthropological Series, vol. 8.

———, 1940ms. *Einige Angabe über die Pau d'Arco-Horde der Nördlichen Kayapó.* Unpublished manuscript (65 p).

———, 1946. *The Eastern Timbira.* Berkeley & Los Angeles: University of California Publications in American Archaeology and Ethnology, vol. 46.

———, 1948. Tribes of the lower and middle Xingú River. *Handbook of South American Indians* (Steward, ed.), vol. 3:213-244.

——, 1952. Os Gorotire: Relatório apresentado ao Serviço de Proteção aos Índios em 18 de abril de 1940. *Revista do Museu Paulista*, nova série, vol. 6:427-453.

——, 1956. Os Apinayé. *Boletim do Museu Paraense Emílio Goeldi*, Antropologia (nova série), n°12 (150p).

OLIVEIRA JUNIOR, Adolfo Neves de, 1995. *O faccionalismo Caiapó: um exercício de investigação antropológica.* Unpublished PhD dissertation, Universidade de Brasília (100 p.).

OTTERBEIN, Keith F., 1968. Internal War: A Cross-Cultural Study. *American Anthropologist*, vol. 70:277-289.

——, 1973. The Anthropology of War. *Handbook of Social and Cultural Anthropology* (Honigmann, *ed.*), pp. 923-959.

OVERING, Joanna, 1986. Images of Cannibalism, Death and Domination in a "Non-Violent" Society. *Journal de la Société des Américanistes,* Paris, vol. 72:133-156.

PERET, João Américo, 1965ms. *População Kayapó do Xingu.* Unpublished manuscript.

——, 1975. *População indígena do Brasil.* Rio de Janeiro Civilização Brasileira.

POSEY, Darrell, 1979a. Pykatôtí: Kayapó mostra aldeia de origem. *Revista da Atualidade Indígena,* vol. 15:50-57.

——, 1979b. *Ethnoentomology of the Gorotire Kayapó of Central Brazil.* Unpublished PhD dissertation, University of Georgia.

——, 1981ms. *Contact before Contact: Typology of post-Colombian Interaction with the Northern Kayapó of the Amazon Basin.* Unpublished manuscript (23p.)

——, 1984. A Preliminary Report on Diversified Management of Tropical Forest by the Kayapó Indians of the Brazilian Amazon. *Advances in Economic Botany,* vol. 1:112-126.

PREIHS, Ari, 1952ms. *Relatório, síntese e histórico do local em que foi fundado a base da turma volante Curuá, na margem direita do rio que dá o nome, afluente do Iriri, Xingú: trabalhos de atração dos índios Kayapó (grupo Mentuktire) naquela zona radicadas e trabalhos de construção do campo para aterizagem de aviões. Relatório para o SPI.* Unpublished manuscript (5 p.)

RADCLIFFE-BROWN, A.R., 1933. *The Andaman Islanders.* Cambridge: University Press.

RADIN, Paul, 1923. The Winnebago Tribe. *Bureau of American Ethnography, 37th Annual Report (1915-1916).* Washington.

RIBEIRO, Darcy, 1970. *Os Índios e a civilização.* Rio de Janeiro: Editora Civilização Brasileira.

RIBEIRO, Fransisco de Paula, 1841. Memória sobre as nações gentias que presentemente habitam o Continente do Maranhão; analyse de algumas tribus mais conhecidas; processo de suas hostilidades sobre os habitantes; causas que lhes tem dificultado a reducção; e único methodo que seriamente poderá reduzil-as. *Jornal do Instituto Histórico e Geográphico Brasileiro*, vol. 3:184-197, 297-322, 442-456.

——, 1874. Descripção do território de Pastos Bons, nos sertões do Maranhão. *Jornal do Instituto Histórico e Geográphico Brasileiro*, vol. 12:41-86.

RUBINSTEIN, Robert A & Mary LeCRON FOSTER (eds.), 1988. *The Social Dynamics of Peace and Conflict: Culture in International Security*. Boulder & London: Westview Press.

SEBASTIÃO THOMAS, Dom, 1936. *Os Gorotirés*. Rio de Janeiro: Prelazia de Conceição do Araguaya.

SEEGER, Anthony, 1975. The meaning of Body Ornaments: a Suia Example. *Ethnology*, vol. 14:211-224

——, 1977. Fixed Points on Arcs in Circles: the Temporal Processual Aspect of Suia Space and Society. *Actes du XLII Congrès International des Américanistes*, vol. 2:340-359.

——, 1981. *Nature and Society in Central Brazil: the Suia Indians of Mato Grosso*. Cambridge: Harvard University Press.

SEEGER, Anthony, Roberto DA MATTA & Eduardo VIVEIROS DE CASTRO, Renate VIERTLER & Manuela CARNEIRO DA CUNHA, 1979. A Construção da pessoa nas sociedades indígenas. *Boletim do Museu Nacional, Antropologia*, vol. 32 (51p.)

SICK, Helmut, 1960. *Tukani. Unter Tieren und Indianern Zentralbrasiliens bei der ersten Durchquerung von SO nach NW*. Hamburg & Berlin: Parey. Re-edition of 1957.

SIVERTS, Henning, 1979. Jivaro Headhunters in a Headless Time. *Peasants, Primitives and Proletariats: The Struggle for Identity in South America* (Browman & Schwarz, eds.). The Hague, Paris & New York: Mouton.

STEWARD, Julian H. (ed.), 1946. *Handbook of South American Indians, vol. 1: The Marginal Tribes*. Washington, Smithsonian Institution: Bureau of American Ethnology.

——, 1948. *Handbook of South American Indians, vol. 3: The Tropical Forest Tribes*. Washington, Smithsonian Institution: Bureau of American Ethnology.

TAYLOR, Anne-Christine, 1985. L'art de la réduction. La guerre et les mécanismes de la différenciation tribale dans la culture Jivaro. *Journal de la Société des Américanistes*, Paris, vol. 71:159-173.

TORNAY, Serge, 1979. Armed Conflicts in the Lower Omo Valley, 1970-1976: An Analysis from within Nyangatom Society. *Warfare among East African Herders* (Fukui K. & D. Turton, eds.), Senri Ethnological Studies, vol.

3:97-117.

TURNER, Terence, 1965. *Social Structure and Political Organization among the Northern Cayapó*. Unpublished PhD dissertation, Harvard University (580 p.).

——, 1969. Tchikrin: A Central Brazilian Tribe and its Symbolic Language of Bodily Ornament. *Natural History,* vol. 78:50-59, 70-71.

——, 1974ms. *Social Structure of the Northern Kayapó.* Unpublished manuscript (208 p.).

——, 1979a. The Gê and Bororo Societies as Dialectical Systems: a General Model. *Dialectical Societies: the Gê and Bororo of Central Brazil* (Maybury-Lewis, *ed.*), pp. 147-178.

——, 1979b. Kinship, Household and Community Structure among the Kayapó. *Dialectical Societies: the Gê and Bororo of Central Brazil* (Maybury-Lewis, *ed.*), pp. 179-246.

——, 1980. The Social Skin. *Not Work Alone* (Cherfas, *ed.*). London.

——, 1987ms. *The Kayapo of Southeastern Para.* Unpublished manuscript (132p).

——, 1992. Os Mebengokre Kayapó: história e mudança social. De comunidades autônomas para a coesistência interétnica. *História dos Índios no Brasil* (M. Carneiro da Cunha, *ed.*), pp. 311-338.

TURNER, Victor, 1967. *The Forest of Symbols.* Ithaca (Cornell University Press).

VERSWIJVER, Gustaaf, 1977. Os Mekrãgnotí. *Revista da Atualidade Indígena,* vol. 6:64.

——, 1978a. *Enquête ethnographique chez les Kayapó-Mekrãgnotí: contribution à l'étude de la dynamique des groupes locaux (scissions et regroupements).* Unpublished Masters dissertation, École des Hautes Études en Sciences Sociales - Paris (138p.)

——, 1978b. Séparations et migrations des Mekrãgnotí, groupe Kayapó du Brésil Central. *Bulletin de la Société Suisse des Américanistes,* vol. 42:47-59.

——, 1978c. A história dos Índios Kayapó. *Revista da Atualidade Indígena,* vol. 12:9-16.

——, 1981. Les gens aux bracelets noirs: un rite de passage chez les Indiens Kayapó du Brésil Central. *Naître, vivre et Mourir: actualité de Van Gennep* (Museum Catalogue, Musée d'ethnographie, Neuchâtel), pp 95-118.

——, 1982a. Les femmes peintes: une cérémonie d'imposition de noms chez les Kayapó-Mekrãgnotí du Brésil Central. *Bulletin de la Société Suisse des Américanistes,* vol. 46:41-59.

——, 1982b. Intertribal Relations between the Jurúna and the Kayapó Indians (1850-1920). *Jahrbuch des Museums für Völkerkunde* (Leipzig), Band 36:305-315.

—— , 1983a. Essai sur l'usage de la parure chez les Indiens Kaiapó du Brésil Central. *Bulletin du Musée d'ethnographie de la Ville de Genève,* vol. 25-26:23-62.

—— , 1983b. Cycles in Kaiapó Naming Practices. *Communication and Cognition* (Ghent), vol. 16(3):301-323. Also in *New Perspectives in Belgian Anthropology* (Rik Pinxten, *ed.*), Edition Herodot, Forum 6:113-135 (1984).

—— , 1984. Cíclos nas práticas de nominação Kaiapó. *Revista do Museu Paulista,* vol. 29:97-124.

—— , 1985. *Considerations on Mekrãgnotí Warfare.* Unpublished Doctoral dissertation, Rijksuniversiteit Gent (463p.)

—— , 1988a. Migration um zu überleben: die spezielle ökonomische Anpassung der Kaiapó-Indianer in Zentralbrasilien. *Geograhica Helvetica* (Zurich), vol. 43(4):194-202.

—— , 1988b. Chants individuels et chants collectifs chez les Kaiapó du Brésil Central. *Cahiers de Musiques Traditionelles* (Genève), vol. 1:13-27.

—— , 1989. Chants et danses des Indiens Kaiapó (Brésil Central) - 2 compact discs. *Archives Internationales de Musique Populaire* (AIMP), Genève, vol. XIV-XV.

—— , 1989ms. *Post-War Adaptative Process in Kayapo Society.* Unpublished manuscript (26 p.)

VIDAL, Lux, 1977. *Morte e vida de uma sociedade indígena Brasileira.* Os Kayapó-Xikrin do Rio Cateté. São Paulo (Hucitec/Edusp).

—— , 1978. A pintura corporal entre Índios Brasileiros. *Revista de Antropologia,* vol. 21(1):87-93.

—— , 1981. Contribution to the Concept of Person and Self in Lowland South American Societies: Body Painting among the Kayapo-Xikrin. *Contribuições à Antropologia em homenagem ao Professor Egon Schaden, Coleção Museu Paulista, Série Ensaios,* vol. 4:291-303.

—— , 1988. Die Körperbemalung und die Zeichenkunst der Xikrín-Kayapó von Cateté. *Die Mythen Sehen: Bilder und Zeichen von Amazonas. Roter Faden zur Ausstellung* (Frankfurt: Museum für Völkerkunde), vol.14:331-389.

VILLAS BÒAS, Cláudio & Orlando, 1954. Atração dos índios Txukahamãi. *Relatório das atividades do Serviço de Proteção aos Índios durante o ano de 1954* (Rio de Janeiro: Ministério da Agricultura, Serviço de Proteção aos Índios), pp. 79-88.

VON DEN STEINEN, Karl, 1886. *Durch Central Brasilien. Expedition zur Erforschung des Schingú im jahre 1884.* Leipzig: Brockhaus.

WAGLEY, Charles, 1977. *Welcome of Tears: the Tapirapé Indians of Central Brazil.* New York: Oxford University Press.

WERNER, Dennis, 1980. *The Making of a Mekranotí Chief: the Psychological and Social Determinants of Leadership in a Native South American Society.*

Unpublished PhD dissertation, City University of New York.

— —, 1981. Are Some People more Equal than Others? Status Inequality among the Mekranoti Indians of Central Brazil. *Journal of Anthropological Research,* vol.37:360-373.

— —, 1981. Gerontocracy among the Mekranoti, Brazil. *Anthropological Quarterly,* vol. 54(1):15-27.

— —, 1982. Chiefs and Presidents: a Comparison of Leadership Traits in the United States and among the Mekranoti-Kayapo of Central Brazil. *Ethos: Journal of the Society for Psychological Anthropology,* vol. 10(2):136-148.

— —, 1983. Fertility and Pacification Among the Mekranoti of Central Brazil. *Human Ecology,* vol. 11(2):227-245.

WILBERT, Johannes (*ed.*), 1978. *Folk Literature of the Gê Indians* (vol. 1). Los Angeles: UCLA Latin American Center Publications, University of California.

WILBERT, Johannes & Karin SIMONEAU (*eds.*), 1984. *Folk Literature of the Gê Indians* (vol. 2). Los Angeles: UCLA Latin American Center Publications, University of California.

Maps

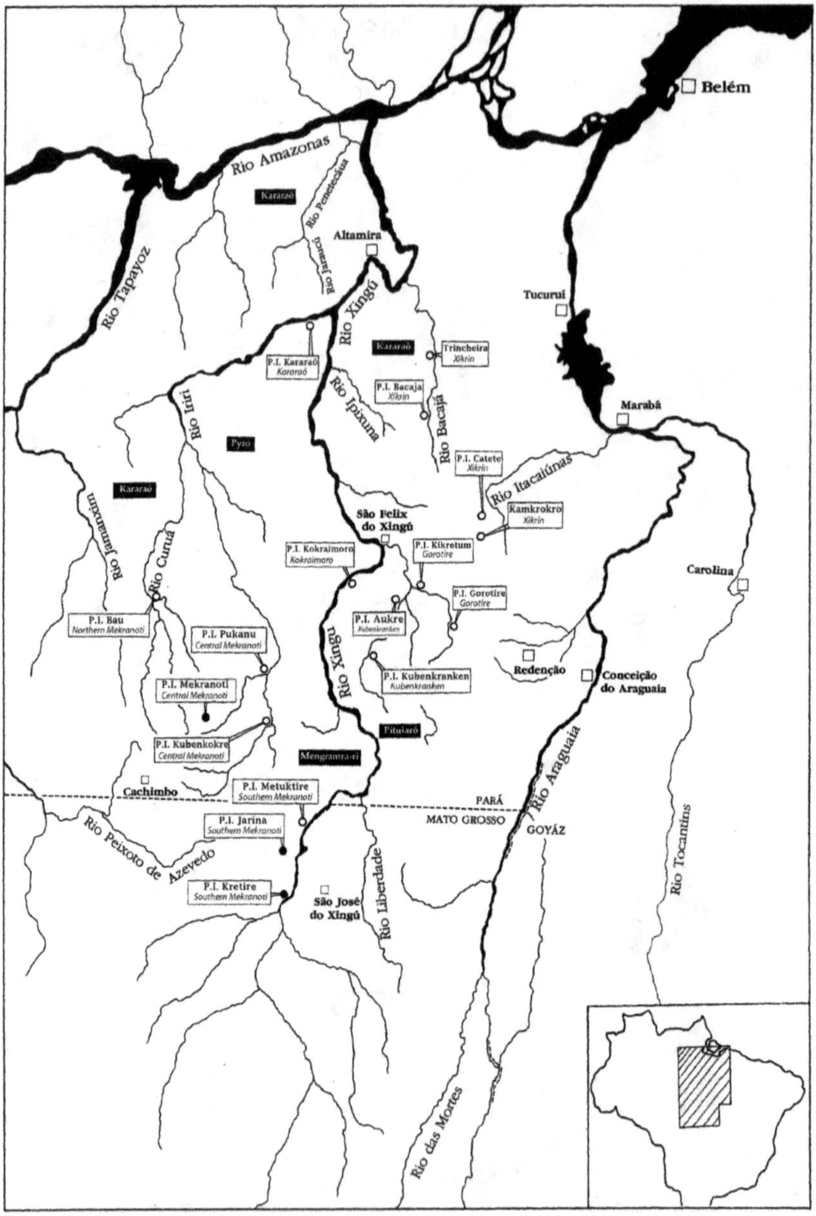

Map . 1. — Distribution of all contemporary Kayapo villages (situation as recorded in 1988).
Names in black boxes refer to still isolated groups; black circles refer to recently abandoned Mekranoti villages often mentioned throughout this essay.

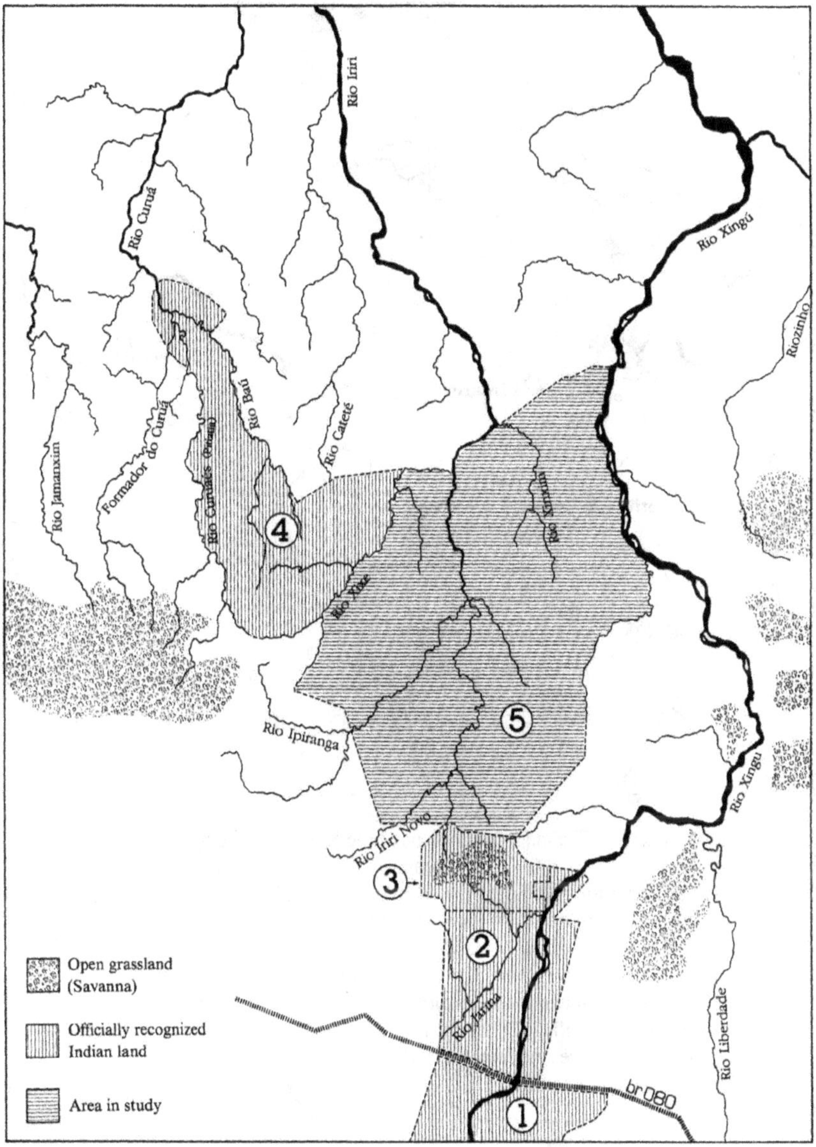

Map . 2. — Legal situation of Mekranoti land (Source: CEDI 1987).
(1) "Xingu Indigenous Park" (2,642,008 ha), created in 1961 and
modified several times; (2) "Jarina Indigenous Reserve" (407,813 ha)
created in 1976 and modified in 1984; (3) "Capoto Indigenous Area"
(186,000 ha) created in 1984; (4) "Bau-Menkranoti Indigenous Reserve"
(665,600 ha) proposed in 1985; (5) proposed additional area of the
"Bau-Menkranoti Indigenous Reserve" (2,366,000 ha).

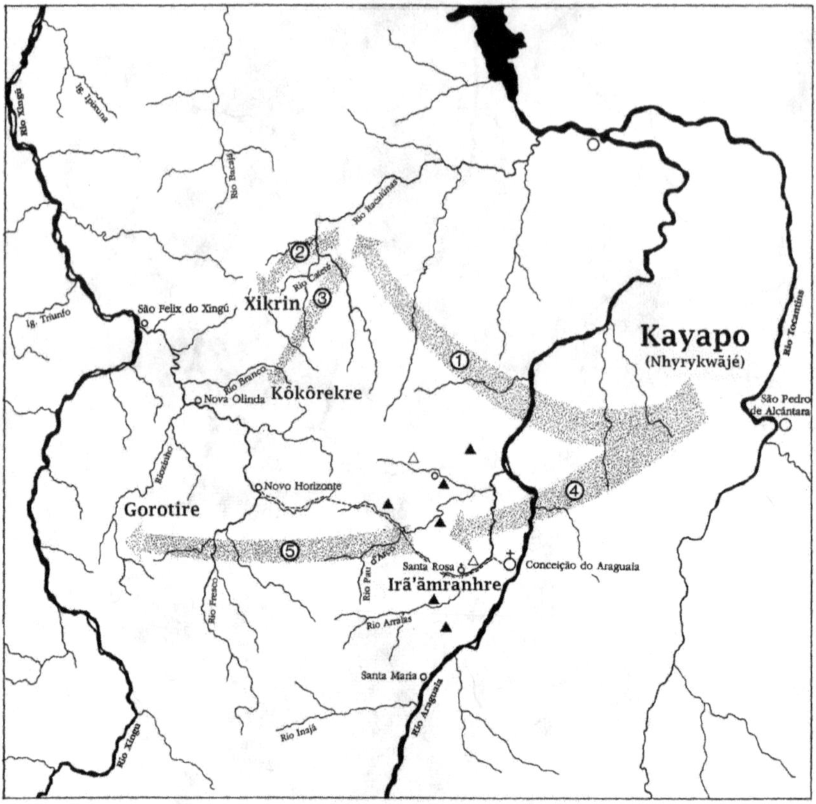

Map . 3. — The major migrations of the Kayapo in the nineteenth century.
(1) the separation and the northwest migration of the Porekry;
(2) the separation of the Pytkarot (Xikrin);
(3) the separation of the Kôkôrekre;
(4) the westward migration of the Goroti Kumrĕnhtx;
(5) the separation and the westward migration of the Gorotire.
▲ Irã'ãmranhre villages in about 1900;
△ last Irã'ãmranhre settlements (1911);
o Brazilian agglomerations;
† Missions.

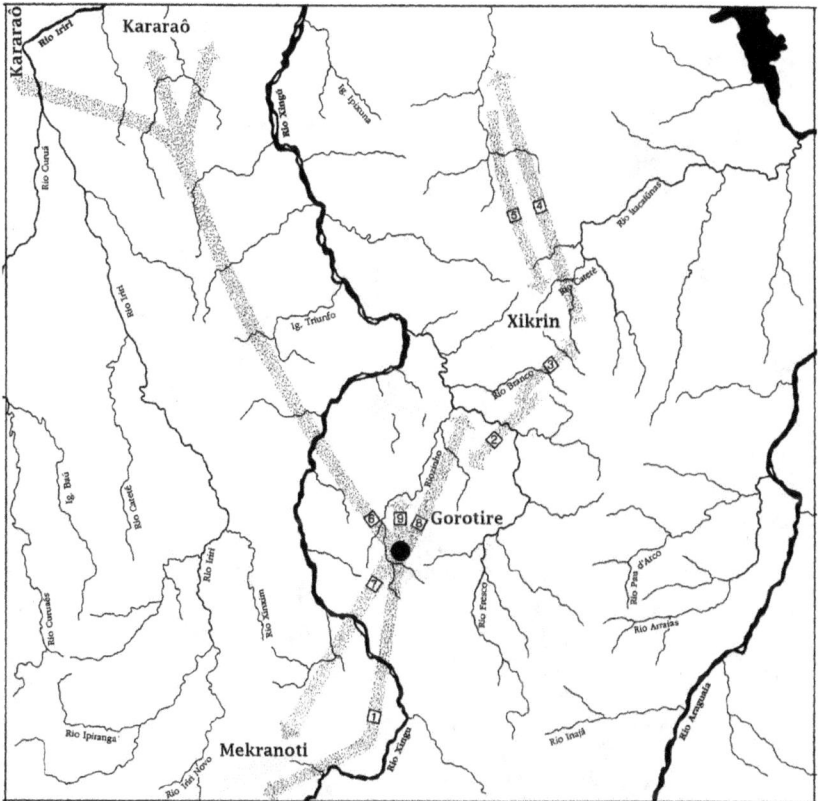

Map . 4. — The major migrations of the Kayapo in the early twentieth
century.
(1) the separation of the Mekranoti led by Mote-re and Panhkĩ;
(2) the Djo-re separate from the Kôkôrekre and move to the Rio Branco;
(3) the Kôkôrekre move to join the Pytkarot (Xikrin);
(4) the Pytkarot (Xikrin) move towards the Bacaja River;
(5) part of the Pytkarot (Xikrin) returns to the Catete River;
(6) the Kararaô separate from the Gorotire and move to the north, where
they split up into several minor groups;
(7) Tàpjêt and his followers separate from the Gorotire and join the
Mekranoti;
(8) the Gorotire separate from the Kubenkranken and move to the
northeast;
(9) the Kubenkranken move to the north.

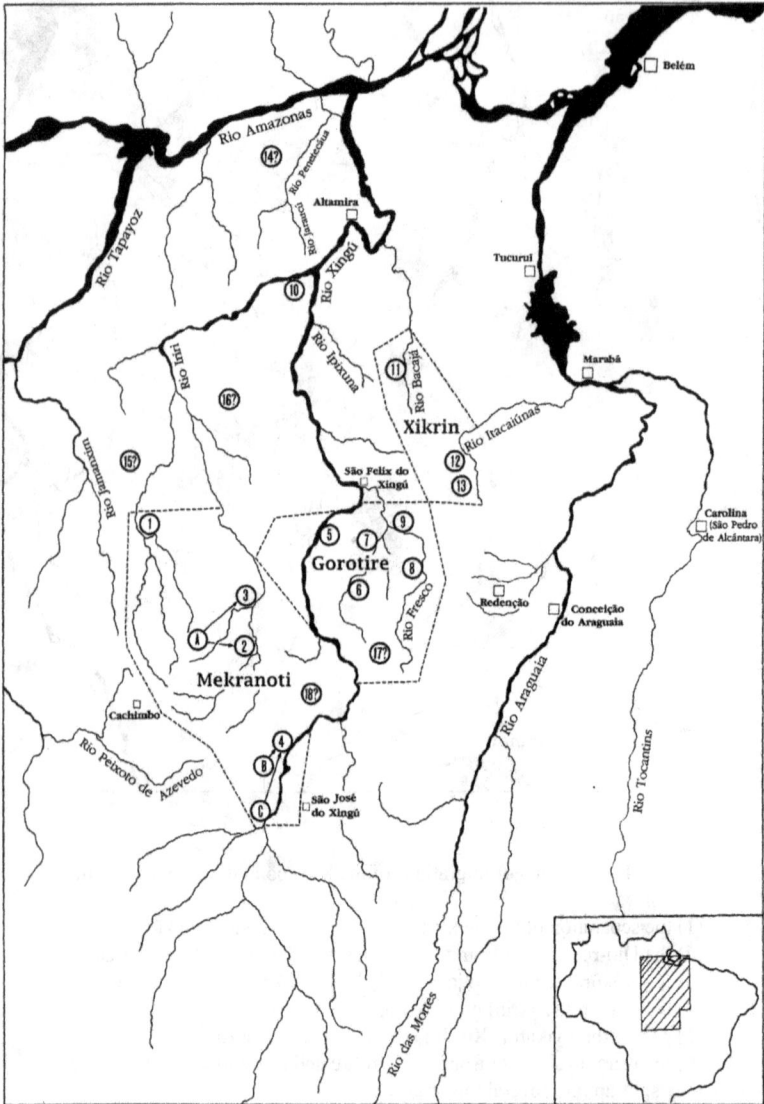

Map . 5. — Distribution of the Kayapo groups: situation in 1986.
KAYAPO - MEKRANOTI: (A) PI Mekranoti (*pi'ydjãm*), occupied until
1985; (B) PI Jarina, occupied until 1985; (C) PI Kretire, occupied until
1985; (1) PI Bau; (2) PI Kubenkokre; (3) PI Pukanu; (4) PI Metuktire.
KAYAPO- GOROTIRE: (5) PI Kokraimoro; (6) PI Kubenkranken; (7) PI
Aukre; (8) PI Gorotire; (9) PI Kikretum; (10) PI Kararaô.
KAYAPO - XIKRIN: (11) PI Bacaja; (12) PI Catete; (13) Kamkrôkrô.
GROUPS THAT CONTINUE ISOLATED: (14) Kararaô; (15) Kararaô;
(16) Pyro; (17) Pitujarô; (18) Mengramra-ri

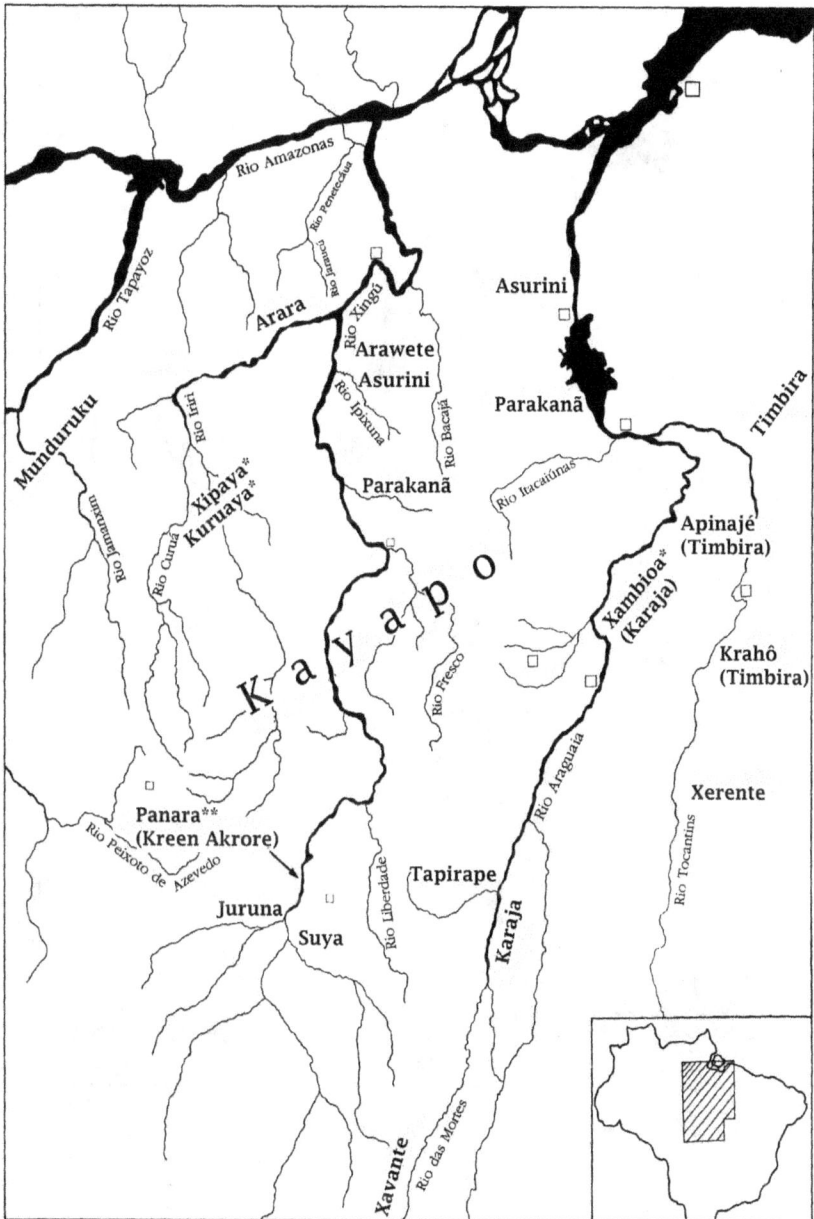

Map . 6. — Ethnic groups in Central Brazil.
* Groups with only a handful of survivors;
** The Panara (Kreen Akrore) were moved into the Xingu Indigenous
Park in 1974

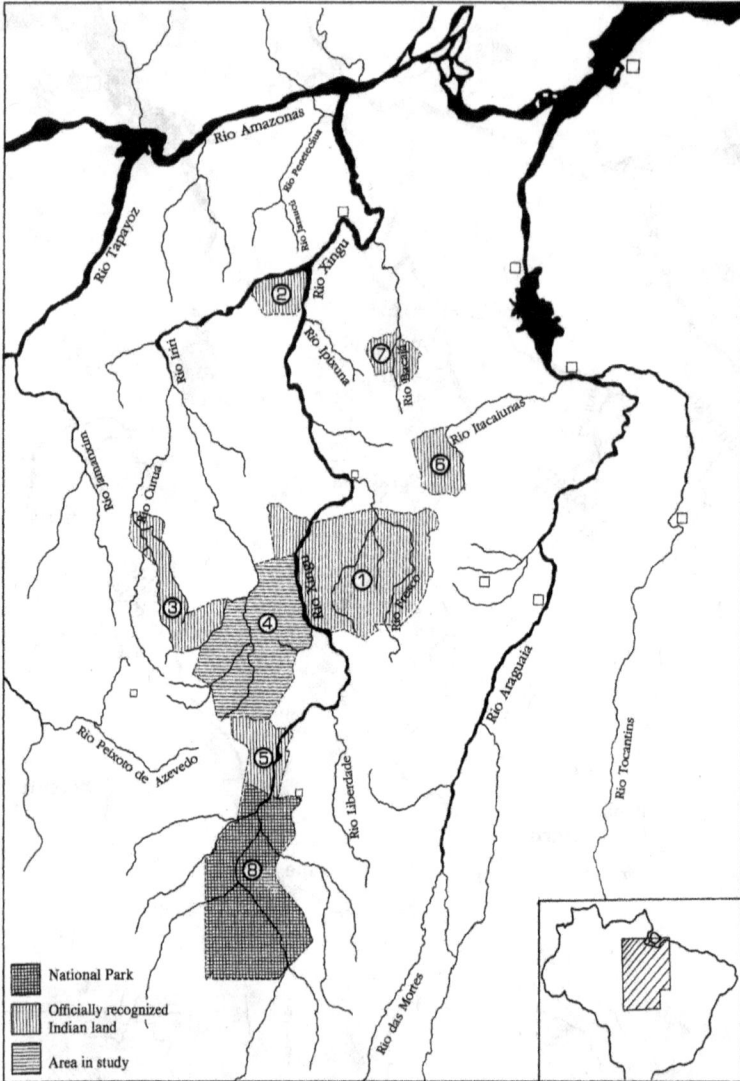

National Park

Officially recognized
Indian land

Area in study

Map . 7. — Legal situation of Kayapo land (Source: CEDI 1987).
(1) "Kayapo Indigenous Area" (3,262,960 ha) created in 1985; (2)
"Kararaô Indigenous Reserve" (224,000 ha) created in 1971; (3) "Bau-
Menkranoti Indigenous Reserve" (665,600 ha) proposed in 1985; (4)
proposed additional area of the "Bau-Menkranoti Indigenous Reserve"
(2,366,000 ha); (5) "Jarina Indigenous Reserve" (407,813 ha) created in
1976 and modified in 1984, and the "Capoto Indigenous Area" (186,000
ha) created in 1984; (6) "Catete Indigenous Area" (439,151 ha) created
in 1977; (7) "Bacaja Indigenous Area" (192,126 ha) created in 1980; (8)
"Xingu Indigenous Park" (2,642,008 ha), created in 1961 and modified
several times

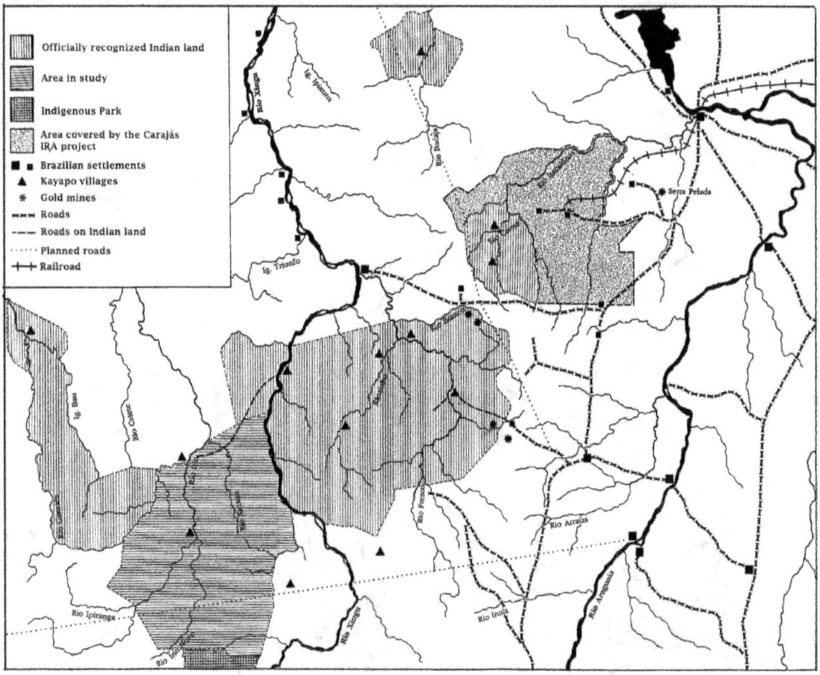

Map . 8. — Map showing the effects of the encroaching colonization
into Kayapo land (situation in 1985)

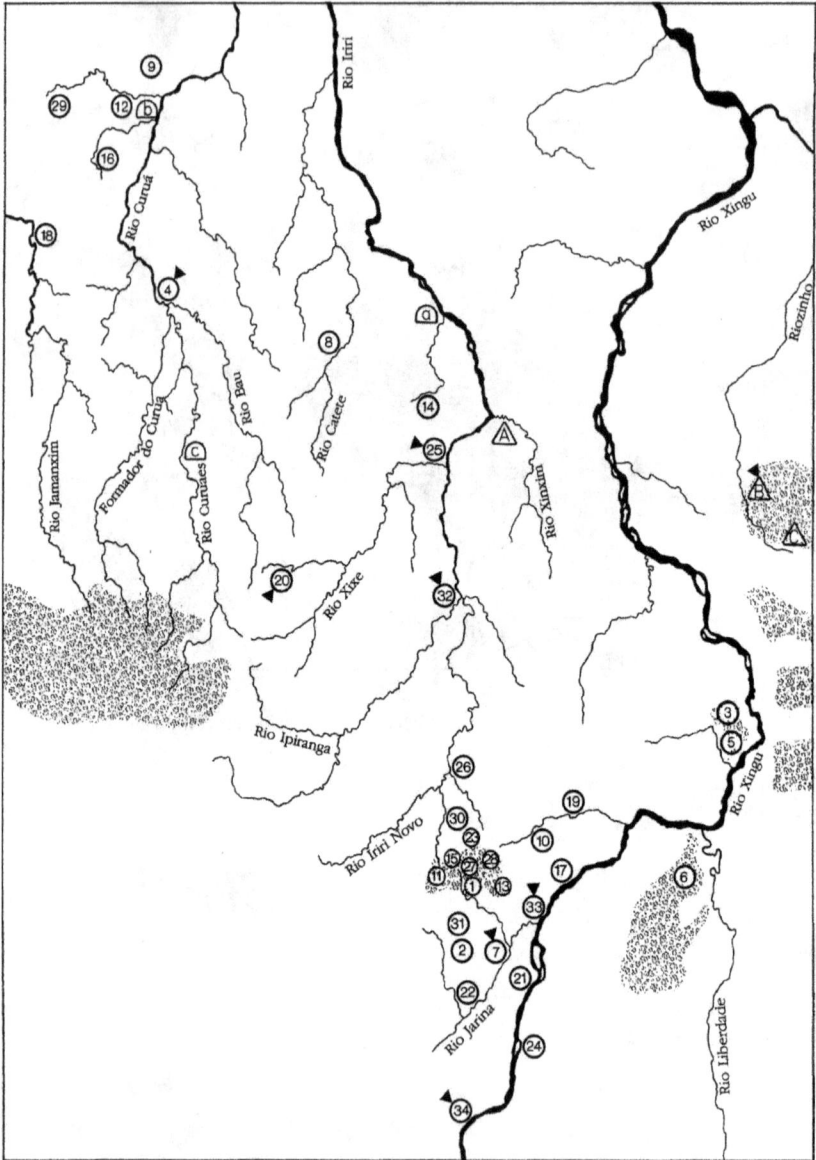

Map . 9. — Approximate location of all Mekranoti villages occupied in
the period 1905-1990 (black triangles indicate airstrips).

(1) *adytirekrekỳ*

(2) *akranhĩnkrô*

(3) *arerek-re*

(4) *baú* [PI Bau]

(5) *djwỳkapĩdjà*

(6) *kapôtnĩnõr*

(7) *kenngà* [PI Jarina]
(8) *kenpoti*
(9) *krãnhkaê*
(10) *krãnhkrax*
(11) *krãnhmrôpryjaka*
(12) *krãnhnĩnõ*
(13) *krãnhtykti*
(14) *krôdjãm-re*
(15) *kŭmjêkô*
(16) *kwỳrỳdjỳti*
(17) *ngôrãrãnk*
(18) *ngôkamrêkti*
(19) *ngrwakre-re*
(20) *pi'ydjãm* [PI Mekranoti]
(21) *porori*
(22) *pykabãr*
(23) *pykakrãkumex*
(24) *pykanhikànhkàry*
(25) *pykany* [PI Pukanu]
(26) *rikrekô-re*
(27) *ropkakô*
(28) *rojkô-re*
(29) *ron'ôkrĩdjà*
(30) *rõntinõr*
(31) *tekàdjỳtidjãm*
(32) ? [PI Kubenkokre]
(33) ? [PI Metuktire]
(34) ? [PI Kretire]
(A) *kendjãm* (old Kokraimoro village site)
(B) *krã'ãbõm* (site of Kubenkranken village)
(C) *pykatoti* (site of ancient village of the Goroti Kŭmrẽnhtx)
(a) P. Candoca
(b) P. Bom Futuro
(c) P. Pitiatia

PLATES

Plate 1. — View at *pi'ydjãm* with its neo-Brazilian style huts
and its platforms to dry leaves, seeds, and so on in the sun.
PI Mekranoti, 1976

Plate 2. — Aerial photograph of the new Central Mekranoti
village with, in its centre, the men's house and the circular
dancing track.
PI Kubenkokre, 1990

Plate 3. — A woman weeding the area in front of her hut.
PI Mekranoti, 1977

Plate 4. — Nhàktu carrying one son in a sling, and another on
her shoulders.
PI Mekranoti, 1980

Plate 5. — Children playing soccer with a self-made fibre-ball.
PI Mekranoti, 1975

Plate 6. — During the final phase of the *menibijôk* naming ceremony, two "police men" (here wearing sun glasses) supervising a ritual act.
PI Mekranoti, 1976

Plate 7. — The dance of the jaguar, similar to the one
performed by returning warriors.
PI Kretire, 1974

Plate 8. — Nhàkti painting her daughter with the black
genipap colour dye, using a fine stem of the central rib of a
palm leaf.
PI Mekranoti, 1980

Plate 9. — The *mei'ītyk-re* boys being painted by their
"substitute father during the *tàkàk* ceremony.
PI Mekranoti, 1975

Plate 10. — During the *tàkàk* naming ceremony, the men
carry long pyte palm poles and perform a dance on a cleared
area outside the village circle.
PI Mekranoti, 1975

Plate 11. — One of the major dances during the corn
ceremony. The man on the right wears the *kubẽkàkamrêk*
("red dress"), and the one on the left the *krãdjêkamrêk* ("red
hat"). Both ornaments were introduced as booty during
attacks on settlements of national colonists.
PI Mekranoti, 1978

Plate 12. — Two *mengrenhõdjwjỳnh* leading the *'ê'êama*
dance during the *memybijôk* naming ceremony.
PI Mekranoti, 1979

Plate 13. — Boys eating the meat of a slain jaguar.
PI Mekranoti, 1976

Plate 14. — The timbo fishing ritual, performed in a creeck
near the village.
PI Mekranoti, 1976

Plate 15. — The ceremonial friends guarding the honoured
children. They are adorned with the ritual costume.
PI Kubenkranken, 1976

Plate 16. — Bepkũm (right) and Pykati-re performing an
aben-o kenh duel.
PI Mekranoti, 1978

Plate 17. — During the *tàkàk* naming ceremony, the men daily race in pairs. At right, Ropni running while carrying his rifle.
PI Kretire, 1974

Plate 18. — The men playing *rõnkrã*, a fairly dangerous native hockey-like game which requires great agility.
PI Mekranoti, 1976

Plate 19. — A group of men returning from a seasonal trek
bringing along buriti palm fibres.
PI Mekranoti, 1979

Plate 20. — Hõ'i preparing buriti palm fibres during one of
the seasonal forest treks.
PI Mekranoti, 1979

Plate 21. — A view of a forest camp with a traditional lean-
to-like hut.
PI Kubenkranken, 1976

Plate 22. — The men returning from a ceremonial migration,
carrying hundreds of forest turtles.
PI. Pukanu, 1997

Plate 23. — Chief Ôket of the Kubenkranken.
Photo between 1955 and 1960.

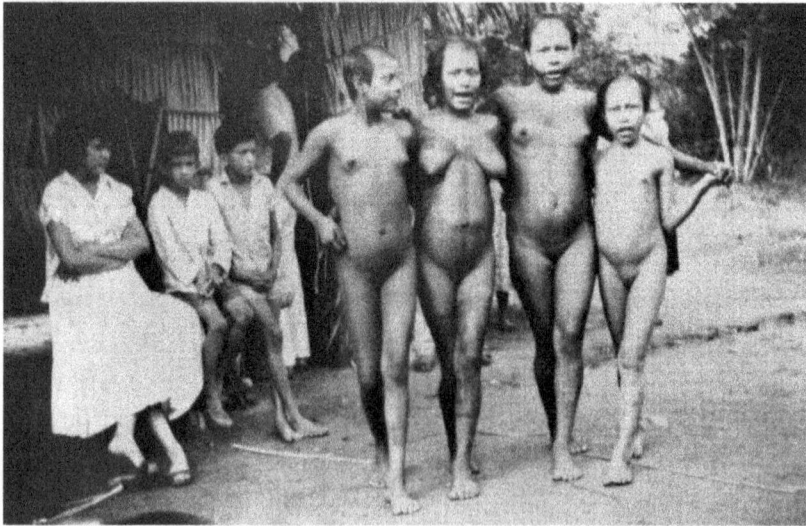

Plate 24. — The "pacification" of the Northern Mekranoti
in 1957: national colonists watching Kayapo women dance
at Posto Curua (?), adjacent to the Brazilian settlement Bom
Futuro.
Courtesy Museu do Índio, Rio de Janeiro.

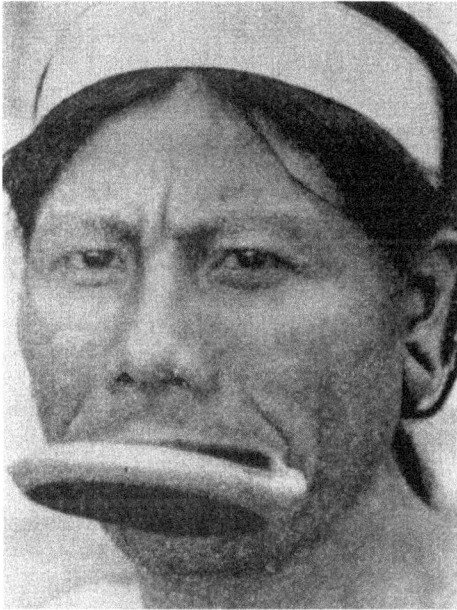

Plate 25. — Chief Bepnox of the Kokraimoro.
Photo between 1957 and 1960.

Plate 26. — Chief Jakuri (at right) and his Kokraimoro
men displaying the rifles they had received from Francisco
Meirelles during so-called "pacification" in 1957.
Courtesy Museu do Índio, Rio de Janeiro.

Plate 27. — A group of Southern Mekranoti men fusing with
the Kubenkranken in 1959.
Courtesy Karl Lukesch.

Plate 28. — Chief Kremôr (at right) and his Southern
Mekranoti followers dancing the *kwỳrỳkangô* to celebrate
their fusion with the Kubenkranken in 1959.
Courtesy Karl Lukesch.

Plate 29. — The 1964 fusion in *porori* of the Southern Mekranoti led by Kremôr with a Central Mekranoti group led by Kreti-re. F.l.t.r.: Kreti-re, Prof. J.-P. Gosse, Ropni, Claudio Villas Bôas, King Leopold III of Belgium.
Courtesy J.-P. Gosse.

Plate 30. — The 1964 fusion of the Southern Mekranoti and an important Central Mekranoti group. F.l.t.r.: King Leopold III of Belgium, Kreti-re, 'Ykakôr, Kremôr and ClaudioVillas Bôas.
Courtesy J.-P. Gosse.

Plate 31. — Old chief Bepgogoti with the winchester he
took as booty upon raiding a Brazilian settlement. He wears
the *krãimrôjakati* headdress, one of the most coveted ritual
privileges (*õ nêkrêx*).
PI Mekranoti, 1976

Plate 32. — Kremôr, a senior Southern Mekranoti chief,
during the meeting at Altamira (1989).

Plate 33. — Kôkôrôti, a senior Central Mekranoti chief.
PI Kubenkokre, 1991.

Plate 34. — Kruma-re wearing a feather headdress.
Altamira, 1989

Plate 35. — Ajol wearing a necklace of mussel shells.
PI Mekranoti, 1975

Plate 36. — Bepkŭm helping his wife to drill holes in the
pieces of mussel shell.
PI Mekranoti, 1980

Plate 37. — Pakyx, one of the founders of PI Mekranoti.
PI Pukanu, 2007

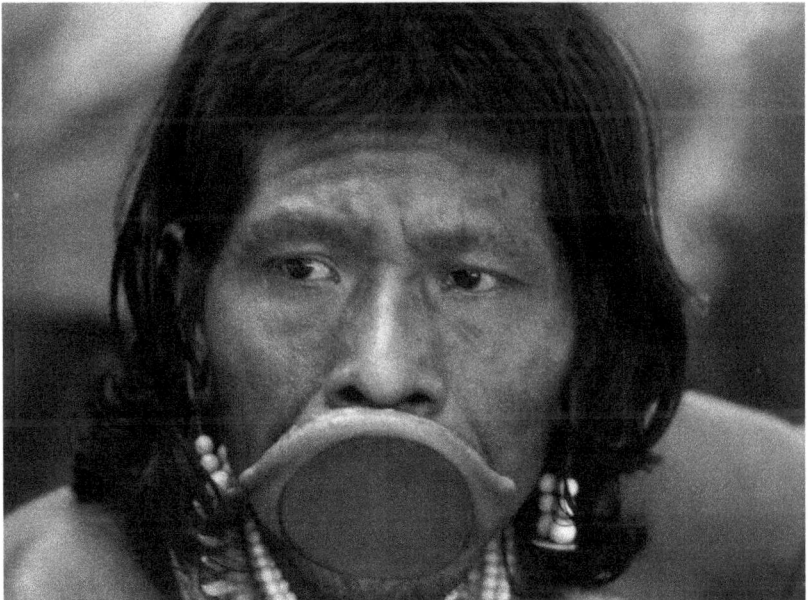

Plate 38. — Ropni (Raoni), a Southern Mekranoti chief.
PI Kretire, 1974

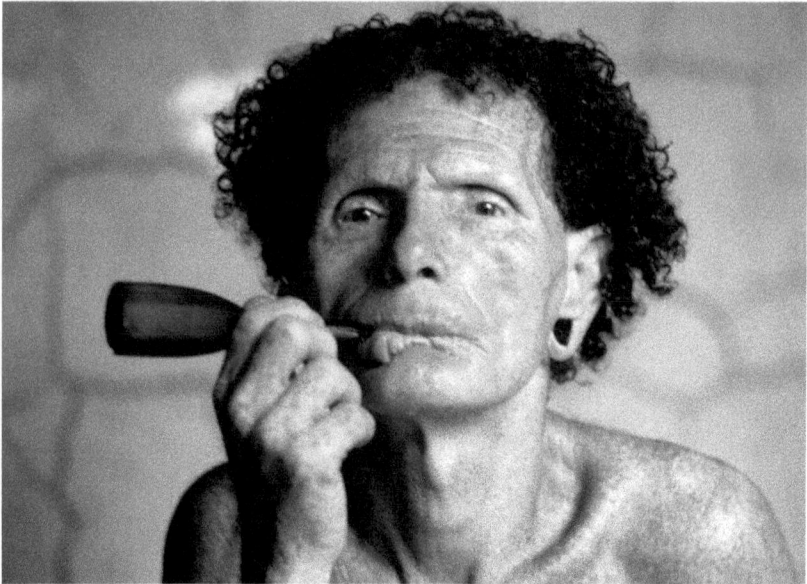

Plate 39. — Bemoti-re, a white man. He was about three years young when the Mekranoti captured him along the Curua River in 1918.
PI Mekranoti, 1974

Plate 40. — Iparemo'i, a Tapirape woman captured in 1947. In the 1990s, she returned to live among the Tapirape.
PI Mekranoti, 1976

Plate 41. — Dance of the *bô* masks during the *memybijôk* naming ceremony. The dance was learned from the Xambioa (Iny Karaja) in the 19th century.
PI Mekranoti 1980

Plate 42. — Women dancing the *kwỳrỳkangô*, a ceremony the Mekranoti learned from the Yudja in the 1890s.
PI Mekranoti, 1974

Plate 43. — A group of Mekranoti watching television
showing video recordings made in another Kayapo village.
PI Kubenkokre, 1990

Plate 44. — New deforestation near São Felix do Xingu, at
the northwestern border of the Kayapo Indian land (1989).

Plate 45. — Paulinho Pajakãn presiding the manifestation at
Altamira in 1989.

Plate 46. — Several hundreds of Kayapo men from different
villages gathered in the meeting room during the 1989
manifestation at Altamira.

Photo credits

Maps, Figures, Tables

www.ingramcontent.com/pod-product-compliance
Lightning Source LLC
Chambersburg PA
CBHW050625280326
41932CB00015B/2528